# UNITED
## ARAB EMIRATES

United Arab Emirates

# INTERNET, E-COMMERCE
# INVESTMENT AND BUSINESS GUIDE
### STRATEGIC AND PRACTICAL INFORMATION, REGULATIONS, OPPORTUNITIES

**International Business Publications, USA**
**Washington DC, USA - United Arab Emirates**

# UNITED ARAB EMIRATES

## INTERNET, E-COMMERCE INVESTMENT AND BUSINESS GUIDE

### STRATEGIC AND PRACTICAL INFORMATION, REGULATIONS, OPPORTUNITIES

**UPDATED ANNUALLY**

**We express our sincere appreciation to all government agencies and international organizations which provided information and other materials for this guide**

**Cover Design: International Business Publications, USA**



**2016 Edition Updated Reprint International Business Publications, USA**
**ISBN 1-4330-5207-5**

For customer service and information, please contact:
in the USA: **International Business Publications, USA**
**P.O.Box 15343, Washington, DC 20003**
**Phone: (202) 546-2103, Fax: (202) 546-3275.**
**E-mail: rusric@erols.com**

Printed in the USA

# UNITED
## ARAB EMIRATES
# INTERNET, E-COMMERCE
## INVESTMENT AND BUSINESS GUIDE
### STRATEGIC AND PRACTICAL INFORMATION, REGULATIONS, OPPORTUNITIES

## TABLE OF CONTENTS

# BUSINESS AND DEVELOPMENT PROFILES

## STRATEGIC PROFILE

| | |
|---|---|
| Capital | Abu Dhabi<br>24°28′N 54°22′E24.467°N 54.367°E |
| Largest city | Dubai |
| Official language(s) | Arabic |
| Ethnic groups | 16.6% Emirati<br>23% Other Arabs and Iranian<br>60.5% South Asian, Indian, Pakistani, Bangladeshi, Chinese, Filipino, Thai, Westerners (2009) |
| Demonym | Emirati |
| Government | Constitutional federation of absolute monarchies with an executive president elected by Emir Council amongst themselves |
| - President | Khalifa bin Zayed Al Nahyan |
| - Vice President and Prime Minister | Mohammed bin Rashid Al Maktoum |
| Legislature | Federal National Council |
| Sovereignty | End of special treaty with the United Kingdom |
| - Constitution | December 2, 1971 |
| | Area |
| - Total | 83,600 [1] $km^2$ (116th)<br>32,278 sq mi |
| - Water (%) | negligible |
| | Population |
| - 2010 estimate | 8,264,070 (93rd) |
| - 2005 census | 4,106,427 |
| - Density | 99/$km^2$ (110th)<br>256/sq mi |
| GDP (PPP) | 2011 estimate |
| - Total | $258.825 billion |
| - Per capita | $48,158 |
| GDP (nominal) | 2011 estimate |
| - Total | $360.136 billion |
| - Per capita | $67,008 |
| Gini (2008) | 36 |
| HDI (2011) | ▲0.846 (very high) (30th) |
| Currency | UAE dirham (AED) |
| Time zone | GMT+4 (UTC+4) |
| - Summer (DST) | not observed (UTC+4) |
| Date formats | dd/mm/yyyy |
| Drives on the | right |
| ISO 3166 code | AE |
| Internet TLD | .ae, امارات. |
| Calling code | 971 |

The **United Arab Emirates** (**UAE**), sometimes simply called the **Emirates**, is a country situated in the southeast of the Arabian Peninsula in Western Asia on the Persian Gulf, bordering Oman to the east and Saudi Arabia to the south, as well as sharing sea borders with Qatar to the west and Iran to the north.

The UAE is a federation of seven emirates (equivalent to principalities), each governed by a hereditary emir, with a single national president. The constituent emirates are Abu Dhabi, Ajman, Dubai, Fujairah, Ras al-Khaimah, Sharjah, and Umm al-Quwain. The capital is Abu Dhabi, which is also the state's center of political, industrial, and cultural activities.

Prior to independence in 1971, the UAE was known as the Trucial States or Trucial Oman, in reference to a 19th-century truce between the local sheikhs, hereditary rulers of the territories, and the United Kingdom. The term *Pirate Coast* was also used by some to refer to the emirates from the 18th to the early 20th century, owing to the preponderance of pirates operating from Emirati ports.

The UAE's political system is based on its 1971 Constitution, which is composed of several intricately connected governing bodies. As a federation of seven monarchies, whose rulers retain absolute power within their emirates, but with a UAE president, it is neither a constitutional monarchy nor a republic. The *emirs* choose one of their members to be the president of the federation, but this does not alter the monarchical character of the government of the individual emirates. The constitution is concerned solely with the relations between the emirates as members of the federation, and does not prescribe a constitutional system of government. Islam is the official religion of the UAE, and Arabic is the official language.

UAE oil reserves are ranked as the world's sixth-largest and it possesses one of the most developed economies in West Asia. It is the thirty-fifth-largest economy at market exchange rates, and ranks among the world's wealthiest nations with per capita GDP (PPP) of US$48,597. It is 15th in purchasing power per capita and has a relatively high Human Development Index for the Asian continent, ranking thirtieth globally. The UAE is classified as a high-income developing economy by the IMF

## GEOGRAPHY

**Location:** Middle East, bordering the Gulf of Oman and the Persian Gulf, between Oman and Saudi Arabia
**Geographic coordinates:** 24 00 N, 54 00 E
**Map references:** Middle East

**Area:**
*total:* 82,880 sq km *land:* 82,880 sq km *water:* 0 sq km

**Area—comparative:** slightly smaller than Maine
**Land boundaries:**
*total:* 867 km *border countries:* Oman 410 km, Saudi Arabia 457 km

**Coastline:** 1,318 km

**Maritime claims:**
*contiguous zone:* 24 nm *continental shelf:* 200 nm or to the edge of the continental margin
*exclusive economic zone:* 200 nm
*territorial sea:* 12 nm

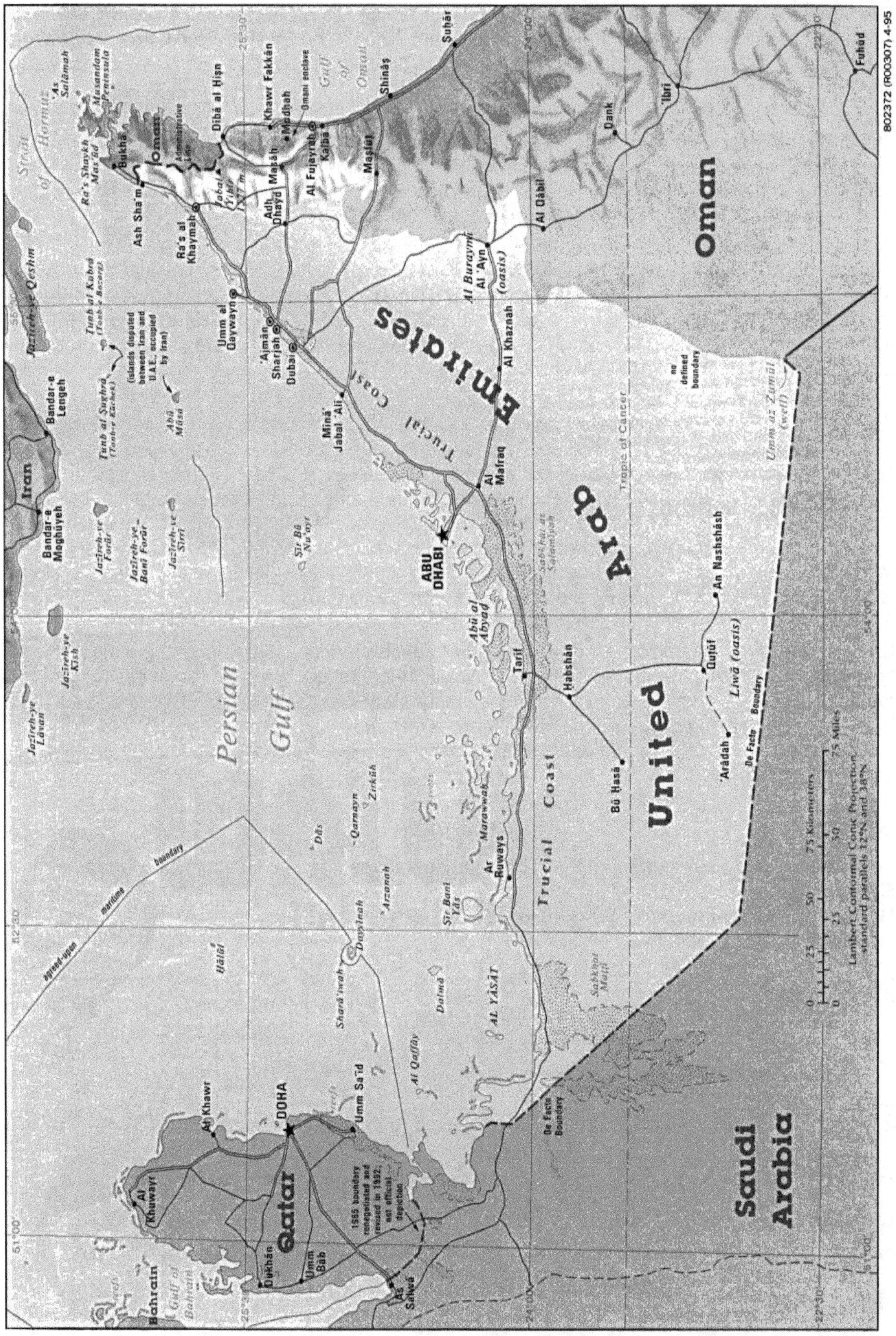


For additional analytical, marketing, investment and business opportunities information, please contact

Global Investment & Business Center, USA
(202) 546-2103. Fax: (202) 546-3275. E-mail: rusric@erols.com

**Climate:** desert; cooler in eastern mountains
**Terrain:** flat, barren coastal plain merging into rolling sand dunes of vast desert wasteland; mountains in east
**Elevation extremes:**
*lowest point:* Persian Gulf 0 m
*highest point:* Jabal Yibir 1,527 m
**Natural resources:** petroleum, natural gas

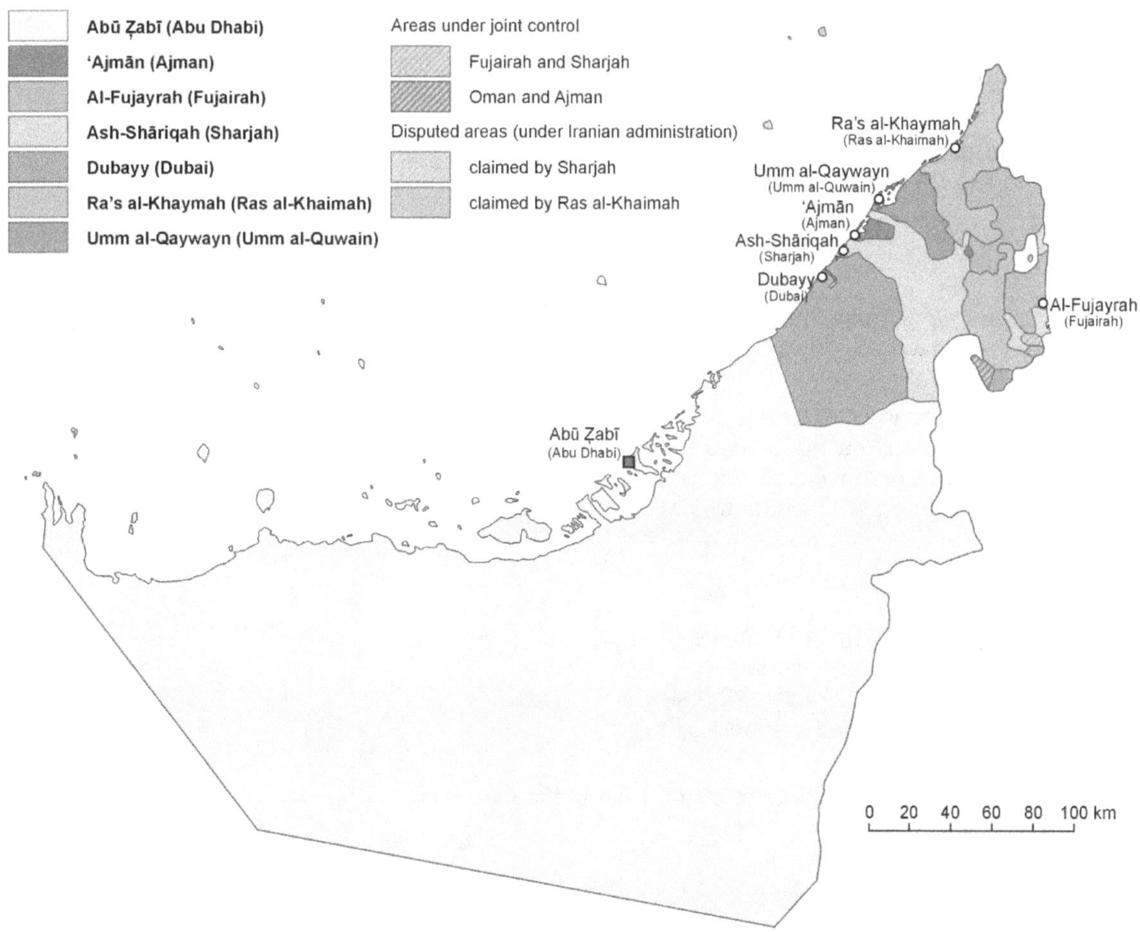


**Land use:**
*arable land:* 0%
*permanent crops:* 0%
*permanent pastures:* 2%
*forests and woodland:* 0%
*other:* 98%

**Irrigated land:** 50 sq km
**Natural hazards:** frequent sand and dust storms

**Environment—current issues:** lack of natural freshwater resources being overcome by des
**Environment—international agreements:**

*party to:* Climate Change, Desertification, Endangered Species, Hazardous Wastes, Marine Dumping, Ozone Layer Protection
*signed, but not ratified:* Biodiversity, Law of the Sea

**Geography—note:** strategic location along southern approaches to Strait of Hormuz, a vital transit point for world crude oil alination plants; desertification; beach pollution from oil spills

## PEOPLE

**Population:** 2,344,402
*note:* includes 1,576,589 non-nationals

**Age structure:**
*0-14 years:* 31% (male 368,844; female 353,183)

*15-64 years:* 67% (male 1,015,690; female 558,902)
*65 years and over:* 2% (male 32,935; female 14,848)

**Population growth rate:** 1.78%
**Birth rate:** 18.86 births/1,000 population
**Death rate:** 3.13 deaths/1,000 population
**Net migration rate:** 2.03 migrant(s)/1,000 population

**Sex ratio:**
*at birth:* 1.05 male(s)/female
*under 15 years:* 1.04 male(s)/female
*15-64 years:* 1.82 male(s)/female
*65 years and over:* 2.22 male(s)/female
*total population:* 1.53 male(s)/female

**Infant mortality rate:** 14.1 deaths/1,000 live births

**Life expectancy at birth:**
*total population:* 75.24 years
*male:* 73.83 years
*female:* 76.72 years
**Total fertility rate:** 3.5 children born/woman
**Nationality:**
*noun:* Emirian(s)
*adjective:* Emirian
**Ethnic groups:** Emiri 19%, other Arab and Iranian 23%, South Asian 50%, other expatriates (includes Westerners and East Asians) 8%
*note:* less than 20% are UAE citizens
**Religions:** Muslim 96% (Shi'a 16%), Christian, Hindu, and other 4%
**Languages:** Arabic (official), Persian, English, Hindi, Urdu

**Literacy:**
*definition:* age 15 and over can read and write

*total population:* 79.2%
*male:* 78.9% *female:* 79.8%

## GOVERNMENT

**Country name:**
*conventional long form:* United Arab Emirates
*conventional short form:* none
*local long form:* Al Imarat al Arabiyah al Muttahidah
*local short form:* none
*former:* Trucial States
*abbreviation:* UAE

**Data code:** TC
**Government type:** federation with specified powers delegated to the UAE federal government and other powers reserved to member emirates
**Capital:** Abu Dhabi

**Administrative divisions:** 7 emirates (imarat, singular—imarah); Abu Zaby (Abu Dhabi), 'Ajman, Al Fujayrah, Ash Shariqah (Sharjah), Dubayy (Dubai), Ra's al Khaymah, Umm al Qaywayn

**Independence:** 2 December 1971 (from UK)
**National holiday:** National Day, 2 December (1971)
**Constitution:** 2 December 1971 (made permanent in 1996)

**Legal system:** federal court system introduced in 1971; all emirates except Dubayy (Dubai) and Ra's al Khaymah have joined the federal system; all emirates have secular and Islamic law for civil, criminal, and high courts

**Suffrage:** none

**Executive branch:**

chief of state: President KHALIFA bin Zayid Al-Nuhayyan (since 3 November 2004), ruler of Abu Zaby (Abu Dhabi) (since 4 November 2004); Vice President and Prime Minister MUHAMMAD BIN RASHID Al-Maktum (since 5 January 2006)

head of government: Prime Minister and Vice President MUHAMMAD BIN RASHID Al-Maktum (since 5 January 2006); Deputy Prime Ministers SAIF bin Zayid Al-Nuhayyan (since 11 May 2009) and MANSUR bin Zayid Al-Nuhayyan (since 11 May 2009)

cabinet: Council of Ministers appointed by the president

note:there is also a Federal Supreme Council (FSC) composed of the seven emirate rulers; the FSC is the highest constitutional authority in the UAE; establishes general policies and sanctions federal legislation; meets four times a year; Abu Zaby (Abu Dhabi) and Dubayy (Dubai) rulers have effective veto power

elections: president and vice president elected by the FSC for five-year terms (no term limits) from among the seven FSC members; election last held 3 November 2004 upon the death of the

UAE's Founding Father and first President ZAYID bin Sultan Al Nuhayyan (next election NA); prime minister and deputy prime minister appointed by the president

election results: KHALIFA bin Zayid Al-Nuhayyan elected president by a unanimous vote of the FSC; MUHAMMAD bin Rashid Al-Maktum unanimously affirmed vice president after the 2006 death of his brother Sheikh MAKTUM bin Rashid Al-Maktum

**Legislative branch:**

unicameral Federal National Council (FNC) or Majlis al-Ittihad al-Watani (40 seats; 20 members appointed by the rulers of the constituent states, 20 members elected to serve four-year terms)

elections: last held on 24 September 2011 (next to be held in 2015); note - the electoral college was expanded from 6,689 voters in the December 2006 election to 129,274 in the September 2011 election; elections for candidates rather than party lists; 469 candidates including 85 women ran for 20 contested FNC seats

election results: elected seats by emirate - Abu Dhabi 4, Dubai 4, Sharjah 3, Ras al-Khaimah 3, Ajman 2, Fujairah 2, Umm al-Quwain 2; note - number of appointed seats for each emirate are same as elected seats

**Judicial branch:** Union Supreme Court, judges appointed by the president
**Political parties and leaders:** none
**Political pressure groups and leaders:** NA

**International organization participation:** ABEDA, AfDB, AFESD, AL, AMF, CAEU, CCC, ESCWA, FAO, G-77, GCC, IAEA, IBRD, ICAO, ICRM, IDA, IDB, IFAD, IFC, IFRCS, IHO, ILO, IMF, IMO, Inmarsat, Intelsat, Interpol, IOC, ISO (correspondent), ITU, NAM, OAPEC, OIC, OPCW, OPEC, UN, UNCTAD, UNESCO, UNIDO, UPU, WHO, WIPO, WMO, WTrO

**Diplomatic representation in the US:**
*chief of mission:* Ambassador Muhammad bin Husayn al-SHAALI
*chancery:* Suite 700, 1255 22nd Street NW, Washington, DC 20037
*telephone:* [1] (202) 955-7999

**Diplomatic representation from the US:**
*chief of mission:* Ambassador Theodore H. KATTOUF
*embassy:* Al-Sudan Street, Abu Dhabi
*mailing address:* P. O. Box 4009, Abu Dhabi; American Embassy Abu Dhabi, Department of State, Washington, DC 20521-6010 (pouch); note—work week is Saturday through Wednesday
*telephone:* [971] (2) 436691, 436692
*FAX:* [971] (2) 434771
*consulate(s) general:* Dubai

**Flag description:** three equal horizontal bands of green (top), white, and black with a thicker vertical red band on the hoist side

## ECONOMY

The UAE has an open economy with a high per capita income and a sizable annual trade surplus. Successful efforts at economic diversification have reduced the portion of GDP based on oil and gas output to 25%. Since the discovery of oil in the UAE more than 30 years ago, the country has undergone a profound transformation from an impoverished region of small desert principalities to a modern state with a high standard of living. The government has increased spending on job creation and infrastructure expansion and is opening up utilities to greater private sector involvement. In April 2004, the UAE signed a Trade and Investment Framework Agreement with Washington and in November 2004 agreed to undertake negotiations toward a Free Trade Agreement with the US; however, those talks have not moved forward. The country's Free Trade Zones - offering 100% foreign ownership and zero taxes - are helping to attract foreign investors. The global financial crisis, tight international credit, and deflated asset prices constricted the economy in 2009. UAE authorities tried to blunt the crisis by increasing spending and boosting liquidity in the banking sector. The crisis hit Dubai hardest, as it was heavily exposed to depressed real estate prices. Dubai lacked sufficient cash to meet its debt obligations, prompting global concern about its solvency. The UAE Central Bank and Abu Dhabi-based banks bought the largest shares. In December 2009 Dubai received an additional $10 billion loan from the emirate of Abu Dhabi. Dependence on oil, a large expatriate workforce, and growing inflation pressures are significant long-term challenges. The UAE's strategic plan for the next few years focuses on diversification and creating more opportunities for nationals through improved education and increased private sector employment.

GDP (purchasing power parity):
$271.2 billion (2012 est.)
country comparison to the world: 50
$260.7 billion (est.)
$247.8 billion (est.)
note: data are in 2012 US dollars

GDP (official exchange rate):
$361.9 billion (2012 est.)

GDP - real growth rate:
4% (2012 est.)
country comparison to the world: 86
5.2% (est.)
1.3% (est.)

GDP - per capita (PPP):
$49,000 (2012 est.)
country comparison to the world: 16
$48,500 (est.)
$47,500 (est.)
note: data are in 2012 US dollars

GDP - composition by sector:
agriculture: 0.8%
industry: 56.1%
services: 43.1% (2012 est.)

Labor force:
4.337 million
country comparison to the world: 88
note: expatriates account for about 85% of the work force (2012 est.)

Labor force - by occupation:

agriculture: 7%
industry: 15%
services: 78% (2000 est.)

Unemployment rate:
2.4% (2001)
country comparison to the world: 17

Population below poverty line:
19.5% (2003)

Investment (gross fixed):
28.5% of GDP (2012 est.)
country comparison to the world: 27

Budget:
revenues: $130.3 billion
expenditures: $113.8 billion (2012 est.)
Taxes and other revenues:

36% of GDP (2012 est.)
country comparison to the world: 66

Budget surplus (+) or deficit (-):
4.5% of GDP (2012 est.)
country comparison to the world: 14

Public debt:
40.4% of GDP (2012 est.)
country comparison to the world: 89
45.9% of GDP (est.)

Inflation rate (consumer prices):
1.1% (2012 est.)
country comparison to the world: 11
0.9% (est.)

Stock of narrow money:
$80.53 billion (31 December 2012 est.)
country comparison to the world: 41
$71.9 billion (31 December 2011 est.)

Stock of broad money:
$234.7 billion (31 December 2012 est.)
country comparison to the world: 36
$224.8 billion (31 December 2011 est.)

Stock of domestic credit:
$313.7 billion (31 December 2012 est.)
country comparison to the world: 36
$293.2 billion (31 December 2011 est.)

Market value of publicly traded shares:

$93.77 billion (31 December 2011)
country comparison to the world: 41
$104.7 billion (31 December 2010)
$109.6 billion (31 December 2009)

Agriculture - products:
dates, vegetables, watermelons; poultry, eggs, dairy products; fish

Industries:
petroleum and petrochemicals; fishing, aluminum, cement, fertilizers, commercial ship repair, construction materials, some boat building, handicrafts, textiles

Industrial production growth rate:
3.2%
country comparison to the world: 84

Current account balance:
$26.76 billion (2012 est.)
country comparison to the world: 15
$30.65 billion (est.)

Exports:
$300.6 billion (2012 est.)
country comparison to the world: 21
$281.6 billion (est.)

Exports - commodities:
crude oil 45%, natural gas, reexports, dried fish, dates

Exports - partners:
Japan 16.2%, India 13.5%, Iran 10.9%, South Korea 5.6%, Thailand 5.5%, Singapore 4.4% (2011)

Imports:
$220.3 billion (2012 est.)
country comparison to the world: 24
$202.1 billion (est.)
Imports - commodities:

machinery and transport equipment, chemicals, food

Imports - partners:
India 19.8%, China 13.7%, US 8.1%, Germany 4.6% (2011)
Reserves of foreign exchange and gold:

$43.77 billion (31 December 2012 est.)
country comparison to the world: 42
$37.27 billion (31 December 2011 est.)

Debt - external:
$158.9 billion (31 December 2012 est.)
country comparison to the world: 32
$156.3 billion (31 December 2011 est.)

Stock of direct foreign investment - at home:
$91.56 billion (31 December 2012 est.)
country comparison to the world: 42
$83.36 billion (31 December 2011 est.)

Stock of direct foreign investment - abroad:
$58.1 billion (31 December 2012 est.)
country comparison to the world: 34
$55.6 billion (31 December 2011 est.)

Exchange rates:
Emirati dirhams (AED) per US dollar -
3.67 (2012 est.)
3.67 (est.)
3.67 (est.)
3.67 (2009)
3.67 (2008)
Fiscal year:
calendar year

## ENERGY

Electricity - production:
83.31 billion kWh (est.)
country comparison to the world: 38

Electricity - consumption:
74.12 billion kWh (est.)
country comparison to the world: 38

Electricity - exports:
0 kWh (est.)
country comparison to the world: 154

Electricity - imports:
0 kWh (est.)
country comparison to the world: 154

Electricity - installed generating capacity:
23.25 million kW (est.)
country comparison to the world: 35

Electricity - from fossil fuels:
100% of total installed capacity (est.)
country comparison to the world: 46

Electricity - from nuclear fuels:
0% of total installed capacity (est.)
country comparison to the world: 35

Electricity - from hydroelectric plants:
0% of total installed capacity (est.)
country comparison to the world: 154

Electricity - from other renewable sources:
0% of total installed capacity (est.)
country comparison to the world: 100

Crude oil - production:
3.087 million bbl/day (est.)
country comparison to the world: 8

Crude oil - exports:
2.036 million bbl/day (est.)
country comparison to the world: 7

Crude oil - imports:
0 bbl/day (est.)
country comparison to the world: 148

Crude oil - proved reserves:
97.8 billion bbl (1 January 2012 es)
country comparison to the world: 8

Refined petroleum products - production:
346,900 bbl/day (est.)
country comparison to the world: 39

Refined petroleum products - consumption:
572,100 bbl/day (est.)
country comparison to the world: 32

Refined petroleum products - exports:
452,400 bbl/day (est.)
country comparison to the world: 17
Refined petroleum products - imports:

377,300 bbl/day (est.)
country comparison to the world: 17

Natural gas - production:
51.28 billion cu m (est.)
country comparison to the world: 19

Natural gas - consumption:
60.54 billion cu m (est.)
country comparison to the world: 14

Natural gas - exports:
7.65 billion cu m (est.)
country comparison to the world: 27

Natural gas - imports:
16.91 billion cu m (est.)
country comparison to the world: 18

Natural gas - proved reserves:
6.089 trillion cu m (1 January 2012 es)
country comparison to the world: 8

Carbon dioxide emissions from consumption of energy:
199.4 million Mt (est.)
country comparison to the world: 27

## COMMUNICATIONS

Telephones - main lines in use:
1.825 million
country comparison to the world: 61

Telephones - mobile cellular:
11.727 million
country comparison to the world: 66

Telephone system:
general assessment: modern fiber-optic integrated services; digital network with rapidly growing use of mobile-cellular telephones; key centers are Abu Dhabi and Dubai
domestic: microwave radio relay, fiber optic and coaxial cable
international: country code - 971; linked to the international submarine cable FLAG (Fiber-Optic Link Around the Globe); landing point for both the SEA-ME-WE-3 and SEA-ME-WE-4 submarine cable networks; satellite earth stations - 3 Intelsat (1 Atlantic Ocean and 2 Indian Ocean) and 1 Arabsat; tropospheric scatter to Bahrain; microwave radio relay to Saudi Arabia (2011)

Broadcast media:
except for the many organizations now operating in Dubai's Media Free Zone, most TV and radio stations remain government-owned; widespread use of satellite dishes provides access to pan-Arab and other international broadcasts (2007)

Internet country code:
.ae

Internet hosts:
337,804 (2012)
country comparison to the world: 61

Internet users:
3.449 million
country comparison to the world: 61

## TRANSPORTATION

**Railways:** 0 km
**Highways:**
*total:* 4,835 km
*paved:* 4,835 km
*unpaved:* 0 km
**Pipelines:** crude oil 830 km; natural gas, including natural gas liquids, 870 km
**Ports and harbors:** 'Ajman, Al Fujayrah, Das Island, Khawr Fakkan, Mina' Jabal 'Ali, Mina' Khalid, Mina' Rashid, Mina' Saqr, Mina' Zayid, Umm al Qaywayn

**Merchant marine:**
*total:* 74 ships (1,000 GRT or over) totaling 1,093,795 GRT/1,757,189 DWT
*ships by type:* bulk 4, cargo 20, chemical tanker 4, container 8, liquefied gas tanker 1, livestock carrier 1, oil tanker 28, refrigerated cargo 1, roll-on/roll-off cargo 7
**Airports:** 41
**Airports—with paved runways:**
*total:* 21
*over 3,047 m:* 8 *2,438 to 3,047 m:* 3 *1,524 to 2,437 m:* 3 *914 to 1,523 m:* 3
*under 914 m:* 4
**Airports—with unpaved runways:** *total:* 20
*over 3,047 m:* 1 *2,438 to 3,047 m:* 1
*1,524 to 2,437 m:* 4 *914 to 1,523 m:* 9
*under 914 m:* 5
**Heliports:** 2

## MILITARY

**Military branches:** Army, Navy, Air Force, Air Defense, paramilitary (includes Federal Police Force)
**Military manpower—military age:** 18 years of age
**Military manpower—availability:** *males age 15-49:* 791,097
*note:* includes non-nationals
**Military manpower—fit for military service:**
*males age 15-49:* 425,248
**Military manpower—reaching military age annually:**
*males:* 23,358
**Military expenditures—dollar figure:** $2.118 billion
**Military expenditures—percent of GDP:** 5%

## TRANSNATIONAL ISSUES

**Disputes—international:** location and status of boundary with Saudi Arabia is not final, de facto boundary reflects 1974 agreement; no defined boundary with most of Oman, but Administrative Line in far north; claims two islands in the Persian Gulf occupied by Iran: Lesser Tunb (called Tunb as Sughra in Arabic by UAE and Jazireh-ye Tonb-e Kuchek in Persian by Iran) and Greater Tunb (called Tunb al Kubra in Arabic by UAE and Jazireh-ye Tonb-e Bozorg in Persian by Iran); claims island in the Persian Gulf jointly administered with Iran (called Abu Musa in Arabic by UAE and Jazireh-ye Abu Musa in Persian by Iran)—over which Iran has taken steps to exert unilateral control since 1992, including access restrictions and a military build-up on the island; the UAE has garnered significant diplomatic support in the region in protesting these Iranian actions

**Illicit drugs:** growing role as heroin transshipment and money-laundering center due to its proximity to southwest Asian producing countries and the bustling free trade zone in Dubai

# IMPORTANT INFORMATION FOR UNDERSTANDING UAE

The **United Arab Emirates** (also the **UAE** or the **Emirates**) is a Middle Eastern country situated in the southeast of the Arabian Peninsula in Southwest Asia on the Persian Gulf, comprising seven emirates: Abu Dhabi, Ajmān, Dubai, Fujairah, Ras al-Khaimah, Sharjah, and Umm al-Quwain. Before 1971, they were known as the **Trucial States** or **Trucial Oman**, in reference of a nineteenth-century truce between Britain and several Arab Sheikhs. It borders Oman and Saudi Arabia. The country is rich in oil.

Few nations on earth have experienced more complete and far-reaching change over the past few decades than the United Arab Emirates. Today a land of six-lane highways and glittering streams of motorcars, where space-age cities of ivory-white and crystal glass emerge like a mirage from the haze of desert and sea, this federation of seven ancient Emirates - Abu Dhabi, Dubai, Sharjah, Ras a]-Khaimah, Umm al Qawain, Ajman and Fujairah - is not only the world's fourth largest oil-producer, but also its richest state per head of population, and the new commercial hub of the Middle East

Yet only fifty years ago, when oil-exploration started, there was no electricity, no plumbing or telephone system, not a single public hospital nor modern school, no bridges, no deep-water harbor, no metalloid roads, no more than a handful of cars and scarcely a building more impressive than the crumbling mud-brick forts and watchtowers of Abu Dhabi and Dubai, where now high-rise stacks, gilded domes and minarets tower over wide boulevards, where cascades of water are flaunted with conspicuous opulence, and where acres of shrubs burgeon on the desert shore, stood sleepy settlements of reed, coral and mud-brick houses, sweltering on sand spits and islands in the most ferocious summer heat.

Life on the Trucial Coast - as it was known until the 1970s - and in its hinterland, was one of considerable hardship. In the towns, fresh water was scarcely available and often had to be drawn by oxen from deep wells, or even brought in barrels from neighboring islands by dhow.

Tribesmen would harvest the unreliable winter rains by stretching a sail with a hole in its center between two poles, and in the merciless heat of the Arabian summer would trap the cooling winds by the ingenious use of wind-towers made of sackcloth or cotton. On the sun-blasted terraces of the Hajar Mountains, subsistence farmers eked out a bitter existence, and in the interior the hardy Bedouin scoured the dunes of the great Empty Quarter for pasture. In the hot months, members of these various groups would come together to work as divers in the pearl-yielding oyster beds which flourished in the warm, shallow waters of the Gulf For almost three millennia the economy of this region was bound up with the pearling fleet, culminating in a boom that was only ended by the invention, in the 1920s of the cultured pearl.

Despite its harsh climate, civilization has flourished in this region since the earliest times. At Jebel Hafit, near al-Ain, lie the remains of a settlement dating back more than five thousand years;

at Hili, not far away, have been found pillbox-shaped tombs of dressed masonry so finely wrought that archaeologists believe they may be connected with the ancient land of Magan, mentioned in ancient Sumerian texts as a land of fabulous wealth, the source of copper, minerals and semi-precious stones.

**COUNTRY**

**United Arab Emirates, federation of seven independent states lying along the east central coast of the Arabian Gulf.**

The states which include Abu Dhabi (capital of the UAE), Dubai, Al Sharjah, Ras Al Khaimah, Ajman, Umm Al Quwain, and Al Fujairah, bounded on the north by the Arabian Gulf, on the east by Sultanate of Oman, and on the west by Qatar and Saudi Arabia. The total area of the UAE is about 83,600 sq. km (with a total of 200 islands) .The area of the U.A.E. excepting the islands is about 77,700 square kilometers and among the G.C.C. states it is the third largest after Saudi Arabia & Oman. United Arab Emirates is a member of the Gulf Co-operation Council (G.C.C.).

## HISTORY

On December 2, 1971, the seven states became independent as the United Arab Emirates. President, His Highness Sheikh Zayed Bin Sultan Al Nahyan who is also Ruler of Abu Dhabi has devoted much of his attention in the intervening years to the development of the federation of the United Arab Emirates.

Each of the states has its own ruler, together they comprise the highest body of the federal government, the Supreme Council of Rulers. The council elects from its members a president and vice president. The federation is also governed by a prime minister and a 40 member consultative assembly called the Federal National Council.

## POPULATION & RELIGION

The population of the UAE grew rapidly in the 1970s, 1980s and 1990s . The population is estimated to be 2.94 million. Growth at present is 6.5 percent per year. This is expected however to slow to 2.9 percent by the year 2005, when the population will number approximately 3.48 million.
The country religion is Islam and official spoken language is Arabic, although English is widely spoken.

## CLIMATIC CONDITIONS

The UAE lies in the arid tropical zone extending across Asia and northern Africa, however the Indian Ocean has a strong influence on the climatic conditions in the area, since the country borders both the Arabian Gulf and the Gulf of Oman. This explains why high temperatures in summer are always accompanied by high humidity along the coast.
Noticeable variations in climate occur between the coastal regions, the deserts of the interior and mountainous areas.

Between the months of November and March a moderate, warm climate prevails during the day at an average temperature of 26°C, and a slightly cooler climate prevails throughout the night at an average temperature of 15°C. The humidity tends to rise in the summer months, between June and August. Prevailing winds, influenced by the monsoons, vary between south or southeast, to west or north to northwest depending upon the season and location. Average rainfall is low at less than 6.5 centimeters annually and more than half of the average rainfall occurs in December and January.

## UAE CURRENCY

Dirhams and fils are the units of currency with 100 fils to the Dirham (Dh). The Dirham is tied to the US Dollar at a steady exchange rate of $US 1= Dh 3.671. Banks usually give the best rates on foreign currency exchange

**but hotels and airports are often quicker and are open outside banking hours. Money changers tend to have a wider range of currencies but their rates may be higher. Exchange rates are published daily.**

### TELEPHONE

| | International areas codes of UAE 00971 + | |
|---|---|---|
| Telecommunications throughout the UAE are modern and efficient. International Direct Dialing is available to most countries. Local telephone calls are free. Local and international dialing codes may be obtained by dialing the operator on 181. | Abu Dhabi | 02 |
| | Dubai | 04 |
| | Al Sharjah | 06 |
| | Ras al Khaimah | 07 |
| | Ajman | 06 |
| | Umm al Quwain | 06 |
| | Al Fujairah | 09 |

### BASIC DATA

**Geography**
Area: 82,880 sq. km. (30,000 sq. mi.); about the size of Maine.
Cities (est.): *Capital*--Abu Dhabi (pop. 1,000,000); Dubai (pop. 860,000).
Terrain: Largely desert with some agricultural areas.
Climate: Hot, humid, low annual rainfall.

**People**
Nationality: *Noun and adjective*--U.A.E., Emirati.
Population : 4.4 million.
Population growth rate : 4.0%.
Ethnic groups: Indian, Pakistani, Bangladeshi, Egyptian, Jordanian, Iranian, Filipino, other Arab; (15-20% of residents are U.A.E. citizens).
Religions: Muslim (96%), Hindu, Christian.
Languages: Arabic (official), English, Hindi, Urdu, Persian.
Education: *Years compulsory*--ages 6-12. *Literacy* (U.A.E. citizens)--about 80%.
Health: *Life expectancy*--about 76 yrs.
Work force 2.968 million (93% foreign in 15-64 age group): *Agriculture*--2.3%; *industry*--61.9%; *services*--35.8%.

**Government**
Type: Federation of emirates.
Independence: December 2, 1971.
Provisional constitution: December 2, 1971.
Branches: *Executive*--7-member Supreme Council of Rulers, which elects president and vice president. *Legislative*--40-member Federal National Council (consultative only). *Judicial*--Islamic and secular courts.
Administrative subdivisions: Seven largely self-governing city-states.

Political parties: None.
Suffrage: State-nominated electors chose half of the Federal National Council seats in 2006.
Central government budget: $7 billion.

**Economy**
GDP : $163 billion.
Annual growth rate : 9.7%.
Per capita GDP : $37,000.
Inflation rate : 10-13%.
Natural resources: Oil and natural gas.
Agriculture (est., 2.0% of GDP): *Products*--vegetables, dates, dairy products, poultry, fish.
Petroleum : 36%.
Manufacturing : 13%.
Services (44% of GDP): Trade, government, real estate.
Trade : *Exports*--$157 billion: petroleum, gas, and petroleum products. *Major markets*--Japan, South Korea, Thailand, India. *Imports*--$126.6 billion: machinery, chemicals, food. *Major suppliers*--Western Europe, Japan, U.S., China, India.
Foreign economic aid (2007): In excess of $5.25 billion.

## PEOPLE

Nationality: Noun and adjective--UAE, Emirian, or Emiri. Population (est.): 1.8 million. Annual growth rate: 2.8%. Ethnic groups: Arab, Pakistani, Indian, Iranian, Filipino (15-20% of residents are UAE citizens). Religions: Muslim (90%), Hindu, Christian. Languages: Arabic (official), English, Hindi, Urdu, Persian. Education: Years compulsory--ages 6-12. Literacy (UAE citizens)--about 60%. Life expectancy: About 63 yrs. Work force 650,000 (90% foreign): Agriculture--6%. Industry and commerce--65%. Services--16%.
Government--13%.

Only 15-20% of the total population of 1.8 million are UAE citizens. The rest include significant numbers of other Arabs--Palestinians, Egyptians, Jordanians, Yemenis, Omanis--as well as many Iranians, Pakistanis, Indians, Filipinos, and West Europeans.

The majority of UAE citizens are Sunni Muslims with a small Shia minority. Most foreigners also are Muslim, although Hindus and Christians make up a portion of the UAE's foreign population.

Educational standards among UAE citizens population are rising rapidly. Citizens and temporary residents have taken advantage of facilities throughout the country. The UAE University in Al Ain had roughly 10,000 students in 1990. A network of technical-vocational colleges opened in 1989.

## HISTORY

The UAE was formed from the group of tribally-organized Arabian Peninsula shaikhdoms along the southern coast of the Persian Gulf and the northwestern coast of the Gulf of Oman. This area was converted to Islam in the 7th century; for centuries it was embroiled in dynastic disputes. It became known as the Pirate Coast as raiders based there harassed foreign shipping, although both European and Arab navies patrolled the area from the 17th century into the 19th century. Early British expeditions to protect the India trade from raiders at Ras al-Khaimah led to campaigns against that headquarters and other harbors along the coast in 1819.

The next year, a general peace treaty was signed to which all the principal shaikhs of the coast adhered. Raids continued intermittently until 1835, when the shaikhs agreed not to engage in hostilities at sea. In 1853, they signed a treaty with the United Kingdom, under which the shaikhs (the "Trucial Shaikhdoms") agreed to a "perpetual maritime truce." It was enforced by the United Kingdom, and disputes among shaikhs were referred to the British for settlement.

Primarily in reaction to the ambitions of other European countries, the United Kingdom and the Trucial Shaikhdoms established closer bonds in an 1892 treaty, similar to treaties entered into by the UK with other Gulf principalities. The shaikhs agreed not to dispose of any territory except to the United Kingdom and not to enter into relationships with any foreign government other than the United Kingdom without its consent. In return, the British promised to protect the Trucial Coast from all aggression by sea and to help out in case of land attack.

In 1955, the United Kingdom sided with Abu Dhabi in the latter's dispute with Saudi Arabia over the Buraimi Oasis and other territory to the south. A 1974 agreement between Abu Dhabi and Saudi Arabia would have settled the Abu Dhabi-Saudi border dispute; however, the agreement has yet to be ratified by the UAE Government and apparently is not recognized by the Saudi Government. The border with Oman also remains unsettled.

In 1968, the UK announced its decision, reaffirmed in March 1971, to end the treaty relationships with the seven Trucial Shaikhdoms which had been, together with Bahrain and Qatar, under British protection. The nine attempted to form a union of Arab emirates, but by mid-1971 they were unable to agree on terms of union, even though the termination date of the British treaty relationship was the end of 1971. Bahrain became independent in August and Qatar in September 1971. When the British-Trucial Shaikhdoms treaty expired on December 1, 1971, they became fully independent. On December 2, 1971, six of them entered into a union called the United Arab Emirates. The seventh, Ras al-Khaimah, joined in early 1972.

# GOVERNMENT

**Principal Government Officials**

| Pres. | KHALIFA bin Zayid Al Nuhayyan |
|---|---|
| Vice Pres. | MUHAMMAD BIN RASHID Al Maktum |
| Prime Min. | MUHAMMAD BIN RASHID Al Maktum |
| Dep. Prime Min. | MANSUR bin Zayid Al Nuhayyan |
| Dep. Prime Min. | SAIF bin Zayid Al Nuhayyan |
| Min. of Cabinet Affairs | Muhammad Abdallah al-GERGAWI |
| Min. of Culture, Youth, & Community Development | Abd al-Rahman Muhammad al-UWAIS |
| Min. of Defense | MUHAMMAD BIN RASHID Al Maktum |
| Min. of Development & Intl. Cooperation | LUBNA al-Qasimi |
| Min. of Economy | Sultan bin Saeed al-MANSURI |
| Min. of Education | Humaid Muhammad Ubayd al-QATAMI |
| Min. of Energy | Suhail bin Muhammad al-MAZROUI |
| Min. of Environment & Water | Rashid Ahmed bin FAHD |
| Min. of Finance | HAMDAN bin Rashid Al Maktum |
| Min. of Foreign Affairs | ABDALLAH bin Zayid Al Nuhayyan |
| Min. of Health | Hanif bin Hassan ALI |
| Min. of Higher Education & Scientific Research | NUHAYYAN bin Mubarak Al Nuhayyan |
| Min. of Interior | SAIF bin Zayid Al Nuhayyan |
| Min. of Justice | Hadef bin Juaan al-DHAHERI |
| Min. of Labor | Saqr Ghobash Saeed GHOBASH |
| Min. of Presidential Affairs | MANSUR bin Zayid Al Nuhayyan |

| | |
|---|---|
| Min. of Public Works | Abdullah Belhaif Al-NUAIMI |
| Min. of Social Affairs | Mariam bint Muhammad Khalfan al-RUMI |
| Min. of State for Federal National Council Affairs | Anwar Muhammad GARGASH |
| Min. of State for Financial Affairs | Obaid Humaid al-TAYER |
| Min. of State for Foreign Affairs | Anwar Muhammad GARGASH |
| Min. of State Without Portfolio | ABDULLAH bin Muhammad Ghobash |
| Min. of State Without Portfolio | Reem Ibrahim al-HASHEMI |
| Min. of State Without Portfolio | Sultan Ahmed Al JABER |
| Min. of State Without Portfolio | Maitha Salem al-SHAMSI |
| Governor, Central Bank | Sultan bin Nasir al-SUWAYDI |
| Ambassador to the US | Yusif bin Mani bin Said al-UTAYBA |
| Permanent Representative to the UN, New York | Ahmad Abd al-Rahman al-JARMAN |

Ambassador to the United States--Saqr Ghobash
Ambassador to the United Nations--Abd al-Aziz Bin Nasir al-Shamsi

The U.A.E. maintains an embassy in the United States at 3522 International Court, NW, Washington, DC8 (tel. 202-243-2400). The U.A.E. Mission to the UN is located at 747 3rd Avenue, 36th Floor, New York, NY 10017 (tel. 212-371-0480).

## POLITICAL CONDITIONS

The relative political and financial influence of each emirate is reflected in the allocation of positions in the federal government. The ruler of Abu Dhabi, whose emirate is the U.A.E.'s major oil producer, is president of the U.A.E. The ruler of Dubai, which is the U.A.E.'s commercial center, is vice president and prime minister.

Since achieving independence in 1971, the U.A.E. has worked to strengthen its federal institutions. Nonetheless, each emirate still retains substantial autonomy, and progress toward greater federal integration has slowed in recent years. A basic concept in the U.A.E. Government's development as a federal system is that a significant percentage of each emirate's revenues should be devoted to the U.A.E. central budget.

The U.A.E. has no political parties. The rulers hold power on the basis of their dynastic position and their legitimacy in a system of tribal consensus. Rapid modernization, enormous strides in education, and the influx of a large foreign population have changed the face of the society. In December 2006, the U.A.E. held its first-ever limited elections to select half the members of the FNC. Ballots were cast by electors selected by the emir of each emirate. One woman was elected to the FNC and seven additional women were appointed to be council members.

## DEFENSE

The Trucial Oman Scouts, long the symbol of public order on the coast and commanded by British officers, were turned over to the U.A.E. as its defense forces in 1971. The U.A.E. armed forces, consisting of 48,800 troops, are headquartered in Abu Dhabi and are primarily responsible for the defense of the seven emirates.

Although small in number, the U.A.E. armed forces are equipped with some of the most modern weapon systems, purchased from a variety of outside countries. The military has been reducing the number of foreign nationals in its ranks, and its officer corps is composed almost entirely of U.A.E. nationals. The U.A.E. air force has about 4,000 personnel. The Air Force has advanced U.S. F-16 BLOCK 60 multi-role fighter aircraft. Other equipment includes French Mirage 2000-9 fighters, British Hawk trainer aircraft, 36 transport aircraft and U.S. Apache and French Puma helicopters. The Air Defense Force is linked into a joint air defense system with the other six Gulf Cooperation Council (GCC) nations aimed at protecting the airspace of the allied states. The U.A.E. Navy is small--about 2,500 personnel--and maintains 12 well-equipped coastal patrol boats and 8 missile boats. Although primarily concerned with coastal defense, the Navy is constructing a six-unit class of blue water corvettes in conjunction with French shipbuilder CMN. The U.A.E.'s Land Forces are equipped with several hundred French LeClerc tanks and a similar number of Russian BMP-3 armored fighting vehicles. The U.A.E. Special Operations Command (SOC) is a small but effective force centered on the counter-terrorism mission within the country. SOC is well-financed, trained, and equipped and is capable of executing its mission with a level of expertise equal to, or above, the rest of the GCC.

The U.A.E. contributes to the continued security and stability of the Gulf and the Straits of Hormuz. It is a leading partner in the campaign against global terrorism, providing assistance in the military, diplomatic, and financial arenas since September 11, 2001

## ECONOMY

| Currency | United Arab Emirates dirham |
|---|---|
| Trade organisations | OPEC and WTO |
| | Statistics |
| GDP | $405 Billion |
| GDP growth | 4% |
| GDP per capita | $48,158 (7th) |
| GDP by sector | Agriculture (0.8%), industry (56.1%), services (43.1%) |
| Inflation (CPI) | 1.4% |
| Population below poverty line | 19.5% |
| Labour force | 4.34 million |
| Labour force by occupation | Agriculture (7%), industry (15%), services (78%) |
| Unemployment | 4.6% |
| Main industries | Petroleum and petrochemicals, fishing, aluminium, cement, fertilizers, commercial ship repair, construction materials, some plane building, handicrafts, textiles. |
| Ease-of-doing-business rank | 26th |
| | External |
| Exports | $314 billion |
| Export goods | Crude oil, natural gas, reexports, dried fish, dates |
| Main export partners | Japan 15.4%<br>India 13.4%<br>Iran 10.7%<br>Thailand 5.5%<br>Singapore 5.5%<br>South Korea 5.3% |
| Imports | $273.5 billion |
| Import goods | Machinery and transport equipment, chemicals, food |
| Main import partners | India 17.0%<br>China 13.7%<br>United States 10.5%<br>Germany 5.1%<br>Japan 4.2% |

| | |
|---|---|
| Gross external debt | $151.8 billion |
| | Public finances |
| Public debt | 40.4% of GDP |
| Revenues | $130.3 billion |
| Expenses | $99 billion |

The **economy of the United Arab Emirates** is the second largest in the Arab world (after Saudi Arabia), with a gross domestic product (GDP) of $377 billion (AED1.38 trillion) in 2012. The United Arab Emirates has been successfully diversifying its economy. 71% of UAE's total GDP comes from non-oil sectors.

Although UAE has the most diversified economy in the GCC, the UAE's economy remains extremely reliant on oil. With the exception of Dubai, most of the UAE is dependent on oil revenues. Petroleum and natural gas continue to play a central role in the economy, especially in Abu Dhabi. More than 85% of the UAE's economy was based on the oil exports in 2009. While Abu Dhabi and other UAE emirates have remained relatively conservative in their approach to diversification, Dubai, which has far smaller oil reserves, was bolder in its diversification policy. In 2011, oil exports accounted for 77% of the UAE's state budget.

Dubai suffered from a significant economic crisis in 2007-2010 and was bailed out by Abu Dhabi's oil wealth. Dubai's current prosperity has been attributed to Abu Dhabi's petrodollars. Dubai is currently in extreme debt. Tourism is one of the main sources of revenue in the UAE, with some of the world's most luxurious hotels being based in the UAE. Although the UAE is now less dependent on natural resources as a source of revenue, petroleum and natural gas exports still play an important role in the economy, especially in Abu Dhabi. A massive construction boom, an expanding manufacturing base, and a thriving services sector are helping the UAE diversify its economy. Nationwide, there is currently $350 billion worth of active construction projects.

The UAE is a member of the World Trade Organization and OPEC

Prior to the first exports of oil in 1962, the U.A.E. economy was dominated by pearl production, fishing, agriculture, and herding. Since the rise of oil prices in 1973, however, petroleum has dominated the economy, accounting for most of its export earnings and providing significant opportunities for investment. The U.A.E. has huge proven oil reserves, estimated at 98.8 billion barrels in 2003, with gas reserves estimated at (212 trillion cubic feet); at present production rates, these supplies would last well over 150 years. In 2006, the U.A.E. produced about 2.8 million barrels of oil per day.

Major increases in imports occurred in manufactured goods, machinery, and transportation equipment, which together accounted for 70% of total imports. Another important foreign exchange earner, the Abu Dhabi Investment Authority--which controls the investments of Abu Dhabi, the wealthiest emirate--manages an estimated $600 billion in overseas investments.

More than 6,000 companies from more than 120 countries operate at the Jebel Ali complex in Dubai, which includes a deep-water port and a free trade zone for manufacturing and distribution in which all goods for re-export or transshipment enjoy a 100% duty exemption. A major power plant with associated water desalination units, an aluminum smelter, and a steel fabrication unit are prominent facilities near the complex.

Except in the free trade zone, the U.A.E. requires at least 51% local citizen ownership in all businesses operating in the country as part of its attempt to place Emiratis into leadership positions.

As a member of the Gulf Cooperation Council (GCC), the U.A.E. participates in a wide range of GCC activities that focus on economic issues. These include regular consultations and development of common policies covering trade, investment, banking and finance, transportation, telecommunications, and other technical areas, including protection of intellectual property rights.

# FOREIGN RELATIONS

The UAE joined the United Nations and the Arab League and has established diplomatic relations with more than 60 countries, including the US, Japan, the Soviet Union, the People's Republic of China, and most Western European countries. It has played a moderate role in the Organization of Petroleum Exporting Countries, the Organization of Arab Petroleum Exporting Countries, the United Nations, and the GCC.

Substantial development assistance has increased the UAE's stature among recipient states. Most of this foreign aid (in excess of $15 billion) has been to Arab and Muslim countries.

Following Iraq's 1990 invasion and attempted annexation of Kuwait, the UAE has sought to rely on the GCC, Syria, Egypt, the US, and other Western allies for its security. The UAE believes that the Arab League needs to be restructured to become a viable institution.

## US-UAE RELATIONS

The United States has enjoyed friendly relations with the UAE since 1971. Private commercial ties, especially in petroleum, have developed into friendly government-to-government ties which include security assistance. The breadth, depth, and quality of US-UAE relations are increasing dramatically as a result of the US-led coalition's campaign to end the Iraqi occupation of Kuwait. The United States was the third country to establish formal diplomatic relations with the UAE and has had an ambassador resident in the UAE since 1974.

## PRINCIPAL US OFFICIALS

**Ambassador-- Barbara A. Leaf**

Barbara A. Leaf was confirmed as the U.S. Ambassador to the United Arab Emirates on November 17, 2014. Prior to that, she served as Deputy Assistant Secretary of State for the Arabian Peninsula in the Bureau of Near Eastern Affairs from 2013-2014, and as Deputy Assistant Secretary for Iraq from 2011-2013. Ambassador Leaf directed the U.S. Provincial Reconstruction Team in the strategic province of Basrah, Iraq from 2010-2011, leaving an assignment as Political Minister Counselor at the U.S. Embassy in Rome, Italy, to oversee the PRT's transition to a U.S. Consulate General. Prior to Rome, Ambassador Leaf served as the first Director of the Department of State's Office of Iranian Affairs.

Deputy Chief of Mission--Martin Quinn
Political Officer--Al Magleby
Economic Officer--Oliver John
Consular Officer--Robert Dolce
Public Affairs Officer--Steven Pike
Management Officer--Stewart Devine
Commercial Officer--Christian Reed

Mailing Address--PO Box 4009, Abu Dhabi; tel: 336691, USIS: 336567, Commercial Office: 345545; fax: 318441, Chancery: 213771, US Labor Office: 391604, Commercial Office: 331374.

Consul General in Dubai--Joseph Le Barron; PO Box 9343; tel: (04) 371115; fax: 379043, Commercial Office: 375121).

## TRAVEL

The U.S. Department of State's Consular Information Program advises Americans traveling and residing abroad through Country Specific Information, Travel Alerts, and Travel Warnings. **Country Specific Information** exists for all countries and includes information on entry and exit requirements, currency regulations, health conditions, safety and security, crime, political disturbances, and the addresses of the U.S. embassies and consulates abroad. **Travel Alerts** are issued to disseminate information quickly about terrorist threats and other relatively short-term conditions overseas that pose significant risks to the security of American travelers. **Travel Warnings** are issued when the State Department recommends that Americans avoid travel to a certain country because the situation is dangerous or unstable.

For the latest security information, Americans living and traveling abroad should regularly monitor the Department's Bureau of Consular Affairs Internet web site at http://www.travel.state.gov, where the current Worldwide Caution, Travel Alerts, and Travel Warnings can be found. Consular Affairs Publications, which contain information on obtaining passports and planning a safe trip abroad, are also available at http://www.travel.state.gov. For additional information on international travel, see http://www.usa.gov/Citizen/Topics/Travel/International.shtml.

The Department of State encourages all U.S citizens traveling or residing abroad to register via the State Department's travel registration website or at the nearest U.S. embassy or consulate abroad. Registration will make your presence and whereabouts known in case it is necessary to contact you in an emergency and will enable you to receive up-to-date information on security conditions.

Emergency information concerning Americans traveling abroad may be obtained by calling 1-888-407-4747 toll free in the U.S. and Canada or the regular toll line 1-202-501-4444 for callers outside the U.S. and Canada.

The National Passport Information Center (NPIC) is the U.S. Department of State's single, centralized public contact center for U.S. passport information. Telephone: 1-877-4USA-PPT (1-877-487-2778). Customer service representatives and operators for TDD/TTY are available Monday-Friday, 7:00 a.m. to 12:00 midnight, Eastern Time, excluding federal holidays.

Travelers can check the latest health information with the U.S. Centers for Disease Control and Prevention in Atlanta, Georgia. A hotline at 877-FYI-TRIP (877-394-8747) and a web site at http://wwwn.cdc.gov/travel/default.aspx give the most recent health advisories, immunization recommendations or requirements, and advice on food and drinking water safety for regions and countries. A booklet entitled "Health Information for International Travel" (HHS publication number CDC-95-8280) is available from the U.S. Government Printing Office, Washington, DC 20402, tel. (202) 512-1800.

# GOVERNMENT OF THE UNITED ARAB EMIRATES

## STRUCTURE OF GOVERNMENT

### Capital: Abu Dhabi

- Type: Federation with specified powers delegated to the UAE central government and other powers reserved to member emirates
- Long Form of Name: United Arab Emirates (no short-form name); abbreviated UAE
- Independence: 2 December 1971 (from UK; formerly Trucial States)
- Administrative Regions: 7 emirates (imarat, singular - imarah); Abu Dhabi (Abu Zaby), Ajman, Fujairah, Sharjah, Dubai (Dubayy), Ras al-Khaimah, Umm al-Quwain
- Constitution: 2 December 1971 (provisional)
- National Holiday: National Day, 2 December (1971)
- Legal System: Secular codes are being introduced by the UAE Government and in several member shaykhdoms; Islamic law remains influential
- Executive Branch: President, vice president, Supreme Council of Rulers, prime minister, deputy prime minister, Council of Ministers
- Legislative Branch: Unicameral Federal National Council (Majlis Watani Itihad)
- Judicial Branch: Union Supreme Court
- Suffrage: None
- Leaders: Chief of State: President Shaykh Zayid bin Sultan Al NUHAYYAN, (since December 1971), ruler of Abu Dhabi; Vice President Shaykh Maktum bin Rashid al-MAKTUM (since October 1990), ruler of Dubai Head of Government: Prime Minister Shaykh Maktum bin Rashid al-MAKTUM (since October 1990), ruler of Dubai; Deputy Prime Minister Sultan bin Zayid Al NUHAYYAN (since November 1990)
- Political Parties: None
- Elections: None
- Defense Expenditures: Exchange rate conversion - $1.47 billion, 5.3% of GDP (1989 est.)
- Military Branches: Army, Navy, Air Force, Federal Police Force
- Manpower Availability: Males 15-49, 974,288; 533,673 fit for military service

## MEMBERSHIP IN OTHER ORGANIZATIONS:

ABEDA, AFESD, AL, AMF, CAEU, CCC, ESCWA, FAO, G-77, GCC, IAEA, IBRD, ICAO, IDA, IDB, IFAD, IFC, ILO, IMF, IMO, INMARSAT, INTELSAT, INTERPOL, IOC, ISO (correspondent), ITU, LORCS, NAM, OAPEC, OIC, OPEC, UN, UNCTAD, UNESCO, UNIDO, UPU, WHO, WIPO, WMO, WTO
**The United Arab Emirates joined the League of Arab States in 1971.**

## COUNCIL OF MINISTERS

The Council of Ministers includes the usual complement of ministerial portfolios, and is headed by the Prime Minister. The Prime Minister, currently the Vice President, although this has not always been the case, then selects the Ministers, who may be drawn from any of the Federation's component emirates, although, naturally, the more populous emirates have generally provided more members of each CaBenet.

The Council of Ministers is the executive authority of the Federation, and is responsible for dealing with all domestic and foreign affairs. The list of the powers of the Council covers ten points, underlining its legislative capacity. Federal laws are drafted by the Council and then submitted to the National Assembly before presenting to the President. The Council of Ministers also drafts decrees and various decisions. The Prime Minister and fellow members of the Council are responsible for their work under the supreme control of the President of the Federation and the Supreme Council.

## RELATIONSHIP BETWEEN FEDERAL AND LOCAL GOVERNMENTS

The powers of the various federal institutions and their relationship with the separate institutions in each emirate, laid down in the constitution, have evolved and changed since the establishment of the state.

Under the terms of the Constitution, Rulers may, if they wish, relinquish certain areas of authority prescribed as being the responsibility of individual emirates to the federal government. One significant such decision being that to unify the Armed Forces in the mid-1970s. The 1971 Constitution also permitted each emirate to retain or to take up membership in the Organization of Petroleum Exporting Countries and the Organization of Arab Petroleum Exporting Countries, although none have done so; the only emirate to be a member in 1971, Abu Dhabi, having chosen to relinquish its memberships in favour of the Federation.

Over the course of the 25 years since the Federation was established, the United Arab Emirates has grown dramatically as a result of a sustained development programme, which has not only seen the completion of a modern infrastructure that reaches into the remotest mountain villages, but has also seen population rise more than ten fold. With such a pace of growth, the organs of government, both federal and local, have also developed impressively, and their influence now affect almost all aspects of life, for both UAE citizens and expatriates. As with other relatively young states, new institutions that were created for the first time, have derived their legitimacy and status from the extent of their activities and achievements, and from acknowledgement and appreciation of their role by the people.

The relationship between the new systems of government, federal and local, has itself evolved in a constructive manner. As the smaller emirates have benefited from development in terms of, for example, education, so they have been able to find the personnel to extend the variety of services provided by their own local governments, which had once been handled on their behalf by federal institutions, such as tourism.

At the same time, in other areas, such as the judiciary, there has been an evolving trend towards a further voluntary relinquishment of local authority to the federal institutions. These new systems of government have not, however, replaced the traditional forms. which coexist and evolve alongside them.

## UAE GOVERNMENT STRATEGY 2011-2013

The UAE Government Strategy 2011-2013 lays the foundations to achieve the UAE Vision 2021, launched by HH Sheikh Mohammed Bin Rashid Al Maktoum, Vice President and Prime Minister of the UAE and Ruler of Dubai. It forms the basis upon which the Federal Entities develop their strategic and operational plans, and consists of seven general principles, seven strategic priorities and seven strategic enablers.

The strategic priorities and enablers are not fully comprehensive but comprise the major focus areas for the government. Each strategic priority and enabler includes general main directions and specific sub-directions - which combined lead to the fulfillment of the relevant main direction - and which the government will work to achieve during this strategy cycle.

### GENERAL PRINCIPLES THAT GUIDE THE UAE GOVERNMENT STRATEGY

The UAE Government Strategy 2011-2013 strives to ensure that all Government work is conducted according to a set of guiding principles that puts citizens first and promotes an accountable, lean, innovative, and forward-looking Government.

The seven general principles that will steer Government work are as follows:

- Enhance the role of Federal Entities in devising effective regulations and integrated policies by successful planning and enforcement
- Enhance effective coordination and cooperation among Federal Entities and with Local Governments
- Focus on delivering high-quality, customer-centric and integrated government services
- Invest in human resource capabilities and develop leaders
- Promote efficient resource management within Federal Entities and leverage dynamic partnerships
- Pursue a culture of excellence through strategic thinking, continuous performance improvement, and superior results
- Enhance transparency and accountable governance mechanisms throughout Federal Entities

## STRATEGIC PRIORITIES OF THE UAE GOVERNMENT

The seven strategic priorities are the themes that define the priorities of the UAE Government over the coming three years:

- Cohesive Society and Preserved Identity
- First-Rate Education System
- World-Class Healthcare
- Competitive Knowledge Economy
- Safe Public and Fair Judiciary
- Sustainable Environment and Infrastructure
- Strong Global Standing

## STRATEGIC ENABLERS OF THE UAE GOVERNMENT

The seven strategic enablers direct how the machinery of the UAE Government must operate in order to fulfill its strategic priorities:

- Skilled Human Capital
- Customer-Centric Service
- Efficient Financial Management
- Good Institutional Governance
- Dynamic Government Networks
- Effective Legislative Process and Integrated Policy-Making
- Effective Government Communication

## TRAVEL

Customs: A visa is required for entry. Business or visitor visas can be arranged with only a few days' notice through local sponsors or major hotels. Hotels levy a varying surcharge for this service. No immunizations are required. Health requirements change; check latest information.

Health: No unusual precautions in food and drink are necessary. Water is potable. For travel to some areas, malaria suppressant is advisable. Many Western-trained doctors practice in the UAE.

# INTERNET AND ELECTRONIC COMMUNICATION IN UAE: STRATEGIC INFORMATION

The UAE is a federation that consists of seven emirates located on the Arabian Peninsula between the Arabian Gulf and the Gulf of Oman. The capital is Abu Dhabi. The federation consists of the Emirates of Abu Dhabi, Dubai, Sharjah, Ajman, Umm Al Quwain, Ras Al Khaima and Al Fujairah. It is bordered from the North and North West by the Arabian Gulf, from the East and South by the Sultanate of Oman and the Gulf of Oman, and from the West by the Kingdom of Saudi Arabia and Qatar occupying a total area of 83.600 m². The population of the UAE has exceeded 4,104,695 according to the 2005 census. This can be contributed to the UAE having an open economy with one of the highest annual individual incomes in the world; it also has a large trade exchange with various countries worldwide that contributes sufficiently to its national income. However, crude oil and natural gas are the main sources of the country's income, forming approximately 33% of the annual local production. In addition, the UAE has joined the World Trade Organization in 1996.

The population of the UAE is estimated to be 4,496,000, with a growth rate of around 6.5 per cent a year. UAE citizens account for a little over 20 per cent of the population, with the rest coming from the rest of the Arab world, the Indian sub-continent, the Far East, Europe and elsewhere. The national language is Arabic, although English and several Asian languages are widely used, particularly in commerce. Islam is the state religion. The main population centers are the cities of Abu Dhabi (the capital) and Dubai.

The UAE lies in the arid tropical zone extending across Asia and northern Africa, however the Indian Ocean has a strong influence on the climatic conditions in the area, since the country borders both the Arabian Gulf and the Gulf of Oman. This explains why high temperatures in summer are always accompanied by high humidity along the coast. Noticeable variations in climate occur between the coastal regions, the deserts of the interior and mountainous areas.

Between the months of November and March a moderate, warm climate prevails during the day at an average temperature of 26C, and a slightly cooler climate prevails throughout the night at an average temperature of 15C. The humidity tends to rise in the summer months, between June and August. Prevailing winds, influenced by the monsoons, vary between south or southeast, to west or north to northwest depending upon the season and location. Average rainfall is low at less than 6.5 centimeters annually and more than half of the average rainfall occurs in December and January.

Dirhams and fils are the units of currency with 100 fils to the Dirham (Dh). The Dirham is tied to the US Dollar at a steady exchange rate of $US 1= Dh 3.671. Banks usually give the best rates on foreign currency exchange but hotels and airports are often quicker and are open outside banking hours. Money changers tend to have a wider range of currencies but their rates may be higher. Exchange rates are published daily.

Internet Users in the Middle East and the World[3]

| Middle East | Population (2011 Est.) | Pop. % of World | Internet Users 31 Dec 2011 | % Population (Penetration) | Users % World | Facebook 31-03-2012 |
|---|---|---|---|---|---|---|

| | | | | | | |
|---|---|---|---|---|---|---|
| Region | | | | | | |
| Total Middle East | 216,258,843 | 3.1 % | 77,020,995 | 35.6 % | 3.4 % | 20,247,900 |
| Rest of the World | 6,713,796,311 | 96.9 % | 2,190,212,747 | 32.6 % | 96.6 % | 815,277,380 |
| World Total | 6,930,055,154 | 100.0 % | 2,267,233,742 | 32.7 % | 100.0 % | 835,525,280 |

Overall, GCC countries have maintained leadership in eGovernment readiness among Arab peers. They have taken serious steps to support the diffusion of eGovernment in their societies (Al-Khouri & Bachlaghem, 2011; Al-Khouri & Bal, 2007). Several UNDP reports confirmed that the growing efforts of GCC governments to promote digital transformation and literacy have helped further enhance the region's collective ranking in the UN eGovernment Readiness Surveys (UNDP, 2010; UNDP 2012). These reports indicated that GCC countries played various roles for eGovernment in addressing the global financial crisis.

Governments of the GCC countries are considered to be in intense competition with each other to develop a new knowledge-based economy, away from the current dependence on oil, and to make their products and services competitive on a global scale (Awan, 2003). GCC countries are proceeding at a rapid space to use more service oriented and citizen-centric operating models. This rapid reform is bringing a paradigm shift in the way citizens in the GCC are interacting with their governments. There are serious efforts in these countries to develop electronic operating environments, with advanced capabilities to build the right conditions for the eCitizens concept to evolve.

The next section provides an overview of the eGovernment strategy of one of the GCC countries, namely the UAE government's strategic framework that aims to electronically transform all public services through a two-year action plan.

**UAE eGovernment Strategic Framework**

Although local initiatives in the UAE started earlier, the federal eGovernment programme started in 2001. One of the early eServices offered at a federal level was the electronic card known as the eDirham in 2001, which was issued to collect government services fees (Figure 4). Today, the UAE is considered to have one of the most advanced and world-class information and communication technology infrastructures.

The UAE is among the highest investing governments in adopting and implementing progressive ICT in its government and private sectors. The UAE has made a remarkable worldwide achievement in the field of eGovernment according to the UN eGovernment Survey 2012, which focuses on the role of eGovernment in sustainable development. The UAE achieved the 28th rank overall according to the survey against the 49th rank in the 2010 Survey. It scored 7th on online service index against 99th in the 2010 survey and 6th in the eParticipation index against 86th in the 2010 survey

The UAE has recently announced a revised eGovernment Transformation Strategic Framework. This framework comprises numerous strategic initiatives at a federal level to transform all government services and make them available electronically through various channels. The following section will provide an overview of this strategy.

### 5.1 UAE Federal eGovernment Strategic Framework

The United Arab Emirates has developed a federal eGovernment Strategic Framework for 2012-2014 that charts out the initiatives and courses of action the government intends to take over a period of three years. The framework is aimed to contribute to:

1. UAE Vision 2021: which drives the UAE to be one of the best countries in the world, see also Table 3; and

2. UAE Government Strategy 2011-2013: that aims at putting citizens first and developing an accountable and innovative government.

The framework also makes reference to some of the existing federal strategies to ensure alignment with government strategic intents and plans. See also Table 3.

The seven primary references in the UAE eGovernment strategy

| Description | References |
|---|---|
| Is the highest reference strategy and provides the strategic vision of the country, for which the eGovernment strategy needs to be aligned with, and contribute to its realisation. The UAE vision 2021 envisages development of a knowledge-based economy that will be diverse and flexible led by skilled professional Emiratis. The vision contains four important components with detailed objectives related to national identity, economy, education and health. It seeks to make the UAE a land of ambitious and confident people who hold on to their heritage; a strong federation; a competitive economy led by creative and knowledgeable Emiratis; and finally a high quality of life in a generous and sustainable environment.<br><br>http://www.vision2021.ae/ | UAE Vision 2021 |
| Provides a phased plan for the Federal Government to progress towards the UAE Vision 2021.<br><br>http://uaecabinet.ae/English/Documents/PMO%20StrategyDocEngFinV2.pdf | UAE Strategy 2011-2013 |
| Government strategy to regulate the telecommunications sector. It represents the basis on which the eGovernment strategy was developed, as it defines and details the three dimensions of service, environment and readiness. | UAE Government ICT Strategy |
| Provides an analysis of the current state of federal government services, as well as detailed guidelines on how to develop them. It also includes many of the strategic initiatives that fall under the eGovernment programme. | Services Development Strategy |
| Alignment of eGovernment budget with the federal budget.<br><br>http://www.mof.gov.ae/En/Budget/Pages/ZEROBudgeting.aspx | Federal government budget |
| Covers three dimensions (environment, readiness and services), and contributes to the identification of gaps and opportunities that can be addressed through the objectives and specific initiatives in the eGovernment strategy.<br><br>http://www.emiratesegov.ae | Current Situation Analysis |
| Comparisons of best practices in the field of eGovernment to support the development of the new strategy and define its primary objectives and initiatives. | Benchmarking |

Figure 9: UAE eGovernment 2011-2014 initiatives Source: http://www.emiratesegov.ae

In order to achieve its goals, the government has identified 38 initiatives to be implemented as part of the eGovernment strategy. Figure 9 depicts the initiatives for each of the four work streams. These 38 initiatives cover four vital eGovernment areas:

1. **Strengthening the regulatory framework and governance mechanisms for eGovernment in the country.** This is related to the legal and regulatory environment governing acquisition and use of information systems in government agencies, eGovernment services, and a high level plan for the overall development of the public sector in the country. Regulations and laws are considered primary enablers to support eGovernment and ensure security, reliability and data privacy. As such, this area also includes the development of strong governance structure to facilitate communication between the different stakeholders and attempts to capture their needs and turn them into electronic service systems.

2. **Infrastructure support of information systems in the United Arab Emirates.** This theme deals with creating a solid infrastructure for information systems to enable the delivery of world-class eGovernment services. It also focuses on aspects such as facilitation of exchange and sharing of data between government agencies.

3. **Launching and providing eGovernment applications and services.** This theme focuses on a set of applications and services to be provided to government agencies to support them in providing eGovernment services effectively and efficiently.

4. **Development of effective mechanisms for performance management.** This theme focuses on improving overall effectiveness and actual levels of performance of departments of information technology within government agencies. It also deals with developing automated tools and reports to monitor performance indicators and overall performance management.

## NATIONAL IDENTITY MANAGEMENT

The UAE national identity management infrastructure is a strategic initiative to enhance homeland security and develop a federated identity management system enabling secure eGovernment transactions (Al-Khouri, 2012b). A federated identity is the means of linking a person's electronic identity and attributes, stored across multiple distinct identity management systems (Madsen, 2005). Such systems would allow individuals to use the same user name, password or other personal identification to sign in to the networks of more than one enterprise in order to conduct transactions (Bertino & Takahashi, 2011; Roebuck, 2011; Windley, 2005).

As part of the programme, the UAE issues smart identity cards for all of its population. The UAE national identity card is one of the world's most advanced and secure smart cards. The card is provided with identification parameters stored securely in the smart chip. It thus enables establishing a person's identity on-site (physically) and remotely (virtually), enabling secure and trusted transactions. The multi factor authentication which provides both match-on-card4 and match-off-card5 features, facilitates validation, verification and authentication of any given identity.

The UAE ID card capabilities of on-site identification, remote identification and authentication are available to be used across the different applications enabling various forms of electronic transactions e.g., G2C, B2C, etc. These are facilitated by PIN verification, biometric authentication (match on card and match off card features) and digital signatures

The UAE national identity management system eliminates the need to maintain distinct user credentials in separate systems. In an eGovernment context, this should result in greatly simplified administration and streamlined access to resources.

Government agencies in the UAE's federated identity management (FIM) system will depend on the National Identity Validation Gateway to authenticate their respective users and vouch for their access to services. Agencies will be able to share applications without needing to adopt the same technologies for directory services, security and authentication. This is enabled by the active directory services part of the FIM that allows government agencies to recognise their users through a single identity

UAE is currently taking rapid steps in integrating its identity management infrastructure and its smart card capabilities in various public sector systems and applications. Some of the current deployments for card usage include the eGate service at the airports that allows cardholders to pass through immigration control using biometric authentication.

In addition, citizens in Abu Dhabi[6], for example, have the ability to login to the online local government portal and avail themselves of various eServices and utility payments. Some additional services provided through the Abu Dhabi portal include viewing and modifying details of one's personal traffic profile with Abu Dhabi Police, such as address, licence plate, etc.

There is increasing motivation in the UAE's public sector to rely on the new identity card to provide its services. It is expected that all eGovernment services would eventually require registering for the UAE identity card and PIN to access online government services. Integration of the national identity card is ongoing in all the federal and local authorities.

The design of the UAE federated identity management system ensures reliable and secure access from multiple locations, and hence provides advanced mobility. This supports the vision set in the UAE eGovernment strategic framework to deliver public sector services through different channels; whether it is the internet, kiosk machines, mobile phone applications or any other electronic channel. The UAE national identity card is viewed as the cornerstone for enabling successful deployment of eGovernment and eServices strategy in the country.

## UAE ICT FUND AND INVESTMENT OPPORTUNTIES

**P.O. Box 116688,Dubai,United Arab Emirates,- Dir: +971 4 2300169 , Tel: +971 4 2300089, Fax: +971 4 2300161, Website: www.ictfund.gov.ae,Email: apply@ictfund.gov.ae**

The ICT Fund has a determined mission to provide targeted funding and advisory services to companies, organisations and individuals to empower them to develop the innovation and knowledge capital of the UAE ICT sector with their research, education and entrepreneurship.

The Fund strives to promote a culture of entrepreneurship in the UAE ICT sector and improve linkage between industry and academia to ultimately promote the involvement of UAE nationals in the realm of scientific and technology research to foster self-reliance of the UAE in technology creation and development.

The Fund is driven by a strong vision to make the ICT sector the leading sector in the Middle East through enabling and fostering progressive innovation in the field. At ICT Fund, we believe that a global leadership position for the UAE ICT sector can be attained by investing in innovative ideas that contribute to the intellectual growth of the sector, yielding measurable results.

The Gulf region has become home to the third-fastest growing

Information Technology market in the world. At the heart of this progress is the UAE IT sector, having expanded by an impressive 27.5% in 2005, with significant growth projected to continue.

Helping to drive this momentum is the Information and Communication Technology (ICT) Fund. A new venture dedicated to advancing the UAE ICT sector both regionally and globally, the ICT Fund proudly shares the UAE's commitment to innovation and progress. The first of its kind in the Middle East, the ICT Fund is designed to fuel innovative research & development projects within the UAE ICT sector as well as support education and training in the field.

Aiming to promote the involvement of UAE nationals in the realm of scientific and technology research, the Fund strives to create a culture of entrepreneurship in the sector and improve linkage between industry and academia. With the firm belief that technology is the creative engine of all new opportunities, the ICT Fund offers funding to drive results, introducing innovation with impact to the region.

## APPLICATION GUIDELINES – INCUBATORS

The objective of this document is to provide guidelines to applicants for development of their proposals for the setting up of Incubators focusing on the ICT (Information and Communication Technology) sector in the UAE.

In addition to the requirements within this document, the applicant may also provide any additional information that would further support the application.

The application will be screened for eligibility (applicant status, nationality requirements, etc.) and then evaluated across the different components – applicant details, technical proposal and commercial proposal. Evaluation criteria will include applicant qualifications, technical feasibility, alignment of commercial proposal with technical proposal, among others.

The ICT Fund reserves the right to request for any clarification on the submitted information or seek any additional information. The ICT Fund also reserves the right to summarily reject an application for funding without assigning any reason whatsoever.

1 Executive Summary
2 Applicant Details
Applicant No: _______
(for office use)

PLEASE COMPLETE USING CAPITALS

2.1 Lead Applicant Name
2.2 Address
Postcode
Country

Tel. No.
Fax No.
Email
Website

2.3 For Companies, please provide:· Company Registration No. and Date· Registration documents and copies of Articles of Association/Memorandum of Association· Details of owners/promoters/shareholders and respective funding/shareholding· Details of Board of Directors and Senior Management and Financial Statements for the past 5 years (if available)

2.4 For Consortiums/Partnerships:Please provide details of Memorandum of Understanding (MoU)/Partnership Agreement between members

2.5 Proof of UAE representation (extent and form of participation of UAE nationals/companies)

2.6 Qualifications of the applicant to establish/operate an Incubator

3 Technical Proposal

A Technical background information on the incubator

3.1 Infrastructure details (R&D, testing and prototype development)

3.2 Processes (for business plan review, mentoring, business review, and exit processes with criteria)

3.3 Support services and processes (business advisory, technology commercialisation, investors & academic networks and industry exposure)

3.4 Incubation performance targets with timelines

B Details of relevant assets/resources

3.5 Committed third party support (if applicable)

3.6 Premises, equipment, experts, partnerships, agreements, etc.

C Capability of the incubator

3.7 Management team's detailed profiles and experience in Technology, Entrepreneurship, Incubation, Financing

3.8 Quality of industry expertise

3.9 Quality of scientific expertise

D Feasibility

3.10 Management's views on alignment of incubator infrastructure and capabilities with planned results, along with justifications

3.11 Management's views on incubator's planned timelines, along with justifications

3.12 Management's views on adequacy of access to all forms of expertise required, along with justifications

E Key Performance Indicators (KPIs)
3.13 Proposed KPIs to measure the success of the incubator
4 Commercial Proposal

A Marketing strategy and plan to ensure sourcing of clients

B Five-year projections
4.1 Revenue model with plans (All service fees, IP ownership fees) , and related projections
4.2 Infrastructure and other resource cost estimates
4.3 Human Resources cost estimates
4.4 Technology cost estimates
4.5 Other costs
4.6 Detailed expenditure plans
4.7 Detailed expenditure plan
C Incubator financial statements and projections (past 5 years if available and next 5 years) – Balance Sheet, Income Statement, Cash Flow Statement
D Detailed related funding plan (including future years)
E Details of other funding partners
F Contribution to the ICT Fund, if any, in the future

Checklist

Please ensure you have attached the following documentation:

0 In case of companies, details of owners / promoters / shareholders along with registration documents and copies of Articles of Association / Memorandum of Association

0 In case of companies, details of Board of Directors and Senior Management and Financial Statements for the past 5 years (if available)

0 In case of consortiums / Partnerships, details of Memorandum of Understanding (MoU) / Partnership Agreement between members

0 Proof of UAE representation (extent and form of participation of UAE nationals / companies)

0 Technical background information on the incubator: Infrastructure details (R&D, testing and prototype development); Processes (for business plan review, mentoring, business review, and exit processes with criteria); Support services and processes (business advisory, technology commercialisation, investors & academic networks and industry exposure); Incubation performance targets with timelines

0 Details of relevant assets / resources: Committed third party support (if applicable); Premises, equipment, experts, partnerships, agreements, etc.
0 Marketing strategy & plan to ensure sourcing of clients
0 Five-year projections: Revenue model with plans (All service fees, IP ownership fees) , and related projections; Infrastructure and other resource cost estimates; Human Resources cost estimates; Technology cost estimates; Other costs; Detailed expenditure plans
0 Technology cost estimates; Other costs; Detailed expenditure plans

0 Incubator financial statements and projections (past 5 years if available and next 5 years) – Balance Sheet, Income Statement, Cash Flow Statement
0 Detailed related funding plan (including future years)

5 Undertaking

I, , hereby declare that:

· I am duly authorized to sign this application

· The information and documents provided for this application is complete, true and accurate and no material details with potential adverse effects for this application has been withheld and that it is an offence to provide false or misleading information

· Once I am granted with the funding, I understand and agree that any output of the Incubator will be primarily utilized for the development of the UAE ICT sector

Signature:
Name:

**APPLICATION GUIDELINES – RESEARCH AND DEVELOPMENT PROJECTS**

The objective of this document is to provide guidelines to applicants for development of their proposals for funding of Research and Development Projects focusing on the ICT (Information and Communication Technology) sector in the UAE.

In addition to the requirements within this document, the applicant may also provide any additional information that would further support the application.

The application will be screened for eligibility (applicant status, nationality requirements, etc.) and then evaluated across the different components – applicant details, technical proposal and commercial proposal. Evaluation criteria will include applicant qualifications, technical feasibility, alignment of commercial proposal with technical proposal, among others.

The ICT Fund reserves the right to request for any clarification on the submitted information or seek any additional information. The ICT Fund also reserves the right to summarily reject an application for funding without assigning any reason whatsoever.

1 Executive Summary

2 Applicant Details

Applicant No: _______

(for office use)

PLEASE COMPLETE USING CAPITALS

2.1 Lead Applicant Name

2.2 Address

Postcode
Country

Tel. No.
Fax No.
Email
Website

2.3 For Companies, please provide:· Company Registration No. and Date· Registration documents and copies of Articles of Association/Memorandum of Association· Details of owners/promoters/shareholders and respective funding/shareholding· Details of Board of Directors and Senior Management and Financial Statements for the past 5 years (if available)

2.4 For Consortiums/Partnerships: Please provide details of Memorandum of Understanding (MoU)/Partnership Agreement between members

2.5 Proof of UAE representation (extent and form of participation of UAE nationals/companies)

2.6 Qualifications of the applicant vis-à-vis project requirements

3 Technical Proposal

A Description of the project

3.1 Research objectives
3.2 Literature / Existing research survey
3.3 Research methodology
3.4 Proposed results
3.5 Proposed plan
3.6 Description of resources required
3.7 Team members for execution of the project

B Details of relevant assets/resources

3.8 Committed third party support (if applicable)
3.9 Premises, equipment, experts, partnerships, agreements, etc.

C Output feasibility
3.10 Management's views on the project's potential of success, along with justifications
3.11 Management's views on project timeframes, along with justifications
3.12 Management's assessment of impact on existing technology / project output environment

D Commercialisation feasibility (if applicable)

3.13 Commercial implications of the proposed outputs of the project (if project is seeking commercial benefits)

E Key Performance Indicators (KPIs)

3.14 Proposed KPIs to measure the success of the project

4 Commercial Proposal

A Two-year projections

4.1 Revenue model (if applicable)
4.2 Infrastructure and other resource cost estimates
4.3 Human Resources cost estimates
4.4 Technology cost estimates
4.5 Project registration / IP protection costs
4.6 Other costs

4.7 Detailed expenditure plan

B Details of other funding partners
C Detailed funding plan (including future years)
D Contribution to the ICT Fund, if any, in the future

Checklist

Please ensure you have attached the following documentation:

0 In case of companies, details of owners / promoters / shareholders along with registration documents and copies of Articles of Association / Memorandum of Association

0 In case of companies, details of Board of Directors and Senior Management and Financial Statements for the past 5 years (if available)

0 In case of consortiums / Partnerships, details of Memorandum of Understanding (MoU) / Partnership Agreement between members

0 Proof of UAE representation (extent and form of participation of UAE nationals / companies)

0 Qualifications of the applicant vis-à-vis project requirements

0 Description of the project: Research Objectives; Literature / Existing research survey; Research Methodology; Proposed results; Proposed plan; Description of resources required; Team members for execution of the project

0 Details of relevant assets / resources: Committed third party support (if applicable); Premises, equipment, experts, partnerships, agreements, etc.

0 Two-year projections: Revenue model (if applicable); Infrastructure and other resource cost estimates; Human Resources cost estimates; Technology cost estimates; Project registration / IP protection costs; Other costs; Detailed expenditure plan

0 Detailed funding plan (including future years)

5 Undertaking

I, , hereby declare that:

· I am duly authorized to sign this application

· The information and documents provided for this application is complete, true and accurate and no material details with potential adverse effects for this application has been withheld and that it is an offence to provide false or misleading information

· Once I am granted with the funding, I understand and agree that any output of the project will be primarily utilized for the development of the UAE ICT sector

Signature:
Name:
Date:

# STRATEGIC STATISTICS

## IAM STATISTICS

| Description of Blocked Content | Jan – October 2011 |
|---|---|
| Internet Content that contradicts with the ethics and morals of the UAE including Nudity and Dating | 88% |
| Internet Content that contains material which expresses hate to religions | 2% |
| Internet Content that is not in line with UAE Laws | 2% |
| Internet Content that allow or assist Users to access Blocked Content | 2% |
| Internet content that directly or indirectly Constitute a risk on UAE internet users such as Phishing websites, Hacking tools & Spywares | 6% |
| Internet Content that is relevant to gambling | 0% |
| Internet Content that provide information on purchasing, manufacturing, promoting and using illegal drugs. | 0% |

# GENERAL POLICY FOR THE TELECOMMUNICATIONS SECTOR IN THE STATE OF THE UNITED ARAB EMIRATES (2006-2010)

This document describes the General Policy for the Telecommunication Sector (the "GTP") of in the State of the United Arab Emirates (the "Government"). The GTP will function as a catalyst towards accelerating the growth and development of the telecommunication sector in its efforts to support the Government's goal of developing the country as the premier Information and Communication Technology ("ICT") hub in the region and beyond.

The Government recognizes that the provision of a world-class competitive telecommunication infrastructure is of critical importance to the economic development of the country. This sector is a key enabler for the other sectors of the economy and a critical catalyst for national progress. It forms the backbone of industries such as trade, financial services, technology-based services, tourism, media, education, oil, manufacturing, transportation and health services.

The policies contained herein will serve as guidelines to all parties involved in the telecommunications sector, including consumers, service providers, operators, investors and the Government.

## 2. GOVERNMENT OBJECTIVES

The key government objectives of relevance to the GTP are:

• To develop the non-oil sector of the
• economy including the areas of trade, financial services, technology-based services, tourism, media, education, manufacturing, transportation and health services. To reinforce the utilization of advanced technology.

• To support and promote economic growth while maintaining economic and social stability.
• To increase the participation of UAE

- • nationals in the economy.
- To catalyze the policies that lead to
- building a comprehensive strategy aimed at developing a diverse economic infrastructure.

## 3 THE GENERAL POLICIES

In order to help achieve the above-mentioned objectives, the Government has outlined the following policies for thetelecommunications sector:

### 1.3 ESTABLISH POLICIES AND REGULATORY FRAMEWORK

The Government will establish a regulatory and policy framework that facilitates the development of the country's telecommunications and ICT infrastructure and services in order to meet national, regional and international objectives through:

1-Gradually introducing competition in 1. the telecommunications sector to achieve greater efficiency, ever increasing quality, diverse choices and availability of services. Ensuring that such competition is

2. sustainable, through providing an appropriate regulatory framework to protect the rights of the enterprises operating in this sector and to protect the rights of the consumers in the Telecommunications services.

3. Ensuring that all reasonable demands for telecommunications services are met and in particular, that ubiquitous and affordable access to basic telecommunications services is provided to all segments of society.

Transforming the economy through accelerated development of the national telecommunication and ICT infrastructure.

(Managing scarce national resources such as but not limited to spectrum, numbering and rights of way in a transparent and non-discriminatory manner, .having regard for the need to foster efficient use of such resources to enable sustainable competition.

6. Encouraging all segments of society to use the Internet to access and contribute to information, ideas and knowledge while promoting responsible use thereof in accordance with the social and moral values of the country.

7-Encouraging participation and investment by local and international companies in the development of the telecommunications sector and the innovative applications of advanced and emerging technologies.

1. Ensuring that adequate protection is given to the rights and interests of all consumers of telecommunications services, including but not limited to data protection, privacy and resolution of complaints.
2. Encouraging the scarce individual highly skilled experts in the ICT sector.
3. Encouraging the convergence of the Telecommunications sector with other national sectors through establishing a fully integrated relationship on both vertical and horizontal levels.
4. Educating the society on the proper and responsible use of the different Telecommunication services.

### 3.2 Promote and Develop New Technologies

The Government will promote the use of new technologies in the UAE through:

1. Leading the Region with existing and future e-government initiatives
2. Facilitating the development of e-commerce and value-added services utilizing an advanced telecommunications infrastructure.

3. Encouraging the development and deployment of infrastructure taking advantage of the convergence of information technology, media, and telecommunication.

### 3.3 Become the Regional ICT Hub The Government will support the development of the UAE as a regional ICT and telecommunications hub by:

1. Encouraging the establishment and growth of competitive ICT based enterprises.
2.Encouraging the development of value-added and enhanced services that make use of broadband, wireless and other innovative technologies.

3. Ensuring a secure environment in telecommunication applications and usage, including information security and network security, authentication, privacy and .consumer protection by developing Policies and Regulatory Framework for this subject.

### 3.4 Develop the Country's Human Capital

The Government will facilitate the development of human capital in the telecommunications and ICT sector to meet the demands of the economy, serving both local and regional requirements by:

1. Investing in national capability development in order to improve the demand-supply of telecommunications and ICT national human resources and build national capabilities in emerging areas of growth in this sector.

2. Promoting the use of ICT in all stages of education, training and human resource development.

3. Encouraging content creators, publishers, producers, teachers, trainers, archivists,librarians and learners to play an active role in promoting ICT.

### 3.5 Encourage Research and Development

The Government will encourage research and development activities within an integrated complex, and establish relationships with international academic institutions.

## 4 POLICY REVIEWS

The Government believes that it is important that its policies continue to be relevant in a rapidly changing and dynamic environment. The Supreme Committee for the Supervision of the Telecommunications Sector will monitor both local and global telecommunications sector trends in order to provide timely and relevant advice for the Government policy reviews. This is to ease facilitate the creation of opportunities and sound investment environment and to encourage making use of the expertise of other developed countries.

Since the introduction of competition in the UAE telecoms sector in February 2007, the TRA has issued numerous directives, regulations and decisions that resulted in significant developments in telecoms services. In 2008, the TRA continued to support such developments by introducing more regulations and policies that would further enhance the sector.

The year saw such milestones as the Corporate Communications & Practices Policy, the Regulatory Instruments Designations, and the Regulatory Policy on the Internet Access Management. TRA directives during 2008 included a resolution regarding the Licensing Framework; followed by a resolution on Licensing Regulations. The UAE national domain ".ae" was the focus of much regulatory work in 2008, with no less than 16 regulatory policies and resolutions issued by the TRA to govern Domain Administration.

The TRA also prepared other relevant instruments and guidelines, including the eArchiving Guidelines and the Online Consumer Protection Guidelines. The TRA has also been working with the UAE Central Bank on the possible introduction of eMoney regulations, and with the Dubai eGovernment on the Trust ae initiative. Both parties have signed an MoU to work together on setting out the terms and conditions under which qualified websites are allowed to use a "Trustae" seal.

In 2008, the TRA also issued two Service License templates: one for the Global Mobile Personal Communications by Satellite (GMPCS), and another for Public Mobile Radio. The TRA also ratified the Articles of Association for two companies set up to operate ICT-related services: Satellite Communications Company (Yahsat), and Star Satellite Communications. The licensing of a third company, Specialized Telecommunications Corporation (Nidaa), was also approved by the TRA during the year.

As the TRA is running the UAE search and rescue frequencies database, the TRA represented the UAE in joining the COSPAS-SARSAT system. Aimed at providing accurate, timely, and reliable distress alert and location data, the global system is intended to help search and rescue authorities in locating and assisting persons in distress.

The eCommerce at the TRA completed the first phase in 2008. This entailed conducting a detailed study on licensing, approval, monitoring and overseeing CSP activity. The study investigated international best practices, and compared the regulations applied in 10 different countries around the world. Based on the study's outcome, the eCommerce Department produced a draft framework for the regulation of CSPs, along with a licensing template, which were subsequently approved and issued by the TRA.

In parallel with its eCommerce initiatives, the TRA also completed a number of eGovernment initiatives in 2008. During the year, the TRA signed an MoU with the Dubai eGovernment (DeG), leading to a partnership on the Trustae initiative. Designed in line with the UAE government's strategy on electronic commerce and transactions; the initiative aims to boost confidence in the electronic business environment in the UAE.

Managed as a joint-venture between the TRA and DeG, the initiative would lead to the introduction of an electronic seal, "Trustae", which would be granted to online eProviders who meet its criteria. As proposed by the initiative, the "Trustae" seal would be an indication that an electronic site applies a stringent code of conduct for online business.

The Be'tha initiative was launched in response to the increasing demand in the country for national human resources specialized in telecoms and related fields. Following an assessment of the current supply-demand scenario, the TRA found that the number of the UAE graduates in ICT-related fields was insufficient to meet the growing needs of a sector that continues to grow year after year. Thus, the TRA launched its initiative, through which academic scholarships will be given to distinguished students – both male and female

## UAE TELECOM AND INTERNET MARKET

The UAE's telecom market was still a monopoly, with government owned operator Etisalat the loan choice. But the entrance of telecom operator du in February marked a vital shift.

In less than a year du has managed to grab a 15 per cent of the mobile telecom market and analysts predict that it will continue to grow in the years to come. "Du is a start-up in a mature market, but because of the commercially driven management, we expect du's market share to reach 30 per cent in 2010," said Marise Ananian, telecom research analyst at investment banking firm EFG-Hermes.

For now, Etisalat will continue to dominate the market, having both a strong foundation and infrastructure which dates back to 1976. "One of the biggest challenges was competing with a company that already had infrastructure set up for more than a decade," admits Osman Sultan, CEO of du.

Another challenge du faced is not having a sister company in the market to guide the way. "Unlike other telecom companies in the region we didn't have a back to rely on, like Mobinil in Egypt had Orascom and Vodafone Egypt had Vodafone International," he added. Being a "stand alone" company du had to rely entirely on finding its own niche in the market and to attract both existing and new subscribers.

There were initial reports of unhappy customers struggling to get a connection when they wanted to make calls. Sultan told AME Info that "bad connection" problems are no longer an issue for customers.

"The stage of being a new-comer network is now behind us," he said. Currently du covers 85 per cent of its population on its own network, while the remaining 15 per cent is covered under a National Roaming Agreement with Etisalat.

Du currently claims it has more than one million mobile subscribers, while Etisalat registered 6.3 million subscriptions, which put the rate of penetration at an all time high of 150 per cent, telecom officials said. Sultan expects further growth by year end.

According to government statistics in 2006, the UAE's population is 4.6 million, which means that there are about 178 mobile numbers in circulation per 100 people, or about two sim cards per person. "With [this] penetration rate, the UAE is among the world's most technologically advanced countries in the world," Mohammad Hasan Omran, Etisalat chairman told a telecom conference last month.

But Andrawes Snobar, Senior Research Analyst at Jordan-based telecoms consultancy Arab Advisors Group, believes that these rates are "over inflated" by the companies, as no definition was set by the country's Telecommunications Regulatory Authority (TRA).

"The penetration rate is inflated because companies just lump active, non-active and prepaid subscribers together without any set definition from the TRA," he told AME Info.

Wael Ziada, telecom analyst at Egypt's EFG Hermes agrees. "Due to the lack of an active subscriber definition, I believe that about 25 per cent or less of du's reported mobile subscribers are non-active," he said.

Sultan admitted that du counts both active and non-active subscribers in its numbers. "We do follow the international definition of an active subscriber, which is basically an individual who makes at least one call over a period of 90 days," he said.

But he was not prepared to reveal the true active users figure unless competing telecom giant Etisalat does the same. "Both companies have to reveal these numbers together so people would be able to compare apples with apples," he said.

"I am in favour of disclosing the number of active users, but the decision has to be taken from the Regulatory Telecom Authority for both companies to do so," added Sultan.

Snobar suggested that going forward operators should abide with what the three months rule. "This means that if subscribers don't use their lines for three months they would be considered non-active," explained Snobar.

Seemly mobile saturated the UAE has a relatively high standard of living in comparison to other Middle Eastern countries, so many people could afford to have more than one mobile line. "People in the UAE market are always attracted to new products and services, so when du was launched they wanted to benefit from the price difference," said Snobar.

As a result of the public's sheer curiosity and desire for added benefits about 300,000 customers subscribed to du on the day it launched. "There is no magic recipe for success...people just want more value for money and that's were we came in by introducing per second billing, mobile TV, e-shopping and other services," said Sultan.

But it is not expected to turn a profit until 2009. "You have to understand that profits don't happen over months, it takes time and I believe that in 2009 we will start acquiring profit," said Sultan. Earlier this year the World Economic Forum ranked the UAE the most competitive economy in the Middle East and North Africa, based on IT resources. But many analysts today are becoming more skeptical about the TRA's intension towards liberalising the telecom sector. "The government owns about 40 per cent in the stakes of both operators so there is a vested interest in both as they are not independent companies," said Snobar.

He felt this might lead du to become a carbon copy of Etisalat. "The two companies might end up being exactly the same in everything which cancels about diversity in the market," he said.

So this "muzzled" competition still leaves the UAE a few steps back from being WTO compliant. "I think that there is room in the market for added competition, in other words du should yield positive results for everyone," said EFG's Ananian.

Sultan said he welcomes competition, even if at the moment the TRA faces a few obstacles in terms of distributing telecom towers in the country. "It's true that in some areas users are forced to use one of the operators without having any other choice, but this is because of technical issues with regards to sharing infrastructure which the TRA is working on," said Sultan.

"At the end of the day, we want people to have a choice in what operator to use and I have confidence that the regulator's regime will give full competition to the nation," he added.

In the meantime, full liberalisation of the telecom sector remains a mirage. "Liberalising the telecom market at this point is difficult and will take time," said Sultan. Analysts have there own doubts about the real intension of the TRA. "The government knows that this a strong revenue generating sector so that's why they will find it hard to let go," said Snobar.

Last year alone, Etisalat revenues hit Dhs16.2m ($4.4m) versus Dhs12.8m last year "So maybe in 2013 we will start to see a more liberal telecom sector in the UAE," Snobar added.

**MOVING ACROSS BORDERS**

While competition is sizzling at home Etisalat has already moved across the borders by operating in 14 countries in Africa and Asia with a total of 28 million international subscribers. It's most recent licence win was in Egypt in July 2006, costing LE16.7bn ($3bn), plus six per cent of annual revenues paid to the government as licence fees.

"I think that we will be seeing a slow down in EBITDA for Etisalat next year, due to losses at the level of the Egyptian start-up," said Ananian.

Overall forecasts for the coming five years are positive and indicate that the UAE will still remain ahead of the game as further growth in population and number of expats moving in will boost telecom profits. And in terms of mobile tele-density, the UEA still tops MENA charts. "This is a time for growth and making a difference," said Sultan.

Despite several attempts made by AME Info no one from Etisalat was available to comment.

The UAE ICT sector has seen significant growth in recent years in terms of revenue and subscribers, as demonstrated in the charts below.

## ECOMMERCE

*Federal Law No. 1 of 2006 on Electronic Commerce and Transactions* (the "Act") was published in the Arabic language in the Official Gazette of the United Arab Emirates, Volume 442, 36th year, Muharam 1427 H/January 2006. Shortly thereafter and in line with the UAE Government National Strategy Plan and the Act, the Ministry of Economy issued two Ministerial Decisions (114) & (406) of 2006, to establish a committee to oversee the implementation of the Act and recommended to the Cabinet to appoint the Telecommunications Regulatory Authority of the UAE as the authority entrusted with overseeing certification services in the UAE pursuant to Article 20 of the Act. The Cabinet approved this recommendation pursuant to its decision no. 8/291 on October 15th, 2006.

The mission of the Telecommunications Regulatory Authority eCommerce Department is "to promote economic development and technological innovation within the defined parameters of a fair eCommerce regulatory regime in line with international standards."

The key objectives of the TRA are to license, monitor, approve, and oversee the activities of Certification Service Providers and to continue providing strategic advice to current and new stakeholders who choose to conduct business online, while working towards fulfilling the objectives of Article 3 of the Act.

These objectives are as follows:

1. Protect the rights of persons doing business electronically and determine their obligations.
2. Encourage and facilitate Electronic Transactions and Communications by means of reliable Electronic Records.
3. Facilitate and eliminate barriers to Electronic Commerce and other Electronic Transactions resulting from uncertainties over writing and signature requirements, and promote the development of the legal and business infrastructure necessary to implement secure Electronic Commerce.
4. Facilitate the electronic filing of documents with governmental and non-governmental agencies and departments and promote efficient delivery of the services of such agencies and departments by means of reliable Electronic Communications.
5. Minimize the incidence of forged Electronic Communications, alteration of Communications and fraud in Electronic Commerce and other Electronic Transactions.
6. Establish uniform rules, regulations and standards for the authentication and validity of Electronic Communications.
7. Promote public confidence in the validity, integrity and reliability of Electronic Transactions, Communications and Records.
8. Promote the growth of Electronic Commerce and other transactions on the national and international level through the use of Electronic Signatures.

| **Fixed Statistics** | **March 2009** | **April 2009** | **May 2009** | **June 2009** | **July 2009** | **Aug 2009** | **Sep 2009** |
|---|---|---|---|---|---|---|---|
| Number of Fixed Lines | 1,576,725 | 1,574,828 | 1,571,819 | 1,564,489 | 1,559,189 | 1,560,009 | 1,558,629 |
| Fixed lines per 100 inhabitants | 31.6 | 31.4 | 31.2 | 30.9 | 30.6 | 30.5 | 30.3 |

| **Mobile Statistics** | **March 2009** | **April 2009** | **May 2009** | **June 2009** | **July 2009** | **Aug 2009** | **Sep 2009** |
|---|---|---|---|---|---|---|---|
| Active Mobile Subscriptions | 9,633,565 | 9,654,927 | 9,682,537 | 9,680,468 | 9,719,456 | 9,781,246 | 9,903,852 |
| Mobile Subscriptions per 100 inhabitants | 193.0 | 192.5 | 192.1 | 191.1 | 190.9 | 191.2 | 192.6 |
| *Post paid* | *837,205* | *841,710* | *853,757* | *869,547* | *878,317* | *891,044* | 907,732 |
| *Pre-paid* | *8,796,360* | *8,813,217* | *8,828,780* | *8,810,921* | *8,841,139* | *8,890,202* | 8,996,120 |
| **Internet Statistics** | **March 2009** | **April 2009** | **May 2009** | **June 2009** | **July 2009** | **Aug 2009** | **Sep 2009** |
| Internet Subscribers | 1,253,981 | 1,264,914 | 1,277,743 | 1,285,907 | 1,296,180 | 1,312,444 | 1,330,037 |
| *Dial-up subscribers* | *660,948* | *664,521* | *668,580* | *670,616* | *674,122* | *680,624* | *684,700* |
| *Broadband subscribers* | *593,033* | *600,393* | *609,163* | *615,291* | *622,058* | *631,820* | *645,337* |
| Internet subscribers per 100 inhabitants | 25.1 | 25.2 | 25.3 | 25.4 | 25.5 | 25.6 | 25.9 |
| Internet Users per 100 Inhabitants | 62.8 | 63.0 | 63.4 | 63.5 | 63.6 | 64.1 | 64.7 |

## PRICES

The TRA sets interconnection prices for a range of interconnection services. The publicly available prices set by the TRA are as follows:

| **Service** | **Interconnect Price** |
|---|---|
| Single Transit Origination | 3.8 fils per minute |
| Single Transit Termination | 3.7 fils per minute |
| Double Transit Origination | 5.6 fils per minute |
| Double Transit Termination | 5.3 fils per minute |
| E1 Network Interconnection Links (up to 40kms long): Set Up Charge | 2,370 AED per link |
| E1 Network Interconnection Links (up to 40kms long): Per Month Rental Charge | 987.50 AED per link; 96 AED per km |

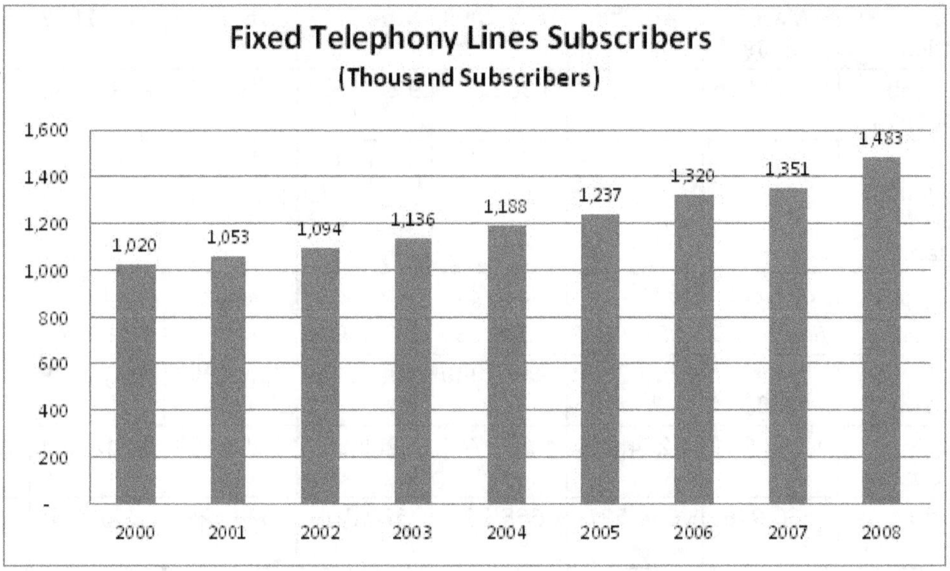
Fixed Telephony Lines Subscribers
(Thousand Subscribers)
1,600
1,400
1,200
1,000
800
600
400
200
-
1,020
1,053
1,094
1,136
1,188
1,237
1,320
1,351
1,483
2000
2001
2002
2003
2004
2005
2006
2007
2008

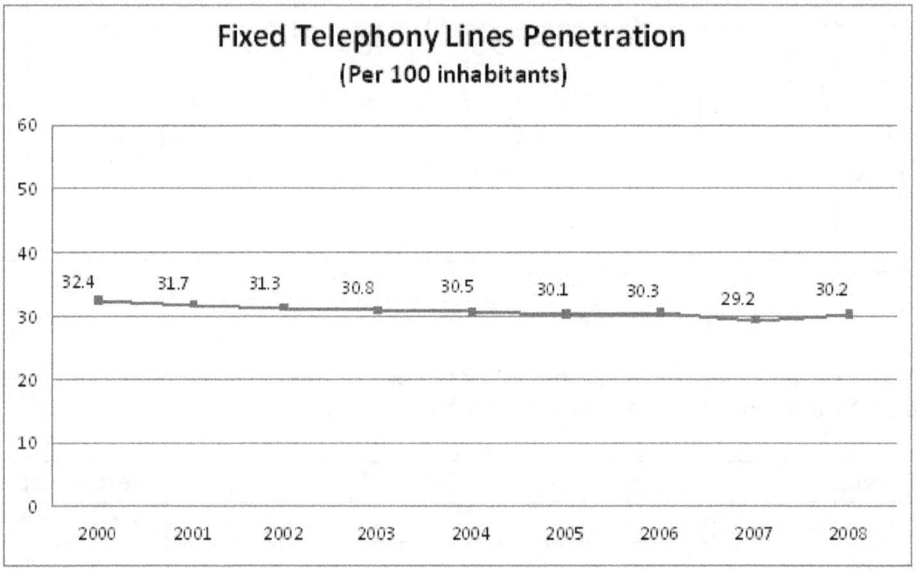
Fixed Telephony Lines Penetration
(Per 100 inhabitants)
60
50
40
30
20
10
0
32.4
31.7
31.3
30.8
30.5
30.1
30.3
29.2
30.2
2000
2001
2002
2003
2004
2005
2006
2007
2008

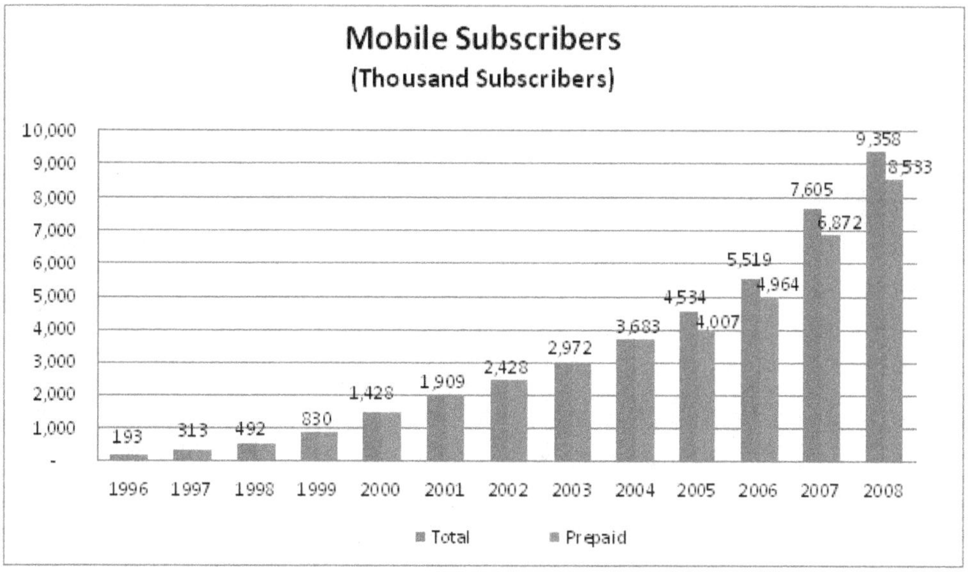


*Includes active mobile subscribers only. "Active" is defined by any subscriber who has made or received a voice or video call in the preceding 90 days, or has sent an SMS or MMS during that period*

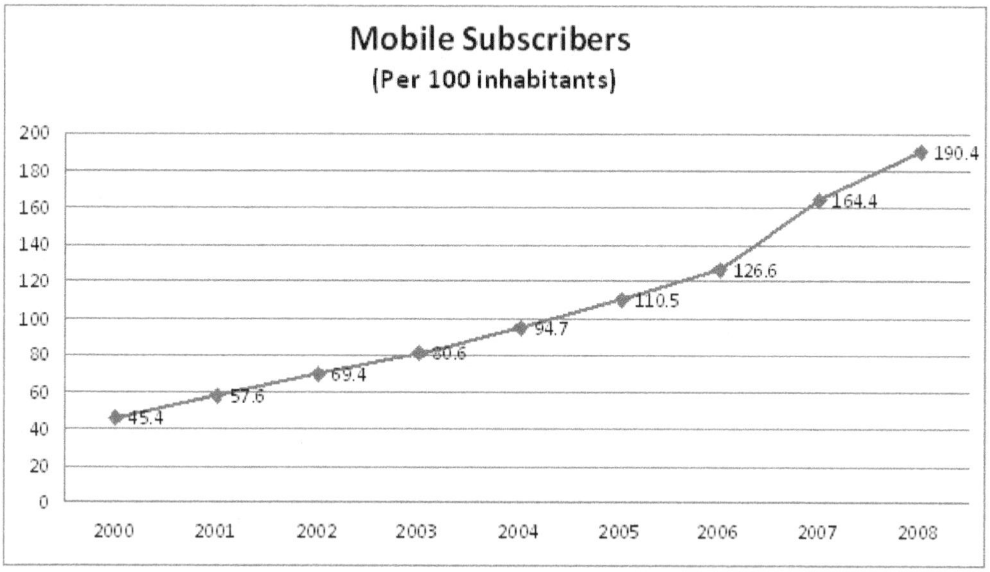


*Includes active mobile subscribers only. "Active" is defined by any subscriber who has made or received a voice or video call in the preceding 90 days, or has sent an SMS or MMS during that period*

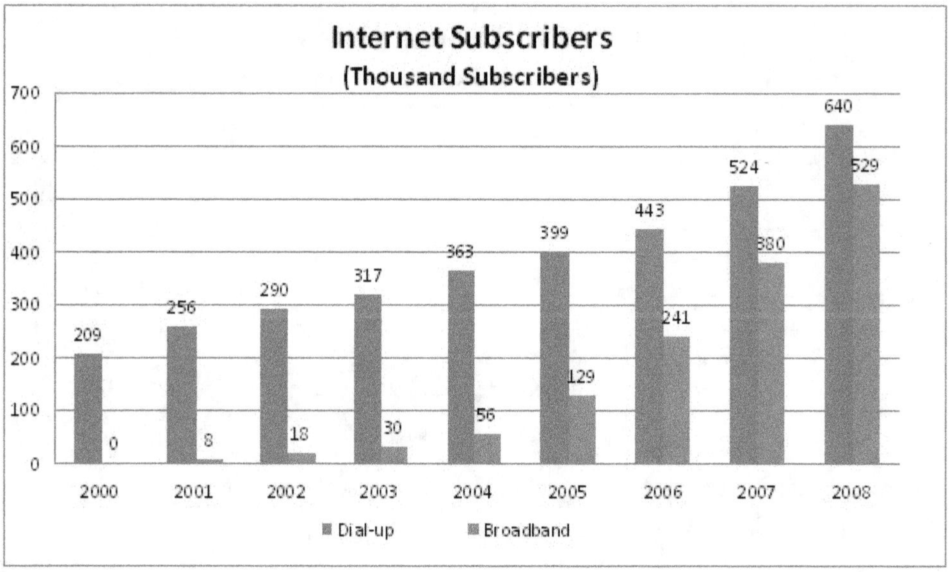


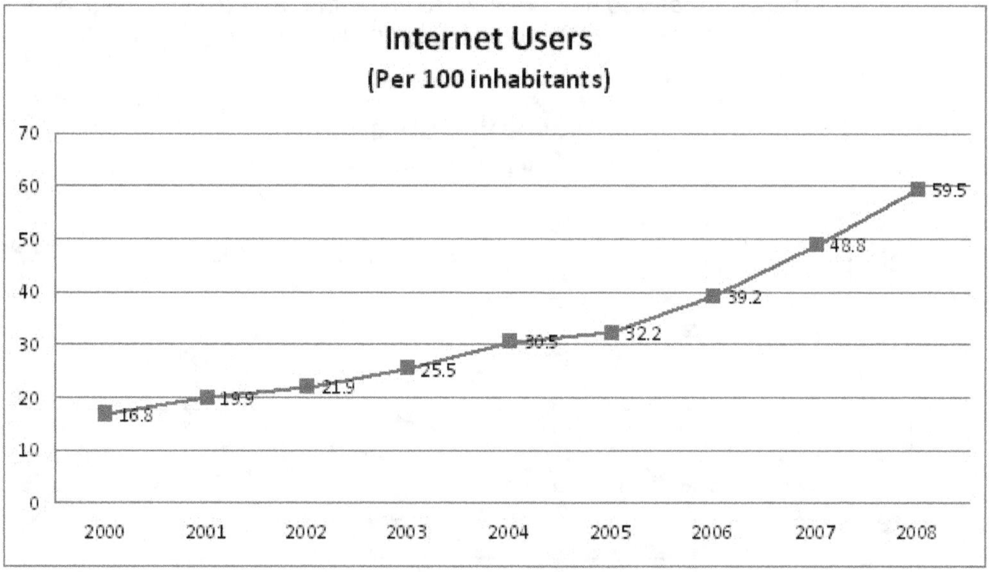


**Chart based on the ITU method of calculating penetration rates, which assumes there are 2.5 users per Internet subscription.*

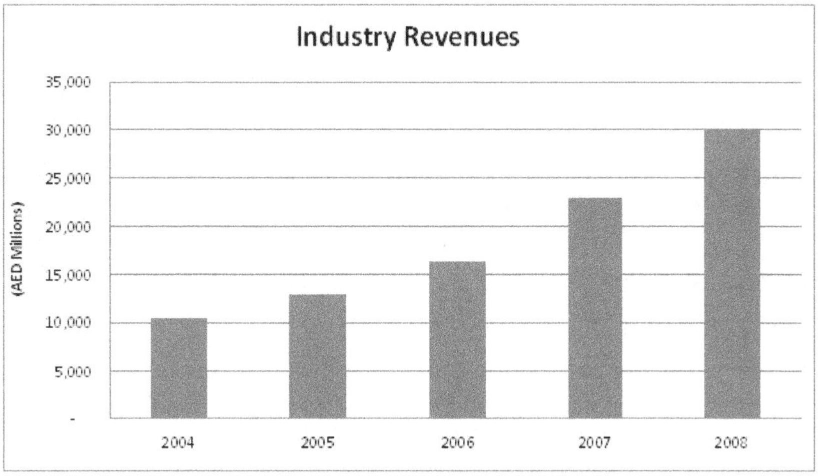


# INTERNET SECTOR DEVELOPMENTS

The UAE is very progressive in it's policies towards and adoption of ICT technology. The government has viewed an advanced ICT infrastructure as a way to attract foreign investment and to diversify the economy of the country. The country has an established National Telecom Policy in place to advance development and innovation within the UAE, especially in Dubai. In 2005 the Government also sponsored an ICT Development Fund, the first of its kind in the Middle East specifically geared towards the promotion of ICT in the country. Finally the government has supported the development of ICT through investment in infrastructure like the Dubai Technology E-Commerce & Media Freezone (TECOM).

In a relatively short time it is my assessment that Dubai's investment in ICT and open and progressive ICT policies (with the exception of some censorship of the Internet) have assisted the company in transitioning a portion of its economy to this area of business.

## GOVERNMENT POLICY ON ICT

The UAE is perhaps the most aggressive country in the region when it comes to censorship on the Internet. The Emirates Telecommunications Corporation (Etisalat), which was established by the government, was until very recently the sole internet service provider in the country. All connections in the country either dial-up or broadband are through a proxy server which filters Web sites by URL based on a list of banned sites. The government claims it has adopted this censorship to prevent access to pornographic Web sites, according to the Open Net Initiative however, a analysis of filtered content in 2005 revealed much more rigorous filtering. (6)

"The UAE uses the SmartFilter filtering software to block nearly all pornography, gambling, religious conversion, and illegal drugs sites tested. The state also blocks access to all sites in the Israeli top-level domain. ONI's testing of the UAE filtering regime also found blocking of sites on the Bahai faith, Middle East-oriented gay and lesbian issues, and English-language (though not Arabic-language) dating sites. While our results did not indicate that UAE uses its filtering system to block political sites, or news and media sources, we conclude that the state's broad content controls unintentionally block information unrelated to UAE's stated goals. The imprecision of the

UAE filtering regime underscores the difficulty of extensive technical filtering of Internet content." (5)

## NATIONAL TELECOM POLICY FOR UAE

The UAE has a General Policy for the Telecommunication Sector (GTP). The GTP is a forward looking document for 2006-2010. The GTP is designed to function as a catalyst towards accelerating the growth and development of the telecommunication sector in its efforts to support the Government's goal of developing the country as the premier Information and Communication Technology hub in the region and beyond.

The Policy recognized the government's view that a world-class competitive telecommunication infrastructure is of critical importance to the economic development of the country. It acknowledges that ICT forms the backbone of industries such as trade, financial services, technology-based services, tourism, media, education, oil, manufacturing, transportation and health services. The policy document is designed to serve a a guideline to all individuals involved in the telecommunications sector, including consumers, service providers, operators, investors and the Government.

The policy consists of 5 main objectives.

**3.1 Establish Policies and Regulatory Framework -** The Government will establish a regulatory and policy framework that facilitates the development of the country's telecommunications and ICT infrastructure and services in order to meet national, regional and international objectives.

**3.2 Promote and Develop New Technologies -**The Government will promote the use of new technologies in the UAE.

**3.3 Become the Regional ICT Hub -** The Government will support the development of the UAE as a regional ICT and telecommunications hub.

**3.4 Develop the Country's Human Capital -** The Government will facilitate the development of human capital in the telecommunications and ICT sector to meet the demands of the economy, serving both local and regional requirements.

**3.5 Encourage Research and Development -** The Government will encourage research and development activities within an integrated complex, and establish relationships with international academic institutions. (7)

## ICT DEVELOPMENT FUND

In September 2005 the UAE launched an "ICT Development Fund" to advance the ICT Policies of the country. The "ICT Development Fund" is a first of its kind in the region and aims to position the UAE to be among the most advanced ICT countries in the World.

The cabinet of United Arab Emirates (UAE) has approved "UAE ICT Strategy 2021". It would increase broadband 15 times. It is one of the main pillars of its knowledge based economy. It has multiplier effects on socio-economic growth as well as national income of the UAE in the days to come. It would speed-up education ratios among the common people. It would promote connectivity which is crucial for rapid economic growth and massive industrialization. It would increase social awareness, sense of duties and responsibilities. It is a counterproductive development strategy which would definitely pay its dividends in the days to come.

While chairing a Federal Cabinet session at the Presidential Palace His Highness Shaikh Mohammed bin Rashid Al Maktoum, Vice-President and Prime Minister of the UAE and Ruler of Dubai approved the UAE's ICT Strategy 2021.

It was formulated by the UAE ICT Development Committee on instructions by Shaikh Mohammed, was approved by the Cabinet as part of national efforts to enhance previous successes and align all component of the sector with the federal government strategy and vision for 2021.

It is a comprehensive strategy which covers each and every possible aspect of the production, regulatory mechanism, price control, speed, infrastructure, employment, education and the last but not the least, innovation. To achieve these goals the committee has already developed 36 strategic performance indexes in the plan towards 2021.One of the main aims of this long term strategy is to elevate the UAE ranking in the global ICT indexes.

UAE cabinet has provided many incentives for all the sectors in the country. A set of initiatives are also given.

**Features**

(a) Speeds of broadband will be increased by 15 times

(b) Number of safe servers will be increased by 20 times

(c) Subscribers will be increased by five times.

(d) The sector is projected to generate 45,000 job opportunities between 2014 and 2021.

"The ICT sector constitutes the foundation for development of our human resources, and the key driver for the growth of our economy as well improvement of quality of life in our community. Development of this sector will be under continuous follow up," Shaikh Mohammed added.

**UAE ICT Sector**

The UAE ICT sector is one of the advanced markets in the Gulf Cooperation Council (GCC), and Middle East and North Africa Region (MENA). The UAE lead the world in terms of mobile penetration rates reaching over 200 percent penetration rate by the end of 2009 as well as sector readiness and regulatory environment.

1. **2013-2014 Networked Readiness Index (NRI)**

Networked Readiness Index (NRI) study issued by the World Economic Forum ranked the UAE 2$^{nd}$ of all the Arab states in the 2014 and 24$^{th}$ among all 148 countries assessed, moving up by one position from 25$^{th}$ in the previous ranking of 2013

The NRI measures the capacity of an economy to fully leverage ICT for increased competitiveness and development. The NRI study was published in The Global Information

Technology Report 2014 and is based on data collected by organizations such as the International Telecommunications Union (ITU), the World Bank, and the United Nations (UN). In terms of the individual indicators analysed, the UAE ranked first among the Arab states in terms of:

| UAE ICT Ranking (Arab World) | UAE ICT Ranking |
|---|---|
| The availability of latest technologies | Use of virtual social networks |
| E-Participation Index | Secure Internet servers |
| low Software piracy rates | Percentage of software installed |
| Business-to-consumer Internet use | Business-to-business Internet use |
| Global Ranking | |
| 1st equal in mobile network coverage, | In terms of the percentage of the population covered |
| 1st in the importance of ICT to the Government's vision of the future | 2nd in Government success in ICT promotion |
| 2nd in ICT use and Government efficiency | 2nd in the impact of ICT on access to basic services |
| 3rd oin Government procurement of advanced technologies products | 4th in laws relating to ICTs |
| 4th oin impact of ICTs on new services and products | 4th in impact of ICTs on new services and products |
| 9th- in the Government Online Service Index | 9th in the impact of ICTs on new organisational models. |
| Source: TRA, UAE (2013-14) | |

## E-GOVERNMENT IN THE UNITED ARAB EMIRATES

The United Arab Emirates (UAE) once largely known for its oil exports today has a diverse and highly developed economy. According to the UAE Economic Report 2009 released by the UAE Ministry of Economy in May 2010 the non-oil sector contributed 71.6 per cent to the UAE's GDP, compared to 66.5 per cent in 2008, underscoring the success of the nation's economic diversification initiatives.

The UAE is investing heavily in adopting and implementing Information and Communication Technology (ICT) in its government and private sectors. The Global Information Technology Report 2010-2011 indicates that the UAE leads the MENA region in leveraging ICT for increased economic diversification and competitiveness. The contribution of telecommunications sector in the UAE's economy rose from 4.1 per cent in 2007 to 5.3 per cent in 2010 according to 'UAE Telecommunications Sector Developments & Indicators (2007-2010)', issued in May 2011 by Telecommunications Regulatory Authority (TRA), UAE. Abu Dhabi Department of Economic Development estimates that investments in IT and Telecom sectors are likely to reach AED18.4 billion (USD5 billion) in 2011, as against AED16.1 billion in 2010.

The eGovernment programme in the UAE is a key initiative of the UAE Government Strategy 2011-2013 that lays the foundation to achieve UAE Vision 2021

## INCEPTION AND TIMELINE

The UAE started some of its eServices such as eDirham in as early as the year 2001. The service initiated by the Ministry of Finance replaced the traditional way of paying and collecting fees for government services. The government gradually made more services available online.

| # | Year | Service | Summary | Initiated by |
|---|---|---|---|---|
| 1 | February 2001 | eDirham | The first online service launched by the Ministry of Finance in the federal government to replace the traditional means of fees collection for government services. | Ministry of Finance |
| 2 | November 2002 | eGovernment Program | The Coordinating Committee for the Federal eGovernment Programme was formed and led by the Ministry of Finance and Industry | Ministry of Finance |
| 3 | March 2003 | eGovernment strategy | IBM was assigned to conduct an assessment study for the federal agencies and to develop an implementation plan | Ministry of Finance |
| 4 | June 2004 | The eGovernment Implementation Plan | A memorandum of understanding was signed with the Emirates Telecommunications Corporation (Etisalat) to provide the infrastructure for the eGovernment. The plan was divided into three phases ending in 2007 | Ministry of Finance |
| 5 | March 2005 | eGovernment Portal | The launch of the first eGovernment portal in cooperation with Etisalat, which was exclusively assigned to implement the plan | Ministry of Finance |
| 6 | March & July 2006 | Assigning the Ministry of Government Sector Development to oversee the eGovernment Programme | A ministerial decree was issued to move the eGovernment programme from the Ministry of Finance to the Ministry of Government Sector Development | Ministry of Governmental Sector Development |
| 7 | June 2008 | Development of the Information Systems Strategy of the Federal Government | A ministerial decree was issued to assign the TRA to lead the efforts to develop a strategy for the information systems in the State. TRA, in cooperation with Booz Allen Company, developed the Information Systems Strategy of the Federal Government | Telecommunications Regulatory Authority |
| 8 | 2010 | Development of the Government Service Development Strategy | The Office of the Prime Minister developed a Government Service Development Strategy, which was the third foundational element of the eGovernment Strategy | Prime Minister's Office |

**THE OFFICIAL PORTAL OF THE UAE GOVERNMENT**

The official portal of the UAE Government is www.government.ae. It is part of the federal eGovernment programme and a major milestone in the process of eTransformation in the UAE.

This portal brings all eServices provided by the UAE federal and local government bodies under one umbrella. It also provides information regarding accessing the government services through mobile phones and other similar electronic devices, and other means such as ATMs and public payment machines.

The aim of the portal is to provide more and better online services to the people of the UAE and involve them in the government's policies, laws, and public interest initiatives with the ultimate goal of achieving transparency.

## FUNCTIONS

The function of the official portal is to act as a single window or a single entry-point for users to access the different federal and local government eServices. The portal also facilitates to boost communication between the customers and the government representatives and eParticipation through forums, blogs, surveys, polls and social media. Government.ae is the parent portal for the sub-portals on eParticipation, eServices, mServices and UAE Open Data.

## ESERVICES

The UAE Government provides a range of services through its official portal www.government.ae. The eServices are classified into services for individuals, businesses and visitors. Through the eServices, it is now very easy for the people of the UAE to avail a variety of services without leaving their home or office spaces. The portal has an advanced search facility to help people look for the services they want to access. The portal also contains a section on alternate means for accessing government services.

## MSERVICES

The portal also provides adequate information on the various services that are available through mobile devices and how to avail them with the help of specially developed short codes and mobile applications. The portal has links to download smart phone applications for Blackberry, iPhone and Android.

Innovative and facilitating option for the business was launched in 2013 when a smart phone app for business registration and licensing was unveiled in Dubai.

## EPARTICIPATION

One of the major features of the enhanced portal is the inclusion of eParticipation channels. The federal portal has engaged multiple platforms like forums, blogs, chats, surveys, polls and social media tools like Facebook, Twitter, Flickr and YouTube to reach out to the general public and engage them in active communication with the government with regard to their opinions and experiences on government services, policies etc.

## OPEN DATA

Under Open Data, government data and information is made available to the public. People can now have access to economic data, population statistics, etc. Open Data could benefit students, economists and researchers in particular and the public in general.

## ICT INFRASTRUCTURE AND PENETRATION

The UAE has one of the most advanced Information and Communication Technology infrastructures not only in the region but also across the globe.

According to Telecommunications Regulatory Authority's (TRA) May 2011 figures, the UAE has 196.3 mobile phone subscriptions per 100 inhabitants and with 1,417,519 internet subscribers, the UAE has 62.4 internet users per 100 inhabitants.

The UAE has excellent broadband service and this was ratified by Cisco's broadband quality survey in the year 2010, placing the UAE on eighth position globally.

## EREADINESS RANKING

eReadiness or Networked Readiness Index (NRI) measures the level of preparedness of a country's government to deliver services and information online and the overall value it delivers to the public. eReadiness or the Readiness Index involves the government's ability to use Information and Communication Technology (ICT) to boost their socio-economic conditions and overall public welfare.

## GLOBAL INFORMATION TECHNOLOGY REPORT (GITR)

According to The GITR 2010-2011, UAE was ranked first amongst Arab countries and stood 24th amongst 138 countries reviewed in the Networked Readiness Index (NRI), indicating the importance the country gives to Information and Communication Technology as a crucial instrument for economic diversification, enhanced efficiency and modernisation. The same report showed Qatar's position at 25, Bahrain's position at 30, Saudi Arabia at 33 and Oman at 41.

As per GITR 2010-2011, the UAE scored third rank in government readiness and fifth rank in individual readiness to use ICT, 18th rank for ICT-friendly market environment and 28th rank for ICT infrastructure in the UAE.

The UAE is one of the few countries in the region that has maintained its steady climb in the eReadiness ranking chart. The UAE shot up six positions in NRI; from 29th position amongst 127 countries reviewed in 2007–2008 to 23rd amongst 133 countries reviewed in 2009–2010.

## UN EGOVERNMENT SURVEY

United Nations Public Administration Network (UNPAN) also conducts a similar survey and publishes its report on eGovernment ranking. The report called UN eGovernment Survey was published annually until 2005 but later became a biennial publication.

The UAE's overall ranking as per the UN eGovernment Survey has gone through many ups and downs. UAE's rank rose for two consecutive surveys; it leapt from 60th rank in 2004 by 18 ranks to be at 42nd position in the year 2005 and then rose by 10 ranks to be at 32nd position in the year 2008. However, its rank took a steep dip in 2010 attaining 49th position. However, overall, UAE was ranked fourth in the region in 2010 report.

## UAE VISION 2021

Under the banner of Vision 2021, the UAE aspires to be among the best countries in the world by 2021. Vision 2021 states: In a strong and safe union, knowledgeable and innovative Emiratis will confidently build a competitive and resilient economy. They will thrive as a cohesive society bonded to its identity and enjoy the highest standards of living with a nurturing and sustainable environment.

Vision 2021 lays down its objectives in four categories: United in responsibility, United in destiny, United in knowledge and United in prosperity. Vision 2021 also charts out responsibilities for the UAE Government, extracts of which are:

- The UAE will not slow the pace of its drive for improvement. In the economic and government sphere, the UAE will build on sectors of excellence to export its model abroad, while constantly evolving to create new competitive advantages.

- Legal frameworks and government services will be designed to provide businesses with the efficient environment that they need in order to grow, thrive and commercialise innovative ideas. Regulations will promote efficient markets and protect intellectual property. Partnerships will flourish between the public and private sectors, spurring growth and maximising opportunities. The UAE will become one of the best places in the world to do business.

- The UAE will nurture high quality of life built on world-class public infrastructure, government services, and a rich recreational environment. The UAE government should provide citizens with world-class infrastructure, services, and leisure resources, creating a rich environment in which they can enjoy well-rounded and fulfilling lives.

- Emiratis will benefit from customer-focused government services whose quality is rigorously monitored and constantly improved. Interactive eGovernment will provide citizens with an especially responsive and efficient channel of service from public authorities.

- We want the UAE to transform its economy into a model where growth is driven by knowledge and innovation. Productivity and competitiveness will come to rival the best in the world, as a result of investment in science, technology, research and development throughout the fabric of the UAE economy.

- Outstanding information and communication infrastructure will network our businesses together and give them a leading edge as they transact and interact with the world. Individual citizens will also reap the benefits of efficient connectedness in their digital lives as they search online for knowledge and the fulfilment of intellectual curiosity.

## UAE GOVERNMENT STRATEGY 2011-2013

UAE Government Strategy highlights the priorities for the government during the years from 2011 to 2013. It forms the basis upon which the federal entities could develop their strategic and operational plans. UAE Government Strategy lays the foundation for Vision 2021.

The strategy is divided into seven general principles, seven strategic priorities and seven strategic enablers.

The seven general principles are:

- Enhance the role of federal entities in devising effective regulations and integrated policies by successful planning and enforcement
- Enhance effective coordination and cooperation among federal entities and with local governments
- Focus on delivering high quality, customer-centric, and integrated government services
- Invest in human resource capabilities and develop leaders
- Promote efficient resource management within federal entities and leverage dynamic partnerships
- Pursue a culture of excellence through strategic thinking, continuous performance improvement, and superior results
- Enhance transparency and accountable governance mechanisms throughout the federal entities

UAE Government Strategy 2011-2013 details its obligations in the field of eGovernment under strategic enabler, customer–centric service. All Federal Entities will move towards focusing on their customers and understanding their needs. Government services will be designed, re-engineered, and streamlined to meet all the needs of different customer segments and their expectations. These government services will be provided through innovative and effective channels, which address their customer's requirements and ensure their access to high quality services.

The UAE Government will satisfy its customers by transforming its services to provide a seamless and high-quality customer experience by accelerating transition towards eGovernment, adopting customer segmentation, enabling convenient access to Government services through innovative and customer-friendly delivery channels, re-engineering and streamlining processes for quality and timely government service delivery, and integrating government service delivery.

## EMIRATES EGOVERNMENT

Emirates eGovernment is responsible for developing, implementing and maintaining the eGovernment programme at the federal level in the UAE. This involves renovating and upgrading the conventional methods of delivering the government services and having the services delivered electronically through the deployment of modern Information and communication technologies (ICT).

### VISION, MISSION AND VALUES

**Vision:** An optimal enabling environment in which the UAE's ICT sector will emerge as a leader in the global market place.

**Mission:** To support the UAE ICT sector by safeguarding competition, to protect the interests of subscribers, to enhance the readiness of eServices, to encourage investment, innovation, development and education, to meet our corporate social responsibility, and to implement best practices in regulation and supervision.

**Values:**

- Transparency

- Fairness
- Team Spirit
- Loyalty and Belonging
- Excellence Culture
- Governance

## SERVICES

Emirates eGovernment has set up the UAE's official portal www.government.ae, which is a major milestone in the process of eTransformation in the UAE. This portal brings all eServices and information provided by the UAE federal and local government bodies under one umbrella.

Emirates eGovernment provides services on G2G, G2B and G2C levels. The UAE's official portal www.government.ae falls under the G2B and G2C level. Under G2G services, the entity provides cloud and Government Website Evaluation Index (GWEI) services.

## INITIATIVES AND AWARDS

Emirates eGovernment pioneers various initiatives that aid the development of the eGovernment programme in the UAE. It is actively involved in projects that promote the usage of eServices and Information and Communication Technology (ICT) tools by the federal government entities and the public in a safe and effective way to achieve better delivery of services and good governance.

Emirates eGovernment regularly holds workshops for internal staff and federal government employees on topics relating to eGovernment, cloud services such as Morasalate and Malafate, IT trends, effective use of ICT to achieve the entity's goals etc.

## POLICIES AND GUIDELINES

Emirates eGovernment drafted a number of guidelines for federal government entities in the UAE. These guidelines deal with websites, social media usage, web content. Emirates eGovernment also issued draft documents related to eParticipation and open data. These guidelines comprise recommendations on the content style, design, layout, accessibility features etc. to make the federal government websites in accordance with the international standards of web content and design as laid down by World Wide Web Consortium.

The Guidelines for Social Media Usage won Emirates eGovernment the 2011 'Social Media Initiative of the Year' award. The guidelines document was prepared in partnership with and extensive support from Dubai School of Government's Governance and Innovation Program and in collaboration with the UAE Government entities. Senior Advisors at Information Technology research firm Gartner Inc. and United Nations eGovernment Programme also offered their assistance and recommendations in preparing this document.

## AWARDS

Emirates eGovernment has received several awards and honours in recognition of its efforts in the field of eGovernment.

**GCC eGovernment Award** The UAE is actively involved in the GCC eGovernment Award. The award is held biennially in one of the GCC countries.

**The second GCC eGovernment Award** The second GCC eGovernment Award was held in Kuwait from November 13 to 15, 2011. UAE entities have bagged most of the awards. They have achieved the first place in three out of the six categories of the Award.

The federal portal of the UAE government (www.government.ae) has achieved the first place among the six GCC government portals.

Dubai Health Authority (DHA) achieved first place for Best eContent and Roads and Transport Authority (RTA) achieved first place in the Best eService category.

Appreciation Awards were presented to Zakat Fund for (Best public eService) and the General Civil Aviation Authority (GCAA) for Best Portal in the Development Sector for its portal www.gcaa.gov.ae.

**The first GCC eGovernment Award** The first GCC eGovernment Award was held in Muscat in the year 2009. The UAE won five awards that year.

Dubai Electricity and Water Authority (DEWA) won 2nd prize for eBill Payment under the category of best eService. General Civil Aviation Authority (GCAA) won the 3rd prize for the best eContent on their website.

Roads and Transport Authority (RTA) won the 2nd prize for eRTA under the category of best eMaturity. eMaturity awards are given to those initiatives that display best ICT infrastructure maturity in providing a standard, reliable and secure infrastructure for managing information.

The UAE won the 3rd prize for utilising SAP (IS-Utilities) for Billing and Customer Relationship Management (CRM) under the category of best eProject. The official portal of the Abu Dhabi eGovernment got a Special Mention for its eContent.

**Arab eGovernment Web Award** The Arab e-Government Web Award organised by the Arab Administrative Development Organization (ARADO) recognises Arab governments for their efforts in promoting the eGovernment portals. The Award seeks to encourage creativity in the design of eGovernment websites, deploy the best information and communication technology to make their services easily available to the public and create a transparent and secure digital environment.

**Technological Innovation Award** Emirates eGovernment has received the 'Technical Innovation Award' in the category of Information and Communication Technology (ICT) for its corporate website (www.emiratesegov.ae).

**Best Strategic Website Award** Emirates eGovernment has received the 'Best Strategic Website' in the category of official government entities websites for the UAE government official portal (www.government.ae).

**Awards won by other UAE government entities:** Government entities in the UAE have won a number of awards in the eGovernment Web Awards. The list of awardees is as follows:

1. The General Authority for Islamic Affairs and Endowments - Technical Innovation Award, official and government entities websites category
2. Ministry of Public Works - Structural Innovation Awards, ministries' websites category
3. Abu Dhabi Tourism Authority – Visual Innovation Award, official and government entities websites category
4. Dubai Airport Free Zone - Interactive Innovation Award, official and government entities websites category
5. Sharjah Government Directorate of Town Planning and Survey – Design Innovation Award, official and government entities websites category

## LOCAL EGOVERNMENT PROGRAMMES

eGovernment in the UAE has been launched and is successfully operating at local levels as well. The governments of six out of the seven emirates, Abu Dhabi, Dubai, Sharjah, Ras Al Khaimah, Ajman and Fujairah have launched their official portals.

These portals are implemented to bring the services and information of the respective government's entities under one umbrella with the aim to provide quick and easy access to the service seeker.

The portals offer many interactive and transactional services such as bill payments, licence renewals etc. In addition, Abu Dhabi and Dubai government portals offer information and advice to residents, businesses and visitors on related matters such as how to apply for health card, how to obtain drivers' license, or how to apply for visa.

The portals aim to be functionally convenient. They strive to adhere to the various guidelines on website content developed by Emirates eGovernment based on the recommendations laid down by World Wide Web Consortium (W3C).

Many local eGovernments are also active on social media such as Facebook and Twitter; providing the public with easy access to government entities and officials. The government entities keep the public informed about their services and initiatives, reply to their queries and engage them in stimulating discussions relating to the government services, policies etc.

The UAE Government is aiming for the electronic transformation or eTransformation of many of its services at the federal level. The UAE government is taking many steps to achieve this. H. H. Sheikh Mohammed bin Rashid Al Maktoum, Vice President and Prime Minister of the UAE and Ruler of Dubai stressed, while launching the federal portal of the UAE that "eTransformation in the UAE and the provision of federal and local services through one portal contributes to enhance the state's competitiveness and opens up broader prospects for direct communication with community groups and works to enhance the effectiveness and efficiency of governmental work in the country

# E-COMMERCE IN UAE - IMPORTANT DEVELOPMENTS AND BASIC REGULATIONS

*Federal Law No. 1 of 2006 on Electronic Commerce and Transactions* (the "Act") was published in the Arabic language in the Official Gazette of the United Arab Emirates, Volume 442, 36th year, Muharam 1427 H/January 2006. Shortly thereafter and in line with the UAE Government National Strategy Plan and the Act, the Ministry of Economy issued two Ministerial Decisions (114) & (406) of 2006, to establish a committee to oversee the implementation of the Act and recommended to the Cabinet to appoint the Telecommunications Regulatory Authority of the UAE as the authority entrusted with overseeing certification services in the UAE pursuant to Article 20 of the Act. The Cabinet approved this recommendation pursuant to its decision no. 8/291 on October 15th, 2006.

The mission of the Telecommunications Regulatory Authority eCommerce Department is "to promote economic development and technological innovation within the defined parameters of a fair eCommerce regulatory regime in line with international standards."

The key objectives of the TRA are to license, monitor, approve, and oversee the activities of Certification Service Providers and to continue providing strategic advice to current and new stakeholders who choose to conduct business online, while working towards fulfilling the objectives of Article 3 of the Act.

These objectives are as follows:

1. Protect the rights of persons doing business electronically and determine their obligations.
2. Encourage and facilitate Electronic Transactions and Communications by means of reliable Electronic Records.
3. Facilitate and eliminate barriers to Electronic Commerce and other Electronic Transactions resulting from uncertainties over writing and signature requirements, and promote the development of the legal and business infrastructure necessary to implement secure Electronic Commerce.
4. Facilitate the electronic filing of documents with governmental and non-governmental agencies and departments and promote efficient delivery of the services of such agencies and departments by means of reliable Electronic Communications.
5. Minimize the incidence of forged Electronic Communications, alteration of Communications and fraud in Electronic Commerce and other Electronic Transactions.
6. Establish uniform rules, regulations and standards for the authentication and validity of Electronic Communications.
7. Promote public confidence in the validity, integrity and reliability of Electronic Transactions, Communications and Records.
8. Promote the growth of Electronic Commerce and other transactions on the national and international level through the use of Electronic Signatures.

The UAE's ICT sector will generate approximately 45,000 job opportunities between 2014 and 2021, forecasts the country's ICT strategy for 2021.

The strategy, which was approved by the UAE Federal Cabinet yesterday (Monday, July 7), is part of national efforts to enhance success and align all components of the sector with the government's overall 2021 strategy and vision. Among other factors, it aims to increase broadband speed by 15 times, the number of safe servers by 20 times and subscribers by five times.

His Highness Sheikh Mohammed bin Rashid Al Maktoum, Vice-President and Prime Minister of the UAE and Ruler of Dubai, chaired the federal cabinet session at the Presidential Palace, where the strategy was approved. The sector continues to be a key economic pillar, growth driver and a source of national income, and "has become, today, part of [our] lifestyles [...]. The development of this sector will contribute to improving life standards of all community segments," he says.

Under the instructions of Sheikh Mohammed, the strategy was devised by the UAE ICT Development Committee, which has developed 36 strategic performance indexes in areas such as quality, speed, prices, infrastructure, employment, education and innovation, in a bid to boost UAE's status in global ICT indexes.

SMEs can potentially play an important role in boosting the ICT sector in the future.

In an earlier interview with SMEinfo.me, Ammar Malik, director of business development for Dubai Internet City and Dubai Outsource Zone, said that the UAE and the Middle East can expect to see a rise in SME ICT companies providing localised content and services, such as payment gateways and e-commerce.

According to International Data Corporation's United Arab Emirates Vertical Markets 2013-2017 IT Spending Forecast report, ICT spending in the UAE is expected to grow by 8.3 per cent year on year in 2014 to reach $4.63 billion.

Over the years, the UAE has steadily established itself as a leader in electronic governance throughout the Middle East. Dubai in particular has made great strides in this field, complementing its growth into the region's commercial hub. I would like to honor the contributions of the people and the organizations that champion the use of technology in facilitating trade and achieving progress for this emirate and the entire country.

I would like to commend Dubai World's Dubai Trade for successfully carrying out its role as the premier end-to-end online service provider and trade facilitator for the emirate. Your work exemplifies the forward-thinking vision of the Dubai Strategic Plan 2015 and presents Dubai as a top global destination for doing business.

The government fully supports your vision of transforming Dubai's end-to-end trade supply chain and developing this emirate into a leading international trade and logistics hub. The UAE Government has been actively pursuing enhancements to its information and communications technology (ICT) infrastructure in a bid to establish a knowledge-based economy and a truly digital society.

This is within the framework of the UAE Vision 2021 development plan which aims to transform the Emirates into one of the best countries in the world within the next decade. Several international studies affirm the steady growth of the UAE's ICT domain. For example, the latest Global Information Technology Report jointly commissioned by the World Economic Forum and the INSEAD international graduate business school ranks the Emirates first in the MENA region in terms of ICT development.

We currently lead all Middle Eastern and African countries in IT spending per capita at USD 983 (AED 3,610) and we are on our way to allocating almost USD 1,000 (AED 3,672) per capita or around USD 5 billion (AED 18.36 billion) on IT this year to make us one of the world's most prolific IT spenders. This special attention to ICT expansion has benefitted other domestic sectors as well, among them trade and logistics

The World Bank's 'Doing Business' report for 2011 ranks the Emirates among the world's top three countries for enabling trade across borders. This is a very impressive leap from our 5th position in 2010 and 13th ranking in 2009 and reflects how technology has played a huge role in enhancing our international commercial relations.

Over the past three years, The World Bank has been consulting with Dubai Trade as a key source of information for the 'Doing Business' report. Dubai Trade in turn has been closely coordinating with the UAE Competitiveness Council to ensure the integrity of the data and communications provided to the World Bank. Through the efforts of Dubai Trade I am hopeful that the UAE will continue to enjoy its competitive position in global trade.

Dubai has blossomed into the UAE's trade hub, accounting for 75% of our non-oil trade. Its total non-oil foreign exchange was worth around USD 205.33 billion (AED 754.14 billion) in 2009, making it the prime commercial catalyst of the entire Gulf. As a global city and business hub, it leads the country's diversification efforts, drawing its main revenues from growth sectors such as tourism, real estate and financial services. Through strategic business and economic adjustments Dubai is expected to achieve a real GDP growth of over 2% in 2011.

# FEDERAL LAW ON ELECTRONIC COMMERCE AND TRANSACTIONS[1]

We, Khalifa bin Zayed Al Nahyan, President of the United Arab Emirates, In cognisance of the Constitution, and

The Federal Law No. (1) of 1972 Regarding the Functions of Ministries and the Powers of Ministers and the amending laws thereof, and
The Federal Law No. (5) of 1975 Regarding the Commercial Register, and
The Federal Law No. (8) of 1980 on the Regulating Working Relationship and the amending laws thereof, and
The Federal Law No. (10) of 1980 on the Central Bank and the Monetary system and regulating the banking profession and the amending laws thereof, and
The Federal Law No. (8) of 1984 on Commercial Companies and the amending laws thereof, and
The Federal Law No. (9) of 1984 on Insurance Companies and Agencies and the amending laws thereof, and
The Civil Transaction Law issued by the Federal Law No. (5) of 1985, and
The Penal Law issued by the Federal Law No. (3) of 1987, and
The Federal Law No. (22) of 1991 on the Justice Registrar and the amending laws thereof, and
The Civil and Commercial Transactions Evidence Law issued by the Federal Law No. (10) of 1992, and
The Civil Procedure Law issued by the Federal Law No. (11) of 1992, and
The Penal Procedure Law issued by the Federal Law No. (35) of 1992, and
The Federal Law No. (37) of 1992 on the Trademarks and the amending laws thereof, and
The Commercial Transactions Law issued by the Federal Law No. (18) of 1993, and
The Federal Law No. (17) of 2002 on Regulating and Protecting the Industrial rights of Patents, and
The Federal Law by Decree No. (3) of 2003 on the Organization of the Telecommunications Sector, and

On the basis of the proposal of the Minister of Commerce and Planning, and the agreement of the Council of Ministers, and the approval of the High Federal Council, have issued the following Law:

## CHAPTER ONE - GENERAL

### Article (1)

The following words and expressions shall have meaning set out opposite unless the context shall require otherwise:

| UAE: | United Arab Emirates |
|---|---|
| Government Departments: | Federal ministries, local departments and authorities and local and federal public entities and corporations |
| Ministry: | Ministry of Economy & Planning |
| Minister: | Minister of Economy & Planning |
| Competent Local Authority: | Competent local authority in each of the Emirates of the UAE |

[1] No. (1) of 2006

| | |
|---|---|
| Electronic: | Relating to modern technology having electrical, digital, magnetic, wireless, optical, electromagnetic, automated, photonic or similar capabilities |
| Electronic Information: | Electronic data and information in the form of text, codes, sounds, graphics, images, computer programs or otherwise |
| Electronic Information System: | A group of software and systems for creating, generating, sending, receiving, storing, displaying or otherwise processing and managing messages electronically |
| Electronic Record or Document: | A record or document that is created, stored, generated, copied, sent, communicated or received by electronic means, on a tangible medium or any other Electronic medium and is retrievable in perceivable form |
| Computer: | An electronic, magnetic, optical, electrochemical or other device used to process information and perform logical and arithmetic operations or storage functions, including any connected or directly related facility which enables the computer to store information or communication |
| Originator: | A natural or legal person by whom, or on whose behalf, a Data Message is sent, whichever the case, but does not include a person who provides services in relation to producing, processing, sending or storing such Data Message and other related services |
| Addressee: | A natural or legal person who is intended by the Originator to receive the Data Message, but not a person who provides services in relation to receiving, processing or storing such Data Message and other related services |
| Computer Program: | A set of computer executable information, instructions and orders designed to accomplish a specific task |
| Data Message: | Electronic Information sent or received by Electronic means, whatever the method of retrieval at the place of receipt |
| Electronic Communication: | The sending and receipt of Data Messages |
| Electronic Signature: | Any letters, numbers, symbols, voice or processing system in Electronic form applied to, incorporated in, or logically associated with a Data Message with the intention of authenticating or approving the same |
| Secure Electronic Signature: | An Electronic Signature which meets the requirements set out in Article (18) of this Law |
| Signatory: | A natural or legal person who holds an Electronic Signature Creation Device and by whom or on whose behalf a signature is applied to a Data Message by use of the device |

| | |
|---|---|
| Signature Creation Device: | A uniquely configured device or Electronic Information that is required, alone or in conjunction with other devices or Electronic Information, in order to create an Electronic Signature attributable to a specific person including systems or devices which generate or capture unique information such as codes, algorithms, letters, numbers, private keys, personal identification numbers or personal attributes |

| | |
|---|---|
| Automated Electronic Agent: | A computer program or Electronic means used independently to initiate an action or response in whole or in part without review or action by an individual at the time of the action or response |
| Automated Electronic Transactions: | Transactions concluded or performed, in whole or in part, by Electronic means or Electronic records, in which the acts or records are not monitored or reviewed by an individual |
| Certification Service Provider: | An accredited or authorized person or organization that issues Electronic Attestation Certificates or provides other services in this connection and in relation to Electronic Signatures regulated by this Law |
| Electronic Attestation Certificate: | A certificate issued by a Certification Service Provider confirming the identity of the person or entity holding an Electronic Signature Creation Device |
| Secure Authentication Procedures: | Procedures aimed at verifying that a Data Message is that of a specific person and detecting error or alteration in the communication, content or storage of a Data Message or Electronic Record since a specific point in time, which may require the use of algorithms or codes, identifying words or numbers, encryption, answerback or acknowledgement procedures, or similar information security devices |
| Relying Party: | A party that acts in reliance on an Electronic Signature or Electronic Attestation Certificate |
| Electronic Transaction: | Any deal, contract or agreement concluded or performed, in whole or in part, through Electronic Communication |
| Electronic Commerce: | Commercial activities conducted through Electronic Communication |

## CHAPTER TWO APPLICATION AND OBJECT OF THE LAW

### Article (2)

1- Matters for which no specific provision is laid down in this Law shall be governed by the international commercial laws affecting Electronic Transactions and Commerce and the general principles of civil and commercial practice

2- This Law applies to Electronic Records, Documents and Signatures that relate to Electronic Transactions and Commerce but does not apply to:

a) Transactions and issues relating to personal law such as marriage, divorce and wills;

b) Deeds of title to immoveable property;

c) Negotiable instruments;

d) Transactions involving the sale, purchase, lease (for a term of more than 10 years) and other disposition of immoveable property and the registration of other rights relating to immoveable property;

e) Any document legally required to be attested before a notary public; and

f) Any other documents or transactions exempted by special provision of law

3- The Cabinet may decide upon an addition, deletion or modification to the list of transactions and matters appearing in subsection (2) of this article

**Article (3)**

The objects of this Law are as follows:

1- To protect the rights of persons doing business electronically and determine their obligations

2- To encourage and facilitate Electronic Transactions and Communications by means of reliable Electronic Records

3- To facilitate and eliminate barriers to Electronic Commerce and other Electronic Transactions resulting from uncertainties over writing and signature requirements, and promote the development of the legal and business infrastructure necessary to implement secure Electronic Commerce

4- To facilitate the electronic filing of documents with governmental and non-governmental agencies and departments and promote efficient delivery of the services of such agencies and departments by means of reliable Electronic Communications

5- Minimize the incidence of forged Electronic Communications, alteration of Communications and fraud in Electronic Commerce and other Electronic Transactions

6- Establish uniform rules, regulations and standards for the authentication and validity of Electronic Communications

7- Promote public confidence in the validity, integrity and reliability of Electronic Transactions, Communications and Records

8- Promote the growth of Electronic Commerce and other transactions on the national and international level through the use of Electronic Signatures

## CHAPTER THREE REQUIREMENTS FOR ELECTRONIC TRANSACTIONS

### One: Electronic Communications

### Article (4)

1- A Data Message is not without legal force and effect merely on the grounds that it is in Electronic form

2- A Data Message that refers to information, without providing details of that information, is not without legal force, so far as this information is accessible within the context of the Electronic System of the Originator and the Message indicates the method of access

### Two: Retention of Electronic Records

### Article (5)

1- Where the law requires that certain documents, records or information be retained for any reason, that requirement is met by retaining Electronic Records, provided that the following conditions are satisfied:

a) the Electronic Record is retained in the format in which it was generated, sent or received, or in a format which can be demonstrated to represent accurately the information generated, sent or received;

b) the information contained therein is accessible so as to be usable for subsequent reference; and

c) such information, if any, is retained as enables the identification of the origin and destination of the Data Message and the date and time when it was sent or received

2- An obligation to retain documents, records or information in accordance with paragraph (c) of subsection (1) does not extend to any information necessarily or automatically generated solely for the purpose of enabling a message to be sent or received

3- A person may satisfy the requirement referred to in subsection (1) by using the services of any other person, if the conditions in that subsection are complied with

4- Nothing in this section shall:

a) apply to any rule of law which expressly provides for the retention of documents, records or information in the form of Electronic Records in accordance with a specific Electronic Information System or through specific procedures, or their retention or communication through a specific Electronic Agent

b) preclude any department of the Government from specifying additional requirements for the retention of Electronic Records that are subject to the jurisdiction of such department

### Three: Admissibility of Electronic Transactions

### Article (6)

1- Nothing in this Law shall require any person or employee to use or accept information in Electronic format, but a person's consent to do so may be inferred from his affirmative conduct

2- As between persons involved in generating, sending, receiving, storing or otherwise processing Electronic Records, the provisions of Chapters Two-Four of this Law may be varied by agreement

3- Notwithstanding the provisions of subsection (1), the Government must give explicit consent to dealing electronically in transactions to which it is a party

### Four: Writing

### Article (7)

If a rule of law requires a statement, document, record, transaction or evidence to be in writing or provides for certain consequences if it is not, an Electronic Document or Record satisfies the requirement if the provisions of subsection (1) of Article (5) of this Law are complied with

### Five: Electronic Signature

### Article (8)

1- Where a rule of law requires a signature on a document, or provides for certain consequences in the absence of a signature, that rule is satisfied if the document contains a reliable Electronic Signature within the meaning of Article (18) of this Law

2- Absent contrary statutory provision, a person may use any form of Electronic authentication

### Six: Electronic Original

### Article (9)

Where a rule of law requires a Data Message to be presented or retained in its original form, or provides for certain consequences if not so presented or retained, that requirement is met by a Data Message if:

1- there exists reliable assurance as to the integrity of the information contained in the Data Message from the time when it was first generated in its final form, as an Electronic Document or Record. The criteria for assessing integrity shall be whether the information has remained complete and unaltered, apart from the addition of any endorsement and any change which arises in the normal course of communication, storage and display; and

2- if the message allows, when required, the display of the information sought to be presented

### Seven: Admissibility and Evidential Weight of Electronic Records

### Article (10)

1- In any legal proceedings, nothing in the application of the rules of evidence shall apply so as to prevent the admission of a Data Message or Electronic Signature in evidence:

a) on the grounds that the message or signature is in Electronic format; or

b) if it is the best evidence that the person adducing it could reasonably be expected to obtain, on the grounds that the message or signature is not original or in its original form

2- In assessing the evidential weight of Electronic Information, regard shall be given to:

a) the reliability of the manner in which one or more of the operations of executing, entering, generating, processing, storing, presenting or communicating was performed;

b) the reliability of the manner in which the integrity of the information was maintained;

c) the reliability of the source of information, if identifiable;

d) the reliability of the manner in which the Originator was identified;

e) any other factor that may be relevant

3- Absent proof to the contrary, it shall be presumed that a Secure Electronic Signature:

a) is reliable;

b) is the signature of the person to whom it correlates; and

c) was affixed by that person with the intention of signing or approving the Data Message attributed to him

4- Absent proof to the contrary, it shall be presumed that a Secure Electronic Record:

a) remained unaltered since creation; and

b) is reliable

## Chapter Four

## Electronic Transactions

### One: Formation and Operation of Contracts

### Article (11)

1- For the purpose of contracting, an offer or the acceptance of an offer may be expressed, in whole or in part, by Electronic Communication

2- A contract is not invalid or unenforceable solely by reason that Electronic Communication was used in its formation

## Two: Automated Electronic Transactions

### Article (12)

1- A contract may be formed by the interaction of Automated Electronic Agents that include two or more Electronic Information Systems preset and preprogrammed to carry out these tasks. Such contract would be valid and enforceable even if no individual was directly involved in the conclusion of the contract within such systems

2- A contract may be formed between an Automated Electronic Information System in the possession of a natural or legal person and another natural person, where the latter knows or has reason to know that the such a system will automatically conclude or perform the contract

## Three: Attribution

### Article (13)

1- A Data Message is that of the Originator if it was sent by the Originator himself

2- As between the Originator and the Addressee, a Data Message is deemed to be that of the Originator if it was sent:

a) by a person who had the authority to act on behalf of the Originator in respect of the Data Message;

b) by an Automated Information System programmed by or on behalf of the Originator to operate automatically

## Four: Acknowledgement of Receipt

### Article (14)

1- The provisions of subsections (2), (3) and (4) of this Article shall apply where, on or before sending a Data Message, or by means of that Data Message, the Originator has requested or has agreed with the Addressee that receipt of the Data Message be acknowledged

2- Where the Originator has not agreed with the Addressee that the acknowledgement be given in a particular form or by a particular method, an acknowledgement may be given by:

a) any communication by the Addressee, electronic, automated or otherwise; or

b) any conduct of the addressee, sufficient to indicate to the Originator that the Data Message has been received

3- Where the Originator has stated that the Data Message is conditional on receipt of the acknowledgment, the Data Message is treated as though it had never been sent until the acknowledgment is received

4- Where the Originator has asked for an acknowledgement but has not stated that the Data Message is conditional on receipt of the acknowledgment within the time specified or agreed, or if no time has been specified or agreed within a reasonable time, the Originator:

a) may give notice to the Addressee stating that no acknowledgment has been received and specifying a reasonable time by which the acknowledgment must be received; and

b) if the acknowledgement is not received within the time specified in para (a) of this subsection, may treat the Data Message as though it has never been sent, or exercise any other rights it may have

5- Where the Originator receives the Addressee's acknowledgment of receipt, it is presumed, unless evidence to the contrary is adduced, that the related Data Message was received by the Addressee, but that presumption does not imply that the content of the Data Message sent by the Originator corresponds to the content of the message received from the Addressee

6- Where the acknowledgment received by the Originator states that the related Data Message met technical requirements, either agreed upon or set forth in applicable standards, it is presumed, unless evidence to the contrary is adduced, that those requirements have been met

7- Except as it relates to the sending or receipt of the Data Message, this Article is not intended to address the legal consequences that may flow either from that Data Message or from the acknowledgment of its receipt

**Article (15)**

One: Unless otherwise agreed by the Originator and the Addressee:

1- The dispatch of a Data Message occurs when it enters an Information System outside the control of the Originator or the person who sent the message on behalf of the Originator

2- The time of receipt of a Data Message is determined as follows:

a) if the Addressee has designated an information system for the purpose of receiving Data Messages, receipt occurs at the time when the Data Message enters the designated Information System; or if the Data Message is sent to an Information System of the Addressee that is not the designated Information System, at the time when the Data Message is retrieved by the Addressee;

b) if the Addressee has not designated an Information System, receipt occurs when the Data Message enters an Information System of the Addressee

Two: Clause (2) of Section One of this Article shall apply notwithstanding that the place where the Information System is located may be different from the place where the Data Message is deemed to be received under Section Three of this Article

Three: Unless otherwise agreed between the Originator and the Addressee, a Data Message is deemed to be dispatched at the place where the Originator has its place of business, and is deemed to be received at the place where the Addressee has its place of business

Four: For the purposes of this Article:

a) if the Originator or the Addressee has more than one place of business, the place of business is that which has the closest relationship to the underlying transaction or, where there is no underlying transaction, the principal place of business;

b) if the Originator or the Addressee does not have a place of business, reference is to be made to the usual place of residence; and

c) "usual place of residence" in relation to a body corporate, means the place where it is incorporated or otherwise legally constituted

## CHAPTER FIVE SECURE ELECTRONIC RECORDS AND SIGNATURES

### One: Secure Electronic Records

### Article (16)

1- If a prescribed Secure Authentication Procedure or a commercially reasonable Secure Authentication Procedure agreed to by the parties involved has been properly applied to an Electronic Record to verify that the Electronic Record has not been altered since a specified point in time, such record shall be treated as a Secure Electronic Record from such specified point in time to the time of verification

2- For the purposes of this Article and Article 17 of this Law, the determination of whether Secure Authentication Procedures are commercially reasonable shall take into account these procedures in the light of the commercial circumstances existing at the time the procedures were used, including:

a) the nature of the transaction;

b) the experience and skill of the parties;

c) the volume of similar transactions conducted by either or both of the parties;

d) the availability of alternative procedures and their cost; and

e) the procedure generally used for similar types of transactions

### Two: Secure Electronic Signature

### Article (17)

1- A signature shall be treated as a Secure Electronic Signature if, through the application of a prescribed Secure Authentication Procedure or a commercially reasonable Secure Authentication Procedure agreed to by the parties involved, it can be verified that an Electronic Signature was, at the time it was made:

a) unique to the person using it;

b) capable of identifying such person;

c) was, at the time of signing, under the sole control of the Signatory in terms of the creation data and the means used; and

d) linked to the Electronic Record to which it relates in a manner which provides reliable assurance as to the integrity of the signature such that if the record was changed the Electronic Signature would be invalidated

2- Absent proof to the contrary, reliance on a Secure Electronic Signature is deemed reasonable

### Three: Reliance on Electronic Signatures and Electronic Attestation Certificates

### Article (18)

1- A person may rely on an Electronic Signature or Electronic Attestation Certificate to the extent that such reliance is reasonable

2- Where an Electronic Signature is supported by a certificate, the Relying Party in respect of such signature shall bear the legal consequences of its failure to take reasonable and necessary steps to verify the validity and enforceability of the certificate, as to whether it is suspended or revoked, and of observing any limitations with respect to the certificate

3- In determining whether it was reasonable for a person to have relied on an Electronic Signature or Certificate, regard shall be had, if appropriate, to

a) the nature of the underlying transaction that Electronic Signature was intended to support;

b) the value or importance of the underlying transaction, if this known to the party relying on the Electronic Signature;

c) whether the Relying Party in respect of the Electronic Signature or the Electronic Attestation Certificate had taken appropriate steps to determine the reliability of the Electronic Signature or the Electronic Attestation Certificate;

d) whether the Relying Party in respect of the Electronic Signature had taken appropriate steps to ascertain whether the Electronic Signature was supported or was reasonably expected to have been supported by an Electronic Attestation Certificate;

e) whether the Relying Party in respect of the Electronic Signature or the Electronic Attestation Certificate knew or ought to have known that the Electronic Signature or the Electronic Attestation Certificate had been compromised or revoked;

f) any agreement or course of dealing which the Originator has with the Relying Party in respect of the Electronic Signature or the Electronic Attestation Certificate, or any trade usage or practice which may be applicable;

g) any other relevant factor

4- Absent proof to the contrary, the party relying on an Electronic Signature or Electronic Attestation Certificate assumes the risk that the Electronic Signature or the Electronic Attestation Certificate is forged, if reliance on the Electronic Signature or the Electronic Attestation Certificate is not reasonable under the circumstances, having regard to the factors in subsection (2) of this Article

**Four: Duties of Signatory**

**Article (19)**

One: A Signatory shall:

1- not unlawfully use its Signature Creation Device;

2- exercise reasonable care to avoid the unauthorized use of its Signature Creation Device;

3- without undue delay, notify concerned persons if:

a) the Signatory becomes aware that the security of its Signature Creation Device has been compromised;

b) the circumstances known to the Signatory give rise to a substantial risk that the security of the Signature Creation Device may have been compromised; and

4- where an Electronic Attestation Certificate is used to support a Signature Creation Device, exercise reasonable care to ensure the accuracy and completeness of all material representations made by the Signatory which are relevant to the Electronic Attestation Certificate throughout its life cycle

Two: A Signatory shall bear the legal consequences of its failure to satisfy the requirements of Section One of this Article

## CHAPTER SIX PROVISIONS RELATING TO ELECTRONIC ATTESTATION CERTIFICATES AND CERTIFICATION SERVICES

### One: Certification Services Controller

### Article (20)

For the purpose of this Law, the Cabinet shall appoint an authority to oversee certification services particularly in relation to the licensing, approval, monitoring and overseeing of the activities of Certification Service Providers

### Two: Duties of the Certification Service Provider

### Article (21)

One: A Certification Service Provider shall:

a) act in accordance with representations made by it with respect to its policies and practices;

b) exercise reasonable care to ensure the accuracy and completeness of all material representations made by it that are relevant to the Electronic Attestation Certificate throughout its life cycle or that are included in the certificate;

c) provide reasonably accessible means which enable a Relying Party to ascertain:

1) the identity of the Certification Service Provider;

2) that the person identified in the Electronic Attestation Certificate holds, at the relevant time, the Signature Creation Device referred to in the certificate;

3) the method used to identify the Signatory;

4) any limitation on the purpose or value for which the Signature Creation Device may be used;

5) that the Signature Creation Device is valid and has not been compromised;

6) whether means exist for the Signatory to give notice pursuant to this Law;

7) whether a timely signature revocation service is offered;

d) provide a means for Signatories to give notice that the Signature Creation Device has been compromised and ensure the availability of a timely signature revocation service;

e) utilize trustworthy systems, procedures and human resources in performing its services;

f) be licensed by the Certification Services Controller if operating in the UAE

Two: For the purposes of para (e) under Section One above, in determining whether any systems, procedures and human resources are trustworthy, regard shall be had to the following factors:

a) financial and human resources, including the existence of assets within the jurisdiction;

b) quality of hardware and software systems;

c) procedures for processing and issuing Electronic Attestation Certificates and applications for certificates and retention of records;

d) availability of information to Signatories identified in Electronic Attestation Certificates and parties relying on certification services;

e) regularity and extent of audit by an independent body;

f) the existence of a declaration by the UAE, an accreditation body, or the Certification Service Provider regarding compliance with or existence of the foregoing;

g) certification Service Provider's susceptibility to the jurisdiction of the courts of the UAE;

h) the degree of discrepancy between the law applicable to the conduct of the Certification Service Provider and the law of the UAE;

Three: An Electronic Attestation Certificate shall state:

a) the identity of the Certification Service Provider;

b) that the person identified in the Electronic Attestation Certificate holds, at the relevant time, the Signature Creation Device referred to in the certificate;

c) that the Signature Creation Device was effective at or before the date when the certificate was issued;

d) any limitations on the purposes or value for which the Signature Creation Device or the Electronic Attestation Certificate may be used;

e) any limitation on the scope or extent of liability which the Certification Service Provider accepts to any person

Four: If damage has been caused as a result of the Electronic Attestation Certificate being incorrect or defective, a Certification Service Provider shall be liable for damage suffered by either:

a) a party who has contracted with the Certification Service Provider for the provision of an Electronic Attestation Certificate; or

b) any person who reasonably relies on an Electronic Attestation Certificate issued by the Certification Service Provider

Five: A Certification Service Provider shall not be liable for any damage if:

a) it included in the Electronic Attestation Certificate a statement limiting the scope or extent of its liability to any relevant person according to the regulations issued in this regard; or

b) it proves that it was not at fault or negligent or that the damage occurred for reasons beyond its control

## Three: Regulation of the Conduct of Certification Service Providers

### Article (22)

The Minister shall, at the recommendation of the Controller, issue rules for the regulation and licensing of Certification Service Providers operating in the UAE. These rules shall include:

a) applications for licenses or renewal of licenses of Certification Service Providers and their authorized representatives and matters incidental thereto;

b) specifying the activities of Certification Service Providers including the manner, place and method of soliciting business from the public;

c) specifying the standards and rules which Certification Service Providers have to maintain and follow in their business;

d) specifying appropriate standards with respect to the qualifications and experience which Certification Service Providers should possess and the training of their employees;

e) specifying the conditions subject to which Certification Service Providers shall conduct their business;

f) specifying the contents of written, printed or visual materials and advertisements that may be distributed or used in respect of an Electronic Attestation Certificate and the digital key;

g) specifying the form and content of an Electronic Attestation Certificate and the digital key;

h) specifying the form and manner in which accounts shall be maintained by Certification Service Providers;

i) specifying the qualification which auditors and Certification Service Providers should possess;

j) laying down regulations governing the inspection and auditing of the activities of Certification Service Providers;

k) specifying the terms and conditions for the establishment of any electronic system by a Certification Service Provider either solely or jointly with other Certification Service

Providers and enforcing and revising those terms and conditions pursuant to the recommendation of the Controller and in coordination with the relevant authorities;

l) specifying the manner in which the licensee shall conduct its dealings with the subscribers including its conflict of interest policy and duties towards subscribers with respect to digital signature certificates;

m) specifying the fees to be paid in respect of any matter required under this Article based on a decision from the Cabinet;

n) prescribing any forms for the purpose of this Article;

o) specifying the fines and penalties applicable to breach of the rules governing the activities of Certification Service Providers;

**Recognition of Foreign Certificates and Electronic Signatures**

**Article (23)**

1- In determining whether an Electronic Attestation Certificate or an Electronic Signature is legally effective, no regard shall be had to the place where the Certificate or the Electronic Signature was issued, nor to the jurisdiction in which the issuer of the Electronic Attestation Certificate or Signature had its place of business

2- Electronic Attestation Certificates issued by a foreign Certification Service Provider are recognized as legally equivalent to Certificates issued by Certification Service Providers operating under this Law, if the practices of the foreign Certification Service Provider provide a level of reliability at least equivalent to that required of Certification Service Providers operating in accordance with this Law, as provided under Article (21), and taking into consideration recognized international standards

3- Signatures complying with the requirements of laws of another state may be recognized as legally equivalent to signatures under this Law if the laws of the other state require a level of reliability at least equivalent to that required for such signatures under this Law

4- In relation to the admissions specified in subsections 2 and 3 above, regard must be had to the factors stated in Section Two of Article (21) of this Law

5- In determining whether an Electronic Signature or Electronic Attestation Certificate is legally effective, regard shall be had to any agreement between the parties in relation to the transaction in which that Signature or Certificate was used

6- Notwithstanding subsections (2) and (3) above:

a) Parties to commercial and other transactions may specify that a particular Certification Service Provider, class of Certification Service Providers or class of certificates must be used in connection with Data Messages or signatures submitted to them

b) Where parties agree, as between themselves, to the use of certain types of Electronic Signatures or Electronic Attestation Certificates, that agreement shall be recognized as sufficient for the purpose of cross-border recognition between the various jurisdictions of states, unless that agreement would not be valid or effective under applicable law of the UAE

## CHAPTER EIGHT GOVERNMENT USE OF ELECTRONIC RECORDS AND SIGNATURES

### Article (24)

1- Government Departments may, within the scope of their legal duties:

a) accept the filing, submission, creation or retention of documents in the form of Electronic Records;

b) issue any permit, license, decision or approval in the form of Electronic Records;

c) accept fees and other payments in Electronic form;

d) put out tenders and receive bids relating to Government procurement by Electronic means

2- In any case where the Government decides to perform any of the functions in subsection (1), the Government may specify:

a) the manner and format in which such Electronic Records shall be created, filed, retained, submitted or issued;

b) the manner, method and process by which Government tenders are put out , bids are received, and Government procurement is made;

c) the type of Electronic Signature required (including, if applicable, the requirement that the sender use a digital signature or other Secure Electronic Signature);

d) the manner and format in which such signature shall be affixed to the Electronic Record, and the criteria that shall be met by any Certification Service Provider to whom the document is submitted for filing and retention;

e) control processes and procedures as appropriate to ensure adequate integrity, safety, security and confidentiality of Electronic Records, payments or fees; and

f) any other required attributes, conditions or rules for Electronic Records of payments and fees that are currently specified for corresponding paper documents

### Article (25)

No person shall publish a certificate with reference to a Certification Service Provider listed in the certificate, with the knowledge that:

a) the Certification Service Provider listed in the certificate has not issued it;

b) the subscriber listed in the certificate has not accepted it; or

c) the certificate has been revoked or suspended, unless such publication is for the purpose of verifying an Electronic Signature or digital signature used prior to such suspension or revocation

## CHAPTER NINE PENALTIES

### Article (26)

The penalty shall be imprisonment for a period of not less than 1 year and a fine of not less than AED 50,000 and not more than AED 250,000 or either for anyone who knowingly creates, publishes, offers or provides any Electronic Attestation Certificate containing or referring to incorrect information

### Article (27)

The penalty shall be imprisonment for a period not exceeding 6 months and a fine not exceeding AED 100,000 or either for anyone who deliberately provides incorrect information to a Certification Service Provider when requesting an Electronic Attestation Certificate or requesting the revocation or suspension of an Electronic Attestation Certificate

### Article (28)

1- The penalty shall be imprisonment for a period of not less than 6 months and a fine of the not less than AED 20,000 and not more than AED 200,000 or either for anyone who, pursuant to any powers conferred under this Law, obtains access to information in Electronic Records, Documents or Communications and discloses the same

2- Excluded from subsection (1) of this Article shall be cases of disclosure that are made for the purpose of this Law or judicial proceedings

### Article (29)

The penalty shall be imprisonment for a period not exceeding 6 months and a fine not exceeding AED 100,000 or either for anyone who, through the use of Electronic means, commits an act which constitutes an offence under the laws in force

### Article (30)

1- The penalty shall be imprisonment or a fine of not less than AED 10,000 and not more than AED 100,000 where an offence under this Law has been committed with the consent, or connivance of, or is attributable to any act of a chairman or member of board of directors or manager of a body corporate

2- The penalty shall be imprisonment or a fine of not less than AED 10,000 and not more than AED 100,000 where an offence under this Law or any of its implementing regulations has been committed by an employee of a body corporate, and it is proved that the offence has been committed with his consent or connivance, or is attributable to any negligence on his part

3- In case of conviction per subsections (1) or (2) of this Article, the body corporate employing the convicted parties shall be ordered to pay a fine equivalent to the fine ordered against any of them

**Article (31)**

A court convicting per this Law shall direct the confiscation of the tools and devices used in the commission of the offence without prejudice to the rights of bona fide third parties

**Article (32)**

A court sentencing a foreign national to imprisonment per this Law shall also order him deported

**Article (33)**

The penalties prescribed under this Law shall be enforced without prejudice to any severer penalty provided for by any other law

## CHAPTER TEN CLOSING PROVISIONS

**Article (34)**

Employees of the Ministry and the Competent Local Authority appointed by the Minister of Justice, Islamic Affairs & Awqaf shall act as law enforcement officers for the purpose of detecting and establishing offences which are committed in violation of this Law and its implementing regulations

**Article (35)**

The Minister shall issue the regulations and decisions necessary to enforce this Law

**Article (36)**

All provisions contravening the provisions of this Law are hereby repealed

**Article (37)**

This Law shall be published in the Official Gazette and shall take effect from the date of publication

# INTERNET AND TELECOM SECTOR LAWS AND REGULATIONS

## FEDERAL LAW BY DECREE REGARDING THE ORGANISATION OF THE TELECOMMUNICATION SECTOR

We, Zayed bin Sultan Al Nahyan, President of the State of the United Arab Emirates, In cognisance of the Constitution, and Federal Law No. (1) of 1972 Regarding the Functions of Ministries and the Powers of Ministers and the amending laws thereof, and Federal Law No. (7) of 1973 Regarding Radio Communications and Apparatus and the amending laws thereof, and Federal Law No. (7) of 1976 Regarding the Audit Bureau as amended, and

Federal Law No. (8) of 1984 Regarding Commercial Companies and the amending laws thereof, and Federal Law No. (5) of 1985 Issuing the Civil Transactions Code and the amending laws thereof, and Federal Law No. (3) of 1987 issuing the Penal Code, and

Federal Law No. (1) of 1991 Regarding Emirates Telecommunications Corporation, and Federal law No. (10) of 1992 Issuing the Law of Evidence in Civil and Commercial Transactions, and

Federal Law No. (18) of 1993 Issuing the Commercial Transactions Code, and Federal Law No. (7) of 1999 Regarding Pensions and Social Security, and on the basis of the proposal of the Prime Minister and the agreement of the Council of Ministers, have issued the following Federal Law by Decree:

### CHAPTER 1 INTERPRETATION

### Article (1)

**Definitions**

In applying this Federal Law by Decree, the following terms shall have the following meanings unless the context requires otherwise:

“Authority” the General Authority for Regulating the Telecommunication Sector.

“Board” the Board of Directors of the Authority.

“Board Members” such persons as may be appointed to the Board in accordance with the provisions of this Federal Law by Decree.

“Chairman” the chairman of the board of directors of the Authority.

“Director General” the Director General of the Authority.

“Etisalat” the Emirates Telecommunications Corporation regulated by Federal Law No. (1) of 1991 Regarding Emirates Telecommunications Corporation.

“Executive Order” the executive order issued pursuant to this Federal Law by Decree.

"Government" the government of the State of the United Arab Emirates.

"Interconnection" the linking by whatever means of Telecommunication Networks in order to allow users of one entity to communicate with users of the same or another entity or enabling the users to make use of Telecommunication Services provided by another entity.

"Interconnection Agreement" an agreement under which the interconnection will be achieved pursuant to the rules and conditions issued by the Authority.

"Licence" a licence issued pursuant to the provisions of this Federal Law by Decree and its Executive Order which allows the Licensee to carry out any of the Regulated Activities.

"Licensees" Etisalat and such entities as may be licensed by the Supreme Committee pursuant to the provisions of this Federal Law by Decree and its Executive Order.

"Private Land" any land owned by, granted to or leased to any person other than any Public Institution.

"Private Telecommunication Network" a Telecommunication Network operated exclusively to serve the requirements and to benefit one person or a group of persons who have a common ownership.

"Public Institution(s)" all federal ministries and local departments, authorities and public organisations linked thereto, including the armed forces, the police, the intelligence and security services of the State but excluding any commercial company or establishment owned by any of the foregoing or in which any of the foregoing may have an interest.

"Public Land" all land under the control or ownership of any Public Institution but excluding any Private Land.

"Public Telecommunication Network" a Telecommunication Network operated by the Licensee for the provision of Public Telecommunication Services by the Licensee pursuant to the provisions of this Federal Law by Decree.

"Public Telecommunication Service" any Telecommunication Service provided to users or a part thereof in consideration of a fee.

"Regulated Activity" either the operation of a Public Telecommunication Network or the supply of a Telecommunication Service to users and all other types of services specified by the Supreme Committee pursuant to the provisions of this Federal Law by Decree.

"State" the United Arab Emirates.

"Supreme Committee" the committee established for the supervision of the telecommunication sector pursuant to the provisions of Article (2) of this Federal Law by Decree.

"Telecommunication Apparatus" apparatus made or adapted for use in transmitting, receiving or conveying any of the Telecommunication Services through a Telecommunication Network.

"Telecommunication Network" a system comprising one or more items of apparatus or means of communication medium for broadcasting, transmission, switching or receiving of Telecommunication Services, by means of electric, magnetic, electro-magnetic, electro-chemical or electro-mechanical energy and any other means of communication medium.

"Telecommunication Service" the service of transmitting, broadcasting, switching or receiving by means of a Telecommunication Network of any of the following:

1. wired and wireless cable and radio telecommunications;

2. voice, music and other sounds;

3. visual images;

4. signals used in transmission other than the production and broadcasting of programmes;

5. signals used to operate or control any machinery or apparatus;

6. the installation, maintenance, adjustment, repair, replacement moving, or removal of apparatus which is or will be connected to a Public Telecommunication Network;

7. the installation, maintenance and operation of networks for telegraph, telephone, telex, leased circuits, domestic and international data networks, internet and wireless transmission;

8. any other Telecommunications Services approved by the Supreme Committee.

but does not include any services used in the production and broadcasting of programmes.

"Wireless Transmission" the transmitting or receiving of electro-magnetic energy which may be used for the conveyance of data, or messages or voice or visual images, or for the operation or control of machinery or apparatus.

## CHAPTER 2 SUPREME COMMITTEE FOR THE SUPERVISION OF THE TELECOMMUNICATION SECTOR

### ARTICLE (2)

*It is hereby established a committee for the purposes of supervising the telecommunication sector called the "Supreme Committee for the Supervision of the Telecommunication Sector". It shall be comprised of four members (including the Chairman) representing the Ministry of Presidential Affairs, the Court of the Vice President of the State, Ruler of the Emirate of Dubai and the Council of Ministers. The members of the Supreme Committee shall be appointed by a Federal Decree and shall be remunerated for their membership in the Supreme Committee. The Supreme Committee shall have all powers necessary for it to carry out its authorities as prescribed by this Federal Law by Decree.

### ARTICLE (3)

The Supreme Committee shall have the sole and exclusive authority to:

1. issue the Executive Order of this Federal Law by Decree;
2. establish and oversee the general policy for the telecommunication sector in the State;
3. issue any general guidance or instructions relating to the telecommunication sector and necessary for national security or international relations;
4. issue resolutions, rules, regulations, and instructions regarding the implementation of this Federal Law by Decree and its Executive Order including resolutions for establishing entities operating in the telecommunication sector and determining the fees of the services and facilities provided to Licensees and to whom such fees should be paid;
5. issue, extend, revoke and suspend Licences pursuant to the provisions of this Federal Law by Decree and its Executive Order;
6. determine fees for Licences;
7. determine the fees for the authorisations, consents and services secured or provided by the Authority pursuant to the provisions of this Federal Law by Decree or its Executive Order; and
8. any other authorities vested in it pursuant to this Federal Law by Decree.

The Supreme Committee may delegate some of its authorities to the Authority

### ARTICLE (4)

The funds required to enable the Supreme Committee to meet its financial needs and obligations shall be allocated in the general budget of the State.

*This article was amended by the Federal law by Decree no. (1) of 2005

### ARTICLE (5)

The Supreme Committee shall, by resolution, issue its internal rules regarding the conduct of its business and the procedures for its meetings, the terms, conditions and remuneration for its employees. The Supreme Committee shall not be subject to the control of the Audit Bureau according to the law establishing such Bureau.

## CHAPTER 3 THE GENERAL AUTHORITY FOR REGULATING THE TELECOMMUNICATION SECTOR

### Part 1 – Establishment of the Authority

### ARTICLE (6)

It is hereby established an independent public authority, called the "General Authority for Regulating the Telecommunication Sector" for the purpose of performing the functions and implementing the duties given to it under this Federal Law by Decree and its Executive Order.

### ARTICLE (7)

The Authority shall have an independent legal personality and shall have full capacity to act accordingly and to perform legal actions in accordance with this Federal Law by Decree, including the capacity to enter into contracts of all types and to own and lease movable and immovable assets of all types and the capacity to sue. The Authority shall have financial and administrative independence in carrying out its affairs.

### Article (8)

The headquarters of the Authority shall be in Abu Dhabi and it shall also have an office in Dubai. The Board may establish other offices for the Authority within the State.

### Article (9)

The Authority shall conduct its business in accordance with this Federal Law by Decree and its Executive Order, and shall have the power to issue its financial and internal policies, contracting, purchasing policies, and all personnel and disciplinary policies for the employees of the Authority without the need to abide by the governmental laws, decisions, rules and regulations applicable in this regard.

### Article (10)

The Authority shall be managed by a board of directors, comprised of five Board Members, including the Chairman and the Director General. The Board shall be appointed by resolution of the Supreme Committee for a period of four years renewed for other similar periods pursuant to the same appointing instrument.

### Article (11)

Board Members cannot be removed from their positions before completing their period of appointment except by a resolution of the Supreme Committee and because of any of the following reasons: -

1. Conviction of dishonour or dishonesty related criminal offence or felony.
2. Disciplinary reasons.
3. Health incapacity which prevents that Board Member from carrying out his duties.

## Part 2 – Functions, Duties and Powers of the Authority

### Article (12)

The Authority is the competent body to oversee the telecommunications sector in the State and all Licensees in accordance with this Federal Law by Decree, its Executive Order and the instructions of the Supreme Committee. The Authority may provide to the Supreme Committee any necessary proposals in relation to the general policy of such sector and shall, at the end of each financial year, submit to the Supreme Committee a report on its activities and business performance during that year.

### Article (13)

The Authority shall exercise its functions and powers under this Federal Law by Decree and its Executive Order to:

1. ensure that the Telecommunication Services provided throughout the State, are sufficient to satisfy the public demands of those who wish to make use of such services;
2. enhance the level of service provided by the telecommunication sector in order to promote the interest of users;

3. ensure that Licensees meet quality standards of performance and adhere to the terms and conditions of the Licences granted to them;
4. encourage, promote, and develop the telecommunications and information technology industries in the State;
5. promote and enhance the telecommunication system in the State as indicated by the development and the establishment of industry related training institutions and through the availability of the latest apparatus, equipment and facilities provided by telecommunications technology.

**ARTICLE (14)**

Considering Articles (3) and (12) of this Federal Law by Decree the Authority shall have the power to issue regulations, orders, resolutions and procedures in relation to:

1. tariff, charges and fees levied by Licensees as determined by the Supreme Committee;
2. the Interconnection of and access to Telecommunication Networks and Telecommunication Services provided by the Licensees, and the co-location of assets and sharing of infrastructure by such Licensees, including the terms, conditions and prices of such Interconnection, access, co-location and sharing, the time-scales and rules for the negotiation and finalisation between such operators of agreements in relation to the foregoing matters and the dispute resolution policies between the parties to such agreements;
3. the terms and level of services provided by the Licensees to users, including the standards and quality of service provided, the terms and conditions of supply of such services, the handling and resolution of user complaints and disputes, the provision of information to users, the use of user information and the rendering of bills to users;
4. the specification of the equipment used by the Licensees including the technical standards and types thereof;
5. the importation, manufacture, dealing in, use and approval of Telecommunication Apparatus;
6. the allocation of telephone numbers, numbering plans and number portability;
7. the radio spectrum which has been allocated to the telecommunication sector under this Federal Law by Decree, including the allocation, re-allocation and use thereof;
8. the terms of preparation and provision of directory services and directory enquiries services;
9. provisions to limit interference with telecommunications in the State by radio waves or electrical or other means;
10. training persons in installing, connecting, adjusting and maintaining Telecommunication Apparatus;
11. the publication and announcements of information relating to Telecommunication Apparatus; and
12. performing such other functions as the Supreme Committee may determine.

## PART 3 – FINANCIAL AFFAIRS

**ARTICLE (15)**

The financial year of the Authority shall commence on the first day of January and end on the last day of December of each year, except that the first financial year of the Authority shall commence on the date this Federal Law by Decree comes into force and shall end on the last day of December of the following year.

### ARTICLE (16)

The Authority shall have an independent budget. In respect of the first financial year of the Authority, the budget shall be set by resolution of the Supreme Committee. In respect of the succeeding financial years of the Authority, the budget of the Authority shall be prepared by the Director General, approved by the Board and submitted to the Supreme Committee for approval.

### ARTICLE (17)

The financial resources of the Authority are derived from the following:

1. any funds assigned to the Authority in the general budget of the State;
2. such License fees as charged by the Supreme Committee pursuant to the provisions of this Federal Law by Decree and its Executive Order and the issued regulations accordingly;
3. such fees as may be charged by the Supreme Committee for any services provided by the Authority or the authorizations or approvals granted by the Authority pursuant to the provisions of this Federal Law by Decree, its Executive Order and the resolutions issued by the Supreme Committee;
4. any other revenues the Authority collects in pursuance of its activities and functions; and
5. any other financial resources approved by the Supreme Committee.

### ARTICLE (18)

The Authority shall collect the fees imposed by the Supreme Committee in relation to the Licenses issued by the Supreme Committee and the authorizations approvals, services of the Authority and any other amounts regarding radio spectrum.

### ARTICLE (19)

Following the approval of the Supreme Committee, the Authority may raise loans from the Government or raise loans from banks and other financial institutions (whether in the State or elsewhere) and may create and issue debentures or bonds on such terms as determined by the Board.

### ARTICLE (20)

The funds of the Authority may invest its fund in the manner approved by the Board.

### ARTICLE (21)

The Authority and it's dealings thereof shall be exempted from all Government fees and taxes.

### ARTICLE (22)

The Authority shall be exempted from the prior control of the Audit Bureau as set out in Federal Law No. (7) of 1976 Regarding the Establishment of the Audit Bureau as amended. The Audit Bureau shall not interfere in the business of the Authority and the decisions of its Board or in the policies determined by the Supreme Committee as applied by the Authority.

### ARTICLE (23)

1. The Board shall appoint an independent auditor, registered with the appropriate authorities in the State, to audit the annual accounts of the Authority and prepare reports regarding the results of the audit.
2. As soon as the accounts of the Authority have been audited, a copy of the accounts approved by the Board with a copy of the auditor's report attached to it shall be forwarded by the Authority to the Supreme Committee.

## CHAPTER FOUR RESTRUCTURING OF THE TELECOMMUNICATION SECTOR

### PART 1 – ETISALAT

### ARTICLE (24)

The exclusive privilege of undertaking the transmission of wire and wireless communications, their operation and maintenance and the development of a general communications system within the State and between the State and foreign countries conferred on Etisalat by Article 4 of Federal Law No. (1) of 1991 Regarding Emirates Telecommunications Corporation shall hereby cease to exist but without prejudice to the fees payable for services and facilities provided by the Government to Etisalat and which are payable to the Government pursuant to the provisions of the regulations and decisions in force at the date this Federal Law by Decree is issued, the right to impose and amend such fees shall transfer to Supreme Committee.

### ARTICLE (25)

Subject to the provisions of any transitional provisions of this Federal Law by Decree, all functions conferred on Etisalat by Federal Law No. (1) of 1991 Regarding Emirates Telecommunications Corporation that conflict with the powers, competences and functions of the Supreme Committee and the Authority under this Federal Law by Decree shall cease to be performed by Etisalat.

### ARTICLE (26)

*The Ministry of Communications shall have responsibility for representing the Government as a shareholder in Etisalat, and shall, accordingly have the power to exercise all rights in that regard.

### ARTICLE (27)

Etisalat shall be required, within a period of ninety days of this Federal Law by Decree coming into force, to take all such steps as shall be necessary to amend its Articles of Association and its applicable rules and regulations to comply with the provisions contained in this Federal Law by Decree and any regulations or decisions issued by the Supreme Committee.

*This article was amended by the Federal law by Decree no. (1) of 2005

### PART 2 – LICENSEES

### ARTICLE (28)

The Supreme Committee shall, by resolution, determine the various types of Regulated Activities for which Licences may be issued and the required terms for prospective Licensees.

In all cases no licence shall be issued to any entity unless such entity is a juridical entity established pursuant to a resolution issued by the Supreme Committee. Such juridical entity may, after obtaining the approval of the Supreme Committee, establish subsidiary companies to carry out certain Regulated Activities.

### ARTICLE (29)

With exception to acquiring the nationality of the State, the provisions of Federal Law No (8) of 1984 regarding Commercial Companies and the amending or replacement laws thereof shall not apply to juridical Licensee licensed pursuant to this Federal Law by Decree and its Executive Orders to the extent provided in their memoranda and articles of association as approved by the Supreme Committee. The competent authorities shall be under an obligation to register such juridical persons.

### ARTICLE (30)

All Licensees shall take into account the special needs and requirements regarding the type of service and Telecommunication Apparatus and ensure non-discrimination when providing such services and apparatus.

### ARTICLE (31)

It is not permitted to conduct any Regulated Activity unless authorised by a Licence or exempted in accordance with the provision of this Federal Law by Decree or its Executive Order.

### ARTICLE (32)

The Supreme Committee shall determine the form and substance of each Licence granted pursuant to this Federal Law by Decree, and shall include conditions specifying the duration of the Licence and may include conditions required by the Supreme Committee.

### ARTICLE (33)

The application for a Licence must be submitted to the Authority in the form prescribed by the Authority and must fulfil all the conditions set out by the Supreme Committee. The Authority shall within a maximum period of thirty days from the date of submitting the application, review the application and report its findings and recommendations thereto to the Supreme Committee.

### ARTICLE (34)

The Supreme Committee shall have the authority to grant or refuse a Licence to an applicant. The Supreme Committee's decision in this regard shall be final and binding on the applicant and may not be challenged or appealed in any way whatsoever.

### ARTICLE (35)

Obtaining a Licence pursuant to the provisions of this Federal Law by Decree shall not operate to relieve a person from any obligation to obtain any licences or authorisations that may be required from any other Government Institution for purposes connected with the conduct of its business.

### PART 3 – EXEMPTIONS AND EXCLUSIONS

#### ARTICLE (36)

The Supreme Committee may, if required, perform the following authorities:

1. exempt any Licensee from the performance of the Licence conditions for such periods and on such terms as specified in the exemption order;
2. issue a general exemption from the performance of the Licence conditions in favour of some, all or such classes of Licensees for such periods, and on such terms as specified in the exemption order.

The Supreme Committee may revoke, amend or extend any specific exemption or general exemption granted pursuant to this Article.

#### ARTICLE (37)

1. No person (whether an individual or a juridical person) nor any Public Institution may provide Telecommunication Services to clients or users through a Public Telecommunication Network unless licensed by the Supreme Committee pursuant to the provisions of this Federal Law by Decree. The establishment and operation of Private Telecommunication Networks shall be regulated by the Executive Order and the decisions issued by the Supreme Committee.
2. In all cases, the persons covered by the above paragraph must comply with the terms, conditions and requirements associated with the use of the frequencies allocated to them pursuant to the provisions of this Federal Law by Decree.

## CHAPTER 5 NETWORKS, APPARATUS AND NUMBERING

### PART 1 - NETWORK INTERCONNECTION AND SITES CO-LOCATION

#### ARTICLE (38)

The Authority shall take any needed action as deemed necessary to facilitate the process of Interconnection and to monitor the compliance of all parties to the provisions of the Interconnection Agreements. The Authority shall have all the powers which will enable it to achieve the foregoing.

#### ARTICLE (39)

1. Where there is a dispute in relation to Interconnection the parties to the dispute may refer the dispute to the Authority for adjudication and the issuance of binding resolutions.
2. The Authority shall adjudicate disputes referred in accordance with this Article as specified in the Executive Order.

#### ARTICLE (40)

1. Where there is a dispute between a Licensee and another Licensee for co-location or the sharing of facilities or sites either party may refer the dispute to the Authority for adjudication. The Authority must adjudicate the dispute referred to it.
2. The Authority shall make such investigations and request any information it deems necessary to resolve the disputes referred in accordance with this Article.

3. The adjudication may specify the steps to be taken by the parties in order to resolve the dispute, determine the terms on which a Licensee shall offer the sharing of facilities, order one or both parties to enter into a facility sharing agreement on terms specified in the decision.

In all cases the Authority's decision shall be final and binding.

### ARTICLE (41)

Etisalat and any of its subsidiaries shall, at the direction of the Authority, satisfy in a timely, efficient and least cost manner all requests from a Licensee for Interconnection, co-location or sharing of sites and facilities at the best point as determined by the Authority. In particular Etisalat shall:

1. comply with any regulations, guidelines or licence conditions issued pursuant to the provisions of this Federal Law by Decree or its Executive Order relating to Interconnection, co-location or sharing of sites and facilities;
2. subject to the regulations issued pursuant to the provisions of this Federal Law by Decree or its Executive Order, offer and provide Interconnection, co-location or sharing of sites and facilities on terms and conditions (including as to cost and quality) which are in accordance with best international practice;
3. Facilitate, provide facilities and information concerning Interconnection, co-location and sharing of sites to Licensees and their subsidiaries under the same conditions and of the same quality as Etisalat provides for its own services or those of its subsidiaries or companies.

## PART 2 – TELECOMMUNICATION APPARATUS APPROVAL

### ARTICLE (42)

The Authority shall be exclusively competent in issuing all authorisations and approvals in relation to Telecommunication Apparatus comprised in or intended for use in connection with a Telecommunication Network or in the provision of a Telecommunication Service in accordance with the Executive Order issued pursuant to this Federal Law by Decree and the instructions of the Supreme Committee to the Authority.

No person shall use, sell, offer for sale or connect to any Telecommunication Network any Telecommunication Apparatus which has not been approved by the Authority.

### ARTICLE (43)

Public Institutions shall be exempted from obtaining the approval of the Authority in respect of Telecommunication Apparatus used or to be used by the Public Institutions.

## Part 3 - Numbering

### ARTICLE (44)

The Authority shall be responsible for allocating prefixes, private telephone numbers and numbering ranges to Licensees in accordance with the provisions of this Federal Law by Decree, its Executive Order and the conditions set by the Authority and approved by Supreme Committee.

## CHAPTER 6 FREQUENCY MANAGEMENT AND ALLOCATION

### ARTICLE (45)

The Ministry of Communications shall ensure that sufficient and appropriate radio spectrum is designated for use for the provision of Telecommunication Services to satisfy demand for such services.

### ARTICLE (46)

A committee called the "Co-ordination Committee" shall be established by resolution from the Supreme Committee chaired by the Director General and representatives from the following institutions:

1. The Ministry of Communications;
2. The Ministry of Information and Culture;
3. The Ministry of the Interior;
4. Armed Forces;
5. The security and intelligence bodies in the State;
6. The Civil Aviation Authority; and
7. The Authority.

The Co-ordination Committee shall be responsible for putting in place a national frequency plan for radio spectrum used in Telecommunication Services to be approved by the Supreme Committee in order to ensure the efficient and proper use of radio spectrum without any interference. The Ministry of Communications or the Authority may request the Co-ordination Committee, from time to time, to review and amend the plan when the need arises.

### ARTICLE (47)

The national frequency plan shall be drawn up in conformity with the international regulations governing radio spectrum and the international or regional agreements concluded or acceded to by the State. It shall include provisions for: -

1. the designation, on the recommendation of the Authority, of bands of radio spectrum for the provision of Telecommunication Services over Telecommunication Networks;
2. the amendment of allocations to existing users of radio spectrum to allow for the development of new services; and
3. the reassignment of radio spectrum on expiry of existing licences or authorisations relating thereto.

### ARTICLE (48)

The Authority shall be responsible for allocation of radio spectrum designated for Telecommunication Services. Any such allocation of radio spectrum shall be made in accordance with the national frequency plan and on the basis of objective procedures and criteria, details of which shall be set out in regulations issued by the Authority.

### ARTICLE (49)

The Authority shall, within nine months of the date this Federal Law by Decree comes into force, and after notifying the Ministry of Communications and the Co-ordination Committee, prepare and publish a plan for the reallocation of radio spectrum currently authorised for use in the provision of Telecommunication Services.

### ARTICLE (50)

The establishment and use of Wireless Transmission stations and the installation and use of any Wireless Transmission shall be prohibited unless permitted by a radio spectrum authorisation issued by the Authority pursuant to the provisions of this Federal Law by Decree, its Executive Order or the regulations and instructions issued by the Authority.

### ARTICLE (51)

On the issue or renewal by the Authority of a radio spectrum authorisation, there shall be paid to the Authority by the entity to whom the authorisation is issued such sums as prescribed by the provisions of this Federal Law by Decree, its Executive Order or the decisions, regulations or instructions issued pursuant thereof.

## CHAPTER 7 OPERATION AND PROTECTION OF TELECOMMUNICATION NETWORKS AND LINES

### PART 1 – OPERATION OF NETWORKS

### ARTICLE (52)

Public Institutions shall, in accordance with their respective jurisdictions, grant all Licensees of Public Telecommunication Networks, without payment, rights to occupy and use Public Land as well as right of way and rights of access to Public Land so as to enable them to perform their activities as set out in their respective Licences, including:

1. the construction of buildings and other installations;
2. the installation of equipment and apparatus;
3. the establishment, extension, development and maintenance of Public Telecommunication Networks including the laying and extension of ground and aerial cables and service lines.

### ARTICLE (53)

The provisions of Article (52) of this Federal Law by Decree shall not apply to any Public Land occupied by any of the Public Institutions to be determined by a resolution of the Supreme Committee.

### ARTICLE (54)

A Licensee licensed to operate a Public Telecommunication Network, may after obtaining the approval of the Supreme Committee in co-ordination with the relevant competent authority, remove or relocate a tree, group of trees or other vegetation if such tree, group of trees or vegetation:

1. obstructs the installation or maintenance of aerial wires by Licensees;

2. materially interferes with or obstructs any signals required to be emitted or received by the equipment or apparatus of a Licensee; or
3. prevents or interferes with a Licensee establishing, maintaining, developing or operating a Public Telecommunication Network,

provided that such removal or relocation is necessary to enter Public Land to carry out necessary works.

### ARTICLE (55)

Licensees operating Public Telecommunication Networks shall be exempted from all duties and taxes applicable to Public Land and public ways which are required for any of the purposes referred to in Article (52) of this Federal Law by Decree.

### ARTICLE (56)

The Supreme Committee may issue regulations authorising Licensees to enter to Private Land and any buildings or premises thereon for any of the purposes referred to in Article (52) of this Federal Law by Decree. The Executive Order shall prescribe the manner in which and/or the terms on which they may do so.

## PART 2 – PROTECTION OF TELECOMMUNICATION LINES AND NETWORKS

### ARTICLE (57)

Any person working close to service line routes, cables, wires, apparatus or equipment belonging to any Licensee, shall take all precautions and arrangements to prevent causing the damage or encroachment to the safety of these lines, cables, wires, apparatus or equipment.

### ARTICLE (58)

If the completion of the works of any person or party necessitates cutting the route of any of the service lines, wires, cables, apparatus or equipment of the Licensees or molest it in any way, the person carrying out the work shall immediately report the same to the Licensee and the Authority. It is prohibited to proceed with the work before the representative of the Licensee determines the manner of completing the work without molesting the safety of such lines, wires, cables, apparatus or equipment.

### ARTICLE (59)

In addition to the penalties prescribed by this Federal Law by Decree or any other law, any person that damages any service line, cable, wires, apparatus or equipment of a Licensee shall be liable to pay the compensation prescribed by regulations issued by the Authority.

## CHAPTER 8 TRANSITIONAL PROVISION

### ARTICLE (60)

The Supreme Committee may issue any company owned by Etisalat a temporary Licence for the purpose of authorising any such company to continue conducting Regulated Activities conducted by them at the date this Federal Law by Decree comes into force pending the issue of its formal Licence pursuant to the provisions of this Federal Law by Decree and its Executive Order.

**Article (61)**

Etisalat may continue to use, for the purposes for which it is allocated and subject to the terms and conditions of such allocation, such radio spectrum which is allocated for its use by the Ministry of Communications until such time as the Authority reallocates any such radio spectrum pursuant to the provisions of this Federal Law by Decree and issues a frequency authorisation to Etisalat.

**ARTICLE (62)**

Etisalat shall within a maximum period of ninety days from the date this Federal Law by Decree comes into force provide to the Authority with:

1. copies of all licences and special approvals relating to certain types of apparatus as specified in such current licences, type approvals and permissions relating to telecommunications equipment or other matters issued by Etisalat under Federal Law No. (1) of 1991 Regarding Emirates Telecommunications Corporation;
2. copies of all current resolutions and regulations containing technical standards specifications for telecommunications equipment issued by Etisalat under the law referred to in the previous paragraph; and
3. such other information as shall be in the possession or control of Etisalat and as the Authority shall require for the purposes of assessing the existing status of the telecommunications sector in the State.

**ARTICLE (63)**

The Ministry of Communications shall, within a maximum period of ninety days from the date this Federal Law by Decree comes into force, furnish to the Authority such information and documents as the Authority shall request for the purposes of assessing the existing status of the telecommunications sector in the State.

**ARTICLE (64)**

Etisalat shall, within a maximum period of ninety days from the date this Federal Law by Decree comes into force, transfer to the Authority ownership of all books, records, registers, databases, documents and other information which were owned or maintained by Etisalat in connection with any function carried out by Etisalat which is now given to the Authority or Supreme Committee under this Federal Law by Decree and, it shall be the duty of Etisalat to deliver all such books, records, registers, databases, documents and other information which the Authority deems necessary to enable it to carry out the powers prescribed to it pursuant to the provisions of this Federal Law by Decree and its Executive Order. Etisalat may retain copies of any such items as may be necessary to enable it to carry out certain functions as approved by the Authority in accordance with the provisions of this Federal Law by Decree.

**ARTICLE (65)**

1. The Supreme Committee is authorised and empowered to issue necessary orders, to transfer to the Authority from Etisalat, with effect from the date ordered by the Supreme Committee, such assets and rights as the Supreme Committee considers necessary to

enable the Authority to carry out the functions determined by this Federal Law by Decree which were carried out by Etisalat. This provision shall apply to Etisalat and third parties.
2. Any such resolutions concerning the transfer effected thereby may include penalties for failure to comply with the transfer and the decision of the Supreme Committee in this regard shall be final and binding.

### ARTICLE (66)

The Supreme Committee shall adjudicate in any matter arising out of the interpretation or application of any of the provisions of Article 65 of this Federal Law by Decree.

### ARTICLE (67)

All Public Institutions shall, on request, take all necessary steps to facilitate the transfer or the registration of any assets or rights from Etisalat to the Authority pursuant to the instructions issued by the Supreme Committee in accordance with Article (65) of this Federal Law by Decree.

### ARTICLE (68)

The Supreme Committee may instruct Etisalat to perform some of the functions given to the Authority under the provisions of this Federal Law by Decree for a period not more than one year after this Federal Law by Decree comes into force. Etisalat shall keep proper records of, and keep the Authority fully and promptly informed of all actions taken by Etisalat and, in particular, shall provide to the Authority copies of all documents relating to such actions taken by Etisalat when requested to do so by the Authority.

### ARTICLE (69)

A determination or regulation concerning technical specifications or standards of telecommunications equipment issued by Etisalat which is effective on the date this Federal Law by Decree comes into force shall continue in force until such time as it expires or is invalidated, revoked, cancelled or until the Authority takes any other decision it deems appropriate thereon.

### ARTICLE (70)

1. Any licence or permission granted or approved by Etisalat under Articles 4(f), 10(1) or 10(2) of Federal Law No. (1) of 1991 Regarding Emirates Telecommunications Corporation or by the Ministry of Communications under Federal Law No. (7) of 1973 Regarding wire and wireless Communications and Apparatus shall, to the extent that it is not inconsistent with the provisions of this Federal Law by Decree, continue in force until such licence shall expire or be replaced by a new licence, authorisation or permit issued by the Authority pursuant to the provisions of this Federal Law by Decree.
2. The Authority shall have the power to determine as to whether such licence or permission so granted or approved is compatible with the provisions of this Federal Law by Decree.

## CHAPTER 9 PENALTIES

### ARTICLE (71)

A person shall be punished with imprisonment of not more than two years and a fine of not less than Dirhams 50,000 and not more than Dirhams 200,000, or either of these punishments if:

1. he conducts any of the Regulated Activities without being licensed to do so or being exempted from the necessity to obtain a licence pursuant to the provisions of this Federal Law by Decree;
2. he intentionally alters, destroys or otherwise suppresses a document or information required by the Supreme Committee or the Authority pursuant to this Federal Law by Decree;
3. he does not amend his status pursuant to the provisions of this Federal Law by Decree within the period specified in Article 81.

### ARTICLE (72)

A person shall be punished with imprisonment of not more than one year and a fine of not less than Dirhams 50,000 and not more than Dirhams 200,000 or either of these punishments if he:

1. provides or contributes to the provision of Telecommunication Services in violation of public order or public morals;
2. uses Telecommunication Services or Apparatus in a grossly offensive or nuisance manner towards others or any other unlawful use;
3. copies, discloses, or spreads the content of any communication through a Public Telecommunication Network without having the right to do so;
4. intentionally and unlawfully accesses a Telecommunication Network or obstructs any Telecommunication Services;
5. abuse or unlawfully use Telecommunication Services without authorisation or permission;
6. intercepts the contents of telephone calls without prior permission by the competent judicial authorities;
7. violates the provisions of Article (50) of this Federal Law by Decree.

### ARTICLE (73)

A person shall be punished with imprisonment of not more than one year and a fine of not more than Dirhams 200,000 or either of these punishments if he:-

1. manufactures, uses, sells or offers for sale or use, to be connected to a Public Telecommunication Network, any Telecommunication Apparatus which he knows has not been approved in accordance with the provisions this Federal Law by Decree.
2. intentionally contravenes Article 57 of this Federal Law by Decree and such violation results in damage to lines, wires, cables, apparatus or equipment owned by or under the management or disposal of a Licensee.

### ARTICLE (74)

A person shall be punished with a fine of not less than Dirhams 50,000 and not more than Dirhams 200,000 if he:

1. manufactures, supplies or offers to supply Telecommunication Apparatus which does not conform to any regulations or guidelines or instructions or decisions issued by the Authority pursuant to the provisions of this Federal Law by Decree or its Executive Order.
2. Refrains from submitting the Telecommunication Apparatus which is under his control for testing and assessment in accordance with the provisions of this Federal Law by Decree, its Executive Order or the regulations, decisions and instructions issued pursuant

thereto, or if he prevents any official or authorised employee from entering his premises in accordance with the provisions of this Federal Law by Decree or its Executive Order.
3. knowingly uses or employs any person who is unqualified for the installation, setting up, connection, modification or maintenance of any Telecommunication Apparatus in accordance with the rules issued by the Authority.
4. presents a description or publishes an advertisement in respect of any Telecommunication Apparatus in order to promote such apparatus in the course of any trade or business which does not comply with the requirements imposed by the Authority.
5. fails to comply with the provisions of this Federal Law by Decree or its Executive Order or the regulations, decisions, instructions or rules issued pursuant thereto.

### ARTICLE (75)

A Licensee may, after obtaining prior approval from the Authority, place an apparatus or any other medium under surveillance if such Licensee had reasonable justifications to lead such Licensee to believe that the apparatus is being used in performing any of the offences prescribed in Article 72 of this Federal Law by Decree.

### ARTICLE (76)

An order shall be issued to seize the Telecommunication wire and wireless Apparatus and any other equipment or apparatus used in contradiction of this Federal Law by Decree, its Executive Order, or the regulations, decisions, instructions or rules issued pursuant thereto. The court may, when necessary, order the destruction of such apparatus and equipment.

### ARTICLE (77)

Where a juridical person is guilty of an offence under this Chapter such juridical person shall be punished with the fine specified for such offence under this Chapter.

### ARTICLE (78)

The application of the punishments prescribed by this Federal Law by Decree shall not prejudice a stricter punishment prescribed by any other law.

### ARTICLE (79)

The punishment of the offences prescribed by this Federal Law by Decree shall be doubled if the offence is repeated.

## CHAPTER 10 FINAL PROVISIONS

### ARTICLE (80)

Federal Law No. (1) of 1991 regarding the Emirates Telecommunications Corporation shall be amended as set out hereunder subject to any relevant transitional provisions under this Federal Law by Decree:

1. Articles 10, 11, 12, 13, 14, 15, 16, 17, 18, 19, 40, 42, 43, 44, 45, 46 and 48 shall be repealed.
2. Article 1 shall be amended by deleting reference to, and definition of,

(A) "the Minister";
(B) "Communications Equipment";
(C) "the Schedule"; and
(D) "Service Lines".
3. Article 24 of Federal Law No. (1) of 1991 referred to shall be amended by inserting the following sentence at the beginning of the said Article:

"subject to the regulations, instructions, decisions and policies issued by the General Authority for Regulating the Telecommunication Sector".

4. The second paragraph of Article 41 of Federal Law No (1) of 1991 referred to shall be amended as follows:

"The Articles of Association shall be issued pursuant to a resolution by the Council of Ministers and the amendment of the Articles and the replacement thereof shall be pursuant to a resolution issued by the Supreme Committee for the Supervision of the Telecommunication Sector".

5. The provisions of Articles 4, 21, 25, 31, 33 and 47 of Federal Law No (1) of 1991 shall be replaced with the following provisions:

**Article 4**

(1) Etisalat shall undertake telecommunications services, operate, maintain and develop the entire public telecommunications system in the State and also between the State and the foreign countries in accordance with the provisions of any laws relating to telecommunications and may exercise the powers to achieve its objectives including:

(A) to establish, maintain and operate local and international telegraphic, telephonic, telex, leased circuits and data networks.

(B) to establish, maintain and operate TV transmission excluding production and broadcasting of programmes.

(C) to administer, connect, hire and deal in telephonic services.

(D) to plan, construct, and possess equipment and stations of transmitters and receivers related to Etisalat's activity.

(E) to offer consultancy and training services in the field of wire and wireless telecommunications.

(F) to prepare, publish, distribute and promote the telephone directory, commercial directory (yellow pages), bulletins, information and data and other matters related to the telecommunications activity or the services provided by Etisalat whether for the purpose of information, trade, publicity or any other purposes.

(2) Etisalat may without prejudice to its basic objects, invest, utilise and employ its funds in any other commercial, financial or servicing fields which in the opinion of the Board shall enhance such funds or reap profits to Etisalat in accordance with the applicable rules in the State.

(3) Etisalat may, for the purpose of achieving the objects provided for in this section:

(A) conclude contracts and agreements,

(B) establish companies, enter into or share in partnerships in accordance with the applicable rules in the State.

**Article (21)**

The Board shall, pursuant to the regulations issued by the Telecommunication Regulatory Authority, determine the charges for the services provided by Etisalat, controls and conditions for provision of such services and the formula and forms of contracts to be concluded with the beneficiaries.

**Article (25)**

*The administration of Etisalat shall be undertaken by a Board of Directors comprised of eleven members, seven thereof including the Chairmanship shall represent the Government and shall be appointed by a Federal Decree. The other members shall be elected by the shareholders. Appointments and elections for Board Members might be for more than one time pursuant to the articles of association.

*This article was amended by the Federal law by Decree no. (1) of 2005

**Article (31)**

Each shareholder of Etisalat shall have the right to attend the General Meeting, discuss the topics listed on the Agenda and question the members of the Board who shall be bound to reply to the questions in so far as it shall not expose Etisalat's interest for damage. The shareholder may resort to the General Meeting if he considers the reply to his questions as insufficient and the decision of the General Meeting shall be obligatory for implementation.

The Government shall be represented in the General Meeting by the State's Minister for Finance and Industry.

**Article (33)**

Etisalat shall comply with the general policy of the Supreme Committee for the Supervision of the Telecommunication Sector and obey any general or specific directives issued by the Supreme Committee in this respect.

**Article (47)**

The Board shall issue the financial and administrative by-laws for management of Etisalat and shall determine the staff's conditions of service which do not conflict with the decisions issued by the Supreme Committee for the Supervision of the Telecommunication Sector.

**ARTICLE (81)**

All juridical persons existing at the time this Federal Law by Decree comes into force which carry out any of the Regulated Activities must conform their status in accordance with the provisions of this Federal Law by Decree within ninety days from date it comes into force. The Supreme Committee may by resolution extend such period to other similar periods.

### ARTICLE (82)

Any provision which contravenes any of the provisions of this Federal Law by Decree shall hereby be repealed.

### Article (83)

The Supreme Committee shall issue the Executive Order, regulations, resolutions and necessary instructions to implement the provisions of this Federal Law by Decree.

### ARTICLE (84)

This Federal Law by Decree shall be published in the Official Gazette and shall become effective on the date of such publication.

## FEDERAL LAW BY DECREE NO. 3 OF 2003 REGARDING THE ORGANIZATION OF THE TELECOMMUNICATIONS SECTOR

by Decree No. (1) of 2005 **Amending the Provisions of the Federal Law by Decree No. (3) of 2003, published in the** Official Gazette; Edition 435, Year 35, Shaban 1426H, September 2005; and

Amended by Federal Law by Decree No. (5) of 2008 Amending the Provisions of the Federal Law by Decree No. (3) of 2003 Regarding the Organization of the Telecommunications Sector, published in the Official Gazette: Edition 485 (repeated), Year 38, Shawal 1429H, October 2008.

Please note that some articles of Federal Law by Decree No. 3 of 2003 have been amended, and some have been retranslated. In this regard, please refer to Endnotes on page No. 41.

We, Zayed bin Sultan Al Nahyan, President of the State of the United Arab Emirates, having regard to the Constitution, and

Federal Law No. (1) of 1972 Regarding the Functions of Ministries and the Powers of Ministers and the amending laws thereof, and

Federal Law No. (7) of 1973 Regarding Radio Communications and Apparatus and the amending laws thereof, and

Federal Law No. (7) of 1976 Regarding the Audit Bureau and its amendments, and Federal Law No. (8) of 1984 Regarding Commercial Companies and the amending laws thereof, and

Federal Law No. (5) of 1985 Issuing the Civil Transactions Code and the amending laws thereof, and

Federal Law No. (3) of 1987 Issuing the Penal Code, and

Federal Law No. (1) of 1991 Regarding Emirates Telecommunications Corporation, and Federal Law No. (10) of 1992 Issuing the Law of Evidence in Civil and Commercial Transactions, and Federal Law No. (18) of 1993 Issuing the Commercial Transactions Code, and

Federal Law No. (7) of 1999 Regarding Pensions and Social Security, and on the basis of the proposal of the Prime Minister and the approval of the Cabinet,

have issued the following Law by Decree:

## CHAPTER 1 - DEFINITIONS

### Article (1)[1]

In applying this Federal Law by Decree, the following terms shall have the following meanings unless the context requires otherwise:

**State**: the United Arab Emirates;

**Government**: the government of the United Arab Emirates;

**Governmental Entities** : federal ministries and local departments, authorities and public organizations linked thereto, including the armed forces, the police, the intelligence and security services of the State but excluding any commercial company or establishment owned by any of the foregoing or in which any of the foregoing may have an interest;

**Authority**: the General Authority for Regulating the Telecommunications Sector;

**Board**: the Board of Directors of the Authority;

**Chairman**: the chairman of the Board of Directors of the Authority;

**Board Members**: the persons appointed to the Board in accordance with the provisions of the Law;

**Director General**: the Director General of the Authority;

**Executive Order**: the executive order issued in accordance with the Law;

**Regulated Activities**: either the operation of a Public Telecommunications Network or the supply of Telecommunications Services to subscribers[2] and all other types of activities specified by the Board in accordance with the provisions of the Law;

**Licensees**: Etisalat Corporation and such entities as may be licensed by the Authority pursuant to the provisions of the Law and its Executive Order;

**License**: a license issued pursuant to the provisions of the Law and its Executive Order which allows the Licensee to carry out any of the Regulated Activities;

**Interconnection**: the linking by whatever means of Telecommunications Networks in order to allow users of one entity to communicate with users of the same or another entity or enabling the users to make use of Telecommunications Services provided by another entity;

**Interconnection** an agreement under which the **Agreement**: Interconnection will be achieved pursuant to the rules and conditions issued by the Authority;

**Telecommunications** a system comprising one or more items of **Network**: apparatus or means of communication medium for broadcasting, transmission, switching or receiving of Telecommunications Services, by means of electric, magnetic, electro-magnetic, electro-chemical or electro-mechanical energy and any other means of communication medium;

**Public Telecommunications** a Telecommunications Network operated **Network**: by the Licensee for the provision of Public Telecommunications Services by the Licensee pursuant to the provisions of the Law;

**Private Telecommunications** a Telecommunications Network operated **Network**: exclusively to serve the requirements of and to benefit one person or a group of persons who have a common ownership;

**Telecommunications** the service of transmitting, broadcasting, **Services**: switching or receiving by means of a Telecommunications Network of any of the following:

1- wired and wireless telecommunications;

2- voice, music and other sounds;

3- visual images;

4- signals used in radio and TV broadcasting;

5- signals used to operate or control any machinery or apparatus;

6- the installation, maintenance, adjustment, repair, replacement, moving or removal of apparatus which is or will be connected to a Public Telecommunications Network;

7- the construction maintenance and operation of networks for telegraph, telephone, telex, leased circuits, domestic and international data networks, Internet and Wireless Transmission; and

8- any other Telecommunications Services approved by the Board;

**Public Telecommunications** any Telecommunications Services **Services**: provided to all subscribers or a part thereof in consideration of a fee;

**Wireless Transmission**: the transmitting or receiving of electro-magnetic energy which may be used for the conveyance of data, messages, voice or visual images, or for the operation or control of machinery or apparatus;

**Telecommunications** apparatus made or adapted for use in **Apparatus**: transmitting, receiving or conveying any of the Telecommunications Services through a Telecommunications Network;

**Etisalat Corporation**: the Emirates Telecommunications Corporation regulated by Federal Law No. (1) of 1991 Regarding Emirates Telecommunications Corporation;

**Private Lands**: any land owned by, granted to or leased to any person other than Governmental Entities;

**Public Lands**: all lands under the control or ownership of any Governmental Entity, excluding Private Lands; and

**Law**: the Federal Law by Decree No. (3) of 2003 Regarding the Organization of the Telecommunications Sector and its amendments.

## CHAPTER 2 - SUPREME COMMITTEE FOR THE SUPERVISION OF THE TELECOMMUNICATIONS SECTOR[3]

### Article (2)

[Repealed]

### Article (3)

[Repealed]

### Article (4)

[Repealed]

### Article (5)

[Repealed]

## CHAPTER 3 - THE GENERAL AUTHORITY FOR REGULATING THE TELECOMMUNICATIONS SECTOR

### Part 1 – Establishment of the Authority

### Article (6)

It is hereby established an independent public authority, called the "General Authority for Regulating the Telecommunications Sector" for the purpose of performing the functions and implementing the duties given to it under this Federal Law by Decree and its Executive Order.

### Article (7)

The Authority shall have an independent legal personality and shall have full capacity to act accordingly and to perform legal actions in accordance with this Federal Law by Decree, including the capacity to enter into contracts of all types and to own and lease movable and immovable assets of all types and the capacity to sue. The Authority shall have financial and administrative independence in carrying out its affairs.

### Article (8)

The headquarters of the Authority shall be in Abu Dhabi and it shall also have an office in Dubai. The Board may establish other offices for the Authority within the State.

### Article (9)

The Authority shall conduct its business in accordance with this Federal Law by Decree and its Executive Order, and shall have the power to issue its financial and internal policies, contracting, purchasing policies, and all personnel and disciplinary policies for the employees of the Authority without the need to abide by the governmental laws, decisions, rules and regulations applicable in this regard.

### Article (10)[1]

A. The Authority shall be managed by a Board of Directors that shall be created and its special provisions defined by a federal decree for a period of four years renewable for other similar periods. The Board shall have jurisdiction to:

1- issue the Executive Order of the Law after approval from the Cabinet;

2- establish the general policy for the telecommunications sector in the State, presenting it to the Cabinet for approval and overseeing its implementation after the approval;

3- issue any general directives or instructions relating to the telecommunications sector and necessary for national security or international relations after approval from the Cabinet;

4- issue decisions, rules, regulations, and instructions regarding the implementation of the Law and its Executive Order including issuing decisions for establishing legal entities operating in the telecommunications sector, determining the fees of the services and facilities provided to the Licensees and to whom such fees should be paid;

5- issue, extend, revoke and suspend Licenses pursuant to the provisions of the Law and its Executive Order;

6- determine fees of Licenses, authorizations, approvals and services issued or provided by the Authority pursuant to the provisions of the Law, its amendments or its Executive Order;

7- issue the internal rules for its conduct of business; and

8- any other functions delegated to it by the Law and its Executive Order.

B- The Authority shall have a Director General appointed by a federal decree, who shall be the Authority's legal representative and be responsible before the Board for managing the daily business of the Authority. The Executive Order shall determine the functions of the Director General.

### Article (11)[4]

[Repealed]

## Part 2 – Functions, Duties, and Powers of the Authority

### Article (12)

The Authority is the competent body to oversee the telecommunications sector in the State and all Licensees in accordance with this Federal Law by Decree, its Executive Order and the instructions of the Board[5]. The Authority may provide to the Board[5] any necessary proposals in relation to the general policy of such sector and shall, at the end of each financial year, submit to the Board[5] a report on its activities and business performance during that year.

### Article (13)

The Authority shall exercise its functions and powers under this Federal Law by Decree and its Executive Order to:

1- ensure that the Telecommunications Services provided throughout the State, are sufficient to satisfy the public demands of those who wish to make use of such services;

2- enhance the level of service provided by the telecommunications sector in order to promote the interests of subscribers[2];

3- ensure that Licensees meet quality standards of performance and adhere to the terms and conditions of the Licenses granted to them;

4- encourage, promote, and develop the telecommunications and information technology industries in the State; and

5- promote and enhance the telecommunications system in the State as indicated by the development and the establishment of industry related training institutions and through the availability of the latest apparatus, equipment, and facilities provided by telecommunications technology.

### Article (14)[1]

The Authority shall have the competence to issue Licenses in accordance with the provisions of the Law, as well as issue regulations, instructions, decisions and rules regulating the following:

1- tariffs, charges and fees levied by Licensees as determined by the Board;

2- anything related to the use and Interconnection of Telecommunications Networks and Telecommunications Services provided by the Licensees, co-location and sharing of infrastructure by such Licensees, including the special conditions for costs of such Interconnection, access, site-sharing, time-scales and principles for negotiations and completion of agreements between concerned entities in relation to the foregoing matters. It shall also issue dispute resolution policies to resolve disputes between the parties to such agreements;

3- the conditions, level and scope of services provided by the Licensees to subscribers, universal service and emergency services including the standards and quality of the provided services, terms of supply, the handling of subscriber[2] complaints and disputes, provision of information to subscribers, usage of subscriber personal information and the provision of bills to subscribers;

4- regulating and ensuring competition in the telecommunications sector without prejudice to the applicable laws and regulations;

5- requesting any information required for the activities of the Authority;

6- setting out the specifications of the equipment used by the Licensees, including their technical standards and types;

7- importing, manufacturing, using and managing Telecommunications Apparatus and issuing their respective approvals;

8- the allocation of telephone numbers, numbering plans and number portability;

9- regulating the usage of radio spectrum pursuant to the Law, including the allocation, re-allocation, usage of these frequencies and granting their authorizations;

10- the terms of provision and preparation of directory services and directory enquiries services;

11- issuing rules to prevent interference with telecommunications in the State by radio or electrical waves or any other means;

12- qualifying persons in installing, connecting, adjusting and maintaining Telecommunications Apparatus;

13- publishing announcements relating to Telecommunications Apparatus; and

14- performing such other functions as the Cabinet may determine.

## Part 3 – Financial Affairs

### Article (15)

The financial year of the Authority shall commence on the first day of January and end on the last day of December of each year, except that the first financial year of the Authority shall commence on the date this Federal Law by Decree comes into force and shall end on the last day of December of the following year.

### Article (16)

The Authority shall have an independent budget. In respect of the first financial year of the Authority, the budget shall be set by decision of the Board[6]. In respect of the succeeding financial years of the Authority, the budget of the Authority shall be prepared by the Director General, and approved and issued by the Board.

### Article (17)

The financial resources of the Authority are derived from the following:

1- any funds assigned to the Authority in the general budget of the State;

2- such License fees as charged by the Board[5] pursuant to the provisions of this Federal Law by Decree and its Executive Order and the issued regulations accordingly;

3- such fees as may be charged by the Board[5] for any services provided by the Authority or the authorizations or approvals granted by the Authority pursuant to the provisions of this Federal Law by Decree, its Executive Order and the decisions issued by the Board[5];

4- any other revenues the Authority collects in pursuance of its activities and functions; and

5- any other financial resources approved by the Board[5].

**Article (18)**

The Authority shall collect the fees imposed by the Board[5] in relation to the Licenses issued by the Board[5] and the authorizations, approvals, services of the Authority and any other amounts regarding radio spectrum.

**Article (19)**

Following the approval of the Cabinet or its delegate[7], the Authority may raise loans from the Government or raise loans from banks and other financial institutions (whether in the State or elsewhere) and may create and issue debentures or bonds on such terms as determined by the Cabinet or its delegate[7].

**Article (20)**

The Authority may invest its funds in any form of investment approved by the Board[12].

**Article (21)**

The Authority and its dealings thereof shall be exempted from all Government fees and taxes.

**Article (22)**

The Authority shall be exempted from the prior control of the Audit Bureau as set out in Federal Law No. (7) of 1976 Regarding the Establishment of the Audit Bureau, as amended. The Audit Bureau shall not interfere in the business of the Authority and the decisions of its Board or in the policies determined by the Cabinet or its delegate[7] as applied by the Authority.

**Article (23)**

1- The Board shall appoint an independent auditor, registered with the appropriate authorities in the State, to audit the annual accounts of the Authority and prepare reports regarding the results of the audit.

2- As soon as the accounts of the Authority have been audited, a copy of the accounts approved by the Board with a copy of the auditor's report attached to it shall be forwarded by the Authority to the Cabinet or its delegate[7].

## CHAPTER 4 - RESTRUCTURING OF THE TELECOMMUNICATIONS SECTOR

### Part 1 – Etisalat Corporation

### Article (24)

The exclusive privilege of undertaking the transmission of wire and wireless communications, their operation and maintenance and the development of a general communications system within the State and between the State and foreign countries conferred on Etisalat Corporation by Article 4 of Federal Law No. (1) of 1991 Regarding Emirates Telecommunications Corporation shall hereby cease to exist but without prejudice to the fees payable for services and facilities provided by the Government to Etisalat and which are payable to the Government pursuant to the provisions of the regulations and decisions in force at the date this Federal Law by Decree is issued and the right to impose and amend such fees shall transfer to the Board[5].

### Article (25)

Subject to the provisions of any transitional provisions of this Federal Law by Decree, all functions conferred on Etisalat Corporation by Federal Law No. (1) of 1991 Regarding Emirates Telecommunications Corporation that conflict with the powers, competences, and functions of the Board[5] and the Authority under this Federal Law by Decree shall cease to be performed by Etisalat Corporation.

### Article (26)[1]

The Emirates Investment Authority shall assume, as from the date of the coming into force of the provisions of this Law by Decree, responsibility for representing the Government as a shareholder in corporations and companies in the telecommunications sector, and shall exercise the required powers, unless their articles of association state otherwise.

### Article (27)

Etisalat Corporation shall be required, within a period of ninety days of this Federal Law by Decree coming into force, to take all such steps as shall be necessary to amend its Articles of Association and its applicable rules and regulations to comply with the provisions contained in this Federal Law by Decree and any regulations or decisions issued by the Board[5].

## Part 2 – Licensees

### Article (28)

The Board[5] shall, by decision, determine the various types of Regulated Activities for which Licenses may be issued and the required terms for prospective Licensees.

In all cases no License shall be issued to any entity unless such entity is a juridical entity established pursuant to a decision issued by the Board[5]. Such juridical entity may, after obtaining the approval of the Board[5], establish subsidiary companies to carry out certain Regulated Activities.

### Article (29)

With exception to acquiring the nationality of the State, the provisions of Federal Law No (8) of 1984 regarding Commercial Companies and the amending or replacement laws thereof shall not apply to juridical entities[8] licensed pursuant to this Federal Law by Decree and its Executive

Orders to the extent provided in their memoranda and articles of association as approved by the Board[5]. The competent authorities shall be under an obligation to register such juridical persons.

### Article (30)

All Licensees shall take into account the special needs and requirements regarding the type of service and Telecommunications Apparatus and ensure non-discrimination when providing such services and apparatus.

### Article (31)

It is not permitted to conduct any Regulated Activity unless authorized by a License or exempted in accordance with the provision of this Federal Law by Decree or its Executive Order.

### Article (32)

The Board[5] shall determine the form and substance of each License granted pursuant to this Federal Law by Decree, and shall include conditions specifying the duration of the License and may include conditions required by the Board[5].

### Article (33)

An application for a License must be submitted to the Authority in the form prescribed by the Authority and must fulfill all the conditions set out by the Board[5]. The Authority shall within a maximum period of thirty days from the date of submission of the application, review the application and report its findings and recommendations thereto to the Board[5].

### Article (34)

The Board[5] shall have the authority to grant or refuse a License to an applicant. The Board's[5] decision in this regard shall be final and binding on the applicant and may not be challenged or appealed in any way whatsoever.

### Article (35)

Obtaining a License pursuant to the provisions of this Federal Law by Decree shall not operate to relieve a person from any obligation to obtain any licenses or authorizations that may be required from any other Government Institution for purposes connected with the conduct of its business.

## Part 3 – Exemptions and Exclusions

### Article (36)

The Board[5] may, if required, exercise the following powers[9]:

1- exempt any Licensee from the performance of the License conditions for such periods and on such terms as specified in the exemption order; and

2- issue a general exemption from the performance of the License conditions in favor of some, all or such classes of Licensees for such periods, and on such terms as specified in the exemption order.

The Board[5] may revoke, amend, or extend any specific exemption or general exemption granted pursuant to this Article.

**Article (37)**

1- No person (whether an individual or a juridical person) nor any Governmental Entity may provide Telecommunications Services to clients or subscribers[2] through a Public Telecommunications Network unless licensed by the Board[5] pursuant to the provisions of this Federal Law by Decree. The establishment and operation of Private Telecommunications Networks shall be regulated by the Executive Order and the decisions issued by the Board[5].

2- In all cases, the persons covered by the above paragraph must comply with the terms, conditions and requirements associated with the use of the frequencies allocated to them pursuant to the provisions of this Federal Law by Decree.

## CHAPTER 5 - NETWORKS, APPARATUS AND NUMBERING

### Part 1 - Network Interconnection and Sites Co-location

**Article (38)**

The Authority shall take any needed action as deemed necessary to facilitate the process of Interconnection and to monitor the compliance of all parties to the provisions of the Interconnection Agreements. The Authority shall have all the powers which will enable it to achieve the foregoing.

**Article (39)**

1- Where there is a dispute in relation to Interconnection the parties to the dispute may refer the dispute to the Authority for adjudication and the issuance of binding decisions.

2- The Authority shall adjudicate disputes referred in accordance with this Article as specified in the Executive Order.

**Article (40)**

1- Where there is a dispute between a Licensee and another Licensee for co-location or the sharing of facilities or sites either party may refer the dispute to the Authority for adjudication. The Authority must adjudicate the dispute referred to it.

2- The Authority shall make such investigations and request any information it deems necessary to resolve the disputes referred in accordance with this Article.

3- The adjudication may specify the steps to be taken by the parties in order to resolve the dispute, determine the terms on which a Licensee shall offer the sharing of facilities and order one or both parties to enter into a facility sharing agreement on terms specified in the decision.

In all cases the Authority's decision shall be final and binding.

**Article (41)**

Etisalat Corporation and any of its subsidiaries shall, at the direction of the Authority, satisfy in a timely, efficient, and least cost manner all requests from a Licensee for Interconnection, co-location or sharing of sites and facilities at the best point as determined by the Authority. In particular Etisalat Corporation shall:

1- comply with any regulations, guidelines or License conditions issued pursuant to the provisions of this Federal Law by Decree or its Executive Order relating to Interconnection, co-location or sharing of sites and facilities;

2- subject to the regulations issued pursuant to the provisions of this Federal Law by Decree or its Executive Order, offer and provide Interconnection, co-location or sharing of sites and facilities on terms and conditions (including as to cost and quality) which are in accordance with best international practice; and

3- facilitate, provide facilities and information concerning Interconnection, co-location and sharing of sites to Licensees and their subsidiaries under the same conditions, and of the same quality as Etisalat Corporation provides for its own services or those of its subsidiaries or companies.

**Part 2 – Telecommunications Apparatus Approval**

**Article (42)**

The Authority shall have exclusive competence in issuing all authorizations and approvals in relation to Telecommunications Apparatus comprised in or intended for use in connection with a Telecommunications Network or in the provision of a Telecommunications Service in accordance with the Executive Order issued pursuant to this Federal Law by Decree and the instructions of the Board[5] to the Authority.

No person shall use, sell, offer for sale or connect to any Telecommunications Network any Telecommunications Apparatus which has not been approved by the Authority.

**Article (43)**

Governmental Entities shall be exempted from obtaining the approval of the Authority in respect of Telecommunications Apparatus used or to be used by the Governmental Entities.

**Part 3 - Numbering**

**Article (44)**

The Authority shall be responsible for allocating prefixes, private telephone numbers, and numbering ranges to Licensees in accordance with the provisions of this Federal Law by Decree, its Executive Order and the conditions set by the Authority and approved by the Board[5].

**CHAPTER 6 - FREQUENCY MANAGEMENT AND ALLOCATION**

### Article (45)[4]

[Repealed]

### Article (46)[1]

1- A committee called the 'Co-ordination Committee' shall be constituted by a decision by the Cabinet or its delegate chaired by the Director General and having as members representatives of the Authority as well as representatives of the Armed Forces, Ministry of Interior, State Security and the National Media Council. Other entities' representatives may also be included, if required, by a decision by the Board.

2- The Co-ordination Committee shall have the competence to put in place a national frequency plan for radio spectrum allocated to Telecommunications Services to be approved by the Board in order to ensure the efficient and proper use of radio spectrum without any interference or jamming. The Authority may request the Co-ordination Committee, from time to time, to review and amend the plan when the need arises.

### Article (47)

The national frequency plan shall be drawn up in conformity with the international regulations governing radio spectrum and the international or regional agreements concluded or acceded to by the State. It shall include provisions for:

1- the designation, on the recommendation of the Authority, of bands of radio spectrum for the provision of Telecommunications Services over Telecommunications Networks;

2- the amendment of allocations to existing users of radio spectrum to allow for the development of new services; and

3- the reassignment of radio spectrum on expiry of existing licenses or authorizations relating thereto.

### Article (48)[1]

The Authority shall have the competence to distribute, allocate, and revoke radio spectrum. Any such allocation shall be made in accordance with the national frequency plan and on the basis of objective procedures and criteria, details of which shall be set out in regulations issued by the Authority.

### Article (49)

The Authority shall, within nine months of the date this Federal Law by Decree comes into force, and after notifying the competent body[10] and the Co-ordination Committee, prepare and publish a plan for the reallocation of radio spectrum currently authorized for use in the provision of Telecommunications Services.

### Article (50)

The establishment and use of Wireless Transmission stations and the installation and use of any Wireless Transmission shall be prohibited unless permitted by a radio spectrum authorization issued by the Authority pursuant to the provisions of this Federal Law by Decree, its Executive Order or the regulations and instructions issued by the Authority.

### Article (51)

On the issue or renewal by the Authority of a radio spectrum authorization, there shall be paid to the Authority by the entity to whom the authorization is issued such sums as prescribed by the provisions of this Federal Law by Decree, its Executive Order or the decisions, regulations or instructions issued pursuant thereof.

## CHAPTER 7 - OPERATION AND PROTECTION OF TELECOMMUNICATIONS NETWORKS AND LINES

### Part 1 – Operation of Networks

### Article (52)

Governmental Entities shall, in accordance with their respective jurisdictions, grant all Licensees of Public Telecommunications Networks, without payment, rights to occupy and use Public Lands as well as right of way, and rights of access to Public Lands so as to enable them to perform their activities as set out in their respective Licenses, including:

1- the construction of buildings and other installations;

2- the installation of equipment and apparatus; and

3- the establishment, extension, development, and maintenance of Public Telecommunications Networks including the laying and extension of ground and aerial cables and service lines.

### Article (53)

The provisions of Article (52) of this Federal Law by Decree shall not apply to any Public Lands occupied by any of the Governmental Entities to be determined by a decision of the Board[5].

### Article (54)

A Licensee licensed to operate a Public Telecommunications Network, may after obtaining the approval of the Board[5] in co-ordination with the relevant competent authority, remove or relocate a tree, group of trees or other vegetation if such tree, group of trees or vegetation:

1- obstructs the installation or maintenance of aerial wires by Licensees;

2- materially interferes with or obstructs any signals required to be emitted or received by the equipment or apparatus of a Licensee; or

3- prevents or interferes with a Licensee establishing, maintaining, developing or operating a Public Telecommunications Network, provided that such removal or relocation is necessary to enter Public Lands to carry out necessary works.

### Article (55)

Licensees operating Public Telecommunications Networks shall be exempted from all duties and taxes applicable to Public Lands and public ways which are required for any of the purposes referred to in Article (52) of this Federal Law by Decree.

### Article (56)

The Board[5] may issue regulations authorizing Licensees to enter to Private Lands and any buildings or premises thereon for any of the purposes referred to in Article (52) of this Federal Law by Decree. The Executive Order shall prescribe the manner in which and/or the terms on which they may do so.

## Part 2 – Protection of Telecommunications Lines and Networks

### Article (57)

Any person working close to service line routes, cables, wires, apparatus or equipment belonging to any Licensee, shall take all precautions and arrangements to prevent causing the damage or encroachment to the safety of these lines, cables, wires, apparatus or equipment.

### Article (58)

If the completion of the works of any person or party necessitates cutting the route of any of the service lines, wires, cables, apparatus or equipment of the Licensees or molesting it in any way, the person carrying out the work shall immediately report the same to the Licensee and the Authority. It is prohibited to proceed with the work before the representative of the Licensee determines the manner of completing the work without molesting the safety of such lines, wires, cables, apparatus or equipment.

### Article (59)

In addition to the penalties prescribed by this Federal Law by Decree or any other law, any person that damages any service line, cable, wires, apparatus, or equipment of a Licensee shall be liable to pay the compensation prescribed by regulations issued by the Authority.

## CHAPTER 8 - TRANSITIONAL PROVISIONS

### Article (60)

The Board[5] may issue any company owned by Etisalat Corporation a temporary License for the purpose of authorizing any such company to continue conducting Regulated Activities conducted by them at the date this Federal Law by Decree comes into force pending the issue of its formal License pursuant to the provisions of this Federal Law by Decree and its Executive Order.

### Article (61)

Etisalat Corporation may continue to use, for the purposes for which it is allocated and subject to the terms and conditions of such allocation, such radio spectrum which is allocated for its use by the competent body[10] until such time as the Authority reallocates any such radio spectrum pursuant to the provisions of this Federal Law by Decree and issues a frequency authorization to Etisalat Corporation.

**Article (62)**

Etisalat Corporation shall within a maximum period of ninety days from the date this Federal Law by Decree comes into force provide the Authority with:

1- copies of all licenses and special approvals relating to certain types of apparatus as specified in such current licenses, type approvals and permissions relating to telecommunications equipment or other matters issued by Etisalat Corporation under Federal Law No. (1) of 1991 Regarding Emirates Telecommunications Corporation;

2- copies of all current decisions and regulations containing technical standards specifications for telecommunications equipment issued by Etisalat Corporation under the law referred to in the previous paragraph; and

3- such other information as shall be in the possession or control of Etisalat Corporation and as the Authority shall require for the purposes of assessing the existing status of the telecommunications sector in the State.

**Article (63)**

The competent body[10] shall, within a maximum period of ninety days from the date this Federal Law by Decree comes into force, furnish to the Authority such information and documents as the Authority shall request for the purposes of assessing the existing status of the telecommunications sector in the State.

**Article (64)**

Etisalat Corporation shall, within a maximum period of ninety days from the date this Federal Law by Decree comes into force, transfer to the Authority ownership of all books, records, registers, databases, documents and other information which were owned or maintained by Etisalat Corporation in connection with any function carried out by Etisalat Corporation which is now given to the Authority or the Board[5] under this Federal Law by Decree and, it shall be the duty of Etisalat Corporation to deliver all such books, records, registers, databases, documents and other information which the Authority deems necessary to enable it to carry out the powers prescribed to it pursuant to the provisions of this Federal Law by Decree and its Executive Order. Etisalat Corporation may retain copies of any such items as may be necessary to enable it to carry out certain functions as approved by the Authority in accordance with the provisions of this Federal Law by Decree.

**Article (65)**

1- The Board[5] is authorized and empowered to issue necessary orders, to transfer to the Authority from Etisalat Corporation, with effect from the date ordered by the Board[5], such assets and rights as the Board[5] considers necessary to enable the Authority to carry out the functions determined by this Federal Law by Decree which were carried out by Etisalat Corporation. This provision shall apply to Etisalat Corporation and third parties.

2- Any such decisions concerning the transfer effected thereby may include penalties for failure to comply with the transfer and the decision of the Board[5] in this regard shall be final and binding.

### Article (66)

**The Board[5] shall adjudicate in any matter arising out of the interpretation or application of any of the provisions of Article 65 of this Federal Law by Decree.**

### Article (67)

All Governmental Entities shall, on request, take all necessary steps to facilitate the transfer or the registration of any assets or rights from Etisalat Corporation to the Authority pursuant to the instructions issued by the Board[5] in accordance with Article (65) of this Federal Law by Decree.

### Article (68)

The Board[5] may instruct Etisalat Corporation to perform some of the functions given to the Authority under the provisions of this Federal Law by Decree for a period of not more than one year after this Federal Law by Decree comes into force. Etisalat Corporation shall keep proper records of, and keep the Authority fully and promptly informed of all actions taken by Etisalat Corporation and, in particular, shall provide to the Authority copies of all documents relating to such actions taken by Etisalat Corporation when requested to do so by the Authority.

### Article (69)

A determination or regulation concerning technical specifications or standards of telecommunications equipment issued by Etisalat Corporation which is effective on the date this Federal Law by Decree comes into force shall continue in force until such time as it expires or is invalidated, revoked, cancelled or until the Authority takes any other decision it deems appropriate thereon.

### Article (70)

1- Any license or permission granted or approved by Etisalat Corporation under Articles 4(f), 10(1) or 10(2) of Federal Law No. (1) of 1991 Regarding Emirates Telecommunications Corporation or by the competent body[10] under Federal Law No. (7) of 1973 Regarding Wire and Wireless Communications and Apparatus shall, to the extent that it is not inconsistent with the provisions of this Federal Law by Decree, continue in force until such license shall expire or be replaced by a new License, authorization or permit issued by the Authority pursuant to the provisions of this Federal Law by Decree.

2- The Authority shall have the power to determine as to whether such license or permission so granted or approved is compatible with the provisions of this Federal Law **by Decree.**

## CHAPTER 9 - PENALTIES

Article (71)[1]

A person shall be penalized with imprisonment of not more than two years and a fine of not less than AED 50,000 and not more than AED 1,000,000 or either of these penalties if he/she/it:

1- conducts any of the Regulated Activities without being licensed to do so or being exempted from the necessity to obtain a License pursuant to the provisions of the Law;

2- intentionally alters, damages or otherwise suppresses a document or piece of information required by the Board or the Authority pursuant to the provisions of the Law; or

3- does not amend his/her/its status pursuant to the provisions of the Law and within the specified time frame in Article (81) of the Law.

**Article (72)**[1]

A person shall be penalized with imprisonment of not more than one year and a fine of not less than AED 50,000 and not more than AED 1,000,000 or either of these penalties if he/she/it:

1- uses Telecommunications Apparatus in an offensive or disruptive manner, or so as to be a nuisance towards others, or for any unlawful purpose;

2- copies or discloses, without a right to do so, the content of any communication, telephone message or any of the Telecommunications Services whether or not working under any Licensee or related to him/her/it by any relationship enabling him to reveal the contents of any communication or telephone message or any of the Telecommunications Services; or

3- violates the provisions of Article (50) of the Law.

**Article (72) repeated (1)**[11]

A person shall be penalized with imprisonment of not less than one year and a fine of not less than AED 50,000 and not more than AED 1,000,000 or either of these penalties if he/she/it:

1- intentionally and unlawfully accesses a Telecommunications Network or obstructs any Telecommunications Services; or

2- exploits without a right any of the Telecommunications Services.

**Article (72) repeated (2)**[11]

A person who intercepts the contents of telephone calls without prior permission by the competent judicial authorities shall be penalized with imprisonment, a fine, or either of these penalties.

**Article (72) repeated (3)**[11]

A person shall be penalized with imprisonment of not more than one year and a fine of not more than AED 50,000 or either of these penalties if he/she/it uses Telecommunications Services in an offensive or disruptive manner, or so as to be a nuisance towards others, or for any unlawful purpose.

### Article (72) repeated (4)[11]

A person shall be penalized with imprisonment and a fine of not more than AED 1,000,000 or either of these penalties if he/she/it uses fraud or counterfeit documents in order to obtain any of the Telecommunications Services, subscribe to them or make them available for others.

The previous actions shall be considered an aggravating circumstance if committed with the intention to commit a crime.

### Article (72) repeated (5)[11]

A person shall be penalized with imprisonment and a fine of not less than AED 50,000 and not more than AED 1,000,000 or either of these penalties if he/she/it provides others with any of the Telecommunications Services without obtaining the required documents as set out by the Executive Order of this Law.

### Article (73)[1]

A person shall be penalized with imprisonment of not more than one year and a fine of not more than AED 1,000,000 or either of these penalties if he/she/it:

1- manufactures, uses, sells or offers for sale or use Telecommunications Apparatus to connect them to a Telecommunications Network knowing that such apparatus has not been licensed or approved in accordance with the provisions of any applicable laws; or

2- intentionally violates Article (57) of the Law and such violation results in damage to lines, wires, cables, apparatus or equipment owned by or under the management or control of a Licensee.

### Article (74)[1]

A person shall be penalized with a fine of not less than AED 50,000 and not more than AED 1,000,000 if he/she/it:

1- manufactures, supplies or offers any Telecommunications Apparatus to be used in the State and which does not comply with the regulations, directives, instructions and decisions issued by the Authority pursuant to the provisions of the Law or its Executive Order;

2- refrains from submitting the Telecommunications Apparatus which is under its control for testing in accordance with the provisions of the Law, its Executive Order or the regulations, decisions, instructions and rules issued pursuant thereto, or if it does not allow any authorized personnel from accessing its premises in accordance with the provisions of the Law or its Executive Order;

3- a Licensee knowingly uses or employs any person who is unqualified for or inadequately experienced with the installation, setting up, modification or maintenance of any Telecommunications Apparatus in accordance with the rules issued by the Authority; or

4- presents a description or publishes an advertisement in respect of a Telecommunications Apparatus in order to promote such apparatus in the course of a trade or business without complying with the requirements issued by the Authority.

### Article (75)

A Licensee may, after obtaining prior approval from the Authority, place an apparatus or any other medium under surveillance if such Licensee has reasonable justifications to lead such Licensee to believe that the apparatus is being used in performing any of the offences prescribed in Article 72 of this Federal Law by Decree.

### Article (76)

An order shall be issued to seize the Telecommunications wire and wireless Apparatus and any other equipment or apparatus used in contradiction of this Federal Law by Decree, its Executive Order, or the regulations, decisions, instructions or rules issued pursuant thereto. The court may, when necessary, order the destruction of such apparatus **and equipment.**

### Article (77)

Where a juridical person is guilty of an offence under this Chapter such juridical person shall be punished with the fine specified for such offence under this Chapter.

### Article (78)

The application of the punishments prescribed by this Federal Law by Decree shall not prejudice a stricter punishment prescribed by any other law.

### Article (79)

The punishment of the offences prescribed by this Federal Law by Decree shall be doubled if the offence is repeated.

### Article (79) repeated (1)[11]

A person shall be penalized with a fine of not less than AED 50,000 and not more than AED 200,000 if he/she/it violates any other provision of the Law, its Executive Order, regulations, decisions, instructions or rules issued thereto.

### Article (79) repeated (2)[11]

The Board may impose administrative fines against the Licensees for violating the provisions of the Law, its Executive Order, decisions, regulations, policies, or instructions issued by the Board or Authority.

The Cabinet shall issue a decision with the schedule of the violations and fines imposed on the Licensees. Each violation shall not be of more than AED 10,000,000.

## CHAPTER 10 - FINAL PROVISIONS

### Article (80)

Federal Law No. (1) of 1991 regarding the Emirates Telecommunications Corporation shall be amended as set out hereunder subject to any relevant transitional provisions under this Federal Law by Decree:

1- Articles 10, 11, 12, 13, 14, 15, 16, 17, 18, 19, 40, 42, 43, 44, 45, 46, and 48 shall be repealed.

2- Article 1 shall be amended by deleting reference to, and definition of,

(A) "the Minister";

(B) "Communications Equipment";

(C) "the Schedule"; and

(D) "Service Lines".

3- Article 24 of Federal Law No. (1) of 1991 referred to shall be amended by inserting the following sentence at the beginning of the said Article:

"subject to the regulations, instructions, decisions, and policies issued by the General Authority for Regulating the Telecommunications Sector".

4- The second paragraph of Article 41 of Federal Law No (1) of 1991 referred to shall be amended as follows:

"The Articles of Association shall be issued pursuant to a decision by the Council of Ministers and the amendment of the Articles and the replacement thereof shall be pursuant to a decision issued by the Board[5] for the Supervision of the Telecommunications Sector".

5- The provisions of Articles 4, 21, 25, 31, 33 and 47 of Federal Law No (1) of 1991 shall be replaced with the following provisions:

**Article (4)**

(1) Etisalat Corporation shall undertake telecommunications services, operate, maintain, and develop the entire public telecommunications system in the State and also between the State and the foreign countries in accordance with the provisions of any laws relating to telecommunications and may exercise the powers to achieve its objectives including:

(A) to establish, maintain and operate local and international telegraphic, telephonic, telex, leased circuits and data networks;

(B) to establish, maintain and operate TV transmission excluding production and broadcasting of programmes;

(C) to administer, connect, hire and deal in telephonic services;

(D) to plan, construct, and possess equipment and stations of transmitters and receivers related to Etisalat Corporation's activity;

(E) to offer consultancy and training services in the field of wire and wireless telecommunications; and

(F) to prepare, publish, distribute and promote the telephone directory, commercial directory (yellow pages), bulletins, information and data and other matters related to the telecommunications activity or the services provided by Etisalat Corporation whether for the purpose of information, trade, publicity or any other purposes.

(2) Etisalat Corporation may without prejudice to its basic objects, invest, utilize and employ its funds in any other commercial, financial or servicing fields which in the opinion of the Board shall enhance such funds or reap profits to Etisalat Corporation in accordance with the applicable rules in the State.

(3) Etisalat Corporation may, for the purpose of achieving the objects provided for in this section:

(A) conclude contracts and agreements, and

(B) establish companies, enter into, or share in partnerships in accordance with the applicable rules in the State.

**Article (21)**

The Board shall, pursuant to the regulations issued by the Telecommunications Regulatory Authority, determine the charges for the services provided by Etisalat Corporation, controls and conditions for provision of such services and the formula and forms of contracts to be concluded with the beneficiaries.

**Article (25)**

The administration of Etisalat Corporation shall be undertaken by a Board of Directors comprised of eleven members, seven thereof including the Chairmanship shall represent the Government and shall be appointed by a Federal Decree. The other members shall be elected by the shareholders. Appointments and elections for Board Members might be for more than one time pursuant to the articles of association.[13]

**Article (31)**

Each shareholder of Etisalat Corporation shall have the right to attend the General Meeting, discuss the topics listed on the Agenda, and question the members of the Board who shall be bound to reply to the questions in so far as it shall not expose Etisalat Corporation's interest for damage. The shareholder may resort to the General Meeting if he considers the reply to his questions as insufficient and the decision of the General Meeting shall be obligatory for implementation.

The Government shall be represented in the General Meeting by the State's Minister for Finance and Industry.

**Article (33)**

Etisalat Corporation shall comply with the general policy of the Board[5] and obey any general or specific directives issued by the Board in this respect.

**Article (47)**

The Board[14] shall issue the financial and administrative regulations for management of Etisalat Corporation and shall determine the staff's conditions of service which do not conflict with the decisions issued by the Board[5].

## Article (81)

All juridical persons existing at the time this Federal Law by Decree comes into force which carry out any of the Regulated Activities must conform their status in accordance with the provisions of this Federal Law by Decree within ninety days from date it comes into force. The Board[5] may by decision extend such period to other similar periods.

## Article (81) repeated[11]

The Authority, in carrying out its functions, may detect violations of the Law. The Authority's employees, who are selected by a decision by the Minister of Justice and with the co-ordination of the Authority, shall have the power of judicial officers regarding crimes committed in breach of the provisions of the Law, its Executive Order, decisions, regulations, or instructions issued thereof and within the scope of responsibility of each.

## Article (82)

Any provision which contravenes any of the provisions of this Federal Law by Decree shall hereby be repealed.

## Article (83)

The Board[5] shall issue the Executive Order, regulations, decisions, and necessary instructions to implement the provisions of this Federal Law by Decree.

## Article (84)

This Federal Law by Decree shall be published in the Official Gazette and shall become effective on the date of such publication.

**Zayed bin Sultan Al Nahyan**

**President of the State of the United Arab Emirates**

Issued at the Presidential Palace in Abu Dhabi:
Dated: 20 Ramadan 1424H
Corresponding to: 15/11/2003

## ENDNOTES

1- Amended by Federal Law by Decree No. (5) of 2008 Amending the Provisions of the Federal Law by Decree No. (3) of 2003 Regarding the Organization of the Telecommunications Sector.

2- In the translation of this Article, the word "user" used in the previous translation has been replaced by the word "subscriber", not because of a legislative change, but because the word "subscriber" more accurately reflects the meaning of the original Arabic.

3- Chapter 2 (Articles (2) to (5)) was repealed by Federal Law by Decree No. (5) of 2008 Amending the Provisions of the Federal Law by Decree No. (3) of 2003 Regarding the Organization of the Telecommunications Sector.

4- Repealed by Federal Law by Decree No. (5) of 2008 Amending the Provisions of the Federal Law by Decree No. (3) of 2003 Regarding the Organization of the Telecommunications Sector.

5- The term "Supreme Committee" was replaced with the term "Board" pursuant to the Federal Law by Decree No. (5) of 2008 Amending the Provisions of the Federal Law by Decree No. (3) of 2003 Regarding the Organization of the Telecommunications Sector.

6- The term "Supreme Committee" was replaced with the term "Board" pursuant to the Federal Law by Decree No. (5) of 2008 Amending the Provisions of the Federal Law by Decree No. (3) of 2003 Regarding the Organization of the Telecommunications Sector. However, it must be noted that despite this amendment, the first financial budget of the Authority was actually set by a decision of the Supreme Committee, in accordance with the provisions of this law, as it was constituted at that time.

7- The term "Supreme Committee" was replaced with the term "Cabinet or its delegate" pursuant to the Federal Law by Decree No. (5) of 2008 Amending the Provisions of the Federal Law by Decree No. (3) of 2003 Regarding the Organization of the Telecommunications Sector.

8- In the translation of this Article, the phrase "juridical Licensee" used in the previous translation has been replaced with the phrase "juridical entity", not because of a legislative change, but because the substituted phrase more accurately reflects the meaning of the original Arabic.

9- In the translation of this Article, the phrase "perform the following authorities" has been replaced by the phrase "exercise the following powers", not because of a legislative change, but because the substituted phrase more accurately reflects meaning of the original Arabic.

10- The term "Ministry of Communications" was replaced with the term "competent body" pursuant to the Federal Law by Decree No. (5) of 2008 Amending the Provisions of the Federal Law by Decree No. (3) of 2003 Regarding the Organization of the Telecommunications Sector.

11- Added pursuant to Federal Law by Decree No. (5) of 2008 Amending the Provisions of the Federal Law by Decree No. (3) of 2003 Regarding the Organization of the Telecommunications Sector.

12- In the translation of this Article, the phrase "The funds of the Authority may invest its fund in the manner" used in the previous translation has been replaced with "The Authority may invest its funds in any form of investment", not because of a legislative change, but because the substituted phrase more accurately reflects the meaning of the original Arabic.

13- Amended by Federal Law by Decree No. (1) of 2005 Amending the Provisions of the Federal Law by Decree No. (3) of 2003 Regarding the Organization of the Telecommunications Sector.

14- The first reference to "Board" in this Article refers to the Board of Etisalat. The second reference is to the Board of the Authority.

# DECISION OF THE SUPREME COMMITTEE FOR THE SUPERVISION OF THE TELECOMMUNICATIONS SECTOR

## ISSUING THE EXECUTIVE ORDER OF FEDERAL LAW BY DECREE NO. 3 OF 2003 REGARDING THE ORGANISATION OF THE TELECOMMUNICATIONS SECTOR

The Supreme Committee for the Supervision of the Telecommunications Sector,

Having reviewed Federal Law by Decree No. (3) of 2003 Regarding the Organisation of the Telecommunications Sector; and

Federal Decree No. (22) of 2004 Forming the Supreme Committee for the Supervision of the Telecommunications Sector; and

According to the proposal by the member of the Supreme Committee for the Supervision of the Telecommunications Sector and the approval of the Supreme Committee for the Supervision of the Telecommunications Sector,

Have decided as follows:

### INTERPRETATION

### Article (1)

Unless the context requires otherwise, the expressions and wordings appearing in Federal Law by Decree No. (3) of 2003 Regarding the Organisation of the Telecommunications Sector shall have the same meanings ascribed thereto in the above-mentioned Federal Law by Decree, and the following expressions and wordings shall have the following meanings assigned thereto:

| | |
|---|---|
| **"Authority"** | the General Authority for Regulating the Telecommunication Sector. |
| **"Board of Directors" or "Board"** | the Board of Directors Of the Authority. |
| **"Earthworks"** | any works of excavation by whatever means and any works in connection with building , refurbishment or demolition or related to extension or connection of pipes or cables or installation or machines connection or other equipment. |
| **"Federal Law by Decree"** | the Federal Law by Decree No. (3) of 2003 Regarding the Organisation of the Telecommunications Sector. |
| **"Interconnection"** | the linking by whatever means of Telecommunication Networks in order to allow users of one entity to communicate with users of the same or another entity or to access and make use of Telecommunication Services provided by another entity. |

| | |
|---|---|
| **"Interconnection Agreement"** | an agreement under which Interconnection will be achieved pursuant to the rules and conditions issued by the Authority. |
| **"Licence Conditions"** | such conditions as may be imposed by the Supreme Committee as implied in the Licences granted to the Licensees and any modification thereto. |
| **"National Spectrum Database"** | database that contains all the administrative and technical information, services and authorization for spectrum. |
| **"Private Land"** | any land owned by, granted to or leased to any person other than any public institution. |
| **"Private Telecommunication Network"** | Telecommunication Networks operated exclusively to serve the requirements and to benefit one person or a group of persons who have a common ownership. |
| **"Public Telecommunication Network"** | Telecommunication Network operated for the provision of Public Telecommunication Services by the Licensed Operators pursuant to the provisions of the Federal Law by Decree and this Executive Order. |
| **"Public Telecommunication Service"** | any Telecommunication Service provided to users or a part thereof in consideration of a fee. |
| **"Supreme Committee"** | the committee established for the supervision of the telecommunication sector. |
| **"Telecommunication Services"** | Any service of transmitting, broadcasting, switching or receiving by means of a Telecommunication Network of any of the following:<br>1.wired and wireless cable and radio telecommunications;<br><br>2.voice, music and other sounds;<br><br>3. visual images;<br><br>4.signals used in transmission otherwise than the transmission and broadcasting of programmes;<br><br>5.signals used to operate or control any machinery or apparatus;<br><br>6.the installation, maintenance, adjustment, repair, alteration, moving, removal or replacement of apparatus which is or is to be connected to a Public Telecommunication Network;<br><br>7.the installation, maintenance and operation of local and international telegraph, telephone and leased circuits and domestic and international data networks, internet and wireless transmission; or<br><br>8.any other Telecommunication Services approved by the Supreme Committee.<br><br>but does not include any services used in the production and broadcasting of programmes. |
| **"Wireless Transmission"** | the transmitting or receiving of electro-magnetic energy which may be used for the conveyance of data, or messages or voice or visual images, or for the operation or control of machinery or apparatus. |

## CHAPTER 1 THE ORGANISATION OF THE AUTHORITY

### Part 1 –Board of Directors of Directors, Director General and Employees

#### Article (2)

1. The Authority shall be managed by Board of Directors comprised of five members, including the Chairman of the Board and the Director General. The Director General will take act as the Chairman during either his absence or position's vacancy. The Board Members shall be appointed by the Supreme Committee's resolution for four years renewable for successive periods pursuant to the same instrument of appointment. The Board shall select from the Authority's employees a secretary who has no voting power during decision-making.
2. Any experts and consultants, if required by the Board, may be invited to its sessions, in which they shall have no voting powers to the Board decisions.

#### Article (3)

1. The remuneration of the Chairman, the Director General and other Board Members shall be specified by resolution from the Supreme Committee.
2. The Board of Directors shall issue the Authority employees manual by which the salaries, benefits and other terms of employment shall be determined without getting confined to any other regulations or to any Governmental salary's scales.
3. The Board of Directors shall issue the organization chart of the Authority which indicates the functions of each division of this chart.
4. The senior positions employees shall be appointed by the Board of Directors pursuant to the rules of the applicable Authority employees manual.

#### Article (4)

1. The Board of Directors shall meet whenever required upon the Chairman's invitation or in accordance with the directives of the Supreme Committee. In all cases, the Board of Directors shall meet at least once every two months. For valid meetings of the Board, the attendance should be by majority and entertained with the attendance of the Chairman or the Director General in his absence
2. The Board meetings shall be chaired by the Chairman and in his absence by the Director General.
3. Board resolutions shall issue by the overwhelming majority of the attendees, where in case of equal voting the Chairman's side shall prevail.

#### Article (5)

1. The Director General is the legal representative of the Authority who shall be, in front of the Board of Directors, responsible for the day to day management affairs which shall be overseen pursuant to the terms of the law by Decree, this Executive Order, the decisions and directives emanating from the Supreme Committee and the applicable regulations in the Authority including its manual and the Board of Directors resolutions.
2. With consideration to section 4 of Article (3) in this Executive Order, the Director General shall have the power to appoint employees pursuant to the applicable employees that should assure carrying out the Authority's activities in effectiveness and efficiency.

### Article (6)

1. The Board of Directors secretary shall prepare meetings record which registers the minutes of meetings on the date they are held that should be signed by the attendant Board Members. The Board of Director's resolutions shall be issued by the signature of the Chairman, or the Director General in his absence.
2. The Authority shall provide the Supreme Committee within a week with a copy of the minutes of each Board meeting.

### Article (7)

The Board membership shall terminate for one of the following reasons:

1. Dismissal, pursuant to the Supreme Committee's decision pursuant to article (11) of the Federal Law by Decree.
2. Membership Expiry; unless renewed.
3. Resignation.
4. Death.

### Article (8)

1. Any Board Member may resign from his membership in the Board by presenting a written resignation to the Supreme Committee. Board Membership shall only terminate when the Supreme Committee issues a decision of acceptance. If no decision is taken regarding the resignation within sixty days of the resignation submission, the resignation will be considered accepted.
2. The absence of any Board member for three successive meetings for no reason or for unaccepted justification by the Board, shall be considered as resignation submittal as stipulated in paragraph (1) of this Article

### Article (9)

The Supreme Committee shall, within thirty days of the Board Membership's expiry, appoint a new Board Member as a replacement. Till such appointment is achieved, and as long as the Board's quorum is met, the other Board Members shall carry out the functions entrusted to the Board and in compliance with this Executive Order's rules.

### Article (10)

Neither any of the Board Members nor the Authority personnel may bear, in their personal capacity, any civil liability against carrying out or abstaining from carrying out any activity if being conducted upon the Supreme Committee's directions and within the frame of these directions, provided that they performed that in good faith and to enable the Authority to exercise its functions pursuant to the Federal Law by Decree and this Executive Order.

### Article (11)

The Authority may issue regulations, instructions, resolutions and rules to achieve the following:

1. ensure that the Telecommunication Services provided throughout the State are sufficient to the needs of those who wish to make use of these services;

2. enhance the level of the provided service in the telecommunication sector to accomplish the benefit of the users and the security and public safety whether to the users or others;
3. ensure that the Licensees abide by the performance quality standards and adhere to the terms and conditions of the Licences granted to them;
4. encourage, promote, and develop the telecommunications and information technology industries in the State;
5. work on the development and upgrading of the telecommunication system in the State through training, qualifying, establishing relevant educational institutions and attaining the latest releases of the apparatus, equipment and facilities in the telecommunications technology;
6. resolve any disputes that may arise between the Licensees;
7. the Licensees provisioning with free of charge Telecommunication Services in emergency cases;
8. obligate the Licensees to ratify binding agreements that achieves the aims specified in the Licence; and
9. Obligates the licensees to keep separate accounts for the licensed activities and to organise the financial subsidy exchange between these activities.

## Part 2 - Reports

### Article (12)

The Director General shall prepare the Authority's draft annual report and present it to the Board of Directors for approval prior to its submission to the Supreme Committee at the end of each financial year. This report shall include the following:

1. the Authority's activities during that year;
2. developments in respect of matters which fall within the scope of the Authority's functions and responsibilities;
3. plans for it's activities for the next year; and
4. any other matter which the Authority deems appropriate to present to the Supreme Committee.

The Authority may provide any concerned bodies, upon its request with a copy of this report

### Article (13)

The Authority shall provide the Supreme Committee with any other reports related to its functions as the Supreme Committee may request.

## Part 3 - Publication and Certification of Information

### Article (14)

The Authority, in the way it deems appropriate, shall place the needed necessary controls to publish information related to licensing standards and conditions issued by the Supreme Committee and any amendments thereto according to the Federal Law by Decree, this Executive Order and regulations and codes of practice issued by the Authority.

### Article (15)

In consideration with the previous Article, the Authority shall publish the standards and conditions related to the Licences, permits, authorisations, regulations, information and guidelines as it may consider expedient to provide to consumers and others.

**Article (16)**

The Authority shall prepare a general record to document all the information relating to:

1. Licences and exemptions issued by the Supreme Committee and any modifications or revocations thereto;
2. authorisations and permits of the Telecommunication Apparatus, and any modifications or revocations thereto; and
3. any exemption from the obligations of the Licence Conditions and any revocation or modification to such exemption.

**Article (17)**

The Authority may, if required and upon acquiring the Board approval, not document in the general record any of the information mentioned above in the previous article and may document it in a special record prepared for this purpose.

**Article (18)**

The Authority, after acquiring the Board of Directors approval, may permit to the concerned bodies, upon its request, to viewing the recorded information pursuant to the terms of this Executive Order and the conditions specified by the Authority. The Authority may provide these bodies with excerpts containing the required information issued by the Authority.

**Part 4 - Financial Affairs**

**Article (19)**

1. The Authority shall hold regular financial accounts and records for its transactions and affairs, which contains its income, expenditures, its assets and its dues. Within three months after the end of each financial year, the Authority shall prepare its closing accounts for the ended financial year indicating the real financial status of that year and the assets and entitlements of the Authority at the end of such financial year and in accordance with the renowned international accounting principles.
2. The accounting auditor shall disclose if the accounts, assets and its dues of the Authority in that particular year as shown are true and reflect the fact and if the Authority retained in that particular year clean accounts and financial records. The auditor may disclose any other matter he considers to be necessary.

**Article (20)**

1. The draft of the estimated annual budget of the Authority shall be prepared by the Director General to be approved by the Board of Directors and submitted to the Supreme Committee for issuance.
2. The Chairman is the cashing commander for the letter of Credit listed in the Authority's Budget and he shall exercise all the entrusted powers by virtue of the Federal Law by Decree and this Executive Order and the regulations and applicable rules in the

Authority. The Chairman may delegate any of his entrusted powers to the Director General or to any of the senior employees.

### Article (21)

In consideration with all the provisions of this Part 4, the Chairman after obtaining the Board of Directors approval shall issue the Authority's financial internal Regulations which shall imply organizing its accounts and financial records in accordance with the accounting principles.

### Part 5 – Contracts and Purchases

### Article (22)

The purchase of items and supplies and the practice of contracts of work and the supply of needed items that are required by the Authority shall be through general tender invitations in order to obtain the best bids and offers. In certain cases contracting by: limited tender, quotations or direct order is licit.

### Article (23)

The sale of materials, used equipments and items shall be through auction. Sales to equipments that values not exceeding 100,000 DHS can be by quotations or direct order.

### Article (24)

The Director General shall issue the necessary decisions for the formation of committee/s for tenders, quotations and public auctions in which a financial member is in each of these committees.

### Article (25)

With the consideration to the provisions of this Part 5, the Chairman upon the Board 's approval may issue the Authority's regulations for contracting and purchasing

## CHAPTER 2 LICENCES AND APPARATUS APPROVAL

### Part 1 – Licences

### Article (26)

*The Supreme Committee may issue specific and objective standards which accordingly Licences shall be issued thereupon or exempted thereof.

### Article (27)

The license issued by the Supreme Committee shall determine the type of activity a juridical person allowed to practice and the term thereto. The Authority should be notified to acquire its written approval in the event of the license waiving.

## Article (28)

The decisions issued by the Supreme Committee in relation to Licences awarding to juridical persons shall be published in the official gazette.

## Article (29)

The Supreme Committee may issue instructions or directives to any Licensed Operator as it may imply conditions in the Licences it issues relating to the following matters:

1. specifying the fees payable by the Licensee upon issuance of the Licence and during its term ;
2. the circumstances in which the Licence, either in whole or in part, may be revoked or suspended;
3. undertaking the Licensee to do specific matter or abstain from doing specific matters that have specific description within the framework of the exercised licensed activities standards.
4. the method of settling certain matters specified by or arose from the license and issues with special specification that need to be settled by qualified person.
5. setting ceiling limit for the shares of any licensee that could be owned by any other Licensee or by any of its subsidiaries or affiliate companies or bodies.
6. oblige the licensee to provide the Supreme Committee or the Authority with the documents, information and data that might be requested.

## Article (30)

Where it appears to the Authority that any Licensee or any person contravenes or already contravened the Federal Law by Decree or this Executive Order or any regulations issued thereupon or the general policy for the telecommunications sector in the State or any term of the Licence, the Authority may, for the purposes of the exercising its functions pursuant to the Federal Law by Decree and this Executive Order, issue a notification, where required, to the contravening party to submit to the Authority any documents or information which are specified or described in the notification. Upon recognition of that contravention, the Authority may issue directives to the Licensee to oblige him or abstain him from any activity as may be specified in the directives.

## Article (31)

A Licence may not be transferred or assigned to any third party unless the following two conditions are available:

1. the Licence issued by the Supreme Committee implies a provision permitting transfer or assignment to any third party; and
2. the prior consent of the Board of Directors is obtained. The consent might be conditional as the Board deems proper.

Any transfer or assignment to others that doesn't satisfy the abovementioned shall be considered void.

## Article (32)

Upon the Authority's request and within the specified time period indicated therein, the Licensee shall provide a report in the format set by the Authority showing the number of complaints against them and the taken procedures in this regard for the period covered in the report.

**Part 2 – Apparatus Approval**

**Article (33)**

1. The Board of Directors shall issue the technical specifications of the Telecommunication Apparatus. The Board of Directors may delegate this authority to the Director General or to a committee formed for such purpose.
2. When issuing regulatory orders in accordance with this Article, the Authority shall take into consideration any applicable international conventions and agreements or any applicable laws.
3. The Authority may coordinate with the competent customs departments to organise the importation of the Telecommunication Apparatus in accordance with the specified technical standards.

**Article (34)**

1. Authorizations for Telecommunication Apparatus shall be granted upon an application lodged pursuant to the standards and procedures issued by the Authority from time to time in relevance to these authorisations.
2. During the processing of the applications for Telecommunication Apparatus approvals, the Authority may refer the application to any other body or entity as deemed required.
3. The Authority may make variations, or amend or abolish the granted approvals at any time and for any reasons as it deems necessary, provided that the Authority announces that.

**Article (35)**

The Authority shall incorporate the following information to any telecommunication apparatus authorization the:

(A) the name and description of the intended Telecommunication Apparatus for which the approval was issued;

(B) the Telecommunication Network through which the Telecommunication Apparatus may be used;

(C) the specifications and description of the Telecommunication Network through which the Telecommunication Apparatus may be used; and

(D) any other information which the Authority deems necessary to imply in the authorization.

**Article (36)**

The Authority shall when processing the application of the telecommunication apparatus authorization take the following into consideration:

(a) the speculated risks as a result of using the Telecommunication Apparatus;

(b) the potential risks that the employees and workmen may be exposed to during the performance of their duties as a result of dealing with the Telecommunication Apparatus

(c) protection for the Public Telecommunication Network from any contingent damage

(d) the efficiency extent upon usage and the compatibility with the existing Telecommunication Apparatus;

(e) the effective use of the frequency spectrum and orbital resources;

(f) the interference avoidance with terrestrial systems and/or space-based communications systems and any other technical systems;

(g) the possibility for such Telecommunication Apparatus to be used for anti-competitive purposes.

**Article (37)**

The Authority shall document and file all the Telecommunication Apparatus authorizations and permissions granted by the provisions of this Part (2) in the formality and in the way it may determine. The documentation and filing shall contain the following information:

(a) information about every applicant who was granted the Telecommunication Apparatus Authorization, and

(b) information about all the approved Telecommunication Apparatus including technical specifications or standards;

(c) details of any conditions, terms and restrictions stipulated in the telecommunication apparatus authorization including those related to the effectiveness duration

(d) details of all variations and modifications to the telecommunication apparatus authorizations and the reasons thereto;

(e) details of the abolishment to all the telecommunication apparatus authorizations and the reasons thereto; and

(f) any other information the Authority deems necessary to file and document

**Article (38)**

The Authority may issue regulations and guidelines to require the provisioning with information and the manual guidance for the approved Telecommunications Apparatus in the means it deems appropriate; either to be marked on fixed to or joint with the Telecommunication Apparatus.

**Article (39)**

1. The approved Telecommunication Apparatus shall be subject to testing and assessment as may be required by the Authority, provided that the Authority shall conduct the tests and the assessments

2. Upon a written request and when it is deemed necessary, the Authority may designate a technical third party to conduct tests or assessments to the Telecommunication Apparatus concerned, provided that the applicant shall bear all the incurred charges requested by the third party for that as specified by the Authority.

**Article (40)**

The approved Telecommunication Apparatus by the Authority may only be installed, set-up, connected, adjusted and maintained by the licensee that operates Public Telecommunication Network or by any other body Licensed to conduct this work as specified by the Authority.

**Article (41)**

For the purposes of this Part (2), the Authorizations granted to the companies, bodies and commissions shall be considered as an empowerment to the natural persons appointed by them to install, set up, connect, adjust, maintain the concerned Telecommunication Apparatus.

**Article (42)**

The Authority may perform any of the following in case any of the Authorised or concerned persons in the Telecommunication Apparatus breaches the terms and restrictions that the Authorisations were granted upon,:

(a) impose a financial fine against the violator ; (b) abolish the issued Authorization.

**Article (43)**

Without prejudice to any applicable criminal penalties, the Authority may take any of the following actions in case the Authorised or concerned persons violate the technical specifications and standards issued by the Authority relevant to the Telecommunications Apparatus:

1. serve a warning to the violator to modify or change the concerned Telecommunications Apparatus to be compatible with the applicable specifications.

2. serve a warning to the violator to handover or destroy all the concerned Telecommunications Apparatus.

3. request from the relevant police authority to seize and detain all such Telecommunication Apparatus;

4. request from the customs authorities to keep in custody all such Telecommunication Apparatus which falls under its control;

5. issue an order to the violator to promptly and immediately dismantle the concerned Telecommunication Apparatus from the Telecommunication Network, provided that the Authority may seek the assistance of the relevant police authorities in this regard if necessary; and

6. any other procedure that commensurate with the nature of the violation after obtaining approval from the Supreme Committee.

**Article (44)**

The provisions of the previous Article shall be applicable against any person who manufactures, uses or offers for sale, supplies or uses Telecommunication Apparatus which has not been approved by the Authority.

**Article (45)**

A decision from the Board of Directors shall specify the Authority's authorised employees to have access to the manufacturing sites and premises of the Telecommunication Apparatus or to the places its stored or placed on the market, displayed or operated, in order to give effect to their duties relating to inspecting such Telecommunication Apparatus and submitting the same to testing and assessment.

**Article (46)**

Without prejudice to any applicable criminal penalties, where a person fails to submit Telecommunication Apparatus for testing and assessment, or prevents any employee or personnel or any other authorised person by the Authority from entering his premises, the Authority may - after serving a warning take any of the following procedures:

1. revoke the Authorisation for the concerned Telecommunication Apparatus; 2. notify him to handover or to damage the concerned Telecommunication Apparatus.

**Article (47)**

Upon request from the Authority, the authorised persons shall present a report detailing the extent of their adherence to the quality of service stipulated in the instructions and regulations issued by the Supreme Committee or the Authority or pursuant to the Authorizations issued to such persons.

**Article (48)**

If a particular entity makes an announcement about any apparatus useable in the telecommunications sector, the Authority may oblige this entity to present a description including all information related to the efficiency of this apparatus and the way it is used. The Authority may enforce requirements to be included in these announcements to reach the information and guidance which are necessary for the proper use of these apparatus.

## CHAPTER 3 NETWORK INTERCONNECTION, CO-LOCATION AND SHARING OF SITES, EARTHWORKS AND NUMBERING

### Part 1 – Network Interconnection, Co-Location and Sharing of Sites

**Article (49)**

In performing its obligations under the Federal Law by Decree and this Executive Order in relation to network Interconnection, co-location and sharing of sites, the Authority may take any of the following procedures:

1. issue the instructions and guidelines it deems appropriate.

2. issue directives obliging the relevant Licensees to reach an agreement between themselves to accomplish network Interconnection or co-location and sharing of sites during fixed timeframe specified in the directives;

3. intervene where necessary in the negotiation of co-location and sites sharing agreements and when specifying the conditions that should be adhered to reach the agreement between the intended Licensees, or issuing directives to any other Licensee regarding Interconnection and co-location and sites sharing;

4. track all parties compliance with the co-location and sites sharing agreements.

5. issue the regulations, directives, decisions and governing rules for national roaming services.

### Part 2 - Earthworks

### Article (50)

Without prejudice to the terms of the Federal Law by Decree and in this Executive Order, the Authority shall be competent to oblige any of the licensees, when carrying out Earthworks, to any of the following:

1. follow certain arrangements before performing the Earthworks;

2. take the necessary procedures to ensure the safety of all persons during the carrying out of Earthworks;

3. take all what is needed for the reinstatement of all the intended ways, lands and buildings as used to be before the commencement of Earthworks;

4. ensure that accurate documentation is maintained for all of the carried out Earthworks;

5. Take all the required procedures, when Earthworks are carried out, to secure that no interference occurs with other Licensee's Telecommunication Networks or with the owners or suppliers or operators of water, electricity and gas equipment, pipelines, facilities and any other services.

The Authority shall specify the relevant standards for Emergency cases that require Earthworks in different rules than those specified in the applicable rules.

### Part 3 – Numbering

### Article (51)

1. After the approval of the Supreme Committee, the Board of Directors shall be issue Instructions that implies conditions related to the allocation of prefixes, private telephone numbers (including the services telephone numbers) and numbering ranges to Licensees.

2. The prefixes, private telephone numbers and numbering ranges in effect shall remain applicable unless modified pursuant to the rules of the previous paragraph.

**Article (52)**

The Licensees shall provide all the information which the Authority requests according to Authority special numbering plan or pursuant to, or for the purpose of establishing or developing the Authority's numbering plan.

**Article (53)**

1. The Authority may set the organizing procedures for the determination of the prefixes, individual telephone numbers and numbering ranges applications.

2. Upon the determination on the applied applications pursuant to the terms of the previous paragraph of this Article, the Authority shall obtain the fees specified by the Supreme Committee for this purpose.

**Article (54)**

Subject to no contradiction with the technical requirements, the Authority shall oblige Licensees and other persons conducting regulated activities or any other persons, who performs prefixes, private telephone numbers and numbering ranges, to the following:

1. permit subscribers to retain the numbers that were assigned to them when they change their subscription, but without changing the geographical location of the subscribers, to other operator.

2. permit to subscribers to retain a particular number or numbers when changing their subscription to other operator or other geographical location if this is possible.

## CHAPTER 4 FREQUENCY SPECTRUM

### Part 1 – Frequency Spectrum Management

**Article (55)**

1. The frequency spectrum is a national resource that the Authority shall regulate pursuant to the terms of the Federal Law by Decree, provided that such terms as stipulated in the Federal Law by Decree shall apply to any telecommunications system or to any radio Telecommunication Apparatus which uses spectrum frequency.
2. The Authority shall prepare the National Frequencies Database that includes all the information related to the use of the frequency spectrum by the authorised users inside the State and the authorisations granted to them.
**Article (56)**

The use of any radio station on State's land or on a ship or plane registered in the State without obtaining an authorisation pursuant to the provisions of the Federal Law by Decree and this Executive Order is forbidden as well as entering radio station to the State without obtaining the Authority's prior approval.

## Part 2 – Authorisation of Frequencies and Usage Monitoring

### Article (57)

The Authority shall issue the authorisations for using frequencies to those authorised in accordance with the national frequency plan and with the available frequency spectrum, allocation of radio stations and their coverage without any violation to any previous rights determined to the authorised person.

### Article (58)

The authorised person shall use the radio frequencies pursuant to the conditions and standards that the authorisation was granted on, including:

1. the assigned radio spectrum frequencies;
2. the conditions and standards of the radio communication equipments, the location and sphere of its use and the purpose and manner in which the equipment operates;
3. the limits of the authorised geographical area related to the station for movable equipment;
4. the term duration of the authorisation;
5. any other technical conditions that utilize the efficiency of using frequencies.

### Article (59)

The Authority may revoke any granted authorisation if the frequencies have not been used within four months from the issuance day of the authorisation.

### Article (60)

When the spectrum frequency authorisation is renewed, the authorised person shall settle the specified renewing fees

## Part 3 – Co-ordination Committee

### Article (61)

1. The coordination committee shall be established pursuant to the rules in article (46) of the Federal Law by Decree and chaired by the Director General with the membership of the representatives of the following:

- The Ministry of Communication;

- The armed forces;

- The Ministry of Interior;

- The security services in the State;

- The Ministry of Information and Culture;

- The Civil Aviation Authority; and

- The Authority.

2. The co-ordination committee's chairman shall nominate one of the Authority's employees to carry out the responsibilities of the committee's secretary, who shall prepare the working timetable for its meetings, record the minutes and keep in safe the documentation, dealings and management matters mandated to him by the co-ordination committee's chairman.

**Article (62)**

The Authority shall study the needs, the current and future usages of the spectrum frequency and its allocation taking into account any use for military, governmental, security and commercial purposes and present this study to the co-ordination committee to operate the functions in accordance with Article (46) of the Federal Law by Decree.

**Article (63)**

The co-ordination committee shall be responsible for setting the national spectrum plan and setting up the National Spectrum Database for the allocation of frequencies relating to Telecommunication Services in conformity with the international and regional agreements and specifications and with the accredited standards and regulations to be submitted to the Supreme Committee for approval in accordance with Article (46) of the Federal Law by Decree.

**Article (64)**

The Ministry of Communications or the Authority may request from the co-ordination committee to review and amend the National Spectrum plan when it deems necessary, provided that the policies and goals relating to the future usages of the radio frequencies in the State are considered.

**Part 4 – Contravention of the Usage of Frequencies**

**Article (65)**

1. The Authority may suspend or revoke (frequency spectrum authorization) when witnessing that the holder of the authorisation has breached its conditions or when required due to the public interest.
2. The Authority' before suspending or revoking the relevant authorisation shall consider the following:

a. notify the authorised person in writing that his authorisation is about to be suspended or revoked;

b. grant the authorised person a suitable period to rectify the breach, provided that the authorised person shall reply in writing to the Authority clarifying his point of view in this regard.

## CHAPTER 5 INTERNET NETWORKS

### Part 1 – Licensing and Managing Internet Networks

#### Article (66)

The Authority shall prepare a national plan for the management of internet networks to be submitted to the Supreme Committee for approval provided that the internet services to subscribers shall not be provided unless the License is acquired from the Supreme Committee.

#### Article (67)

The Licensee shall be obliged to offer internet services pursuant to the conditions and standards specified in the issued Licence, provided that the Authority shall monitor the services offered by those licensees.

#### Article (68)

The Supreme Committee may revoke any granted Licence to the licensee if the service is not provided within four months from the Licence issuance day.

## CHAPTER 6 FINAL GENERAL PROVISIONS

#### Article (69)

The Board of Directors shall issue the regulations and conditions related to setting up and operating the Private Telecommunication Networks after obtaining the approval of the Supreme Committee,

#### Article (70)

*The Authority shall prepare draft resolution to impose additional fees over the licensees to be approved by the Supreme Committee. The additional fees shall be determined in accordance with the international standards. The returns shall be dedicated to promote research and development in the Telecommunication and Information Technology sector.

#### Article (71)

The Supreme Committee shall issue the regulations related to admitting the Licensees to enter to the Private Lands and any buildings or premises thereupon that enables them to exercise their activities as specified in the issued Licences and the conditions and terms thereto.

The entry to such Private Lands shall be only to the extent necessary to enable the Licensees to carry out necessary activities for a limited period of time and subject to notifying the people living on the Private Lands with a prior notice that specifies as well the names of the persons authorised to enter the Private lands and by taking all the legal procedures pursuant to the law.

### Article (72)

The Authority shall, in co-operation with the related Governmental bodies, represent the State in the international conferences and meetings relating to the telecommunications sector.

### Article (73)

The Authority's employees who are selected by the Board of Directors shall have the power of the official investigation officer in the occasion of exercising their specific functions pursuant to the rules of the Federal Law by Decree and this Executive Order and the regulations and decisions issued by the Board of Directors, provided that the Authority shall take the necessary legal steps pursuant to the law.

### Article (74)

The Supreme Committee shall issue the regulations and resolutions, instructions and directives that are supplementary to this Executive Order.

### Article (75)

This Executive Order shall be published in the official gazette and shall become effective on the date of such publication.

**Chairman of the Supreme Committee for the Supervision of the Telecommunications Sector**
**Dated: 14th Sha'ban 1425H**
**Corresponding to: 28th September 2004**

* This article was amended by the Supreme Committee Resolution no (2) of 2006.
* This article was amended by the Supreme Committee Resolution no (4) of 2005.

# RESOLUTION NO. (6) OF 2008 REGARDING THE LICENSING FRAMEWORK[1]

The General Authority for Regulating the Telecommunication Sector

In cognizance of the Federal Law by Decree No. (3) of 2003 Regarding the Organisation of the Telecommunication Sector and the amending laws thereof; and the

Decision of the Supreme Committee for the Supervision of the Telecommunication Sector No. (3) of 2004 Issuing the Executive Order of the Federal Law by Decree No. (3) of 2003 Regarding the Organisation of the Telecommunication Sector and the amending laws thereof; and the

Cabinet Resolution No. (42/23) of 2008 Session No. (3), Regarding the Abolition of the Supreme Committee for the Supervision of the Telecommunication Sector and delegating its functions to the Board of Directors of the General Authority for Regulating the Telecommunication Sector; and

On the basis of the proposal of the Director General of the General Authority for Regulating the Telecommunication Sector and the approval of the Board of Directors of the Authority, Have issued the following:

## ARTICLE (1) DEFINITIONS

Unless the context requires otherwise, the terms and expressions appearing in Federal Law by Decree No. (3) of 2003 Regarding the Organisation of the Telecommunication Sector and its amendments shall have the same meanings in this resolution The following terms shall have the following meanings:

"Regulatory Framework" the regulations, decisions, directives, regulatory policies, guidelines, recommendations and procedures made by the Supreme Committee and the Authority including any revisions or amendments made to them from time to time.

"Regulated Activity" the operation of a Public Telecommunication Network or the provision of Telecommunication Services to subscribers.

[1] This is an English translation of the official document which is in Arabic. Only the Arabic version may be relied upon for legal purposes.

**"State"** the United Arab Emirates

**"The Authority"** the General Authority for Regulating the Telecommunication Sector.

## ARTICLE (2) REGULATED ACTIVITIES

1. All Regulated Activities in the State are Licensable by the Authority.
2. The introduction of competition will be done gradually. New Licences for networks and services will be introduced gradually as well.

3. The number and scope of such Licences can be restricted due to the scarce resources used (e.g. spectrum and numbers) or the implementation of any technical restrictions to guide the use of these resources and to maximize their utilization for the public interest.
    1. The Authority may grant Licences by the following two methods, without limitation:
        1. considering the merits of the application; or
        2. proposals submitted by way of beauty contests or auctions.
4. The Authority shall create a balance between ease of market entry, merits of competition among different service providers, technical efficiency and consumer protection. As such, the Authority can choose between Licensing methods like, beauty contests, auctions or others in determining the number of new Licensees in a particular market regardless of there being no restrictions due to scarce resources. Where scarce resources are not restricted, the Licences shall be granted based on the merits of the application.
5. The Authority shall evaluate all applications objectively based on clear criteria.

## ARTICLE (3) AWARD PROCEDURES

1. The Authority shall determine the networks and services yet to be Licensed through resolutions issued from time to time.
2. The Authority shall also announce the kind of procedures to be followed in awarding the Licence at the relevant time.
3. The Authority shall enforce all processes required to disclose the true shareholding structure of the applicant including investors. The Authority may require these entities to demonstrate that they have not been found to be materially or repeatedly in breach of the applicable rules and regulations in the State or other jurisdictions.

## ARTICLE (4) INDIVIDUAL AND CLASS LICENCES

**1**. The Authority shall issue two categories of licences:

a. individual Licence; and
b. class Licence.

2. The general rules followed to determine which activity will fall under the individual Licence and which will fall under the class Licence include the following:

a. Individual Licences are issued where scarce resources (e.g. spectrum and numbers) are used or due to the nature of the activity or the significance of the resources to the public more regulatory supervision is required.
b. Class Licences are issued where there is no need to use scarce resources (e.g. spectrum and numbers) or due to the nature of the activity or the insignificance of the activity to the public, less regulatory supervision is required. Competition in these activities will provide the consumer with a greater choice of service providers.

1. The Authority shall in its resolutions issued from time to time indicating which Regulated Activities shall be Licensed, also indicate whether the activities will have an individual Licence or a class Licence.
2. The Licences will have generic conditions which apply to all types of Licensees as well as special conditions on the network, service or service provider. Thus, the draft Licence articles attached to the relevant resolutions announcing new Licences, may be modified to suit issues relating to the network, service or service provider.

3. The Licence conditions shall make reference to the Regulatory Framework that include issues on spectrum or technical approvals, interconnection, access and consumer protection. In case of significant amendments to the Regulatory Framework, due consultation will take place with the relevant parties in accordance with the Authority's consultation procedures.
4. As obtaining the Licence shall not mean the automatic approval to utilize or for the allocation of any scarce resource (e.g. spectrum and numbers), the Licensees shall apply to the Authority in order to be granted authorization to use spectrum or numbers in accordance with the Regulatory Framework.

**ARTICLE 5 TERM OF LICENCE**

**1**. Subject to the Article 5(2), the term of Licences shall be as follows:

a. individual Licences: 10 years; and class Licenses: 10 years

2. Where the award of the Licence is made by way of a beauty contest or auction; the term shall be made clear in the relevant documentation.

**ARTICLE 6 GENERAL**

This resolution shall come into force from the date of its publication and shall be published in the Official Gazette.

# RESOLUTION NO. (7) OF 2008 REGARDING THE LICENSING REGULATIONS[1]

The General Authority for Regulating the Telecommunication Sector

In cognizance of the Federal Law by Decree No. (3) of 2003 Regarding the Organisation of the Telecommunication Sector and the amending laws thereof; and the

Decision of the Supreme Committee for the Supervision of the Telecommunications Sector No. (3) of 2004 issuing the Executive Order of Federal Law by Decree No. (3) of 2003 Regarding the Organisation of the Telecommunication Sector and the amending laws thereof; and the

Cabinet Resolution No. (42/23) of 2008 Session No (3), Regarding the Abolition of the Supreme Committee for the Supervision of the Telecommunications Sector and delegating its functions to the Board of Directors of the General Authority for Regulating the Telecommunication Sector; and

On the basis of the proposal of the Director General of the General Authority for Regulating the Telecommunication Sector and the agreement of the Board of Directors of the Authority, Have issued the following:

**ARTICLE (1) DEFINITIONS**

Unless the context requires otherwise, the terms and expressions appearing in Federal Law by Decree No. (3) of 2003 Regarding the Organisation of the Telecommunication Sector and its amendments shall have the same meanings in this resolution. The following terms shall have the following meanings:

“Regulatory Framework” the regulations, decisions, directives, regulatory policies, guidelines, recommendations and procedures made by the Supreme Committee or the Authority from time to time including any revisions or amendments made to them.

“Regulated Activity” the operation of a Public Telecommunication Network or the supply of a Telecommunication Service to subscribers as

[1] This is an English translation of the official document which is in Arabic. Only the Arabic version may be used for legal purposes.

described in the relevant resolutions issued by the Authority from time to time.

“Individual Licence” a Licence as set out in Resolution No. (6) of 2008.

“Class Licence” a Licence as set out in Resolution No. (6) of 2008.

“State” the United Arab Emirates.

“Authority” the General Authority for Regulating the Telecommunication Sector.

## ARTICLE (2) INDIVIDUAL LICENCE

**1**. An entity shall be eligible for an Individual Licence if it is:

a. A company incorporated under the Commercial Companies Law (Federal Law No. (8) of 1984) and pursuant to Article 28 of the Federal Law by Decree No. (3) of 2003 Regarding the Organisation of the Telecommunication Sector and its amendments or any legal person approved by the Board of the Authority.
b. A company whose shareholding complies with the resolution in which that particular Regulated Activity has been approved to be licensed.

2. The applicant shall comply with the following:

a. Seek the approval for the establishment of the company to be Licensed, pursuant to Article 28 of Federal Law by Decree No. (3) of 2003 Regarding the Organisation of the Telecommunications Sector and its amendments. Approval for establishment shall not indicate approval for any Licence applied for thereafter.
b. If the applicant seeks an exemption from the provisions of the Commercial Companies Law (Federal Law No. (8) of 1984), it is required to submit an application to the Authority for such exemption which shall identify the range of exemptions from the provisions of the Commercial Companies Law and support this with justification.
c. An applicant shall submit the following information to the Authority:
i. Proof of fulfilment of the eligibility criteria for awarding the Licence; ii. Certified true copies of its memoranda and articles of association; iii. Details of shareholding structure including information of any telecommunication licence held by any of the shareholders, whether in the State or elsewhere;

iv. Details of management team including qualifications and experience in the telecommunication field in the State and, if any, in other jurisdictions;

v. Business plan including without limitation:

1. type of networks to be operated and services to be provided;
2. roll out plan for network and services including network diagrams and relevant technical details;
3. whether spectrum or numbers is/are required for the service and if so, details of the requirements;
4. funding proposal;

vi. Benefits to the UAE economy of the proposal; vii. Any other information supporting the application.
d. Additional information may be sought by the Authority from the applicant; such information to be submitted within a specified time. If the deadline is not met it will be deemed that there is no wish on part of the applicant to pursue the procedures.
e. Upon receipt of all required information, the applicant will be asked by the Authority to complete and submit the application form set out as Form A (Appendix 1) along with the required application fee.
f. A recommendation will be made by the Authority to the Board of Directors within thirty days of receipt of the duly completed application form.

## ARTICLE (3) CLASS LICENCE

1. An entity shall be eligible for a Class Licence if it is:

a. A company incorporated under the Commercial Companies Law (Federal Law No. (8) of 1984) and pursuant to Article 28 of the Federal Law by Decree No. (3) of 2003 Regarding the Organisation of the Telecommunications Sector and its amendments or any legal person approved by the Board of the Authority.
b. A company whose shareholding complies with the resolution in which that particular Regulated Activity has been approved to be Licensed.

2. The applicant shall comply with the following

a. Seek the approval for the establishment of the company to be Licensed, pursuant to Article 28 of Federal Law by Decree No. (3) of 2003 Regarding the Organisation of the Telecommunications Sector and its amendments. Approval for establishment shall not indicate approval for any Licence applied for thereafter.
b. If the applicant seeks an exemption from the provisions of the Commercial Companies Law (Federal Law No. (8) of 1984), it is required to submit an application to the Authority for such exemption which shall identify the range of exemptions from the provisions of the Commercial Companies Law and support this with justification.
c. An applicant shall submit the following information to the Authority:
i. Proof of fulfilment of the eligibility criteria for awarding the Licence; ii. Certified true copies of its memoranda and articles of association; iii. Details of shareholding structure including information of any telecommunication licence held by any of the shareholders, whether in the State or elsewhere;

iv. Details of management team including qualifications and experience in the telecommunication field in the State and, if any, in other jurisdictions;
v. Type of networks to be operated and services to be provided;
vi. Any other information supporting the application.
d. Additional information may be sought by the Authority from the applicant; such information to be submitted within a specified time. If the deadline is not met it shall be deemed that there is no wish on part of the applicant to pursue the procedures.

e. Upon receipt of all required information, the applicant will be asked by the Authority to complete and submit the application form set out as Form B (Appendix 2) along with the required application fee.
f. A recommendation will be made by the Authority to the Board of Directors within thirty days of receipt of the duly completed application form.

**ARTICLE 4 SUSPENSION OF LICENCE**

1. An Individual Licence and a Class Licence may be suspended for the following reasons:

a. The Licensee has provided incorrect, false or misleading information at the time of application for the Licence;
b. The Licensee has failed to pay the annual Licence fee;
c. The Licensee is in breach of the Licence conditions and has failed to remedy the breach despite the Authority requiring it to do so;
d. In the national interest.

2. Every suspension of a Licence shall mean the suspension of any resources associated with that Licensed network or service and authorised for use by that Licensee including without limitation spectrum and numbers.

**ARTICLE (5) REVOCATION OF LICENCE**

1. An Individual Licence and a Class Licence may be revoked for the following reasons:

a. The Licensee has provided incorrect, false or misleading information at the time of application for the Licence;
b. The Licensee has failed to pay the annual Licence fee;
c. The Licensee is in breach of the Licence conditions and has failed to remedy the breach despite the Authority requiring it to do so;
d. In the national interest.

2. Every revocation of a Licence shall mean the revocation of any resources associated with that Licensed network or service and authorised for use by that Licensee including without limitation spectrum and numbers.

**ARTICLE (6) RENEWAL OF LICENCE**

1. Every application for renewal of a Licence shall be made in the relevant form not less than six months before the expiry of the Licence and the Licensee shall be granted a renewal of the Licence for a specified term unless:

a. The Licensee has failed to comply with the terms and conditions of the Licence;
b. The Licensee has failed to comply with the law or the Regulatory Framework;
c. It is not in the national interest to do so.

2. The Authority shall consider the application and may seek further information if necessary before deciding:

a. to grant the renewal of the Licence;
b. not to grant the renewal of the Licence.

## ARTICLE (7) REGISTERS

Information on the Licences will be set out in the register established for it pursuant to the Executive Order and extracts including required information may be requested by entities from the Authority.

## ARTICLE (8) POWER TO EXTEND TIME

**Whenever a time period is specified in these Regulations or in a Licence for an act to be done or a condition to be fulfilled, the person affected may request for an extension of such time in writing and the Authority, as the case may be, may grant or refuse such extension of time as it deems fit in its absolute discretion.**

## ARTICLE (9) PUBLICATION

**This resolution shall come into force from the date of its publication and shall be published in the Official Gazette.**

## APPENDIX 1 FORM A APPLICATION FORM FOR INDIVIDUAL LICENCE

(If space is insufficient please attach information as Appendices)

1. Name of Applicant:
2. Registration Number[1]:
3. Address: PO Box No: ______________________________ Floor: _________________________________ Building: _________________________________
   Street: _________________________________
   Emirate: _________________________________
4. Names and details of shareholders (up to and including actual shareholders)[2]: (Please attach as Appendix)
5. Details of capital of applicant:
6. Contact person (Name and Designation):

[1] Please attach certified true copies of incorporation documents. [2] Please include chart showing all shareholders of the applicant.

-Telephone:
-Fax:
-Mobile Phone No.:
-Email address:

1. Applicant website address, if any:
2. Nature of facilities/services to be offered[3]:
   1. Business Plan including[4]:
      - Roll out Plan for networks/services
      - Funding proposal
   2. Details of key management personnel[5] including details of:

      Qualifications;

      Experience;

- Previous experience in telecommunications sector (with name of company, country and period of employment)

3. Will spectrum be required? If so, which frequencies?

[3] Please include network diagram. [4] Please attach details as Appendix. [5] Please attach details as Appendix.

1. Will numbers be required? If so, what numbers?
2. Has the applicant or any of its shareholders any interest in any telecommunications entity licensed in the UAE or any other country?
3. If so, please provide details of name of licensee, licences held, nature of facilities and services provided and details of any fines, charges, and penalties levied by other regulatory bodies[6].
4. Additional information in support of application, if any:
5. Declaration:

I am the duly authorised representative of
________________________________________ and I hereby confirm that all the information submitted in this and all related documents for the purpose of this application for an Individual Licence under the Federal Law by Decree No.

(3) of 2003 and its amendments, is correct and true. Signature:
________________________________________________ Name:
________________________________________________ Designation:
________________________________________________ Date:
________________________________________________ Stamp:

[6] Please attach details as Appendix

### APPENDIX 2 FORM B APPLICATION FORM FOR CLASS LICENCE

(If space is insufficient please attach information as Appendices)

1. Name of Applicant:
2. Registration Number[1]:
3. Address: PO Box No: __________________________ Floor: ______________________________ Building: ______________________________
   Street: ______________________________
   Emirate:______________________________
4. Names and details of shareholders (up to and including actual shareholders)[2]: (Please attach as Appendix)
5. Details of capital of applicant:
6. Contact person (Name and Designation):

[1] Please attach certified true copies of incorporation documents. [2] Please include chart showing all shareholders of the applicant.

-Telephone:
-Fax:
-Mobile Phone No.:
-Email address:

1. Applicant website address, if any:

2. Nature of services to be offered:
    1. Details of key management personnel[4] including details of:
        Qualifications;
        Experience;
        - Previous experience in telecommunications sector (with name of company, country and period of employment)
3. Has the applicant or any of its shareholders any interest in any telecommunications entity licensed in the UAE or any other country?
4. If so, please provide details of name of licensee, licences held, nature of facilities and services provided and details of any fines, charges, and penalties levied by other regulatory bodies[5].

[3] Please include network diagram. [4] Please attach details as Appendix. [5] Please attach details as Appendix

1. Additional information in support of application, if any:
2. Declaration: I am the duly authorised representative of ____________________________________________ and I hereby confirm that all the information submitted in this and all related documents for the purpose of

this application for a Class Licence under the Federal Law by Decree No. (3) of 2003 and its amendments, is correct and true. Signature:

_____________________________________________________ Name:
_____________________________________________________ Designation:
_____________________________________________________ Date:
_____________________________________________________ Stamp:

# STRATEGIC INFORMATION AND CONTACTS FOR UAE

## SEVEN EMIRATES

### ABU DHABI

Abu Dhabi is the largest of all seven emirates with an area of 67,340 square kilometers, equivalent to 86.7 per cent of the country's total area, excluding the islands. It has a coastline extending for more than 400 kilometers and is divided for administrative purposes into three major regions. The first region encompasses the city of Abu Dhabi which is both the capital of the emirate and the federal capital. Sheikh Zayed, President of the UAE resides here. The parliamentary buildings in which the federal Cabinet meets, most of the federal ministries and institutions, the foreign embassies, state broadcasting facilities, and most of the oil companies are also located in Abu Dhabi, which is also the home of Zayed University and the Higher Colleges of Technology. Major infrastructure facilities include Mina (Port ) Zayed and Abu Dhabi International Airport. The city also has extensive cultural, sport and leisure facilities, together with the wonderfully engineered Abu Dhabi Corniche which offers many kilometers of risk-free walking, cycling, jogging and roller-blading along the seashore of Abu Dhabi island. Architecturally speaking the city is also a fascinating place where older buildings such as small mosques have been preserved and sit comfortably in the shade of futuristic modern skyscrapers.

Abu Dhabi's second region, known as the Eastern Region, has as its capital Al Ain city. This fertile area is rich in greenery with plenty of farms, public parks and important archaeological sites. It is also blessed by substantial groundwater resources which feed into numerous artesian wells. Points of particular interest in this region are the Ain Al Faydah Park, Jebel Hafit, the leisure park at Al Hili, Al Ain Zoo and Al Ain Museum. This is also a cultural and educational center and site of the UAE's first university, the UAE University, which includes among its many faculties a vibrant medical school. Internal transport is facilitated by a superb road network and Al Ain is connected to the outside world through Al Ain International Airport.

The Western Region, the emirate's third administrative sector, comprises 52 villages and has as its capital Bida Zayed, or Zayed City. Extensive a forestation covers at least 100,000 hectares, including more than 20 million evergreens. The country's main onshore oil fields are located here, as is the country's largest oil refiner y, at Al Ruwais. In addition to the three mainland regions of Abu Dhabi there are a number of important islands within the emirate including Das, Mubarraz, Zirku and Arzanah, near where the main offshore oil fields are located. Closer inshore are Dalma, Sir Bani Yas, Merawah, Abu al-Abyadh and Saadiyat, together with many other islands.

### DUBAI

The Emirate of Dubai extends along the Arabian Gulf coast of the UAE for approximately 72 kilometers . Dubai has an area of c. 3,885 square kilometers , which is equivalent to 5 per cent of the country's total area, excluding the islands. Dubai city is built along the edge of a narrow 10-kilometre long, winding creek which divides the southern section of Bur Dubai, the city's traditional heart, from the northern area of Deira. The Ruler's office, together with many head offices of major companies, Port Rashid, the Dubai World Trade Center, customs, broadcasting stations and the postal authority are all situated in Bur Dubai. Deira is a thriving commercial center containing a huge range of retail outlets, markets, hotels and Dubai International Airport. Bur Dubai and Deira are linked by Al Maktoum and Al Garhoud bridges, as well as Al Shindagha tunnel which passes under the creek.

Jebel Ali, home of a huge man-made port, has the largest free-trade zone in Arabia housing an ever growing list of international corporations which use the zone for both manufacturing and as a redistribution point.

Jumeirah beach is a major tourism area with a number of spectacular award winning hotels and sports facilities. Inland, the mountain resort town of Hatta is an extremely attractive location. Adjacent to a lake reservoir, the Hatta Fort Hotel is set in extensive parkland and provides a perfect base for exploring the nearby wadis and mountains, which extend into Omani territory.

## SHARJAH

The Emirate of Sharjah extends along approximately 16 kilometers of the UAE's Gulf coastline and for more than 80 kilometers into the interior. In addition there are three enclaves belonging to Sharjah situated on the east coast, bordering the Gulf of Oman. These are Kalba, Khor Fakkan and Dibba al-Husn. The emirate has an area of 2,590 square kilometers, which is equivalent to 3.3 percent of the country's total area, excluding the islands.

The capital city of Sharjah, which overlooks the Arabian Gulf, contains the main administrative and commercial centers together with an especially impressive array of cultural and traditional projects, including several museums. Distinctive landmarks are the two major covered souqs, reflecting Islamic design; a number of recreational areas and public parks such as Al Jazeirah Fun Park and Al Buheirah Corniche. The city is also notable for its numerous elegant mosques. Links with the outside world are provided by Sharjah International Airport and Port Khalid.

Sharjah also encompasses some important oasis areas, the most famous of which is Dhaid where a wide range of vegetables and fruits are cultivated on its rich and fertile soil. Khor Fakkan provides Sharjah with a major east coast port. Two offshore islands belong to Sharjah, Abu Musa, which has been under military occupation by Iran since 1971, and Sir Abu Nu'air.

## AJMAN

Ajman, located a short distance northeast of Sharjah's capital city, has a beautiful 16-kilometre stretch of white sand beach. It is a small emirate in terms of its physical size, covering about 259 square kilometers, which is equivalent to 0.3 per cent of the country's total area, excluding the islands.

The capital city, Ajman, has an historic fort at its center. This has been recently renovated and now houses a fascinating museum. In addition to the Ruler's office, various companies, banks and commercial centers, the emirate is also blessed with a natural harbor in which the Port of Ajman is situated.

Masfut is an agricultural village located in the mountains 110 kilometers to the southeast of the city, while the Manama area lies approximately 60 kilometers to the east.

## UMM AL-QAIWAIN

The Emirate of Umm al-Qaiwain, which has a coastline stretching to 24 kilometers , is located on the Arabian Gulf coast of the UAE, between Sharjah to the southwest, and Ras al-Khaimah to the northeast. Its inland border lies about 32 kilometers from the main coastline. The total area of the emirate is about 777 square kilometers, which is equivalent to 1 per cent of the country's total area, excluding the islands.

The city of Umm al-Qaiwain, capital of the emirate, is situated on a narrow peninsula which encircles a large creek 1 kilometer wide by 5 kilometers long. The Ruler's office, administrative and commercial centers, the main port and a Mari culture Research Center where prawns and fish are reared on an experimental basis, are located here. The city also has the preserved remains of an old fort, its main gate flanked by defensive cannons.

Falaj al-Mualla, an attractive natural oasis, is located 50 kilometers southeast of Umm al-Qaiwain city. Sinayah island, lying a short distance offshore has important mangrove areas together with a breeding colony of Socotra cormorants.

## RAS AL-KHAIMAH

Ras al-Khaimah, the most northerly emirate on the UAE's west coast, has a coastline of about 64 kilometers on the Arabian Gulf, backed by a fertile hinterland, with a separate enclave in the heart of the Hajar mountains to the southeast. Both parts of the emirates have borders with the Sultanate of Oman. In addition to its mainland territory, Ras al-Khaimah possesses a number of islands including those of Greater and Lesser Tunb, occupied by Iran since 1971. The area of the emirate is 168 square kilometers , which is equivalent to 2.2 per cent of the country's total area, excluding islands.

The city of Ras al-Khaimah is divided into two sections by Khor Ras al-Khaimah. In the western section, known as Old Ras al-Khaimah, are Ras al-Khaimah National Museum and a number of government departments . The eastern part, known as Al Nakheel, houses the Ruler's office, several government departments and commercial companies. The two sections are connected by a large bridge built across the khor.

Khor Khuwayr is an industrial region situated approximately 25 kilometers to the north of Ras al-Khaimah city. In addition to its major cement, gravel and marble enterprises, it is also the location for Port Saqr, the main export port for the emirate and the traditional fishing district of Rams. Digdagga district, on the other hand, is a we l l - k n own agricultural area and houses the Julphar pharmaceutical factory, the largest in the Arabian Gulf.

Other important centers within the emirate include: Al-Hamraniah, an agricultural center and also the location for Ras al-Khaimah International Airport, Khatt, a tourist resort that is renowned for its thermal springs, Masafi which is well known for its orchards and natural springs and Wadi al-Qawr, an attractive valley in the southern mountains.

## FUJAIRAH

With the exception of some small enclaves belonging to Sharjah, Fujairah is the only emirate situated along the Gulf of Oman. Its coast is more than 90 kilometers in length and its strategic location has played a key role in its development. The area of the emirate is 1165 square kilometers, which is equivalent to 1.5 per cent of the country's total area, excluding islands.

Fujairah city, the capital of the emirate, is a rapidly developing center which contains the Ruler's office, government departments, many commercial companies and a number of hotels, as well as an airport and the Port of Fujairah, one of the world's top oil bunkering ports.

The physical features of the emirate are characterized by the jagged Hajar mountains which border the fertile coastal plain where most of the settlement has taken place. Blessed with dramatic scenery, Fujairah is well placed to continue building upon its tourism trade.

Attractions include some excellent diving sites, the natural beauty of the mountains and coastline, cultural and historic attractions and, of course, reliable winter sunshine. The historic town of Dibba al-Fujairah, at the northern end of the emirate, is an important center for both agriculture and fishing, while the village of Bidiya has a unique four-domed mosque that is the oldest in the country.

# SELECTED STRATEGIC INFORMATION ON EMIRATES

## DYBAI: BASIC INFORMTION

Lying on the calm, blue waters of the southern Gulf and flanked by majestic desert, Dubai offers year-round sunshine and five-star luxury... plus the adventure of a unique Arabian experience.

One of the seven emirates that make up the United Arab Emirates, Dubai is a place of fascinating contrasts, a distinctive blend of modern city and timeless desert, of East and West, of old and new.

Known in the region as 'the city of merchants', Dubai has welcomed seafarers and traders to its shores for generations. Today, this tradition of courtesy and hospitality lives on. Dubai's streets are clean and safe, and travellers are sure to be charmed by the city's warmth and friendliness.

Dubai has something for everyone, from holidaymakers seeking a relaxing break away from clouds and crowds, to active tourists looking for a new, exciting experience. The emirate is also rapidly emerging as an international conference, exhibition and incentive destination.

Dubai has superb sports, shopping, dining and entertainment facilities. Likewise, its rapidly developing tourism sector is well equipped to cater to the diverse needs of individual travellers, families or incentive groups.

In the following pages, Destination Dubai provides comprehensive details of the emirate's tourist attractions, facilities and services.

### KEY ATTRACTIONS

- A taste of Arabia with a cosmopolitan lifestyle
- Year-round sunshine
- Uncrowded, clean, sandy beaches
- Crime-free environment
- Tolerant and welcoming society

### GETTING THERE

- Dubai is less than eight hours from Europe and the Far East
- Some 80 airlines provide direct links to more than 120 cities worldwide
- Efficient immigration, baggage handling and customs formalities

### ACCOMMODATION

- Wide selection of luxurious, modern hotels offering superb accommodation and facilities for sports, dining and entertainment
- Choice of location — in the city, on the beach or in the mountains
- Furnished holiday apartments for longer stays

### ENTERTAINMENT

- Extensive range of restaurants featuring cuisine from around the world.
- Varied nightlife — bars, cafés and nightclubs
- Family fun at theme parks, a zoo, beaches and country parks

### GROUND ARRANGEMENTS

- Choice of internationally-experienced destination management companies with multilingual guides and well-qualified drivers
- Modern air-conditioned coaches
- Plentiful taxis and hire cars
- Good roads, highways and wide boulevards
- First-rate cruise docking, supply and ground-handling facilities

### TOURS AND EXCURSIONS

- Variety of standard or tailor-made tours available, covering the city, shopping, the desert, the East Coast, mountains, neighbouring emirates, and more
- Limousine, boat and dhow tours
- Special interest packages including golf, watersports, fishing, bird-watching, archaeology

### ARABIAN EXPERIENCES

- Desert safaris, dune driving and exploring wadis (dry river beds) by four-wheel-drive vehicles
- Sand-skiing

- Moonlit Arabian desert barbecues, complete with traditional entertainment
- Camel racing, horse racing and falconry
- Cruises by traditional wooden dhow on Dubai Creek or into the Gulf
- Exploring the old city souks (markets), creekside dhow quays and traditional architecture
- Photographic opportunities galore: majestic mosques, magnificent palaces, brightly dressed children, camel and goat herds, ancient windtowers, dusty Bedouin villages, lush oases and palm groves, and dramatic sunsets

### OUTDOOR ACTIVITIES AND SPORTS

- Superb watersports: sailing, fishing, windsurfing, water-skiing, jet-skiing, scuba-diving and snorkelling
- Golf on three championship-standard grass courses, with two more to open this year
- Wide range of other sports, from squash and tennis to horse riding and trekking, paragliding, cycling, ice-skating, shooting, archery, bowling and go-karting

### SHOPPING

- Dubai's tax-free open market means bargains galore
- Attractive traditional Middle Eastern gifts — coffee pots, rugs, silverware, jewellery, brass, inlaid rosewood furniture and much more
- One of the world's great gold trading centres offering unbeatable value
- Wide selection of low-priced international brand name products including audio equipment, VCRs, cameras, watches, designer clothes, perfumes
- Award-winning Dubai Duty Free complex at the airport.

## BUSINESS CLIMATE

Dubai presents international business with a wide range of opportunities for different activities and operations, including:

- Trade
- Transport and distribution
- Manufacturing and processing
- Regional offices.

### THE MARKET

As the leading regional trading hub, Dubai offers access to a market of outstanding potential for overseas companies in a wide range of sectors. Among its key characteristics are:

- A large market - more than $17 billion in domestic imports annually; gateway to a $150 billion p.a., 1.4 billion population regional import market;
- A growing market - Dubai's imports have more than doubled since 1989; regional economic growth and liberalisation is set to boost demand;
- A prosperous market - strategic location at the heart of one of the world's richest regions;
- A diversified market - wide import requirements; opportunities for suppliers of most products;
- An accessible market - served by more than 170 shipping lines and 86 airlines;
- An open market - no exchange controls, quotas or trade barriers.

Dubai offers incoming business all the advantages of a highly developed economy. Its infrastructure and services match the highest international standards, facilitating efficiency, quality and service. Among the benefits are:

- Free enterprise system
- Highly developed transport infrastructure
- State-of-the-art telecommunications
- Sophisticated financial and services sector
- Top international exhibition and conference venue
- High quality office and residential accommodation
- Reliable power, utilities etc
- First class hotels, hospitals, schools, shops etc
- Cosmopolitan lifestyle.

### THE COSTS

Overseas companies setting up in Dubai can secure cost advantages not generally available internationally. Among the reasons are:

- No corporate taxes
- No income taxes
- No foreign exchange controls
- No trade barriers
- Competitive import duties (4% with many exemptions)
- Competitive labour costs
- Competitive energy costs
- Competitive real estate costs.

### DOING BUSINESS

Dubai offers foreign companies a wide choice of business options, including:

- Direct trade - selling directly to established dealers and distributors
- Commercial agency arrangements - appointee must be a UAE national or company; agreement to be registered with Ministry of Economy and Commerce
- Branch or representative office - 100% foreign ownership permitted; local agent (sponsor) must be appointed; Economic Development Department licence required
- Limited liability company - foreign ownership restricted to 49%; Economic Development Department licence required
- Special free zone investment incentives (see below).

### SPECIAL INVESTMENT INCENTIVES

Dubai's highly successful Jebel Ali Free Zone and new Airport Free Zone provide all the advantages available elsewhere in the emirate, with the following additional benefits:

- 100% foreign ownership and control
- Renewable 15-year guarantee of no taxation
- No customs duties
- Flexible investment options
- Efficient transport and distribution facilities
- Full administrative and recruitmentsupport.

# UAE INDUSTRY INFORMATION AND CONTACTS

Economic development in general, and Industrial development in particular, necessitates all effort and resource mobilization . The U.A.E. has prepared infrastructure that enable the private sector to play the largest and distinct role in this respect. The private sector made good achievement in this field, thanks to the patronage and guidance of H.H. President Sheikh Zayed Bin Sultan Al Nahayan and H.H. Sheikh Maktoum Bin Rashid Al Maktoum Bin Rashid Al Maktoum, Deputy President, Prime Minister and Ruler of Dubai and their Highnesses Members of the Supreme Council, Rulers of the Emirates.

The steady increase in local industry export products to several countries worldwide is and evidence to the quality level these products achieved and their competence in foreign trade markets.

Permanent endeavors targeted at successful national industry will continue in coherence with related industrial structure, and an industry capable of standing against the now economic international changes without any protection or help, an industry whose slogans is high quality and modern technology.

## BASIC FEATURES OF THE INDUSTRIAL SECTOR IN THE UAE

Modern industry in the United Arab Emirates began with the production and export of crude oil and continued to expand as the country started to develop its productive capacity. Economic policies aimed at creating alternative sources of revenue and diversifying the economic base, were adapted by the U.A.E. to reduce its dependency on oil . The development of Industry was a strategic option taken by the U.A.E. on the basis of the availability of the factors necessary for the development of a modern industrial sector such as capital, abundant sources of energy as well as metallic and non-metallic minerals and various raw materials that can be used in building and other industries.

As a result of the huge investments directed towards the development of the industrial sectors, large number of manufacturing and processing industries were established which used hydrocarbons as raw materials such as oil refineries, gas liquefaction and fertilizer plants. In addition, a large number of consumer industries were established in order to satisfy the local consumption demand for food and other consumer products such as meat, milk and other food production industries, textile and garments , metal products and fiber glass.

## EMIRATES INDUSTRIAL BANK

It is a financial and development establishment established in 1982 by the Federal Law No. (1) the year 1982 , so as to contribute to the economy of the country and diversify its productive structure by building new industries and supporting the existing ones through out the country.

The Bank fundamentally directs its efforts to private establishments and companies and mixed economy establishments and companies in the field of industry whose capital is at lest 51% owned by UAE nationals or the State.
The Bank finance the industries having convincing feasibly, technically and profitably on condition that the industrial loan does not exceed 20 % of the capital and reserve of the contributing bank; or 60% of the gross expenses of the project (including the active capital for three months) ; which is less, Financing will be made through loans or by contributing to the capital of the project owning company, This last case includes projects the Bank finds it necessary to establish and encourage, depending on their importance and influence on the development of industry in the state. had started operation and activity assigned to it in the license.

The license is to be given after registration of the project in the register in the name of the project owner. The philosophy of establishing the Bank is closely related to the long term aims and objective of the UAE economy, as the main objective of the Bank is to contribute to activate and support industry in the UAE, for the achievement of a further objective : the diversification of national income sources and creating a firm industrial sector on the long run, In this respect, before giving the loan, the Bank makes a comprehensive economic and technical feasibility study for the proposed industrial project, on the basis of which it can give the clients a specialized assessment that helps them upgrade the efficiency of their projects.

This assessment includes the feasibility study, financial and engineering analysis and marketing and legal consultation research.

Since 1984, the Industrial Bank set up a special branch to study and decide the industrial sectors representing the uncovered power of the industrial investment. In January 1986 the Bank started issuing a regular pamphlet supplying industry businesses with the essential industrial information.

### BANK LOAN TYPES

The Bank offers the following types of loans, as type are needed:

a) Short Term Loans : not exceeding two year duration. These loans are assigned to financing capital, acting in the existing industrial establishments.

b) Short Term Loans: not exceeding five-year duration. These loans are assigned to increase production lines or the renewal of the existing industrial establishments.

c) Long Term Loans : not exceeding eight-year duration. These loans are assigned to establishing new industrial projects.

### OTHER SERVICES AND FACILITIES

1. Providing Renewed Credit Facilities for financing active capital.
2. Private Contracts Financing.
3. Credit Facility Grants for exports.
4. Transferable Loans.
5. Providing Preliminary Guarantee Statements.
6. Providing Preliminary Statements of Guaranteed performance.
7. Preparation of Assessment Studies for Industrial Projects.
8. Preparation of Marketing Studies .
9. Investigating Investment Chances in the Industrial Fields in the Country.
10. Loans Transferable to Participate in Capital.
11. Contribution to the Capital of Companies Acting within the Activity of the Bank. est. of 4% of the amount of the loan, added to a 0.5 % interest for administration fees.

    a) Industrial projects of dense capital insuring importing modern technology to the country.

    b) Industrial projects whose most needs depend on locally available primary material to produce commodities for the UAE market with the capacity of replacing imported ones and gross expenses less than those of the imported ones .

    c) Projects depending on locally available primary material which, rather than locally marketing, can be marketed in Arab and Foreign markets by multi - party by literal long term agreements.

## DUTY FREE TRADING IN DUBAI

Dubai Duty Free retails duty free merchandise at Dubai International Airport temporary sites at sponsored events in Dubai such as golf and tennis tournaments, horse racing, offshore powerboat racing and concerts.

The company is committed to reducing the adverse impacts of its commercial and sponsored event activities on the environment, to prevent pollution and to continually improve its environmental performance.

The company will consider the environmental impacts of storage, display and final packaging of merchandise during the product selection process and will comply with the requirements of CITES.

The Company will comply with relevant UAE environmental legislation and will use its purchasing influence to encourage its local suppliers to also comply.

The company will train its employees to be aware of the Company's Environmental Policy and to be involved in its implementation.

We will, where practical, seek to adopt methods of reducing the consumption of materials and energy and to indicate the re-use and recycling of materials wherever economically viable.

We will encourage our customers to either re-use or dispose of packing material in an environmentally responsible manner.

The Dubai Duty Free Environmental Management System will be used to measure the Company's environmental performance, to set and review environmental objectives and targets and to monitor the progress towards them.

This Environmental Policy is available at our Duty Free Office Reception and to anyone requesting a copy.

Dubai Duty Free got ISO 14001 certificate for Environmental Management

| S.N. | ITEM | QUANTITY SOLD | UNIT OF MEASURE |
|---|---|---|---|
| 1 | CIGARETTES | 820,838 | CARTONS |
| 2 | LIQUOR | 1,013,655 | BOTTLES |
| 3 | GOLD | 1.5 | TONNES |
| 4 | WATCHES | 46,465 | PIECES |
| 5 | PERFUMES | 357,016 | BOTTLES |
| 6 | MOBILE PHONES | 25,136 | PIECES |
| 7 | DVD | 1,738 | PIECES |
| 8 | VIDEO CAMERA | 5,524 | PIECES |
| 9 | DISCMAN | 3,545 | PIECES |
| 10 | WALKMAN | 3,768 | PIECES |

| | | | |
|---|---|---|---|
| 11 | RADIO CASETTE RECORDER | 3,261 | PIECES |
| 12 | AUDIO CASSETTES | 41,807 | PIECES |
| 13 | VIDEO CASSETTES | 7,505 | PIECES |
| 14 | CAMERAS | 86,186 | PIECES |
| 15 | TELEPHONE CARDS | 143,393 | PIECES |
| 16 | GOLF CLUBS | 620 | PIECES |
| 17 | HANDBAGS | 6,611 | PIECES |
| 18 | PASHMINA/SHAWL | 6,310 | PIECES |
| 19 | CAVIAR | 2 | TONNES |
| 20 | NUTS | 284.6 | TONNES |
| 21 | CADBURY | 44 | TONNES |
| 22 | TOBLERONE | 39 | TONNES |
| 23 | KITKAT | 58 | TONNES |
| 24 | MARS | 16 | TONNES |
| 25 | QUALITY STREET | 30 | TONNES |
| 26 | SMARTIES | 9 | TONNES |
| 27 | LINDT | 25 | TONNES |
| 28 | NESTLE | 13.7 | TONNES |
| 29 | TANG | 268 | TONNES |
| 30 | NIDO | 197 | TONNES |

**MILLENNIUM MILLIONAIRE**

- For each Millennium Millionaire Series, 5000 tickets are sold at Dhs 1,000 (US$ 278) each and with no restrictions on the number of tickets that each passenger purchases.
- The prize for each series is US$ 1,000,000.

- Tickets are available from the following outlets:
  - DDF Finest Surprise counters at Departures, Arrivals & Terminal 2.
  - At most sales counters throughout the Dubai Duty Free shop floor.
  - The Newsagent shops in new concourse
  - Arrivals Shop.
  - Online from www.dubaidutyfree.com
- The ticket itself is in the form and size of a plastic credit card with every purchaser receiving the card as their proof of purchase after completing the ticket form. You will be required to produce this card to collect your prize (US$ 1,000,000).
- Cards are limited to 5,000 for each draw.
- Your card is valid for the series number shown on the card and is not transferable. The cash prize will be paid only to the person named on the ticket form, on production of the card and original passport for identification.
- The names of the winners are announced in the local & regional press. Draw dates and names of the winners are also posted on this website. In addition, all participants in a draw are notified by mail of the winning number.
- Dubai Duty Free reserves the right to refuse sale of the cards or cancel the draw and refund all monies.
- The purchaser is required to fill in all their particulars including passport number, nationality and receives as proof of entry into the Millennium Millionaire Draw, the plastic card with coinciding number as printed on the ticket form.
- Each draw is held under the supervision of the Management of Dubai Duty Free.

**Finest Surprise draw**

- Every ticket holder will be kept informed about the drawn date and winning ticket number. This shall also be posted on the web.
- Dubai Duty Free will hand over the car personally to the winner upon furnishing the original ticket proof of purchase and a photocopy of the passport.
- Dubai Duty free will ship the car to the winners country of residence/nearest seaport free of charge , however all local taxes, and custom duties will be the payable by the winner.
- Ticket sales are limited to 1000 per car.
- The car will be stored in the Dubai Duty Free warehouse for a limited period (2 weeks) after the presentation.
- All Dubai Duty Free raffle cars are GCC Specifications.

## CONTACTS

**Customer Support**

E-mail: customerservice@ddf.co.ae
Tel : (971-4)2062453
FAX: (971-4)2244164
Toll Free : 8004443 (UAE)
**Contact Persons**
Emelita Sanchez, Ruby Ballon, Aloha Alfaro,
Edna Credo, Neil Daniel, Gwen Marie Jamili,
Selvyno Fernandez, Joan Suyao
**Marketing Department**

E-mail: marketing@ddf.co.ae
Fax: (971-4) 2244455
**You can correspond with us at:**
Dubai Duty Free
P.O. Box 831
Dubai
United Arab Emirates
Tel : (971-4) 2066444
Fax: (971-4) 2244036

## MAJOR OIL COMPANIES

### GROUP INTRODUCTION

The ADNOC Group of companies consists of three main oil and gas operating companies, five support companies providing services to the oil and gas industry, three joint ventures to fully utilize the produced gas, two maritime transport companies for crude oil, refined product and LNG and one refined product distribution company.

In the field of Exploration and Production of Oil and Gas, Abu Dhabi Company for Onshore Oil Operations (ADCO), the largest crude oil producer in the southern Arabian Gulf, undertakes exploration, drilling, production and export activities in Abu Dhabi's onshore areas, and the shallow coastal waters.

The Company operates on behalf of ADNOC and six industry shareholders and produces oil mainly from five fields:

**ASAB**
**BAB**
**BU HASA**
**SAHIL**
**SHAH**

Abu Dhabi Marine Operating Company (ADMA-OPCO), operates the exploration, development and production activities of oil and gas in Abu Dhabi's offshore concession area. Many fields and reservoirs were discovered by ADMA-OPCO in its concession but oil and gas production comes only from two fields:

**Umm Sheif**
**Zakum**

The output of oil and gas from these fields is transported to the company's center of operations on Das Island for processing, storage and export via the Island's Terminal.

Zakum Development Company (ZADCO), was established in 1977 to develop and operate the Upper Zakum field, one of the largest fields in the world, on behalf of ADNOC and Japan Oil Development Company (JODCO). The development of the Upper Zakum reservoirs is considered to be one of the major technical achievements in Abu Dhabi. Besides Upper Zakum, the company currently operates Umm Al Dalkh, Satah and Arzanah fields.

In the field of Exploration and Production Services, Abu Dhabi Drilling Chemicals and Products Ltd. (ADDCAP), now a fully owned subsidiary of ADNOC, has set up a new base for its activities at Mussafah Industrial area and is now operating totally from there. The drilling chemicals are now produced at their newly constructed grinding plant at Mussafah using the latest technologies.

National Drilling Company (NDC), a leading drilling company with over 24 years of accumulated experience and one of the largest drilling contractors in the Middle East, has successfully carried out all drilling operations requirements and played an important role in the discovery of oil and gas in Abu Dhabi.

Meanwhile, the National Petroleum Construction Company (NPCC), a joint company owned by ADNOC which holds 70% interest, and the Consolidated Contractors Group (S.A.L), which holds the remaining 30%, NPCC offer complete services as a MAJOR EPC International Contractor for the offshore and onshore Oil & Gas production industry.

And for the Abu Dhabi Petroleum Ports Operating Company (ADPPOC), it was incorporated in 1997 to operate in all the petroleum and industrial ports in Abu Dhabi, providing maintenance operations, safety and diving services.

On the other hand, National Marine Services (NMS) is the leading Offshore Support Service Company in Abu Dhabi. The company currently owns 25 offshore vessels of various categories including supply boats, anchor handling and rig moving tugs, safety standby, maintenance vessels and crew boats.

In the field of Natural Gas Processing, Abu Dhabi Gas Liquefaction Company Limited (ADGAS), was established in 1973 to turn gas, extracted from Abu Dhabi's offshore fields crude oil, into a new source of national income and a major source of marketable energy. The fact that gases are no longer used as fuel for oil field flares hs impacted positively on the environment.

Meanwhile, Abu Dhabi Gas Industries Limited (GASCO) is one of the largest gas processing companies in the world, and one of the biggest industrial projects in the UAE. It handles the associated gas from ADCO's onshore crude production and processes it through three NGL extraction plants at Bu Hasa, Bab and Asab.

In the field of Chemicals and Petrochemical Services, Ruwais Fertilizer (FERTIL) was established in 1980 as a joint venture between ADNOC and TOTAL for the construction and operation of a plant to produce fertilizers and market them locally and internationally.

And in the field of Refined Products Distribution, Abu Dhabi National Oil Company for Distribution (ADNOC-FOD) is specialized in marketing and distribution of petroleum products in the United Arab Emirates. ADNOC-FOD operates a vast network of filling stations covering all areas of the UAE.

Finally in the field of Maritime Transportation, National Gas Shipping Company Limited (NGSCO) provides shipping services to ADGAS and manages a fleet of carriers specially designed for LNG/LPG transportation.

Another company, Abu Dhabi National Tanker Company (ADNATCO), provides logistical support and advice on shipping to ADNOC and its Group of Companies.

| | |
|---|---|
| Exploration & Production of Oil & Gas | ADCO<br>ADMA-OPCO<br>ZADCO |
| Exploration & Production Services | NPCC<br>ADDCAP<br>ADPPOC<br>NDC<br>NMS |
| Natural Gas Processing | GASCO<br>ADGAS |
| Chemicals & Petrochemicals | FERTIL |
| Refined Products Distribution | ADNOC-FOD |
| Maritime Transportation | ADNATCO<br>NGSCO |

| | |
|---|---|
| ADCO | Onshore exploration, development and production on behalf of the partners.<br><br>Address: P.o. Box 2700, Abu Dhabi, UAE.<br>Tel. 6040000, Tlx 22222 EM, Fax:669785 |
| ADMA | Offshore exploration, development and production on behalf of the partners.<br><br>Address: P.O. Box 303, Abu Dhabi, UAE.<br>Tel. 6060000, Tlx 22284 EM, Fax720099 |
| ZADCO | Development and production from the Upper Zakum field; also operates Umm Al-Dalkh, Satah and Arzanah fields on behalf of the partners.<br><br>Address: P.O. Box 46808, Abu Dhabi, UAE<br>Tel 6050000, Tlx 22948 EM, Fax 669448 |
| NPCC | Construction and fabrication facilities for the oil industry.<br><br>Address: P.O. Box 2058, Abu Dhabi, UAE.<br>Tel 549000, Tlx 22638 EM, Fax 54911 |
| ADDCAP | Production of drilling chemicals and provision of marine base and services.<br><br>Address: P.O. Box 46121, Abu Dhabi, UAE<br>Tel 6029000, Tlx 23267 EM, Fax 6029010 |
| NDC | Provision of onshore and offshore drilling operations<br><br>Address: P.O. Box 4017, Abu Dhabi, UAE<br>Tel 316600, Tlx 22553 EM, Fax 317045 |

| | |
|---|---|
| ADPPOC | Operating Ruwais, Jabel Dhanna and other oil or industrial ports.<br><br>Address: P.O. box 61, Abu Dhabi, UAE<br>Tel 777300, Tlx 22209 EM, Fax 766903 |
| NMS | Owning and operating, chartering or leasing specialized vessels serving the oil industry.<br><br>Address: P.O. Box 7202, Abu Dhabi, UAE<br>Tel 339800, Tlx 22965 EM, Fax 211239 |
| GASCO | Operation of onshore gas gathering and processing plants<br><br>Address: P.O. Box 665, Abu Dhabi, UAE<br>Tel 6041111, Tlx 22365 EM, Fax 6047414 |
| ADGAS | Operation of Das Island gas liquefaction plants<br><br>Address: P.O. Box 3500, Abu Dhabi, UAE<br>Tel 6061111, Tlx 22698 EM, Fax 6065456 |
| FERTIL | Operation of ammonia and urea plant in Ruwais and marketing its products.<br><br>Address: P.O. box 2288, Abu Dhabi, UAE<br>Tel 6021111, Tlx 24205 EM, Fax 728084 |
| ADNOC-FOD | Storage, transporation and domestic distribution of refined products<br><br>Address: P.O. Box 4188, Abu Dhabi, UAE<br>Tel 771300, Tlx 22358 EM, Fax 722322 |
| ADNATCO | Transporting crude oil and refined products<br><br>Address: P.O. Box 2977, Abu Dhabi, UAE<br>Tel 331800, Tlx 22747 EM, Fax 322940 |
| NGSCO | Shipping liquefied gas products from Das Island<br><br>Address: P.O. Box 2600, Abu Dhabi, UAE<br>Tel 311400, Tlx 24457 EM, Fax 328303 |

## AGRICULTURE AND FISHERIES

- Greening & Desert
- Distribution of farms
- Date Palm Cultivation
- Offset tissue culture laboratory
- Chelsea Flower Show
- Horticulture Exports
- Groundwater Project
- Dams in the UAE
- Fishing
- Artificial Reefs
- Fish Farming
- Ras al-Khaimah

***for more information, visit Ministry of Agriculture and Fisheries***

**Greening & Desert**

The UAE has made major strides in developing its agricultural sector and, due to the determination of Sheikh Zayed, the desert has undergone a remarkable transformation. Concerned authorities like Abu Dhabi Municipality and Town Planning Department

and Sheikh Zayed's Private Department have played significant roles in spreading forestation and establishing farms to increase agricultural production, thereby meeting local market requirements as well as providing surplus production for export abroad. Under instructions from Sheikh Zayed, Abu Dhabi Municipality has been extremely busy beautifying the emirate's cities. The municipality has also planted extensive green belts in order to protect these cities from the devastating effects of sandstorms. Examination of the vast areas which the municipality has cultivated under beautification projects, totaling 92,500 hectares in 1998, proves that the difficulties posed by the country's harsh climate have been successfully over come by the municipality's use of advanced technology. To date a total of 39 public parks, occupying an area of 3.7 million square meters, have been established in the emirate. Some of these leisure and entertainment parks are reserved especially for women and children, such as Al Khalidiya Park, Al Mushrif Park and the Women's Beach, all in Abu Dhabi city. The municipality has also planted approximately 2,450 hectares of greenery and flowers on the verges of internal roads and highways. Other projects include Baynunah Forest, which covers an area of 20,000 hectares. In Abu Dhabi, the municipality has also planted 2,500 hectares with palm trees, as at Ras al-Akhdar and Al Ghaf Park. Special nurseries set up by the municipality produce a total of 1.5 million tree saplings, 20 million flowers and 30,000 plants each year, supplying the raw material for the beautification process.

## DISTRIBUTION OF FARMS

In accordance with Abu Dhabi's long-term urban development plan, scheduled for implementation by the year 2010, the Ruler's Representative in the Western Region and Chairman of the Abu Dhabi Municipality and Town Planning Department, Sheik h Mohammed bin Butti Al Hamed, has instructed that farms in Liwa, Ghiyathi and Bida Zayed be established for distribution to UAE nationals. Around 3,000 farms are also being created around Al Ajban where Abu Dhabi Municipality has leveled a 30-kilometre desert area to transform it into cultivable land. These farms will also be distributed to nationals.

With the completion of the project, productive farms in Abu Dhabi and adjoining areas should increase to around 15,000. Meanwhile over the past six years the number of farms has grown 12-fold from approximately 1,000 to more than 12,000. The total number of farms distributed among nationals so far totals 12,021 covering an area of 27,704 hectares.

The municipality also provides farmers with financial assistance to purchase equipment, fertilizer and seeds. As a result of the programme the country's once small-scale traditional farming has been complemented by investment that has seen more than 100,000 hectares of land being brought under the plough.

### DATE PALM CULTIVATION

No. of date palm trees in 1986 was 4.6 million while in 1997 was 35 million
Date production in 1986 was 59,718 (tones) while in 1997 was 388,190 tones As the above figures indicate, Sheikh Zayed's initiatives in date palm cultivation have led to a qualitative and quantitative breakthrough,

The production of rapidly growing trees and the introduction of effective control to combat palm diseases. The UAE has become a world leader in the production of palm tissues having established a tissue culture laboratory at the Emirates University for this purpose. The Ministry of Agriculture and Fisheries plans to develop all aspects of palm cultivation and to improve productivity through the creation of experimental farms, provision of guidance services and equipment, generation of high quality varieties, studies of palm populations and establishment of date processing plants.

### OFFSET TISSUE CULTURE LABORATORY

One new project which will assist in achieving the Ministry's goal is the Dh 5.75 million bio-technology joint venture, Al Wathba Marionnet LLC, which has been set up by France's Giat Industries as part of its military offset obligations. The project, the first of its kind in the UAE, will cultivate date palm seedlings using advanced tissue culture techniques. The cloning of date palms began in January 1999 in the Al Ain laboratory and the process is expected to take about three years before the high-yield trees bear quality dates. The new company, which will produce an initial 200,000 date palms annually 50 per cent of which will be exported, will assist in providing the UAE and the Arab world with disease-free, well rooted plants of selected varieties.

## STATES ECONOMIC PERFORMANCE AND OPPORTUNITIES

World oil prices fluctuations in1997havehad a significantimpact on the GCC economies.Prices sharp drop of 6.0per cent below 1996 levelwas a direct stimulus to the GDP reduction in the GCCStates from 5.9 per cent in 1996 to about 3.0per cent in 1997. The GCCstates GDP'sgrowth rate is projected to drop in 1998 compared with 1997.This could basically beattributed to the fact that these countries rely heavily on oil.

As it was projected that average oil price per barrel is to swing between 12.0 to 15.5 US dollars.In 1997, it was further assumed that the GCCstates oil revenues would drop below 1997 levels, and such drop would be sharp in certain GCC states.Accordingly oil sector'sgrowth is anticipated to decline in 1998 , as these sectors contribute the highest GDP share in theGCC states.Governments would be forced at the same time to adopt austerity economic measures to slash spending, due to fall in oil revenues which would have a negative economic impact on these countries.

With respect to structural adjustments and economic major reformProgrammes been braced to improve internal and outside imbalances, certain GCCstates in 1997 have dropped the policyaiming to diversify and broaden tax revenues base, and reduce services and commodities subsidiesoffered by Governments.Gradual implementation of this policy should be maintained by GCC states to avoid sharp and sudden slumps in their revenues whenever there is a major decline in their oil revenues.

Inflation rates inmost GCC states in 1997 were less than most advanced and developing countries worldwide.Inflation rate recorded in most GCC states was less than3.0 per cent.As all

GCC states currencies are tied to the US dollar, inflation has increased with the rise in the value of the Dollar against the Yen and most European and South EasternCurrencies.GCC commodity import Prices were reduced as a result of this, which helped to contain inflation rates at a low level.

Estimates indicate that GCC total exports were reduced by 4.8 percent in 1997 as a result of oil prices decline by 8.0per cent.It is projected that total exports would drop by 14.4 per cent in 1998 less than 1997 level.GCC imports have increased in 1997 by 3.5 per cent, and it is estimated to make a slight increase of 1.3 per cent in 1998 compared with 1997.

Estimates also indicate that the trade balance which has recorded US 49.8 billion surplus in 1996and increased by 34.2 per cent over its 1995 level, has shown a surplus too in 1997, despite its 16.9 per cent decline.It is estimated that in 1998 trade balance surplus would drop by 46.4 per cent- due to projected decline in oil exports revenues.

It is worth to refer to the staunch efforts exerted by GCC states regarding custom tariffs unification issue, which was recommended by member states.This issue was the basis of all inter-trade negotiations carried out in between GCC states in 1997.In addition to this, the European Union has decided to revive an old trade agreement with GCC states, whereas the only condition stipulated for signing this new trade agreement is to unify custom tariffs.

## DUBAI PORT AUTHORITY

**D**ubai Ports Authority (DPA) is firmly committed to providing Quality Service to its customers. This is underlined by the ISO 9002 certification that we have achieved in our container terminal and general cargo operations. Our focus on continuous improvement has enabled us to maintain our position as the best port in the Middle East and a leading port in the world.

**D**ubai has become a major international center of trade in an evolving region. Dubai's infrastructure development plan spells out the government's commitment to trade and industry.

**A**lways the entrepot, Dubai is the preferred regional headquarters for numerous multinational organizations, and home to a thriving commercial community. Some 50% of container cargo passing through Port Rashid and Jebel Ali terminals is now destined for Dubai whilst the rest is transshipped regionally. While we work to maintain our hub position, we will also increase our focus on the home market for which valuable import and export cargo can be generated. Our quality orientated, competitive service will continue to foster the import, export and transshipment possibilities through DPA, and in so doing, enhance Dubai's position as the center of trade in the region.

**W**hile striving to anticipate our customers' requirements we continue to invest in state-of-the-art cargo handling technology and information management systems, together with skilled personnel to run them. By continuing to develop in advance of need, we will be able to maintain our hub position and the distinction of being the most modern and technologically advanced port in the region.

**Sultan Ahmed bin Sulayem**
Chairman of Jebel Ali Free Zone Authority &
Managing Director of Dubai Ports Authority

## ADVANTAGES

The emirate of Dubai is renowned for its pro-business culture and relative absence of red tape. The buoyant local economy offers increasing business opportunities.

Dubai's strategic location at the crossroads between East and West has made it the leading hub between Europe and the Far East . The city is the acknowledged gateway to a market of an estimated 1.5 billion people in the Gulf countries, Arab world, and surrounding region.

Due to Dubai's traditional trade links with its neighbours, shippers are keen to capitalize on Dubai's proven distribution capabilities.

### GROWING LOCAL MARKET

Exports and re-exports are on the rise from Dubai, and the Jebel Ali Free Zone in particular. DPA has frequently demonstrated its ability to adapt quickly to changing trade patterns by picking up considerable business such as in the re-export of cotton and base metals from CIS countries and the sub-continent.

### PORT PERFORMANCE

DPA is one of the leading transshipment centers in the world, serving more than 125 shipping lines. It is ranked $10^{th}$ among the container ports of the world. In 1997, it handled 2.6 million TEU's, an increase of sixteen per cent on the previous year's achievement. The two terminals of Jebel Ali and port Rashid handled 10,243 vessels including 4,600 container vessels increasing seven per cent over 1996. The total tonnage handled rose to 36.0 million tonnes, up 18 percent over 1996.

### ONE STEP AHEAD

Dubai Ports Authority takes pride in remaining one step ahead of its competition and in step with its customers. Strategic planners in all departments maintain close watch on developments within the industry, and are quick to forecast trends. For this reason, the port has invested in the most technically advanced cranes in the world. As ship builders re-think design, DPA plans for the possibility of handling the larger vessels required to cope with ever- increasing international container traffic. Equipment available with DPA

### EFFICIENCIES OF EDI

The advantages of Electronic Data Interchange (EDI) are recognized globally and DPA has pioneered an electronic manifest system. Working with the shipping community and related government departments, DPA has developed its own system as part of an ambitious plan for paperless cargo clearance in the near future.

### AN AWARD WINNING PLAYER

For container customers, the key consideration is turn-around time and efficiency. DPA leads the region in these respects and was named best seaport in the Middle East for the fourth consecutive year in 1997, and best container terminal operator in the region.

DPA pursues quality in all of its operating areas. It is one of the few ports in the world, with ISO 9002 accreditation for its container and general cargo business. Achieving ISO standards commits the organization to a continual program of improvement in its processes. In June 1998, the Jebel Ali Free Zone Authority, which works in synergy with DPA, achieved ISO 9002 certification.

The service benefit: DPA's customer-driven service is second to none in the Middle East, and the port prides itself in finding creative solutions to the unique requirements of its business partners. DPA Sales and Customer Services departments maintain a close link with all customers to ensure that individual requirements are known and responded to.

DPA maintains an open door policy that encourages feedback and consultation. A business-like attitude permeates the organization from the chief executive to the rank and file. DPA is different, and the difference is service.

## SERVICES

Customer-driven service ensures that Dubai Ports Authority (DPA) consistently listens to its customers' needs and responds by providing superior handling and storage capabilities. These range from cold and cool store facilities in Jebel Ali to a purpose-built berth for import of bulk aluminum oxide and expanded tanker jetties to handle the requirement for petroleum and petrochemical products. A built-in over capacity in container handling equipment gives DPA the flexibility to respond quickly to customers' requests, and to generate additional business

A sophisticated control system for the cargo-handling equipment is also planned. This will increase efficiency of movement about the port, by allocating ample units as required on any given assignment.

Additionally, DPA's efficient commercial trucking department provides cost-effective, reliable transportation anywhere within the United Arab Emirates. This value-added service is available to customers upon request.

## STORAGE

The Container Freight Station (CFS) at Port Rashid terminal provides covered space in seven warehouses with a combined capacity of 52,000 square meters and a total 66,000 square meters of uncovered area. In addition, the CFS offers a 24-hour service to receive and deliver both import & export cargo as per customer requirements. Jebel Ali terminal's CFS has two warehouses and one Dutch barn with a combined capacity of 27,140 square meters of covered space and a total of 50,000 square meters of uncovered area dedicated to this cargo type.

These facilities, together with DPA'S advanced cargo handling equipment, provide an efficient service to LCL consolidators. Unstuffing and cross-stuffing for onward carriage is an attractive, and growing, value-added service to consignees and shippers.

## CONTAINER REPAIR

Each terminal has a well-equipped container repair yard where maintenance is carried out by Emirates Container Repair and Middle East Container Repair Company to IICL standards and approved by Bureau Veritas and the American bureau of Shipping. Both yards can take all types of containers in their paint and blast shop facilities for hot and cold works. Steam cleaning and chemical washing are also available. Combined, the yards have a storage capacity for more than 2,000 units and all container owners and operators have access to the facilities.

## TANKER FACILITIES

Four tanker berth are available at Jebel Ali which can accommodate ships up to 120,000 tons deadweight, with overall length of 275m and draft of 15m. Privately-operated storage tanks are also available for rent by companies who wish to hold stocks of oil for delivery elsewhere in the world.

Within Port Rashid terminal, a jetty operated by Shell can handle tankers of up to 40,000 tonnes, as well as bunker barges. It is protected by the latest safety equipment including plastic-faced

fenders. remote-control fire monitors and high-tech telescopic access ladders.
Bunkering is provided through private vendors at both terminals.

**Dedicated Aluminum Berth**

One of the world's largest aluminum smelters is operated at Jebel Ali by Dubai Aluminum (Dubal). The company imports raw material via its own dedicated berth at the Jebel Ali terminal and exports high-quality ingots to major markets around the world. A US$500 - million expansion which doubled the plant's capacity was inaugurated in early 1997 and further expansion shall take effect in 1999.

## ACTIVITIES AND SERVICES

| TEUs | | | | |
|---|---|---|---|---|
| 2000 | Inbound | Outbound | Transhipment | Total |
| Jan | 66,903 | 54,625 | 106,783 | 228,311 |
| Feb | 67,636 | 55,867 | 116,437 | 239,940 |
| Mar | 70,636 | 56,066 | 118,951 | 245,653 |
| Apr | 70,380 | 59,169 | 113,904 | 243,453 |
| Total | 275,555 | 225,727 | 456,075 | 957,357 |

| Container, General Cargo, Petroleum Tonnage | | | | | | | | |
|---|---|---|---|---|---|---|---|---|
| | | General Cargo Tonnage | | | Petroleum Tonnage | | | |
| 2000 | Container Tonnage | Bulk Cargo | General Cargo | Cold Storage | Oil | Gas | Other Products | Total Tonnage |
| Jan | 1,806,633 | 292,043 | 272,317 | 1,567 | 1,015,082 | 10,465 | 13,308 | 3,411,415 |
| Feb | 1,895,549 | 364,466 | 277,613 | 251 | 1,078,710 | 9,037 | 11,113 | 3,636,739 |
| Mar | 2,020,152 | 426,592 | 223,411 | 708 | 1,137,993 | 23,991 | 9,390 | 3,842,237 |
| Apr | 1,944,368 | 395,080 | 250,349 | 801 | 1,059,761 | 27,410 | 11,003 | 3,688,772 |
| Total | 7,666,702 | 1,478,181 | 1,023,690 | 3,327 | 4,291,546 | 70,903 | 44,814 | 14,579,163 |

| Vessel Calls | | | | | | | |
|---|---|---|---|---|---|---|---|
| 2000 | Container Vessels | Ro - Ro Vessels | Gen. Cargo Vessels | Tankers | Supply Vessels | Others | Total Vessels |
| Jan | 390 | 26 | 70 | 68 | 124 | 174 | 852 |
| Feb | 400 | 23 | 71 | 66 | 164 | 169 | 893 |
| Mar | 414 | 34 | 66 | 73 | 152 | 185 | 924 |
| Apr | 405 | 28 | 70 | 66 | 124 | 183 | 876 |
| Total | 1,609 | 111 | 277 | 273 | 564 | 711 | 3,545 |

# FUJAIRAH

Emirate of Fujairah, one of the seven emirates forming the United Arab Emirates, witnessed a rapid rate of economic and social development and tourism activities under the wise guidance of **H.H.Sheikh Hamad Bin Mohammad Al Sharqi**, Supreme Council member and ruler of Fujairah.

....After the emirate had completed its infrastructure, it set out to implement its ambitious development plan to achieve the ideal exploitation of its resources and to extend the base of industrial, commercial, and agricultural production.

....The historical importance of Fujairah goes back to the period that preceded birth of the christ (peace be upon him), it was known in the old ages as land of the sea giants, and was the first home for immigrants who came from the southeast of Arabian Peninsula and who were later known as the Phoenicians. Some of those immigrants came from Yemen after the collapse of Ma'areb Dam, and of whom the Sharqis tribes descend.

....Emirate of Fujairah lies on the eastern part of the arabian peninsula, bordered from the east by Omani coast, from the west by emirates of Ras Al Khaimah and Sharjah, from the south Kalba and it faces Omani coast. Fujairah extends 70 km. on the Gulf of Oman from Ousla village to Dibba to the north.

..Total aria of Fujairah is 1450 sq.km., made of varying heights mountains and hills, plains, cast, oasis and desert areas.

....The climate in Fujairah is semi tropical with varying temperature, rare rain, high level of evaporation and varying degree of humidity.

....Last census showed that total population of Fujairah was 100,000. Main cities are Al Fujairah, Dibba, Mirbeh, Al Bidiah and Masafi.

## MAJOR CITIES

### DIBBA

Dibba Al Fujairah, considered of the ancient historical civilization areas in the UAE, lies in the far northern frontiers of Fujairah where the coastal plains are rich and fresh water is plenty. Dibba is known of its many ancient castles, fortresses and remains. History of Dibba goes back to the eras of ancient civilizations whenit was an important commercial centre during the phoenician era.

### AL BIDYA

Al Bidya city considered as an important human residence and settlement area all through the old history. Located 38 km north of Fujairah City and 25 km of Dibba City.
Al Bidya mosque is one of the most important archeological sites in Fujairah is surrounded by Al Bidya castle.

## MASAFI

Masafi is located in the Hajar mountains on the crossroads of the highways to Fujairah and Dibba. It is well known for its freshwater springs, which provide water for extensive orchards.

An extensive 'Friday market' has developed near Masafi, with articles as diverse as vegetables, fruits and garden plants, woolen carpets, candy floss and roasted corn-on-the-cob, toys and items of pottery. Most of the fruit is imported, but some of the vegetables are grown locally. The pottery is based on local designs

## QIDFA

Eighteen kilometres north of Fujairah, along the coast road, lies the village of Qidfa. This is where an Iron Age (500 BC) horseshoe-shaped communal tomb was found during bulldozing work. It was excavated in 1986-1987 and yielded an important hoard of bronze weapons and bowls, jewellery, pottery and soapstone boxes and bowls. The collection is on display in Fujairah museum.

## AL BITHNA

Driving from Fujairah into the mountains at the back of the city, the first village on the right set on the plain above Wadi Ham is Bithna. It is the site of a megalithic T-shaped tomb from the second millennium BC, Wadi Suq period, which was reused in the late first millennium BC; and of an impressive Late Islamic fort, commanding a strategic passage to the Wadi Ham, one of the main routes from east to west to the UAE's Hajar mountains.

## HISTORY

...For the historian, Fujairah is a hidden treasure waiting to be discovered The old fort in Fujairah's historic town which is approximately 300 years old and the many small wind towers still standing in neighbouring villages as proud reminders of the town's recent past. However, archaeological ations have shown that man's presence in the region actually dates back to the Iron Age. In fact, some of -the most important archaeological finds in the Arabian Gulf have been made in the area.

### Fujairah Fort

Situated just two km away from the main town. It is a strategically located mud brick structure. A huge castle built in 1670 A.D. which consists of 3 major parts and several halls and towers surrounded by the old Fujairah.
The fort was fully renovated in year 2000.

### Al Bidya Mosque

Dates back 400 years and displays a unique feat of engineering for the time. All four domes are supported by one central pillar and internal decoration combines stone carvings with special

shelves to house the Holy Quran.
Al Bidya Mosque is located close to Al Bidya village about 30 km North of Fujairah.

**Al Heil Castle**

At Al Heil village, 8km south-west of Fujairah city.
One of the most famous castles in the Emirate of Fujairah, it used to be headquarters for the ruler and had been used for patrolling, surveillanc and to defend neibouring area.

**AL Bithnah Forte**

Built in 1735 near Al Bithnah Village 13 km west of Fujairah city, it has guarded the strategic route across the Hajar mountains throught Wadi Ham since the 18th Century, and was considered among the most important forts and castles in eastern part of UAE.

**Archeological Sites**

Some of the most important archeological finds in the Arabian Gulf have made in the area, and archeological excavations have shown that man's presence in the region actually dates back to the Iron Age.

## NATURE

Fujairah's unspoiled natural beauty and have all nice faces of rich and beautiful nature: mountains, waterfalls, oases and long beaches and more than 30 large valleys in addition to several smaller ones. It is also the land of water springs, cold and warm.

...**Ain Madhab Park:** A 50 hectare park and resort for families, is a popular park in Fujairah, looks like a green carpet with the grass and many kinds of trees and flowers planted.
...**Ain Al Ghamour:** Over 20 km south of Fujairah, in a mountains area, the spring water temperature reaches 60 centigrade, and it is visited by tourists and cure seekers from diseases like rheumatism, backache and arthritis.

## IMPORTANT INFORMATION AND CONTACTS

**Fujairah International Airport**
Established in 1987, and since it's operation the airposrt played vital role to link Fujairah worldwide and to develop tourism, the airport designed to take it into the next century.

**Road and Transportation**
Fujairah has established modern new highway network which link the Emirate with other sister's Emirates plus excellent internal roads inside the city of Fujairah.

**Communication**
National and International network as well as phone, Fax and other telecommunication services are available. Direct dialling and international calls are possible throught ground satellite station. Mobile phone and fast Internet connection are easily available.

**Banks**
Fujairah has national and international banks offering professional banking services of all kinds.

**Driving License**
Visitors can easily obtain a one-month temporary license by presenting their valid foreign license, International driving license also acceptable for visitors.

**Visas**
Citizens of GCC and Europe nationals can enter UAE and Fujairah without visas. Other nationalities can get a 14 days transit visa or visit visa throught a hotel, tour operators, travel agencies and Emirates & Gulf Airlines

**Working Hours**
From 8.00 to 2.30, Saturday to Wednesday for the public sector, and Saturday to Thursday for the private sector.
Local Time GMT +4 hours

### GOVERNMENT DEPARTMENTS

| | |
|---|---|
| Fujairah Museum<br>Phone: +971 9 2229085<br>Fax....: +971 9 2229539<br>P.O.Box: 1, Fujairah, UAE. | Fujairah International Airport<br>Phone: +971 9 2226222<br>Fax....: +971 9 2224205<br>P.Box: 977, Fujairah, UAE.<br>Email: fiadgm@emirates.net.ae<br>Web Site:fujairah-airport.com |
| | |
| Port of Fujairah<br>Phone: +971 9 2228800<br>Fax....: +971 9 2228811<br>P.Box: 787, Fujairah, UAE.<br>Email:fujport1@emirates.net.ae | Fujairah Free Zone<br>Phone: +971 9 2228000<br>Fax....: +971 9 2228888<br>P.Box: 283, Fujairah, UAE.<br>Email: freezone@emirates.net.ae<br>Web Site: www.fujairahfree.com |
| | |
| Fujairah Exhibition Centre<br>Phone: +971 9 2231212<br>Fax....: +971 9 2231616<br>P.Box: 1550, Fujairah, UAE.<br>Email: fujcci@emirates.net.ae | Fujairah Trade Centre<br>Phone: +971 9 2222661<br>Fax....: +971 9 2226212<br>P.Box: 1433, Fujairah, UAE.<br>Email:ftcfuj@emirates.net.ae<br>Web Site: |
| | |
| Fujairah Municipality<br>Phone: +971 9 2227000<br>Fax....: +971 9 2222231<br>P.Box: 7, Fujairah, UAE. | Dibba Municipality<br>Phone: +971 9 2444233<br>Fax....: +971 9 2444727<br>P.Box: 11462, Dibba, Fujairah, UAE. |
| | |
| General Post Office<br>Phone: +971 9 2222235 | Fujairah Police<br>Phone: +971 9 2224411 |

| | |
|---|---|
| Fax....: +971 9 2229011<br>P.Box: 760, Fujairah, UAE. | Fax....: +971 9 2222213<br>P.Box: 5, Fujairah, UAE. |
| | |
| Naturalisation & Immigration Administration<br>Phone: +971 9 2222727<br>Fax....: +971 9 2226606<br>P.Box: 6, Fujairah, UAE. | Fujairah Hospital<br>Phone: +971 9 2242999<br>Fax....: +971 9 2229077<br>P.Box: 10, Fujairah, UAE. |

### HOTELS AND RESIDENCE

| | | |
|---|---|---|
| Fujairah Hilton<br>Phone: +971 9 2222411<br>Fax....: +971 9 2226541<br>P.O.Box: 231, Fujairah, UAE. | | Al Diar Siji Hotel<br>Phone: +971 92 2232000<br>Fax....: +971 9 22232111<br>P.Box: 1199, Fujairah, UAE. |
| Ritz Plaza Hotel<br>Phone: +971 9 2222202<br>Fax....: +971 9 2222203<br>P.Box: 1919, Fujairah, UAE. | | Fujairah Beach Motel<br>Phone: +971 9 2228111<br>Fax....: +971 9 2228054<br>P.Box: 283, Fujairah, UAE. |
| Sandy Beach Motel<br>Phone: +971 9 2445555<br>Fax....: +971 9 2445200<br>P.Box: 659, Fujairah, UAE. | | Holiday Beach Motel<br>Phone: +971 9 2445540<br>Fax....: +971 9 2445580<br>P.Box: 1433, Fujairah, UAE. |
| | | |
| Summerland Residents<br>P.O.Box 818, Fujairah, UAE.<br>Tel: +971 9 2232922<br>Fax: + 971 9 2231272 | | Oasis Residents<br>P.O.Box 1325, Fujairah, UAE.<br>Tel: +971 9 2232823<br>Fax: + 971 9 2232813 |
| | | |

### TRAVEL AGENCIES

| | | |
|---|---|---|
| Fujairah Aviation Services<br>Phone: +971 9 2226969<br>Fax....: +971 9 2226949<br>P.O.Box: 989, Fujairah, UAE.<br>Email: fastb@emirates.net.ae | | Fujairah Aviation Services International<br>Phone: +971 9 2222596<br>Fax....: +971 9 2222598<br>P.Box: 2100, Fujairah, UAE. |
| | | |
| Travel Link<br>Phone: +971 9 2226116<br>Fax....: +971 9 2226118<br>P.Box: 1618, Fujairah, UAE.<br>Email:trvllink@emirates.net.ae | | DNATA<br>Phone: +971 9 2222985<br>Fax....: +971 9 2222986<br>P.Box: 445, Fujairah, UAE. |
| | | |
| Fujairah National Air Travel Agency<br>Phone: +971 9 2222524<br>Fax....: +971 9 2222555<br>P.Box: 96, Fujairah, UAE. | | Arabian Travel Agency<br>Phone: +971 9 2221561<br>Fax....: +971 9 2221461<br>P.Box: 638, Fujairah, UAE. |

Email: aliali7@emirates.net.ae

| Email: aliali7@emirates.net.ae | | |
|---|---|---|

## BANKS

**UAE Central Bank**
Phone: +971 9 2224040
Fax...: +971 9 2226805
P.O.Box: 768, Fujairah, UAE.

**Fujairah National Bank**
Phone: +971 9 2224513
Fax....: +971 9 2227992
P.Box: 887, Fujairah, UAE.
Email: fuj@emirates.net.ae
Web Site: www.fujairah.com

**AL Mashreq Bank**
Phone: +971 9 2226018
Fax....: +971 9 2226509
P.Box: 270, Fujairah, UAE.

**Dubai Islamic Bank**
Phone: +971 9 2221550
Fax....: +971 9 2229249
P.Box: 1007, Fujairah, UAE.

**Abu Dhabi Commercial Bank**
Phone: +971 9 2223900
Fax....: +971 9 2224900
P.Box: 770, Fujairah, UAE.

**Abu Dhabi National Bank**
Phone: +971 9 2222633
Fax....: +971 9 2227241
P.Box: 79, Fujairah, UAE.

**Middle East British Bank**
Phone: +971 9 2222221
Fax....: +971 9 2221750
P.Box: 21, Fujairah, UAE.
Email:
Web Site: www.britishbank.com

**Al Arabic Bank**
Phone: +971 9 2222050
Fax....: +971 9 2224024
P.Box: 300, Fujairah, UAE.

**Umm Al Quwain Bank**
Phone: +971 9 2232100
Fax....: +971 9 2232220
P.Box: 1444, Fujairah, UAE.

**Union National Bank**
Phone: +971 9 2222747
Fax....: +971 9 2224851
P.Box: 268, Fujairah, UAE.
Email:
Web Site: www.unb.com.ae

**Middle East Bank**
Phone: +971 9 2223423
Fax....: +971 9 2223433
P.Box: 1472, Fujairah, UAE.
Email: sandrad@emirates.net.ae
Web Site: www.emiratesbank.com

## CAR RENTALS

| Future Rent A Car | | Classic Rent A Car |
|---|---|---|
| Phone: +971 9 2224481 | | Phone: +971 9 2222222 |

P.O.Box: 201, Fujairah, UAE. Fax....: +971 9 2222089

| P.O.Box: 201, Fujairah, UAE. | | Fax....: +971 9 2222089<br>P.Box: 481, Fujairah, UAE. |
|---|---|---|
| | | |
| Avis Rent A Car<br>Phone: +971 9 2225384<br>Fax....: +971 9 2225778<br>P.Box: 6891, Fujairah, UAE. | | Autobahn Rent A Car<br>Phone: +971 9 2232226<br>Fax....: +971 9 2232148<br>P.Box: 1254, Fujairah, UAE. |
| | | |
| Al Massa Rent A Car<br>Phone: +971 9 2229982<br>Fax....: +971 9 2241320<br>P.Box: 481, Fujairah, UAE.<br>Email: aliali7@emirates.net.ae | | Dubai Rent A Car<br>Phone: +971 9 2221318<br>Fax....: +971 9 2221325<br>P.Box: 684, Fujairah, UAE. |

## SHARJAH

Sharjah is the third largest of the seven states which form the United Arab Emirates.

Sharjah is the only Emirate to have land on both the Arabian Sea and the Indian Ocean.

The Emirate covers approximately 2,600 square kilometers.

In addition to Sharjah City which is located on the three mile deep subkhat (salt) strip along the coast, the Emirate has three provinces on the Batinah (the East Coast), Hisn Dibba, Khor Fakkan and Kalba, plus the Islands of Abu Mousa and Sir Abu Nu'air.

The Batinah consists of the spectacular, rugged Hajar mountains rising in places to 2,500 feet, intersected by sheer sided wadis, with gravel beds and rich soil.

Beautiful sandy beaches and the clear blue Indian Ocean have made this coast a haven for diving, fishing and relaxing.

The towns of Dibba and Khor Fakkan have grown steadily with modernization gently nudging out the traditional ways, fortunately not completely.

Khor Kalba, the southern most tip of the UAE's Indian Ocean coastline ends in an extensive mangrove marsh which has recently been designated as a Nature Reserve for several endangered species.

The hinterland is a red sand desert with impressive dunes, becoming a gravel plain along the eastern border which runs along the line of the foothills. This fertile, well watered area, rich in gardens and natural shrub is interspersed by innumerable wadis (steep sided dry valleys) running East to West. There are many small villages in this area where people still live in the traditional manner.

An excellent area for 'wadi bashing' but beware of flash floods in times of heavy rainfall!

Al Dhaid, the peaceful falaj based palm oasis in the center of the Emirate is the third largest town and producer of the renowned Al Dhaid strawberries, in addition to many other fruits and vegetables.

## HISTORY

The earliest settlements found in the Emirates date back 7000 years. Research indicates that Sharjah was probably a mangrove swamp and the settlers were fishermen.

The most important archaeological finds so far have been the tombs and settlements of ***Meliha*** and ***Tell Abraq***.

In 1970, an Iraqi team made the first find at ***Meliha,*** located on the plain close to ***Al Dhaid*** and ***Jebel Fayha***. The civilization, sophisticated for its time, dates back 2000 years. The 12 kilometers of land excavated reveals a palace and a small town with a fair sized tomb cemetery. One tomb has an inscription of old Yemeni writing and is the oldest of its kind to be found in the Emirates.

This once fertile plain lay on the caravan route from the East to West coast and was perhaps the gateway for trade and travel with Oman.

***Tell Abraq*** (dating back approximately 4000 years) is on the border of Sharjah and Umm Al Quwain.

This site is by far the largest settlement to be discovered in the region and the only one to have been inhabited continuously for 2000 years. The settlement contained a circular fort of 40 meters in diameter with its walls still preserved reaching a height of 8 meters, plus nearby a collective tomb built of stone.

An 11 cm long bone comb, surprisingly well preserved, with intricate carvings is a very unusual discovery.

The treasures found here help to piece together the lifestyles of these obviously wealthy and aristocratic people.

The exciting discoveries from these sites include amphorae from Greece, iron weapons, glass jars and coins dating back to Alexander the Great.

These and many other fascinating finds are on display in the Archaeological Museum, in Halwan.

The Islamic Museum, also exhibits magnificent archaeological discoveries found in Sharjah Emirate, dating from the Islamic period

The settlement of Sharjah dates back some 6,000 years when it is believed to have been called ***Sarcoa***. The population was small and people relied on trade and sea faring in addition to, farming, hunting, fishing and pearling. Many of the early settlements were based around the 'falaj', a man-made underground water course.

From the 16th century onwards, times were turbulent. In 1507, the Portuguese savagely took command of the East Coast in order to establish control of the spice trade. They built forts at

***Khor Fakkan***, ***Kalba*** and ***Dibba*** and their reign lasted a century till the Dutch gained supremacy for the same reason.

By the 17th century the British arrived and began trading with the ***Qawassim***, the forefathers of today's ruling family. The Europeans favored the Gulf and the Red Sea as principal routes of communication between the Mediterranean and India.

In the 18th century, the ruling Qawassim tribe became the mighty seafarers who created an important maritime power in the southern Gulf. Their strongholds were based in Ras Al Khaimah and Sharjah. ***Sheikh Sultan bin Saqr bin Rashid Al Qassimi***, the patriarch of today's rulers became the Sheikh of Sharjah in 1804 and governed for over 50 years.

By the turn of the century relationships between the ***Qawassim*** and the British deteriorated. As documented in '***The Myth of Arab Piracy in the Gulf***', ***H.H. Dr. Sheikh Sultan bin Mohammed Al Qassimi,*** member of the Supreme Council and Ruler of Sharjah, has shown, that whilst the British blamed all the attacks on their ships on the Qawassim, the latter were often blamed for the other's misconduct.

In 1809, the British mounted their initial land based attack on the ***Qawassim*** in Ras Al Khaimah. By 1820, the first of several Treaties of Peace was signed guaranteeing peace at sea and protection of the British against attack for 150 years. The coast became known as the ***Trucial Oman*** and the Sheikhdoms as the ***Trucial States***. These names remained from 1853 up until the formation of the ***United Arab Emirates*** in 1971.

Whilst the Emirate prospered from trade and pearling, Sharjah had many 'firsts' to its credit during these years of development.

Between 1823 and 1954, Sharjah was the base for Britain's only political representative on the Trucial Coast.

In 1932, a staging post was established by the British Government in Sharjah, for the ***Imperial Airways*** flights en route from England to India. This was the first airport in the Emirates and is still in use today, as a main road, not a runway!

At the time of its establishment, the airport was located two miles across the desert from the town. All provisions for the air traveler were brought by donkey including the *in-flight catering* and water from wells. Traders traveled from the town by camel to do business with the foreigners.

The ***Sheikh's Fort (Al Hisn)*** was located where Sharjah's modern banking center (***Al Boorj Avenue***) now stands and ***Al Arouba Street*** was used for horse racing.

The importance of the airport helped cushion the collapse of the pearl trade in the 1930's. Sharjah suffered another set back thirty years later when the sea trade also declined due to the silting up of the Creek.

Sharjah remained the regional base for the ***British RAF*** and ***Trucial Oman Scouts*** until British presence officially ended in 1971 with independence.

In 1953, the first properly organized school in the UAE was established in Sharjah attracting students throughout the country.

Sharjah joined the United Arab Emirates as a founder member on 2nd December, 1971.

In 1972, ***His Highness Sheikh Sultan bin Mohammed Al Qassimi*** succeeded as the ruler of Sharjah.

The same year, oil was struck in the ***Mubarak*** field, 80 kms offshore, close to the island of ***Abu Mousa***. Two years later production began and at its peak 35,000 barrels were produced per day. A few years later gas condensate was discovered and drilling started in 1990.

This natural wealth combined with the foresight of ***His Highness Dr. Sheikh Sultan bin Mohammed Al Qassimi*** has allowed Sharjah to enjoy prosperity and vitality whilst retaining the charms and traditional values of an Islamic city.

## CULTURE AND TRADITIONS

The official religion of the United Arab Emirates is ***Islam*** and the call to prayer sounds five times a day on almost every street corner. People adhere closely to the tenets of ***Islam*** in all aspects of their lives.

Family ties are very strong and nearly sacred. National dress for men is the ***kandora (dishdasha)***, the long white robe and headdress. Women wear the traditional ***abbaya*** or black cloak.

The most popular national sports include camel racing, falconry and football.

The ***Sharia' Court*** enforces the law of the land which constitutes a mixture of written and verbal laws passed down from generation to generation.

The laws of the government are passed by ***His Highness Dr. Sheikh Sultan bin Mohammed Al Qassimi,*** through the ***Emiri Diwan,*** to the various ministries and to the Municipality (Baladia) for implementation.

You must understand and respect the traditions of the UAE society in order to settle and to do business here. The cultural traditions go back to the days of the desert tribes and the influence brought upon them by migration.

Whilst the UAE is now a modern thriving entity, 50 years ago the towns were small with few facilities - electricity was powered by generator and water supplied by well. The leap into the developed world has taken place over a very short span of time.

An enormous amount of adjustment and flexibility by the national people, have been key factors sustaining this change. All expatriates are welcome but care must be taken to respect and honor the local traditions which are still very much part of life here.

We can only touch on the fascinating culture and customs of the Arab world but it is worth spending time to discover the hospitality and generosity of the Arab people.

## Islam

Some of the basic values of ***Islam*** include honesty, courtesy and hospitality which help govern the society. One fifth of the world's population are ***Muslims***, the followers of ***Islam*** and 19% of these live in the Arab world.

***The Qur'an,*** God's words revealed to ***The Prophet Mohammed (PBUH)*** by the Angel Gabriel in the 7th century AD, recounts the written law, forms of worship and morality.

***The Prophet Mohammed (PBUH)*** was born in ***Makkah*** around 570 AD (571 AD to 632 AD) and grew up appalled by the corruption around him. At the age of forty he received his first revelation from the God and he set out to spread the words of Islam. By 630 AD he returned to Makkah having gained the submission of most of the Arabian Peninsula's people to Islam.

There are ***FIVE PILLARS OF ISLAM*** on which religious duty rests.

The first is the profession of ***Iman*** or ***Faith***. "There is none worthy of worship, except God and Mohammed (PBUH) is the messenger of God." This simple declaration of faith is called the Shahadah, a simple formula that all the faithful pronounce. The significance of this declaration is the belief that the only purpose of life is to serve and obey God, and this is achieved through the teachings and practices of the Last Prophet, Mohammed (PBUH).

***Prayer*** is the second pillar of faith. ***Salah*** is the name of the obligatory prayers that are performed five times a day, and are a direct link between the worshipper and God. There is no hierarchical authority in Islam and there are no priests. Prayers are led by a learned person who knows the Qur'an and is generally chosen by the congregation.

The five daily calls to prayer are, ***Fajr*** (dawn), ***Dhuhr*** (midday), ***Asr*** (mid-afternoon), ***Maghreb*** (early evening) and ***Isha*** (late evening). Prayer times vary according to sunrise and sunset and are listed in the daily newspapers.

An important principle of Islam is that everything belongs to God and that wealth is therefore held by human beings in trust. The work ***Zakat*** means both *purification* and *growth*. Our possessions are purified by setting aside a proportion for those in need and for the society in general. Like the pruning of plants, this cutting back balances and encourages new growth.

Each Muslim calculates his or her own ***Zakat*** individually. This involves the annual payment of a fortieth of one's capital, excluding such items as primary residence, car and professional tools.

The fourth pillar is ***Fasting*** or ***Sawm.*** Every year, in the month of Ramadan, all Muslims fast from dawn until sundown -- abstaining from food and drink. Non-Muslim expatriates and visitors must also respect the fast by not eating, drinking and smoking in public. Working hours throughout the country are reduced during the Holy Month. The end of Ramadan is marked by the sighting of the new moon and the start of the ***Eid Al Fitr*** festival.

The last pillar of Islam is the Pilgrimage, ***Haj***. The pilgrimage to ***Mekkah*** (the *Haj*) is an obligation only for those who are physically and financially able to do so. Nevertheless over two million people go to Makkah each year from overy corner of the globe providing a unique opportunity for those of different nations to meet one another.

The close of the ***Haj*** is marked by a festival, the ***Id Al Adha***, which is celebrated with prayers and the exchange of gifts in Muslim communities everywhere. This and the ***Id Al Fitr***, a festive day celebrating the end of Ramadan, are the two holidays of the Islamic calendar.

## PEOPLE

The population of the Emirate has risen dramatically during the past 10 years from 159,595 in 1981, to an estimated 450,000 in 1995.

The majority of people living in ***Sharjah*** are based in the city, with an estimated population of 350,000 in 1995, followed by the towns of ***Al Dhaid*** (24,716) and ***Khor Fakkan*** (10,888).

The population of the UAE in 1995 was estimated at 2.5 million.

The national population descends from 4 main tribes:

***Qawassim***
The ruling family are descendants of the ***Qawassim's***. Relatively small in numbers yet very powerful and highly regarded.

***Al-Ali***, ***Shewaihain*** and some mixed tribes
These comprise much of the remaining national population of Sharjah town. These tribes were the settled fishermen of former times.

***Bani Qitab***
These people are the principal tribe of the Sharjah sand desert. Originally semi nomadic, they are mainly based in ***Al Dhaid.*** The ***Tunaij*** are a smaller tribe existing in the same area.

***Naqbiyin***
The principal tribe of many found in the mountainous areas, the ***Naqbiyin*** are also the settled fishermen and gardeners of ***Khor Fakkan***, ***Kalba*** and ***Hisn Dibba***.

***DESERT LAW***
Honor is everything to the strong and courageous bedu tribes who live in the desert. Children learn in the majlis (meeting place) the 'wrongs and rights' of life. The law sets the rules between the man and the family and between the tribes. The strength of the law deters crime, many say more effectively than modern civil law.

## TRAVEL

Sharjah has been a major Middle East tourist Destination since 1932!

Tourists intending to visit Sharjah do not have to go far to get what they are interested in. That's why Sharjah was the first emirate to attract tourist groups in 1980. Since then, tourism has developed in leaps and bounds.

The number of tourists entering Sharjah and the UAE in general in 1981 was about 4,000. However Sharjah has developed and so have its tourist attractions. Today the number of tourists visiting the emirate has reached 250,000.

Since 1997 Sharjah and Tourism Development Authority has been working to develop and promote tourism in Sharjah. This has been possible following the mobilization of all available facilities and services, be it airlines, travel agents and other authorities concerned.

In addition, Sharjah paid special attention to its recreational facilities like hotels, bazaars, parks, restaurants and the attractions of the Emirate are being spread between the two gulfs in the east and west.

The civility of the people of Sharjah and the high standard of its tourist facilities makes it highly attractive to tourists who appreciate the safety and security of the emirate and its free economy.

## CLIMATE

Sharjah's climate is idyllic from November to April with warm sunny days, cool evenings and low humidity. Daytime temperatures range from 18 to 30 degrees C.

You can expect some rainfall and tropical storms during January, February and March. After heavy rains you will need a good pair of rubber boots to negotiate the streets ! (Rainwear can be purchased in Rolla Square)

From May to September the climate is hot with midday temperatures in July and August reaching in excess of 45 degrees C. Even the nights are warm averaging 25 degrees C.

Humidity is often at 100% so all in all, it's stifling! Most people head to cooler climates during the summer.

## PORTS

Khorfakkan Container Terminal (KCT) in recent years has undergone a continuous rolling program of improvements. The multi-million dollar developments have reinforced its acknowledgment position as the logical container transshipment port for the United Arab Emirates, Upper Arabian Gulf States and the Indian Sub Continent.

The most recent project, completed in May 1999, was its 350 meter quay extension. The ultra modern container terminal now has 1,060 meters of berths, dredged to a depth of 15 meters alongside at MLW. The enlarged turning circle and seaward approaches have also been dredged to 15 meters.

Managers and operator of KCT, Gulftainer Co Ltd, have matched the quay construction program with the introduction of sophisticated container handling equipment. The terminal now boasts eight ship-to-shore gantries including four Panamax, two Post Panamax, two Super Post Panamax cranes. The most recent acquisitions are the largest in the region and capable of handling vessels stowed 18 containers across. Additional Super Post Panamax gantry cranes are now under consideration.

On the landward slide, container stacks in KCT's 300,000sq meters plus storage areas can now accommodate 18,000 TEUs. The fourth original rail mounted yard gantries plus six recently introduces rubber tyred gantries (RTGs) serve them. The new RTGs can handle containers one over five high and seven across plus a roadway. Four more enhanced specification Liebherr RTGs will arrive in the port by the end of the year and the number of reefer points has been increased to 214.

The only natural deepwater port in the Middle East, KCT is located on the east coast of the Emirate of Sharjah, close to the main east-west shipping routes and outside the sensitive Straits of Hormuz. Via a modern dual carriage-way Khorfakkan Container Terminal (KCT) - which now has a potential throughput of over 1.5 million TEUs annually - is just three hours form the dynamic commercial and industrial markets on the UAEs Gulf Coast.

**KHORFAKKAN CONTAINER TERMINAL**
PO Box 10326, Sharjah, United Arab Emirates
Tel : +971 (9) 2385604/5 Fax : +971 (9) 2387212
E-Mail : gtlkct@emirates.net.ae

## Port Khalid

The first major port of call within the Arabian Gulf is Port Khalid, on the West Coast of Sharjah, one of the most advanced ports in the region. Here the majority of Sharjah's general cargo traffic is being handled, using the latest in-cargo handling machinery. Its 13-berth deep water harbor is capable of managing vessels of varying draughts.

Many UAE-based importers favor Port Khalid to ship their cargo because of its modern storage facilities - amongst which two berthed cold stores that can handle up to 5,000 tons at any given time. It is also popular because of its proximity to the city, the customer-oriented service, the minimum turnaround time and the absence of customs duties on import and export. Over 40 percent of the UAE's manufacturing is in the Emirate of Sharjah and much of it is less than an hour by truck from SCT. Port Khalid also boasts the only passenger terminal facility in UAE.

Situated on Sharjah's Gulf coast and managed and operated by Gulftainer Co Ltd., it is fully equipped to offer immediate berthing, expert merchandised handling of dry and refrigerated containers, documentary back-up, bonded warehousing and groupage facilities. Gulftainer's NCR 3430 Pentium based computer management system provides complete terminal control, statistical reports, ship planning and EIR functions.

The terminal's 586 meter quay has a minimum depth alongside of 11.5 meters at MLW and can accommodate two third generation container ships simultaneously or two roll-on roll-off vessels. Covering over 150,000 sq. meters the terminal provides storage for 8,000 TEUs and there is a 9,300 sq. meter dedicated transit shed and storage area and a 100 tons capacity weighbridge.

Ship work is handled 24 hours a day, seven days a week by two Liebherr T115, 35 tons capacity gantry cranes. The yard handling equipment inventory includes 30 tons capacity Transtainers, 40 tons SWL top loading forklifts plus a full range of smaller forklifts, flatbeds, skeletal trailers, tractors and other ancillary equipment.

In addition to being one of the most efficient and flexible ports in the region, SCT is cost effective. Gulftainer Co Ltd operates to a keenly competitive scale of charges exercising tight cost control and high productivity.

**SHARJAH CONTAINER TERMINAL**
PO Box 225, Sharjah, United Arab Emirates
Tel : +971 (6) 5284205 Fax : +971 (6) 5284513
E-Mail : gtlsct@emirates.net.ae

**GULFTAINER CO. LTD**
PO Box 225, Sharjah, United Arab Emirates
Tel : +971 (6) 5274201 Fax : +971 (6) 5724711
E-Mail : gtluae@emirates.net.ae

## INTERNATIONAL AIRPORT

Sharjah International Airport, its design reflecting traditional Islamic architecture, is one of the most modern in the region, offering state-of-the art facilities. Situated approximately 10 km from Sharjah town, it is linked by a four lane highway with Port Khalid and Port Khorfakkan, as well as the other Emirates.

The airport boasts modern passenger handling facilities and has an annual capacity of over 2.5 million passengers. The terminal is designed for ultimate comfort and convenience and is comparable to the best in the world.

The Airport's main features include jet ways to the aircraft, full passenger services, including air-conditioned waiting lounges, well-equipped duty-free areas, banks, rent-a-car companies, hotel reservations, restaurants, a well-appointed Airport Hotel and excellent transit facilities with a minimum turnaround time. Apart from these, the Airport boasts modernized first class and business class lounges have been modernized, well coordinated ground services and a high standard of aircraft line maintenance.

Cargo handling facilities include four warehouses, each with a 7,400 sq. meters storage space, separate cargo apron for up to 6 aircraft, 24-hour customs clearance, free zone facilities and speedy and efficient document procedures.The airport handles the largest amount of air cargo in the Middle East and is the main air cargo handling center for Lufthansa Cargo in the region.

Warehouses offer the customer security for his shipment and protect it against cargo handling irregularity, including theft. The warehousing facilities may be utilized as a distribution center for the Gulf. For those operating from Sharjah, goods can be stored at the airport without incurring any liability for duties, unless the goods are for internal distribution, Foreign goods may be stored safely for re-export. Furthermore a repair and spare parts service is offered on a worldwide scale.

The airports facilities have recently been upgraded. The runway has been extended of by 300 meters, making the complete distance available for take off of an aircraft 4060 meters and a 3 site runaway visual range system has been installed. There are individual packages available, tailored to meet the needs of different companies by offering flexible facilities, the airport promises the best possible assistance to companies.

**SHARJAH INTERNATIONAL AIRPORT**
PO Box 8, Sharjah, United Arab Emirates
Tel : +971 (6) 5581111 Fax : +971 (6) 5581167
E-Mail : mktg@shj-airport.gov.ae
http://www.shj-airport.gov.ae

## EXHIBITION CENTER

The Expo Center Sharjah, the exhibition organization of the Sharjah Chamber of Commerce and Industry, has the distinction of having pioneered the exhibition medium in the Gulf. As a consequence it is not only widely respected in the Gulf region, but also has a pioneer's experience in organizing shows that are well attended and successful.

Set up in 1977, the Center has been a conduit not only for the success of thousands of companies in the Middle East and all over the world, but also for many successful products and services. It has been hosting exhibitions that reflect the most opportune lines of business activity at any given time. As a result, the Expo Center's exhibition mix consists of some of the most prestigious trade fairs in the region. The profiles of each exhibition are fine-tuned to optimize its specialist status and exhibitor-trade visitor interaction.

Expo's track record for introducing some of the region's truly-international, specialist fairs is impressive. Leather Expo, for instance, has the distinction of being the Middle East's only professional exhibition to enjoy the prestigious ICHSLTA's (International Council of Hides, Skins and Leather Traders' Associations) sponsorship, as well as the support of the Arab Union of Leather Industries. In addition, its Watch & Jewelry Fair enjoys the sponsorship of the World Gold Council, its International Food Fair has the support of the Arab Federation for Food Industries and UAE's Ministry of Agriculture & Fisheries, and TEXPO (the International Fair for Textiles and Accessories), Image Expo, and Kid Expo, to name a few, are the only events of their kind in the region.

**Expo Center's strong points and specialized services include:**

- A databank which is one of the strongest in the region.
- Fixing of appointments with pre-registered trade buyers.
- Mailing of trade invitations to active world buyers.
- Extensive promotional coverage in international trade publications of the industry.
- Coverage in the regional bilingual media and coverage in Expo Center newsletters published during the exhibitions.

Spread over a sprawling 88,000 sq. meters, Expo Center Sharjah is one of the few exhibition venues anywhere to provide such a complete range of facilities under one roof. The exhibition grounds include both 8000 sq. meters of covered exhibition space and an uncovered area stretching over 10000 sq. meters; ideal for static or moving open-air displays.

The centrally air-conditioned covered area incorporates three high-domed pillar-free exhibition halls whose modular structures allow enormous flexibility in terms of layout and exhibition design. High-vaulted artificial ceilings, and a sophisticated user-friendly lighting and sound system complete the effect.

The state-of-the-art Expo auditorium, the setting for numerous up-market shows and designer fashion presentations in the past, can be purpose-adapted to a wide variety of functions.

**Conferencing**
Instead of having one all-purpose exhibition hall, conference facilities at Expo are divided into distinct need-based units.

The tastefully furnished main conference hall can seat up to 450 people and is equipped with ultra- modem sound and lighting and state-of-the-art audiovisual facilities. The main hall has been the venue for some major conferences and seminars held in the region in the past, and houses a full-fledged interpreter's cabin capable of simultaneous interpretation in three languages.

For large-scale international conferences, the Sharjah Business Club's user-friendly facilities enable anything from personalized across-the-table discussions to larger gatherings. In addition to seminars and conferences that habitually accompany trade exhibitions, the Expo Center also leases out its conference facilities to independent groups of companies, particularly those organizing financial or management seminars.

**Expo Direct Mail & Advertising Services**
Expo Center's trump card is Expo Direct, a fully-equipped Direct Marketing Division geared to off exhibitors and trade visitors a complete range of market-support facilities.

The cornerstone of Expo Direct is one of the region's most comprehensive data banks which, additional support, interfaces with the Sharjah Chamber of Commerce and Industry's database. Moreover, networking tie-ups with international agencies provide powerful global connections. The data bank enables the Listings Department to do a first-rate job with correct audience target in enabling it to arrange exhibitor meetings with firms that fall in the category of activity and line of product the exhibitor is interested in.

The Tele Sales Department works in concert with the Listings Department. An outbound tele-sales unit handles research, data base development and follow-up to direct mail, while an inbound tele-sale team is responsible for response handling.

In addition to servicing Expo Center's in-house requirements, Expo Direct can provide exhibitors and trade visitors an entire range of services, ranging from data base rental and sourcing to direct response advertising and mailing.

A special Product Promotion Cell can handle everything from supermarket promotions and sampling surveys to product launches and fashion or road shows. Expo Center also has a full-fledged Advertising & Promotions Division that performs a complete rang of advertising services both for the Center as well as outside clients.

**A full range of back-up services**
Every trade exhibition at Expo Center Sharjah is backed by a full complement of professional support services. The Center is equipped with the latest communication facilities, offering instant access to any part of the world in a matter of seconds by telephone, fax or electronic mail. The modem administrator building houses a smart reception, sophisticated secretarial services and an impressive Research & Development department. A dedicated team of young professionals is always on the alert to attend to a client's every requirement. They do pre-and post exhibition market surveys, follow up on business leads and provide exhibitors and trade visitors with a comprehensive picture of the regional market.

Expo Center has also introduced a catering service capable of handling large-scale banqueting assignments. The Center's Technical Services Department can provide customized stands for exhibitors at a nominal cost.

Expo Center even has its own design department to plan entire exhibitions. Other services include clearing and forwarding and packing, and a huge parking facility that can accommodate up to 1600 cars. Expo Center also helps business visitors with hotel reservations and sightseeing at special group rates. The Center thus serves as a one-stop exhibition venue, with services extending from market surveys, product promotion and trade tie-ups to in-house catering and conferences. Moreover, since the Center's primary objective is to boost trade and investment, it offers these benefits at a fraction of what it would cost at similar exhibition venues.

The exhibitions calendar runs from September to May each year, with an impressive coverage of specialized shows which support and promote trade and industry in the UAE. The exhibition schedule directly from the Expo Centre web site may be viewed

For more information, contact the Expo Centre.

**EXPO CENTRE SHARJAH**
PO Box 3222, Sharjah, United Arab Emirates
Tel : +971 (6) 5551888 Fax : +971 (6) 5552888
Telex : 68306 EXPO EM
Sharjah, United Arab Emirates
E-Mail : expocs@emirates.net.ae
http://www.expo-centre.co.ae/

## WORLD TRADE CENTER

Sharjah is constructing a world trade center at a cost that exceeds a US$ 100 million. The building rises to 304 meters and consists of 52 floors.
Once complete, it will be visible with its tilting shape and beams made of stainless steel and huge columns of concrete and natural stone from miles away.
The main block will house the Sharjah Chamber of Commerce and Industry, Expo Center, conference halls and other commercial representative offices.
The Expo included in the center would have a capacity to host 7,860 people with exhibition area of up to 20,000 sq. m.
The Trade Center would include also a mosque, a sailing club and parking spaces for 2,500 cars.
The Sharjah World Trade Center is to be built in Al-Khan area. In line with the comprehensive development of the region, H.H. Dr. Sheikh Sultan bin Mohammed Al Qassimi has approved the final stages of the Sharjah World Trade Center.

## HOTELS

The following hotels are located in Sharjah. Please click on the hotel name for more information.

| HOTELS IN SHARJAH | FURNISHED APARTMENTS IN SHARJAH |
|---|---|
| | |
| AL BUSTAN HOTEL | SPARK RESIDENCE |
| AL HARMOODI PALACE | AL BUHEIRA RESIDENCE |
| AL SHARQ HOTEL | BASMA RESIDENCE |
| BEACH HOTEL | CROWN SUITES |
| CITY HOTEL | DIPLOMAT RESIDENCE |
| CORAL BEACH HOTEL | INTERHOME |
| FEDERAL HOTEL | JAWHARAT AL GHUWAIR |
| GOLDEN BEACH HOTEL | KUWAIT TOWER |
| GULF BEACH HOTEL | MINA HOUSE |
| HOLIDAY INN RESORT, SHARJAH | THE SUITES |
| HOLIDAY INTERNATIONAL HOTEL | |
| KHALEEJ TOURIST HOTEL | |
| LOU' LOUA BEACH HOTEL | |
| MARBELLA RESORT | t |
| BREEZE MOTEL | HOTELS IN KHOR FAKKAN |
| MONACO HOTEL | t |
| NOVA PARK HOTEL | OCEANIC HOTEL |

| | |
|---|---|
| ROYAL CROWN HOTEL | |
| SHARJAH AIRPORT HOTEL | |
| SHARJAH CARLTON HOTEL | |
| SHARJAH GRAND HOTEL | |
| SHARJAH ROTANA HOTEL | |
| PRIME TOWER | |

| **TRAVEL AGENCIES** | **CONTACT INFORMATION** |
|---|---|
| AL FAISAL TRAVEL AND TOURISM AGENCY<br>Mr. Yassin Diab, General Manager | Harbour Street, Kithab and Alami Building<br>POB 2275, Sharjah, United Arab Emirates<br>Tel : +971 (6) 5527111 Fax : +971 (6) 5527666 |
| ARABIAN TRAVEL AGENCY LIMITED<br>Mr. RGK Nair, General Manager | POB 1477, Sharjah, United Arab Emirates<br>Tel : +971 (6) 5610000 Fax : +971 (6) 5610202<br>Telex : 68959 ATA EM<br>E-Mail : attravel@emirates.net.ae |
| ARABIAN LINK TOURS<br>Mr. Jerome Gomes, Manager | Airport Road, POB 821, Sharjah, United Arab Emirates<br>Tel : +971 (6) 5726666 Fax : +971 (6) 5721440<br>E-Mail : arablink@emirates.net.ae<br>http://www.arabianlink.com |
| AEROFLOT RUSSIAN INTERNATIONAL AIRLINES | POB 22748, Sharjah, United Arab Emirates<br>Tel : +971 (6) 5721991 Fax : +971 (6) 5721993 |
| AL KHALIDIAH TOURISM AND CARGO | POB 12666, Sharjah, United Arab Emirates<br>Tel : +971 (6) 5610557 Fax : +971 (6) 393082 |
| AL WAHADA TRAVEL AND CARGO AGENCY<br>Mr. Hassan Abbas, Senior Sales Officer | POB 6825, Sharjah, United Arab Emirates<br>Tel : +971 (6) 330477 Fax : +971 (6) 337041 |
| AL ZORA TRAVEL AND CARGO AGENCY<br>Mr. A M Beic, General Manager | POB 328, Sharjah, United Arab Emirates<br>Tel : +971 (6) 5725977 Fax : +971 (6) 5723511 |
| BUHAIRA TRAVEL AGENCY | POB 4841, Sharjah, United Arab Emirates<br>Tel : +971 (6) 5614593 Fax : +971 (6) 5623855 |
| CHINA SOUTHERN AIRLINES | POB 6577, Sharjah, United Arab Emirates<br>Tel : +971 (6) 5371029 Fax : +971 (6) 5366339<br>Telex : 68767 CSN 650 EM |
| CORDIAL TOURS AND CARGO | POB 4614, Sharjah, United Arab Emirates<br>Tel : +971 (6) 5725142 Fax : +971 (6) 5724921<br>Telex : 68898 CORDIA EM<br>E-Mail : cordial@emirates.net.ae |

| DNATA<br>Mr. Jose Cyriac, Sales Executive | POB 4033, Sharjah, United Arab Emirates<br>Tel : +971 (6) 5723131Fax : +971 (6) 5723498<br>SITA : SHJAWTG |
|---|---|
| EMIRATES WORLD TRAVEL, TOURISM AND CARGO<br>Mr. Ali Mohammed Sukker, General Manager | POB 1975, Sharjah, United Arab Emirates<br>Tel : +971 (6) 5735666 Fax : +971 (6) 5733371 |
| EMIRATES TRAVEL AND FREIGHT AGENCY | POB 20, Sharjah, United Arab Emirates<br>Tel : +971 (6) 5361000 Fax : +971 (6) 5364595 |
| FLYING STAR LTD. TRAVEL TOURISM & CARGO | POB 20223, Sharjah, United Arab Emirates<br>Tel : +971 (6) 5736677 Fax : +971 (6) 5736868 |
| INDIAN AIRLINES LIMITED | POB 1477, Sharjah, United Arab Emirates<br>Tel : +971 (6) 5616635 Fax : +971 (6) 5372789 |
| INTERCONTINENTAL TRAVEL AND TOURISM | POB 21220, Sharjah, United Arab Emirates<br>Tel : +971 (6) 5363553 Fax : +971 (6) 5371441 |
| ISIS TRAVEL | POB 4152, Sharjah, United Arab Emirates<br>Tel : +971 (6) 5359555 Fax : +971 (6) 5722214 |
| JARNAS CARGO TOURS<br>Mr. Abdul Kareem Doweedar, Director General | POB 12822, Sharjah, United Arab Emirates<br>Tel : +971 (6) 5725212 Fax : +971 (6) 5725943<br>E-Mail : jarnctrz@emirates.net.ae |
| KANOO TRAVEL<br>Mr. Varghese Daniel, Assistant Travel Manager | POB 153, Sharjah, United Arab Emirates<br>Tel : +971 (6) 5616058 Fax : +971 (6) 5618655 |
| KHALID TRAVEL AND TOURISM AGENCY<br>Mr. Amir Singh, General Manager | POB 21766, Sharjah, United Arab Emirates<br>Tel : +971 (6) 5620166 Fax : +971 (6) 5620788<br>E-Mail : emirus@emirates.net.ae |
| KUWAIT AIRWAYS | POB 17, Sharjah, United Arab Emirates<br>Tel : +971 (6) 5378126 Fax : +971 (6) 5366877 |
| MARHABA TOURISM AND TRAVELS | POB 5394, Sharjah, United Arab Emirates<br>Tel : +971 (6)5355320 Fax : +971 (6) 5355300 |
| MIDDLE EAST EXPRESS LIMITED | POB 622, Sharjah, United Arab Emirates<br>Tel : +971 (6) 5726327 Fax : +971 (6) 5723832 |
| NAPOLI TRAVELING, TOURS AND CARGO AGENCY | POB 6699, Sharjah, United Arab Emirates<br>Tel : +971 (6) 5357545 Fax : +971 (6) 5351257 |
| NATA TRAVEL AND TOURISM | POB 20757, Sharjah, United Arab Emirates<br>Tel : +971 (6) 5723434 Fax : +971 (6) 5723003 |
| ORIENT TOURS | POB 26820, Sharjah, United Arab Emirates<br>Tel : +971 (6) 549333 Fax : +971 (6) 5525077 |

| | |
|---|---|
| | E-Mail : otshj@emirates.net.ae |
| ORIENT TRAVEL, HOLIDAYS AND CARGO<br>Mr. Asim Arshad, General Manager | POB 772, Sharjah, United Arab Emirates<br>Tel : +971 (6) 5549333 Fax : +971 (6) 5725012 |
| PLANET TRAVELS AND TOURISM | POB 8, Sharjah, United Arab Emirates<br>Tel : +971 (6) 5581401 Fax : +971 (6) 5581341 |
| REDLINE TOURIST SERVICES AND EXHIBITIONS | POB 27111, Sharjah, United Arab Emirates<br>Tel : +971 (6) 5740740 Fax : +971 (6) 5740400 |
| SPEED TRAVELS AND TOURS | POB 855, Sharjah, United Arab Emirates<br>Tel : +971 (6) 333222 Fax : +971 (6) 336026<br>E-Mail : speed1@emirates.net.ae |
| STALCO TRAVEL SHARJAH | POB 5283, Sharjah, United Arab Emirates<br>Tel : +971 (6) 5351150 Fax : +971 (6) 5358950 |
| SUNSHINE EMIRATES | POB 23528, Sharjah, United Arab Emirates<br>Tel : +971 (6) 324939 Fax : +971 (6) 324936<br>Telex : 68358<br>E-Mail : sunshine@sharjah-welcome.com |
| SWIFT INTERNATIONAL TOURISM | POB 144, Sharjah, United Arab Emirates<br>Tel : +971 (6) 5539966 Fax : +971 (6) 5539988 |
| SNTTA | POB 17, Sharjah, United Arab Emirates<br>Tel : +971 (6) 5351411 Fax : +971 (6) 5374968<br>Telex : 68021 SNTTA EM<br>E-Mail : sntta@emirates.net.ae<br>http://www.sntta.com |
| SKYLINE TRAVEL AND TOURIST | POB 40085, Sharjah, United Arab Emirates<br>Tel : +971 (6) 5355923 Fax : +971 (6) 5367968<br>Telex : 68812 |
| TRANSAVIA TRAVEL AGENCY | POB 9362, Sharjah, United Arab Emirates<br>Tel : +971 (6) 5522833 Fax : 971 (6) 556600 |
| TRANSWORLD AIR TRAVEL | POB 852, Sharjah, United Arab Emirates<br>Tel : +971 (6) 5725088 Fax : +971 (6) 721781 |
| TOP TOURISM | POB 6722, Sharjah, United Arab Emirates<br>Tel : +971 (6) 5544022 Fax : +971 (6) 5548191 |
| TOP TOURS | POB 6722, Sharjah, United Arab Emirates<br>Tel : +971 (6) 5724022 Fax : +971 (6) 5725191<br>Telex : 68746 TOP TRS EM |
| UZBEKISTAN AIRWAYS | POB 23088, Sharjah, United Arab Emirates<br>Tel : +971 (6) 5543732 Fax : +971 (6) 5548322 |
| VICTORIA TRAVELS | POB 58, Sharjah, United Arab Emirates |

| | Tel : +971 (6) 5617444 Fax : +971 (6) 5617722 |
|---|---|

**RESTAURANTS**

As in any city Sharjah has restaurants and cafes of many nationalities and specialties.

Sharjah is a place for takeaways, any dish can be delivered to your door hot and fresh at almost any time of the day or night. Choosing a favorite restaurant may be the problem.

The following selection of restaurants and cafes offers a cross section of the food available.

## Where to go?

Sharjah's restaurants are dotted throughout the city but the following areas have shops to browse in, and here, the most popular restaurants can be found.

- *Al Wahda Street* for fast food, International restaurants, coffee shops and shawarma stands.
- *Jammal Abdul Nasser Street,* parallel to Al Wahda Street has many restaurants ranging from shawarma stands and coffee shops to medium sized Arabic and International restaurants.
- *Al Wahda and King Faisal Street junction* finds the most popular Arabic restaurants of Al Fawar, Al Nomade and Al Jerash. Other coffee shops and restaurants can be found along both these streets.
- *Al Qassimia Street and roundabout* have most of the Chinese, Filipino and some Arabic restaurants.
- *Rolla Square* and the surrounds have the Indian and Pakistani restaurants.
- *Corniche Road* has a number of juice bars and cafes serving roast chicken on a spit and shawarmas.

**PUBLIC SERVIES**

A wide range of services is being provided by Sharjah Municipality, especially in the infrastructure of the public facilities to keep pace with construction and urban development.

The Municipality is active in road construction, the creation of parks and other public facilities.

The municipality also provides a wide range of public health services and issues trading, professional and industrial licenses. More information on health and hospitals can be found here.

## Sharjah Municipality

Sharjah Municipality includes numerous departments, centers and branches. These include :

- The Engineering Department
- Public Works Department
- Quality Control and Building Research Laboratory
- Solid Refuse Section
- Health Section

- Public Health Clinic
- The Central Laboratory for Food Control and Consultations
- Agriculture Section
- Fertilizer Factory
- Legal Affairs Section
- Information Technology Section
- Garage Section
- Sharjah Driving Institute

The **Department of Planning and Survey** has four sections:

- Planning Section
- Land Registration Section
- Real Estate Registration Section
- Survey Section

**THE SHARJAH MUNICIPALITY**

PO Box 22, Sharjah, United Arab Emirates
Tel : +971 (6) 5623333 or 378392
Fax : +971 (6) 5626455
E-Mail : munitc@emirates.net.ae

Location : Municipality Round About, Down town, Sharjah

Working Hours
Saturday to Wednesday (7:30 am to 2:30 pm)
Thursday and Friday holidays

**HOSPITALS**

Health is an important issue for anyone. In the UAE, there are no specific risks although the climate can be harsh during the summer months. No special immunizations are required.

The quality of health care and facilities in Sharjah is generally good. You have a choice of public and private hospitals, clinics, and individual practitioners to choose from.

## Health Card

It is a requirement for expatriates to have a health card in order to live and work in the UAE. These cards are available to all residents of the UAE for a fee. The medical is usually done at the Public Health Clinic, however some of the private hospitals also offer this service.

Listed below is the necessary paperwork required to apply for a health card:
1. Passport photocopy
2. Covering letter from sponsor
3. Visa application or photocopy
4. 2 passport size photographs
5. Ministry of Health form duly filled

6. Dhs 300 for the health card
7. Dhs 200 for the medical examination

For a renewal:
1. Last health card
2. Passport copy with visa stamp
3. Same as above from Nos. 4 to 7

You will find typists, a photocopier and people to explain and help you through the procedure.

It can be quite hectic and time consuming, so try and go as early in the morning as possible.

A health card will give you access to the government hospitals listed below. If you do not have a health card, the government hospitals are open in case of emergency only and for up to 24 hours stay. If you have health insurance, you can also choose to use the private hospitals and clinics. Without insurance private medical care is costly.

## Government Hospitals

| HOSPITAL NAME | TELEPHONE |
|---|---|
| Kuwaiti Hospital<br>Kuwait Road Open 24 hours for emergency and health card holders. | +971 (6) 5242111 |
| New Al Qassimi Hospital Wasit Road Reserved for national patients. Open 24 hours for emergency and health card holders. | +971 (6) 386444 |
| Al Dhaid Hospital | +971 (6) 8822221 |
| Dibba Hospital | +971 (9) 2446666 |
| Kalba Hospital | +971 (9) 2777011 |
| Khor Fakkan | +971 (9) 2370222 |

## Private Hospitals

| HOSPITAL NAME | TELEPHONE |
|---|---|
| Al Zahra Private Hospital | +971 (6) 5619999 |
| Zulekha Hospital | +971 (6) 5378866 |
| Click on the hospital name for more information. | |

## Clinics

| NAME | TELEPHONE |
|---|---|
| Al Buhairah Medical Center | +971 (6) 5599699 |
| Bhatia Clinic | +971 (6) 5522936 |

| | |
|---|---|
| Al Mueed Clinic | +971 (6) 5522429 |
| Al Salam Clinic | +971 (6) 5614262 |
| Chinese Clinic | +971 (6) 5616446 |
| Click on the name for more information. | |
| Emirates PVT. Poly Clinic | +971 (6) 5551666 |
| Al Siddique Clinic (Dhaid) | +971 (6) 8822046 |

| **Emergency Services** | **Number** |
|---|---|
| Fire | 997 |
| Ambulance | 998 or 999 |
| Police | 999 |
| Anjad (Police Emergency) | 5512222 |
| UAE Coastguard | 5281667 |
| Electricity | 5322511 |
| Water | 5541414 |
| Ministry of Health | 7429333 |
| Kuwaiti Hospital | 5242111 |
| New Al Qassimi Hospital | 5386444 |
| Kalba Hospital | 09-2777011 |
| Khor Fakkan Hospital | 09-2370222 |

For Public Health Clinic at Al Nasseriya, Sheikh Sultan bin Saqr Al Qassimi Road, between Mohammad Abu Khater R/A and Fire Station R/A, dial +971 (6) 5522301 or 5523316.

## GOVERNMENT CONTACTS

| **ORGANIZATION** | **CONTACT INFORMATION** | **TELEPHONE** | **FAX** |
|---|---|---|---|
| **Federal Government Ministries** | | | |
| General Postal Authority | POB 4444, Sharjah | +971 (6) 5722219 | +971 (6) 5722953 |
| Ministry of Agriculture | POB 926, Sharjah | +971 (6) 5522968 | +971 (6) 5526363 |
| Ministry of Communications | POB 3522, Sharjah | +971 (6) 5281234 | +971 (6) 5281764 |
| Ministry of Economy & Commerce | POB 3803, Sharjah | +971 (6) 5745000 | +971 (6) 5745450 |

| | | | |
|---|---|---|---|
| Ministry of Education and Youth | POB 452, Sharjah | +971 (6) 5723082 | +971 (6) 5725866 |
| Ministry of Electricity & Water | POB 1672, Dubai | +971 (6) 5341111 | +971 (6) 5341548 |
| Ministry of Foreign Affairs | POB 155, Sharjah | +971 (6) 5722623 | +971 (6) 5726347 |
| Ministry of Health | POB 2072, Sharjah | +971 (6) 5541117 | +971 (6) 5355473 |
| Ministry of Information & Culture | POB 5051, Sharjah | +971 (6) 5723011 | +971 (6) 5725877 |
| Ministry of Interior (Police HQ) | POB 29, Sharjah | +971 (6) 5541111 | +971 (6) 5541595 |
| Ministry of Islamic Affairs & Endowments | POB 501, Sharjah | +971 (6) 5722328 | +971 (6) 5736573 |
| Ministry of Justice | POB 377, Sharjah | +971 (6) 5541821 | +971 (6) 5351398 |
| Ministry of Labor & Social Affairs | POB 301, Sharjah | +971 (6) 5515777 | +971 (6) 5357369 |
| Ministry of Planning | POB 1134, Sharjah | +971 (6) 5722704 | +971 (6) 5723852 |
| Ministry of Public Works & Housing | POB 1515, Sharjah | +971 (6) 5745577 | +971 (6) 5745588 |
| UAE Armed Forces | POB 162, Sharjah | +971 (6) 5582111 | +971 (6) 5584418 |
| UAE Central Bank | POB 645, Sharjah | +971 (6) 5592592 | +971 (6) 5593977 |
| Government Departments | | | |
| Al Diwan Al Emiri | POB 101, Sharjah | +971 (6) 5725222 | +971 (6) 5723366 |
| Administration Control Dept. | POB 201, Sharjah | +971 (6) 5541999 | +971 (6) 5518886 |
| Department of Civil Aviation | POB 8, Sharjah | +971 (6) 5581158 | +971 (6) 5580880 |
| Committee of Admin. & Technical Development | POB 4693, Sharjah | +971 (6) 5545917 | +971 (6) 5543448 |
| Department of Culture & Information | POB 5119, Sharjah | +971 (6) 5541116 | +971 (6) 5362126 |
| Department of Customs & Ports | POB 510, Sharjah | +971 (6) 5281666 | +971 (6) 5281425 |
| Economic Dept. | POB 829, Sharjah | +971 (6) 5734222 | +971 (6) 5734111 |

| | | | |
|---|---|---|---|
| Finance Dept. | POB 201 , Sharjah | +971 (6) 5541999 | +971 (6) 5518886 |
| Financial Control | POB 201, Sharjah | +971 (6) 5546411 | +971 (6) 5362141 |
| Department of Islamic Affairs & Endowments | POB 501, Sharjah | +971 (6) 5727722 | +971 (6) 5736573 |
| Islamic Center | POB 1087, Sharjah | +971 (6) 5723999 | +971 (6) 5724000 |
| Sharjah Municipality | POB 22, Sharjah<br>E-Mail :<br>munitc@emirates.net.ae | +971 (6) 5623333 | +971 (6) 5626455 |
| Petroleum & Mineral Affairs | POB 188, Sharjah | +971 (6) 5541888 | +971 (6) 5378647 |
| Real Estate Registration | POB 22, Sharjah | +971 (6) 5623333 | +971 (6) 5546455 |
| Sharjah Airport Authority | POB 8, Sharjah | +971 (6) 5581111 | +971 (6) 5581051 |
| Sharjah Chamber of Commerce & Industry | POB 580, Sharjah<br>E-mail :<br>scci@sharjah.gov..ae<br>Website:<br>http://www.sharjah.gov.ae | +971 (6) 5541444 | +971 (6) 5541119 |
| Sharjah Electricity & Water Authority | POB 135, Sharjah<br>E-mail :<br>sewa@emirates.net.ae | +971 (6) 5541414 | +971 (6) 5366515 |
| Sharjah Television | POB 111, Sharjah | +971 (6) 5361111 | +971 (6) 5541755 |
| Social Services Dept. | POB 4424, Sharjah | +971 (6) 5725333 | +971 (6) 5722066 |

**AMERICAN UNIVERSITY**

The American University of Sharjah (AUS) is a non-profit, coeducational American style institution of higher education formed on the American model. It was established and is funded by His Highness, Sheikh Dr. Sultan bin Mohammed Al Qassimi, Member of the Supreme Council, Ruler of Sharjah and Supreme President of the University.

Architecturally distinguished facilities will accommodate 4,000 undergraduate students.

The language of instruction is English.

Bachelor's degrees are offered in 18 majors by the Faculties of four Colleges: Arts and Sciences, Architecture and Design, Business and Management, and Engineering.

The **Continuing Education Center (CEC)** provides businesses and individuals access to the educational resources of AUS and offers quality educational programs to meet the ongoing professional and personal needs of the Northern Emirates' adult community

# FREE ECONOMIC ZONES: LEGAL CLIMATE AND OPPORTUNITIES

## AJMAN FREE ZONE

### ADVANTAGES

Cheap energy
The most economical wage structure and easy access to vast work force
Total exemption from all import and export duties
Total elimination of all service charges and hidden fees
Exceptionally low handling charges
20 years contract renewable to another 20 years guaranteeing 40 years tax and customs free operations
Low lease prices
World class infrastructure
Lowest tariffs in the region

**CORPORATE BENEFITS**
100% foreign ownership
100% repatriation of capital and profits
No personal income tax
No corporate tax

**CUSTOM DUTY EXEMPTION IN GCC COUNTRIES**
Goods produced by companies having a National Industrial License in the Ajman Free Zone with 51% share holding with GCC nationals are eligible for a "UAE Certificate of Origin" from the Ministry of Economy and Commerce, UAE, qualifying them for customs duty exemption in member states of GCC, provided the value addition in Ajman Free Zone has been at least 40% of the total final value of the relevant product.

### QUESTIONS AND ANSWERS

| **Q. Does Ajman Free Zone finance projects?** |
|---|
| A. No, Ajman Free Zone doesn't provide financing services to the projects. |
| |
| **Q. Could I transfer my money outside UAE?** |
| A. Yes, there is no any restriction in this regard. |
| |
| **Q. Is there any Income tax applied on companies or individuals?** |
| A. There is neither any personal income tax nor any corporate tax. |
| |
| **Q. Could my Company compete freely with similar companies?** |
| A. Yes, Ajman Free Zone follows opened and free business policy without any restrictions against |

| competition. |
|---|
| |
| **Q. Do banks and financial institutes provide services to the Companies that are registered in Ajman Free Zone?** |
| A. Yes, but they should obtain the required permission. |
| |
| **Q. Is it possible for more than one company to participate in the rent?** |
| A. No, this is not permitted. |
| |
| **Q. Is it possible for me to be a partner in more than one project inside the free zone?** |
| A. Yes, there is no any restriction regarding number of projects that the investor can participate in. |
| |
| **Q. Do I need a local partner to invest in Ajman Free Zone?** |
| A. No, there are no any restrictions on the Foreigner's exclusive proprietorship. |
| |
| **Q. Is it possible for me to sell my merchandise and services in UAE?** |
| A. Yes, as per the valid-laws. |
| |
| **Q. Is it possible for me to obtain a certificate of origin for the goods that the goods that are manufactured in the Free Zone?** |
| A. Yes, if 40% of production cycle is completed in the Free Zone. |
| |
| **Q. Is it possible for me to freely move from and to Ajman Free Zone?** |
| A. Yes. |
| |
| **Q. Is it possible to change the activities covered in the license?** |
| A. Yes, but after obtaining the approval for such application and pay the necessary fees for change. |
| |
| **Q. What is the validity period of the Ajman Free Zone License?** |
| A. It is valid for one year, renewed annually if the investor is having a valid tenancy contract and paid all the dues. |
| |
| **Q. Could I open a branch for my existing company?** |
| A. Yes, you may open a branch or a representation setup to your existing company. |

| |
|---|
| **Q. What are the types of activities permitted to be practiced in Ajman Free Zone?** |
| A. All good types of activities shall be reviewed. |
| |
| **Q. Is it possible for me to import and export goods?** |
| A. Yes, as per the license granted to you. |
| |
| **Q. What is the validity period for my residence visa?** |
| A. Three years. |
| |
| **Q. Is it possible for my family to stay with me in the U.A.E.?** |
| A. Yes, but you have to follow the official immigration procedures. |
| |
| **Q. Will my family members be allowed to work?** |
| A. Yes, after obtaining residence visas. |
| |
| **Q. Is there any restriction to transport between the Emirates?** |
| A. No you may freely transport. |
| |
| Q. Is there any restriction regarding my departure? |
| A. As soon as you obtain a valid visa, you may enter and leave the country without any restriction. |
| |
| **Q. Do I have to recruit UAE staff?** |
| A. No, companies may recruit staff from nationalities of their choice. |
| |
| **Q. Is my staff allowed to reside in my factory or store?** |
| A. No, they shall be accommodated in residential complexes inside the free zone. |
| |
| **Q. What are the communication services available in the free zone?** |
| A. International and local telephone line services, fax, and e-mail and Internet services through telephone. |
| |
| **Q. Is the hired unit ready for connection?** |
| A. Yes all units for offices, store and land are ready for connection. |

| |
|---|
| **Q. Is there any maximum limit for number of service lines that I may obtain?** |
| A. No, there is no maximum limit. |
| |
| **Q. What are the available international communication lines?** |
| A. To all countries around the world. |
| |
| **Q. Are the communication rates competitive to rates of other countries in the region?** |
| A. Yes, prices are competitive to you and available in the investor's directory. |

## JEBEL ALI FREE ZONE

The Jebel Ali Free Zone offers a unique opportunity to do business in the Middle East. It is the ideal industrial, warehousing & distribution hub for a market of some 1.5 billion people, combining the services of the best port in the Middle East with an efficient, dynamic infrastructure.

Stable regulations, well-developed communications and transportation systems and the pro-business environment of Dubai make this Free Zone one of the best in the world. It is already the base of more than 1600 companies from more than 85 countries, including many global brand leaders - companies such as Sony, Black & Decker, Daewoo, Estee Lauder, Grundig, Colgate Palmolive, Nokia, IBM and Samsung.

so, if you are considering expanding your business, wanting to re-locate your business to a vibrant, stable, safe and prospective location, there can always be a place for you in the 100 sq. km. Jebel Ali Free Zone in Dubai.

For more details about JAFZ, the incentives it offers for prospective investors, please browse through the rest of this site. If you have any comments and/or questions, please feel free to e-mail/fax or call.

## ADVANTAGES

| MAIN ADVANTAGES |
|---|
| No major markets in the Middle East are more than 24 hours drive |
| No major port in the region is more than 48 hours steaming |
| Europe is 14 days, Japan 20 days and South East Asia 9 days away |
| Over 125 of the world's major container shipping lines call into Dubai, including feeder vessels to Iran, Africa and the Indian sub-continent |
| Dubai International airport, just 30 minutes by road from JAFZ is serviced by more than 80 |

| airlines to and from over 130 destinations |
|---|
| Over 175 countries can be reached through direct dialling |

The Jebel Ali Free Zone Authority was created by a Government of Dubai decree on 9th February 1985.

As a Government body, JAFZA is charged with the supervision of the Jebel Ali Free Zone. Its responsibilities include providing companies wishing to operate within the Free Zone: -

Appropriate licences to operate.

Lease facilities such as Office Units, Light Industrial Units, Land Sites and Storage Facilities.
Administration, Engineering and Utility services.
An interface with the Dubai Ports Authority for its services.
A continually improving service by investing in upgrading and updating its equipment, infrastructure, and facilities.

Every Free Zone client can enjoy the combined benefits of the services and facilities offered by the Jebel Ali Free Zone Authority(JAFZA) and Dubai Ports Authority.

## COMPANIES

J ebel is a business base for over 1450 companies from 85 countries. While their businesses span a whole range of activities, they can be broadly classified into three distinct groups, namely Trading, Industrial and Service companies. About 74% of the companies hold trading licences, 22% industrial and the rest 4%, service licences.

Among the countries, the top ten are UAE, India, UK, USA, Iran, Japan, Pakistan, France, Germany and Saudi Arabia.

Several of Free Zone's clients are either Fortune 500 companies, Multinationals or are market leaders in their own fields.

### COMPANIES IN JEBEL ALI FREE ZONE - REGION & COUNTRY-WISE STATISTICS

| REGION | COUNTRY | Total Number of Companies | Industrial Licences | Trading Licences | Service Licences | Sub Total | Total Licences |
|---|---|---|---|---|---|---|---|
| | | | | | | | |
| AUNZ | Australia | 10 | 1 | 10 | 0 | 11 | |
| | New Zealand | 1 | 1 | 0 | 0 | 1 | 12 |
| | | | | | | | |
| CIS | Armenia | 4 | 1 | 3 | 0 | 4 | |
| | Azerbaijan | 1 | 0 | 1 | 0 | 1 | |
| | Russia | 5 | 0 | 5 | 0 | 5 | |
| | Ukraine | 3 | 0 | 3 | 0 | 3 | |

| | | | | | | | |
|---|---|---|---|---|---|---|---|
| | Uzbekistan | 1 | 0 | 1 | 0 | 1 | 14 |
| | | | | | - | | |
| EURO | Austria | 4 | 1 | 3 | 0 | 4 | |
| | Belgium | 4 | 0 | 4 | 0 | 4 | |
| | Bulgaria | 2 | 1 | 1 | 0 | 2 | |
| | Channel Island | 1 | 0 | 1 | 0 | 1 | |
| | Cyprus | 8 | 1 | 7 | 0 | 8 | |
| | Czechoslovakia | 1 | 0 | 1 | 0 | 1 | |
| | Denmark | 7 | 3 | 5 | 0 | 8 | |
| | Finland | 8 | 0 | 8 | 0 | 8 | |
| | France | 35 | 8 | 33 | 1 | 42 | |
| | Germany | 46 | 10 | 41 | 1 | 52 | |
| | Greece | 1 | 0 | 1 | 0 | 1 | |
| | Ireland, Republic | 1 | 0 | 1 | 0 | 1 | |
| | Italy | 14 | 5 | 11 | 0 | 16 | |
| | Liechtenstein | 3 | 0 | 3 | 0 | 3 | |
| | Luxembourg | 1 | 0 | 1 | 0 | 1 | |
| | Malta | 2 | 0 | 2 | 0 | 2 | |
| | Netherlands | 17 | 2 | 17 | 0 | 19 | |
| | Norway | 5 | 1 | 5 | 0 | 6 | |
| | Poland | 1 | 0 | 1 | 0 | 1 | |
| | Portugal | 4 | 3 | 1 | 0 | 4 | |
| | Spain, Canary.Is | 4 | 0 | 4 | 0 | 4 | |
| | Sweden | 4 | 0 | 4 | 0 | 4 | |
| | Switzerland | 19 | 1 | 19 | 0 | 20 | |
| | United Kingdom | 181 | 33 | 165 | 1 | 199 | 411 |
| | | | | | | | |
| FARE | China | 12 | 2 | 11 | 0 | 13 | |
| | Hongkong | 17 | 2 | 16 | 0 | 18 | |
| | Indonesia | 2 | 0 | 2 | 0 | 2 | |
| | Japan | 59 | 2 | 58 | 0 | 60 | |
| | Malaysia | 2 | 0 | 2 | 0 | 2 | |
| | North Korea | 1 | 1 | 0 | 0 | 1 | |
| | Philippines | 1 | 0 | 1 | 0 | 1 | |
| | Singapore | 18 | 1 | 18 | 0 | 19 | |
| | South Korea | 10 | 3 | 8 | 0 | 11 | |

| | | | | | | | |
|---|---|---|---|---|---|---|---|
| | Taiwan, Province | 10 | 4 | 10 | 0 | 14 | |
| | Thailand | 4 | 2 | 2 | 0 | 4 | 145 |
| | | | | | | | |
| FEIN | Afghanistan | 4 | 1 | 3 | 0 | 4 | |
| | India | 158 | 59 | 129 | 1 | 189 | |
| | Mauritius | 3 | 0 | 3 | 0 | 3 | |
| | Pakistan | 30 | 16 | 22 | 0 | 38 | |
| | Sri Lanka | 5 | 2 | 4 | 0 | 6 | 240 |
| | | | | | | | |
| GCCE | Bahrain | 6 | 2 | 4 | 0 | 6 | |
| | Kuwait | 12 | 3 | 9 | 1 | 13 | |
| | Oman | 6 | 1 | 5 | 0 | 6 | |
| | Qatar | 4 | 1 | 4 | 0 | 5 | |
| | Saudi Arabia | 34 | 10 | 25 | 0 | 35 | |
| | U.A.E. | 279 | 66 | 163 | 58 | 287 | 352 |
| | | | | | | | |
| GCME | Egypt | 10 | 1 | 9 | 0 | 10 | |
| | Iran | 86 | 12 | 78 | 0 | 90 | |
| | Iraq | 5 | 2 | 4 | 0 | 6 | |
| | Jordan | 25 | 6 | 22 | 1 | 29 | |
| | Lebanon | 17 | 4 | 15 | 0 | 19 | |
| | Palestine | 1 | 0 | 1 | 0 | 1 | |
| | Syrian Arab Rep | 6 | 2 | 4 | 0 | 6 | |
| | Turkey | 8 | 1 | 8 | 0 | 9 | |
| | Yemen Arab Repu | 5 | 2 | 3 | 0 | 5 | 175 |
| | | | | | | | |
| IACI | Algeria | 6 | 0 | 6 | 0 | 6 | |
| | Djibouti | 1 | 0 | 1 | 0 | 1 | |
| | Kenya | 4 | 1 | 4 | 0 | 5 | |
| | Latvia | 1 | 0 | 1 | 0 | 1 | |
| | Libyan Arab Jam | 3 | 0 | 3 | 0 | 3 | |
| | Morocco | 1 | 0 | 1 | 0 | 1 | |
| | Nigeria | 1 | 0 | 1 | 0 | 1 | |
| | Sierra Leone | 1 | 0 | 1 | 0 | 1 | |
| | South Africa | 4 | 2 | 3 | 0 | 5 | |

| | | | | | | | |
|---|---|---|---|---|---|---|---|
| | Sudan | 10 | 1 | 10 | 0 | 11 | |
| | Tanzania, United | 5 | 4 | 4 | 0 | 8 | |
| | Tunisia | 3 | 0 | 3 | 0 | 3 | |
| | Uganda | 1 | 0 | 1 | 0 | 1 | 47 |
| | | | | | | | |
| USCA | Bahamas | 8 | 2 | 8 | 0 | 10 | |
| | Bermuda | 5 | 0 | 5 | 0 | 5 | |
| | British West In | 2 | 0 | 2 | 0 | 2 | |
| | Canada | 23 | 4 | 23 | 0 | 27 | |
| | Cayman Islands | 2 | 0 | 2 | 0 | 2 | |
| | Chile | 1 | 0 | 1 | 0 | 1 | |
| | Panama | 9 | 0 | 9 | 0 | 9 | |
| | Saint Vincent A | 1 | 0 | 1 | 0 | 1 | |
| | TAHITI | 1 | 0 | 1 | 0 | 1 | |
| | U.S.A. | 114 | 14 | 107 | 1 | 122 | 180 |
| | | | | | | | |
| ZZZZ | Lithuania | 1 | 0 | 1 | 0 | 1 | 1 |
| | | | | | | | |
| 86 COUNTRIES | | 1446 | 308 | 1204 | 65 | 1577 | 1577 |

## THE HAMRIYAH FEE ZONE SHARJAH

The Hamriyah Fee Zone Sharjah, was established by an Emiri Decree issued on November 12, 1995. Since the decree was issued no effort has been spared in fast-tracking the development of the Free Zone to serve as a cornerstone in Sharjah and the United Arab Emirates (UAE) industrial development strategy.

The Hamriyah free Zone Authority (HFZA) manages the Free Zone area, which comprises approximately 10 million square meters of industrial and commercial land. Included in the Free Zone area is a 14m-deep water port, which is designed to incorporate dedicated petrochemical bulk handling and general cargo berths.

### GENEROUS INCENTIVE FRAMEWORK

As a Next Generation Free Zone, the Hamriyah Free Zone's mission is to provide incentives which exceed that of its competitors and which meet the needs of firms competing for market penetration in the new millennium. Taking up this challenge, Hamriyah Free Zone has sought to both match the standard terms offered by competitor Free Zones and to exceed it.

### INVESTMENT INCENTIVES

- 100% Foreign company ownership
- 100% import & export tax exemption

- 100% exemption from all commercial levies
- 100% repatriation of capital and profits
- Leases for 15 years renewable for a further 15 years

## FACILITIES

- **Land for Lease for investor development:** Land is available for lease within the Free Zone in plots of 5,000 square meters and above and can be developed by investors to suit their exact requirements.

- **Pre-built warehouse/factory/office units:** Warehouse, factory and office units have been constructed on the site and are available in two convenient sizes, 416 and 614 square meters.
- **Executive Suite Offices:** The International Business Center provides space for 100 executive suite offices with state-of-the-art conferencing and Internet facilities.

## SPECIAL ADVANTAGES

- Strategic, friendly location
- Access to 3 seaports on the Arabian Gulf & Indian ocean
- Access to Sharjah International Airport, the largest sea-air transit cargo hub in the Middle East
- Rents fixed for 5 years
- Quick and simple procedure for approval of License Applications
- Recruitment and sponsorship of personnel and procurement of visas
- Access to inexpensive workforce
- Access to Internet, secretarial services, vehicle registration services and driving licenses.
- An established abundant and inexpensive energy.

## INDUSTRIES AND ACTIVITIES

Typical activities, which will benefit from being in the Free Zone, include manufacturing, assembling, processing, storage, distribution, general trading, packaging and consolidating.

Hamriyah Free Zone has already signed several contracts over the last 12 months with capital commitments of approximately US$ 350 million. These projects include: oil refining, bulk grain storage, oil blending, Soya bean crushing facility, flour mill, printing ink blending, furniture assembling, furniture restoration, electronics and computer components, clothing recycling, satellite TV systems assembling and distribution, trading and many more.

Click here to go to the official Hamriyah Free Zone web site.

**HAMRIYAH FREE ZONE**
PO Box 1377, Sharjah, United Arab Emirates
Tel : +971 (6) 5263333 Fax : +971 (6) 5263444
E-Mail : hfz@emirates.net.ae
http://www.hamriyahfz.com/

# SAIF ZONE

## An Ideal Business Hub

With the distinction of being the world's first ISO 9001 certified Airport Free Zone, SAIF-Zone has a highly developed infrastructure, providing state of the art services. It is ideally located in the vicinity of Sharjah City, adjacent to Sharjah International Airport. Its close proximity to major UAE Airports and Seaports on the East Coast (Arabian Gulf) and 120 kms to the West Coast (Indian Ocean) of the UAE is a vital strategic advantage especially for export, import and industrial establishments. Located adjacent to the best Airport in cargo operations in the Middle East and North Africa, it is also the Middle East cargo hub for Lufthansa and the Airport International Counsel (ACI) ranks it to be one of the best ranked (ranked 29th) airports in the world in cargo operations. These integral links give investing companies direct access to a potential market covering over 1.6 billion consumers from the Middle East, Iran, Asian subcontinent, East Africa and the emerging markets of the CIS countries. Companies based in SAIF - Zone have direct access to both the East and West coasts and sea-air transfers can be made in 6 to 8 hours. Speed, safety, reliability and cost-effectiveness are Sharjah's unique selling points as a cargo hub. The UAE accounts for the highest volume of sea-air cargo handled in Asia with Sharjah International Airport accounting for the highest volume of sea-air tonnage movement.

## SAIF- Zone Advantages

- 100% foreign ownership and repatriation of funds with no currency restrictions
- No personal income or corporate tax
- Sponsorship/visas for all staff with no restriction to a 100% expatriate workforce along with an economical wage structure
- Low cost accommodation for on-site work force
- Administration and Management services
- Highly qualified bilingual staff
- 24 hour hotline for hire of equipment and cargo movement
- Abundant and inexpensive energy
- Modern telecommunication infrastructure
- Land for unrestricted development, pre-built warehouses in different sizes with office space, furnished office suites with reception and temporary auxiliary warehouses available on lease.

## Our Growth Path

Number of companies registered with SAIF Zone rose from 55 in 1995 to 382 in 1999 representing companies from 50 countries.

**SAIF ZONE**
PO Box 8000, Sharjah, United Arab Emirates
Tel : +971 (6) 5570000 Fax : +971 (6) 5571010
E-Mail : saifzone@emirates.net.ae
http://www.saif-zone.com/

# TRAVEL TO UAE

## US STATE DEPARTMENT SUGGESTIONS

**COUNTRY DESCRIPTION:** The United Arab Emirates (UAE) is a federation of seven independent emirates, each with its own ruler. The federal government exists as a constitutional republic, headed by a president and council of ministers. Islamic ideals and beliefs provide the conservative foundation of the country's customs, laws and practices. The UAE is a modern, developed country, and tourist facilities are widely available. The capital is Abu Dhabi.

**ENTRY REQUIREMENTS:** A passport and visa are required. In addition, an AIDS test is required for work or residence permits; testing must be performed after arrival. A U.S. AIDS test is not accepted. For further information, travelers can contact the Embassy of the United Arab Emirates, Suite 700, 1255 22nd Street, N.W., Washington, D.C. 20037, telephone (202) 955-7999.

**DUAL NATIONALITY:** The UAE Government does not recognize dual nationality. Children of UAE fathers automatically acquire UAE citizenship at birth and must enter the UAE on UAE passports. UAE authorities have in the past confiscated U.S. passports of dual (UAE/U.S.) nationals. This does not constitute loss of U.S. citizenship, but should be reported to the U.S. Embassy in Abu Dhabi or the U.S. Consulate General in Dubai. Dual nationals may be subject to UAE laws that impose special obligations. For additional information, please see the Bureau of Consular Affairs home page on the Internet at http://travel.state.gov for our flyer on dual nationality.

**SAFETY/SECURITY:** Taking photographs of anything that could be perceived as being of military or security interest may result in problems with authorities.

**CRIME INFORMATION:** Crime is generally not a problem for travelers in the UAE. The loss or theft of a U.S. passport should be reported immediately to local police and the nearest U.S. embassy or consulate. Useful information on safeguarding valuables, protecting personal security, and other matters while traveling abroad is provided in the Department of State pamphlets, *A Safe Trip Abroad* and *Tips for Travelers to the Middle East and North Africa*. They are available from the Superintendent of Documents, U.S. Government Printing Office, Washington, D.C. 20402, via the Internet at http://www.access.gpo.gov/su_docs, or via the Consular Affairs home page at http://travel.state.gov.

**MEDICAL FACILITIES:** Basic modern medical care and medicines are available in the principal cities of the UAE, but not necessarily in outlying areas. Serious medical problems requiring hospitalization and/or medical evacuation to the United States can cost thousands of dollars or more. Doctors and hospitals often expect immediate cash payment for health services, and U.S. medical insurance is not always valid outside the United States. U.S. Medicare and Medicaid programs do not provide payment for medical services outside the United States.

**MEDICAL INSURANCE:** Uninsured travelers who require medical care overseas may face extreme difficulties. Please check with your own insurance company to confirm whether your policy applies overseas, including provision for medical evacuation. Please ascertain whether payment will be made to the overseas hospital or doctor or whether you will be reimbursed later for expenses that you incur. Some insurance policies also include coverage for psychiatric treatment and for disposition of remains in the event of death. Useful information on medical emergencies abroad, including overseas insurance programs, is provided in the Department of

State's Bureau of Consular Affairs brochure, *Medical Information for Americans Traveling Abroad*, available via the Bureau of Consular Affairs home page or autofax: (202) 647-3000.

**OTHER HEALTH INFORMATION:** Information on vaccinations and other health precautions may be obtained from the Centers for Disease Control and Prevention's hotline for international travelers at telephone 1-877-FYI-TRIP (1-877-394-8747); fax 1-888-CDC-FAXX (1-888-232-3299) or via the CDC's Internet home page at http://www.cdc.gov.

**TRAFFIC SAFETY AND ROAD CONDITIONS:** While in a foreign country, U.S. citizens may encounter road conditions that differ significantly from those in the United States. The information below concerning the UAE is provided for general reference only and may not be totally accurate in a particular location or circumstance.

Safety of Public Transportation: Good
Urban Road Conditions/Maintenance: Excellent
Rural Road Conditions/Maintenance: Good
Availability of Roadside Assistance: Good

Passers-by are in general very willing to assist in road accidents, but they can be very unprofessional in medical emergencies requiring first-aid treatment. Mobile phones are widely used throughout the UAE, so passers-by usually request emergency police and medical services quickly. Response time by emergency services is adequate. However, medical personnel emphasize transport of the injured to the hospital rather than treatment on site. Traffic accidents are a leading cause of death in the UAE. Unsafe driving practices are common, especially on inter-city highways. On highways, wandering camels, unmarked speed bumps and drifting sand create additional hazards.

Country-wide traffic laws impose stringent penalties for certain violations, particularly driving under the influence of alcohol. Penalties may include hefty jail sentences and fines, and, for Muslims, lashings. Persons involved in an accident in which another party is injured automatically go to jail until the injured person is released from the hospital. Should a person die in a traffic accident, the driver of the other car is liable for payment of compensation for the death (known as "dhiyya"), usually the equivalent of $41,000 (US). Even relatively minor accidents may result in lengthy proceedings, during which both drivers may be prohibited from leaving the country.

In order to drive, UAE residents must obtain a UAE driver's license. Foreign driver's licenses are not recognized, and temporary UAE licenses are no longer issued. However, a non-resident visitor to the UAE can drive if he/she obtains a valid international driver's license issued by the motor vehicle authority of the country whose passport the traveler holds. The UAE recognizes driver's licenses issued by other Gulf Cooperative Council (GCC) states only if the bearer is driving a vehicle registered to the same GCC state. Under no circumstances should anyone drive without a valid license. Non-GCC citizens departing the UAE via land are required to pay a departure fee of UAE dirhams 20 (equivalent to $5.45 US). This fee is payable only in the local UAE dirham currency.

**AVIATION SAFETY OVERSIGHT:** As there is no direct commercial air service by local carriers between the United States and the UAE, the U.S. Federal Aviation Administration (FAA) has not assessed the UAE's Civil Aviation Authority for compliance with international aviation safety standards for oversight of the UAE's air carrier operations. For further information, travelers may contact the Department of Transportation within the U.S. at tel. 1-800-322-7873, or visit the FAA Internet web site at http://www.faa.gov/avr/iasa/.

The U.S. Department of Defense (DOD) separately assesses some foreign air carriers for suitability as official providers of air services. As a result of the August 23, 2000 crash of a Gulf Air flight in the Persian Gulf, DOD has recommended that military commands use air carriers other than Gulf Air for DOD official travel, at least until investigation of the crash is complete. For information regarding the DOD policy on specific carriers, travelers may contact the DOD at tel. (618) 229-4801.

**CUSTOMS REGULATIONS:** UAE customs authorities enforce strict regulations concerning temporary importation into or export from UAE of items such as firearms, including fireworks, pornographic materials, medications, religious materials and communication equipment. It is advisable to contact the Embassy of UAE in Washington for specific information regarding customs requirements. UAE customs authorities also impose additional requirements for the importation of pets into the country. Prior permission in the form of a permit from the UAE Ministry of Agriculture and Fisheries must be secured before the pet's travel. To obtain the permit, the following items will need to be submitted to the UAE Ministry of Agriculture and Fisheries at the following address: P.O. Box 213, Abu Dhabi, UAE, telephone 971-2-662-781 or 971-2-485-438. A) The pet's travel itinerary; B) Copies of veterinary health certificates, showing that the animal is free of disease and indicating all shots which have been given to the pet; C) The sex and color of the pet; and D) A completed import permit application form (available from the Ministry).

**CRIMINAL PENALTIES:** While in a foreign country, U.S. citizens are subject to that country's laws and regulations, which sometimes differ significantly from those in the United States and may not afford the protections available to the individual under U.S. law. Penalties for breaking the law can be more severe than in the United States for similar offenses. Persons violating the UAE laws, even unknowingly, may be expelled, arrested, or imprisoned. The penalties for possession, use, or trafficking in illegal substances are strict in the UAE, and convicted offenders can expect jail sentences and heavy fines. Legislation enacted in January 1996 imposes the death sentence for convicted drug traffickers. A variety of drugs normally taken under a doctor's supervision in the United States are classified as narcotics in the UAE. A doctor's prescription should be carried along with any medication that is brought into the country.

In addition, the UAE's tough anti-narcotics program also includes poppy seeds, widely used in other cultures, including the U.S., for culinary purposes, on its list of controlled substances. The importation and possession of poppy seeds in any and all forms is strictly prohibited. Persons found to possess even very small quantities of the controlled substances listed by the UAE are subject to prosecution by the authorities and may be given lengthy prison terms of up to 15 years. Travelers with questions regarding the items on the list of controlled substances should contact the U.S. Embassy in Abu Dhabi or the U.S. Consulate General in Dubai.

If suspected of being under the influence of drugs, individuals may be required to submit to blood and/or urine tests so that local authorities may make a determination as to usage. UAE authorities have been known to arrest travelers upon their arrival into the UAE and, based on recent prior drug use, to prosecute these travelers.

Crimes of fraud, including passing bad checks and non-payment of bills (including hotel bills), are regarded seriously in the UAE and can result in imprisonment, as well as fines. Penalties are generally assessed according to religious law. If imprisoned, bail is generally not available to non-residents of the UAE.

Drinking or possession of alcohol without a Ministry of Interior liquor permit is illegal and could result in arrest and/or fines and imprisonment. Alcohol is served at bars in most major hotels. However, this alcoholic beverage service is for those persons who are staying at the hotel.

Persons not staying at the hotel who come in to use the facility's bar technically are required to have their own personal liquor license. Liquor licenses are obtainable only by non-Muslim persons who possess UAE residency permits. Drinking and driving is considered a serious offense.

**SPECIAL CIRCUMSTANCES:** American citizens may become involved in disputes of a commercial nature involving the withholding of the American citizen's passport by the local firm or courts. Travel bans may also be enforced on American citizens involved in financial disputes with a local sponsor or firm. These bans, which are rigidly enforced, prevent the individual from leaving the UAE for any reason until the matter is resolved. Although it is customary for a local sponsor to hold an employee's passport, it is not required under UAE law. Most contractual/labor disputes can be avoided by clearly establishing all terms and conditions of employment or sponsorship in the labor contract at the beginning of any employment. Should a dispute still arise, the UAE Ministry of Labor has established a special department to review and arbitrate labor claims. A list of local attorneys capable of representing Americans in such matters is available from the Consular and Commercial sections of the U.S. Embassy in Abu Dhabi and the U.S. Consulate General in Dubai.

Travelers intending to reside and work in the UAE should have their academic and occupational certificates duly authenticated by the Department of State's Office of Authentication in Washington, D.C. before traveling to the UAE. UAE labor law requires local sponsors to produce employees' academic and/or professional certificates duly authenticated by the Foreign Ministry of the individual's country before a work permit can be issued. Travelers intending to bring their families to reside with them in the UAE will also need to have their marriage certificates, and children's birth certificates duly authenticated by the State Department in Washington, D.C.

**CHILDREN'S ISSUES:** Children of UAE fathers automatically acquire UAE citizenship at birth and must enter the UAE on UAE passports. Child custody decisions are based on Islamic law. It is difficult for an American woman, even a Muslim, to obtain custody of her dual national (UAE/U.S.) children through the UAE courts. Custody cases are complex and involve the court's consideration of parents' religion, place of permanent residence, income, and the mother's subsequent marital status. Children involved in custody disputes in local courts are generally subject to travel bans regardless of their nationality. For information on international adoption of children, international parental child abduction, and international child support enforcement issues, please refer to our Internet site at http://travel.state.gov/children's_issues.html or telephone (202) 736-7000.

**REGISTRATION / EMBASSY AND CONSULATE LOCATION:** Americans living in or visiting the UAE are encouraged to register with the Consular Section of the U.S. Embassy in Abu Dhabi or the Consulate General in Dubai where they can obtain updated information on travel and security within the UAE. The U.S. Embassy in Abu Dhabi is located on 11th St., also known as Al-Sudan St., P.O. Box 4009. The telephone number is (971) (2) 443-6691 and the Consular Section fax number is (971) (2) 443-5786. The after hours telephone is (971) (2) 443-4457. The Embassy Internet web site is http://www.usembabu.gov.ae. The U.S. Consulate General in Dubai is located on the 21st floor of the Dubai World Trade Center, P.O. Box 9343. The telephone number is (971) (4) 331-3115 and the Consular Section fax number is (971) (4) 331-6935. The workweek for both the Embassy in Abu Dhabi and Consulate in Dubai is Saturday through Wednesday.

## IMPORTANT INFORMATION

**Population:** With a 1998 estimate of 2.8 million, the population of the United Arab Emirates has been growing about 3.0% annually. Major ethnic groups include Arab, Pakistani, Indian, Iranian,

Afghan, Bangladeshi and Filipino, while exact data is not available. Less than 20 percent of the population are believed to be nationals of the United Arab Emirates.

**Religion (s):** The official religion is Islam, 90 percent of the total population ( including expatriates) are Muslims. The authorities permit worship of other religions. There are Christian churches and Hindu temples in Abu Dhabi, Dubai and Sharjah.

**Government Systems:** The government is a federation of the seven Emirates headed by a president and a vice president ( since its respectively). The rules of each of the Emirates belong to the supreme council, which is the U.A.E.'s highest legal authority and promulgates federal laws. The Federal National Council, consisting of 40 nationals appointed by the rules, acts as an advisory legislative body. The Council of Ministers, appointed by the supreme council, manages the day to day affairs of the federation.

Each Emirates has its own local government involved with municipal affairs, and in some cases major public utilities like power and water.

**Language (s):** The official language is Arabic, but English is widely used in business. Hindi, Urdu, and Farsi (Persian) are also spoken.

**Work Week:** The regular work week is from Saturday to midday Thursday. Most private business offices are also open on Thursday afternoon. Working hours vary. Government offices and banks close for the day at 1:00 pm, but commercial outlets re-open in the afternoon from about 4:30 pm - 8:00pm.
Note: The oil sector in Abu Dhabi works 07:00 a.m. - 15:00 p.m., Saturday through Wednesday. The oil sector in Dubai works 8:00 a.m. - 5:00 p.m., Sunday through Thursday. Many other Dubai companies are trending this way.

Drugs and Crime Penalties: Travelers are subject to the laws and legal practices of the country in which they travel. Penalties for possession, illegal substances are strict in the United Arab Emirates. A variety of drugs normally taken under a doctor's supervision in the United States are classified as narcotics in the U.A.E.. Doctor's prescriptions should be carried along with any medication that is brought into the country.

U.A.E. authorities have been known to arrest travelers upon their arrival here and based on recent prior drug use, to prosecute these travelers.

Crimes of fraud, including passing bad checks and non-payment of bills (including hotel bills), are regarded seriously in the U.A.E. and can result in imprisonment, as well as fines. Penalties are generally assessed according to religious law. If imprisoned, bail is generally not available to non-residents of the U.A.E..

Drinking alcohol without a ministry of interior liquor permit is illegal and could result in arrest or fines and imprisonment. Alcohol is served at bars in most major hotels. However, this alcoholic beverage services is for those persons who are residing at the hotel. Persons not residing at the hotel who come in to use the facility's bar technically are required to have their own personal liquor license. Liquor licenses are obtainable only by persons who possess U.A.E. residency permits. Drinking and driving is considered a serious offense.

**Driver's license:** In order to drive, U.A.E. residents must obtain a U.A.E. driver's license. Foreign driver's licenses are not recognized and temporary U.A.E. licenses are no longer issued. However, a non-resident visitor to the U.A.E. can drive if he/she obtains a valid international driver's license issued by the motor vehicle authorities of the country whose passport the travelers holds. Under no circumstances should anyone drive without a valid license.

Visas are required by all visitors to the UAE, except GCC nationals and UK citizens. Visas may be obtained from the Department of Naturalization and Residence through hotels. Passports must be valid for at least six months from the time of application.

Many people think that because the United Arab Emirates looks very modern and familiar, they should dress as they would in any other hot climate or Western resort destination.

**But the United Arab Emirates is an Islamic country and, as a visitor, please respect that different codes of dress and behavior apply.**

Muslim men and women are generally conservative in their dress and behavior and find it offensive to see too much exposed flesh - which is against their moral beliefs, daily habits and traditional dress codes going back to the beginning of history.

While foreigners are not expected to be fully covered - there are a few simple rules that we would like to ask you to observe in order to get the best out of your visit:

1. Do not wear beach clothes, sleeveless or low cut tops and shorts in public - only at the beach or private clubs.
2. Embracing in public is not acceptable behavior.
3. Women should not first offer their hand for a handshake, but if offered, should shake hands gently.
4. Never take photographs of local citizens, especially women, without asking permission.
5. During the Holy Month of Ramadan, absolutely no eating, drinking or smoking are allowed in public during daylight hours. Meals will be served in the hotel areas or your hotel room.

Following these simple rules will make you an even more welcome guest in one of the world's safest, most secure and friendly vacation destinations.

**VISAS**

Citizens of the Arab Gulf Cooperation Council (GCC) countries and British nationals, with the right of abode in the UK, do not need visas to enter the UAE.
Britons can stay for one month, renewable for a further two months. Generally, all other visitors must obtain a visa from a sponsor, which can be a company, individual or hotel.

For an individual to sponsor a visit visa, you must earn over Dhs 3,000 per month and hold a valid residence visa.

US and German citizens can obtain tourist or business visas through any UAE embassy. It can however, be quicker if you apply in your home country.
A business visitor may enter the UAE on either a transit or visit visa. Visa holders may enter and exit the UAE through any port of entry. Airlines may require evidence that the incoming visitor has a sponsor who holds a valid visa.
Transit and visit visas must be deposited at the airport immigration one hour before the arrival of a flight.

## Visit Visa

A visit visa is valid for 60 days, renewable once up to a total of 90 days. To obtain a visa from a UAE embassy you require the following:

- Passport with at least 6 months validity remaining
- 2 photographs
- Duplicate application form
- Letter or fax from the sponsor in the UAE to the embassy concerned
- A letter from the applicant's company plus photocopy

All nationalities resident in GCC countries, holding a valid resident visa and of a managerial status, can obtain a 30 day visit visa on arrival in the UAE.
You can expect it to take one week to 10 days for a visit visa to be issued. An express service exists.

*Department for Naturalization and Residence - Sharjah*
PO Box 858
King Abdul Aziz Road/Al Istiqlal Road,
Al Qassimia, Sharjah
Tel: +971 (6) 5726777
Fax: +971 (6) 5723572
Open: 7:30 am - 2:30 noon (Saturday through Wednesday. Thursday and Friday holidays)

## Transit Visa

These are issued for 15 days only and cannot be extended or renewed. You must have a UAE company who sponsors your visit. Larger hotels can sponsor transit visas for tourists and business visits.

## Residence Visa

Formalities are normally handled by the company of employment. Dependents (spouse and family) are sponsored usually by the husband, once he has his company sponsorship. A medical, including blood test and chest x-ray, is required for adults before the visa process starts. These are taken at the Public Health Clinic in Nasseriya. Anyone who works in the Emirates must have a valid labor card issued by their employer. It is usual for the employer to hold an employee's passport or labor card. On leaving the Emirates permanently, your residence visa should be canceled and proof of this in writing, is given to the sponsor.

## MONEY

The history and develop[...] n the 18th century , to the Dirham of today, can be explored in the Trade Room of Al Hisn Fort in Sharjah City. Today's currency took over from the rupee when the UAE was formed in 1971.

The UAE Dirham is divided into 100 fils. Coins include Dhs.1, 50 fils, 25 fils, 10 fils and 5 fils. The latter two are rarely used. Notes are of Dhs. 5, 10, 20, 50, 100, 200, 500 and 1000 denominations.

### Currency Exchange

The Dirham is freely convertible, making exchange of travelers checks and currency easy. The local currency is index linked to the US Dollar.
1 US Dollar = Dirhams 3.68 (buying and selling)

### Costs

The UAE is not a low budget country and the cost of living for an expatriate could be on par with New York, depending on life style. Having said that, you can find a meal for less than Dhs 10. Getting around is also cheap, either by purchasing or renting a car or by taxi.

### Banks

Both locally incorporated and International banks are represented in Sharjah. A number of banks are located in Al Boorj Avenue (also called Bank Street). As Sharjah has expanded, some banks have moved to other areas, mainly King Faisal Street, Khalid Lagoon and Old Airport Road.

### Banking Hours

Banks are open to public from Saturday to Wednesday between 8 am and 1 pm and from 8 am to 12 noon on Thursday. Mashreq and Standard Chartered banks are also open from 4.30 pm to 6.30 pm. Banks are closed on Fridays and public holidays.

### Lost Credit Cards

| | |
|---|---|
| AMERICAN EXPRESS | 800 0004 |
| BRITISH BANK | 800 6111 |

| | |
|---|---|
| CITIBANK | 800 4000 |
| EMIRATES BANK INTERNATIONAL | 800 4080 |
| MASHREQ BANK | 800 4010 |
| STANDARD CHARTERED | 800 4884 |
| VISA | 800 4420 |

## Money Changers

The best rate of exchange is usually found in the privately owned bureaux de change. These are open later than the banks which can be very convenient. Working hours are generally 8.30 am to 1 pm and 4.30 pm to 8.30 pm on weekdays (Saturday to Thursday). Most are open on Friday afternoons. The UAE Exchange Center on Al Arouba Street is open on Friday mornings from 8.30 am to 11 am. Closed on public holidays.
In addition to the banks and hotels, money changers are common (Blue Souk, Al Arouba Street and Rolla Square) and it is worth shopping around for the best cash deal. You will find most currencies available. Some accept certain travelers checks, but not all. It is also advisable to check the bank rates before making any transactions with the money changers. The business section of the daily newspapers displays the closing Dirham and dollar exchange rates.

| | |
|---|---|
| Thomas Cook Al Rostamani | +971 (6) 5614656 |
| UAE Exchange Center | +971 (6) 5547725 |
| Wall Street Exchange Center | +971 (6) 5522831 |
| Al Ansari Exchange EST | +971 (6) 5544113 |
| Al Fardan Exchange | +971 (6) 5350371 |
| Habib Exchange CO | +971 (6) 5351885 |
| Western Union Money Transfer Box | +971 (6) 5614028 |

## DRIVING

A vehicle is a necessity as cities tend to be spread out with residential areas set away from schools and shops. Apart from taxis there is no public transport system. Driving is on the right hand side of the road. It can be erratic at times. Try to avoid the rush to Dubai in the mornings, from 7 am - 8.30 am and back, between 6 pm - 8 PM Look out for camels, particularly on highways at night.

Third party insurance is compulsory. The penalty for drinking and driving is severe.

Ladies should always use the Ladies Section at the police station, which tends to speed up the procedure and affords you comfort and privacy. All payments for licenses, fines etc. must be made in cash.

Whenever you drive, you must carry your license and registration document. GCC nationals may drive on their respective licenses within the UAE. Other nationalities see below. Forms must be completed in Arabic. There are typist shops located within the compound walls of the various traffic departments. Typing costs are around Dhs 5 - 10 per form.

## Driving Licence

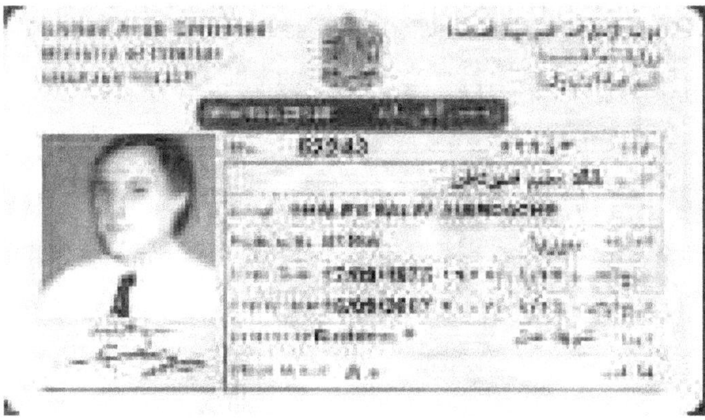

Licenses (full and temporary) are issued at the Traffic Police Headquarters (Murrur) in Abu Tina, (Tel : +971 (6) 5541111). You can only obtain a full driving license, valid for 5 years, if you have a valid Sharjah residence visa. If you are a visitor on a visit visa you can obtain a temporary driving license provided you hold a valid license from a recognized country (see below). This is valid for one month and is renewable for a further two months.

It is not necessary to take a driving test to obtain a license if you hold a valid license from one of the following countries:
EC, USA, Japan, Korea, Ireland, Turkey, Iran, Norway or Czech Republic.

## Documents for a full licence

1. A no objection letter from your sponsor in Arabic.
2. A photocopy of your passport including the visa page.
3. A photocopy of your sponsor's passport.
4. 2 photographs.

Eye and blood tests, necessary for the license, are carried out at the Police Station. Cost: Dhs 140 plus Dhs 50 for the blood test.

## Documents for a temporary licence

Available for visitors from the countries mentioned above only. Other nationalities - refer to International Driving Permits below.
1. A no objection letter from your sponsor in Arabic.
2. Your passport.
3. A photocopy of the visa page.
4. Two photographs

Cost: Dhs 30 per month.

## Procedure

Take all the necessary documents and cash to the Traffic Police.
International Driving Permit.
Valid for one year and issued by the Automobile & Touring Club for the United Arab Emirates (Tel : +971 (6) 5523183). The office is located in Al Arouba Street, 1st floor of the Bank of Cairo Building.
You need 2 photographs and a copy of your driving license plus Dhs 100. The whole procedure

takes 5 minutes. Visitors other than European, Scandinavian, American, Canadian and Japanese can drive a rented vehicle, provided they hold an International Driving License, issued by their home country. Residents must hold a valid UAE license to rent a vehicle.

## Car Registration

For registration of a new vehicle go to the Traffic Police Headquarters in Abu Tina. For a renewal, go to the Traffic Department in Wasit. You must hold a valid residence visa for Sharjah and a valid UAE driving License. Every vehicle must have a fire extinguisher with a validity paper. After registration, you receive a laminated document which must be kept in the vehicle at all times.

## Documents for a new vehicle

1. Letter in Arabic from the dealer to traffic department with all of the car particulars and the name of the buyer.
2. Car registration application form, available at the traffic police, to be typed in Arabic.
3. Passport copy.
4. Driving License copy.
5. One photograph.
6. Insurance valid for one year.
7. No objection letter from your sponsor.

## Procedure for a new vehicle

Take the application form and documents to the registration counter in the main building. Fee is to be paid to the cashier. Back to the Counter where you are given a slip to obtain the number plates. Collect number plates from another building in the main compound. Return in half an hour to collect the laminated registration book from the main building.

Cost : Variable, depending on the model and make of vehicle.

## Car Registration Renewal

Registration renewal to be done at the Traffic Department by Wasit Roundabout Any police tickets (speeding and other traffic violations) have to be paid before the renewal process starts. The police will advise you there and then.

## Documents for renewal

1. Car Insurance certificate valid for a full year.
2. Copy of passport.
3. Registration document.

As you proceed you will collect the following documents:

1. Renewal form typed in Arabic
2. Inspection certificate.
3. Renewal of fire extinguisher, valid for a full year.

## Procedure

The car is first inspected at the testing center. Any faults must be rectified before proceeding. All documents are taken to the counter. The fee is paid and the registration issued for one year.

Cost : Up to Dhs 305 plus traffic fines! The cost is related to the size of the vehicle.

## Ownership transferral and sale of vehicle

Traffic Police Headquarters, Abu Tina.

## Documents

1. Application form completed in Arabic to be signed by the person selling the car.
2. Insurance paper.
3. Driving License or ID.
4. Number plates.
5. Registration Document.
6. Inspection certificate (not necessary if the transfer is within the UAE).
7. 'Malkiya'- ownership document.

## Procedure

Forms and documents to the transfer counter. Fee paid to cashier. If buying, the procedure is as per a new registration.

## Driving test

Traffic Department, Wasit Roundabout. You need to open a file here with :
1. A no objection letter from your sponsor.
2. A copy of your passport (and take along the original).
3. Blood group and eye test certificates.

A date for the test is given and a paper which must be taken to Nasseriya Driving School. Here you pay a fee of Dhs 250 to attend lectures in English or Arabic. An oral test is given, and once you pass, you then apply for driving lessons. These can be taken through the private schools or the Government's Driving Institute. Once completed you wait for your test date.

## Speed Limits

The speed limit in and around built up areas is 60 kph. On highways, cars may drive up to 100 kph, heavy vehicles up to 80 kph. Many areas are controlled by stationary and mobile radar. The fine in Sharjah Emirate is Dhs 200 each time you are caught speeding.

## Accidents and breakdowns

In the event of either of the above you can contact the Anjad (The Special Branch of the Traffic Police) on +971 (6) 5512222. The Anjad patrol the streets to assist the public in all traffic related and security matters. Do not move any vehicles involved in an accident until a report has been made and permission is given by the police. All accidents, no matter how small, must be reported to the police. No repairs can be made without a police report. It is customary to obtain two quotations for repairs. If your car has broken down and obstructs the free flow of the traffic, do your best to move the vehicle to the side of the road, out of the way.

**CUSTOMS REGULATIONS**

The twin ports of Khorfakkan (on the east coast of the UAE); and Port Khalid (the main Sharjah seaport, on the Arabian Gulf) are controlled by common customs laws and management. Goods can be cleared from either port after documentation has been filed and completed from the main Customs Office in Port Khalid.

Airlines using Sharjah International Airport as their hub get special services from the Customs Department. A separate customs office can be made available for these airlines.

Thus regular importers with the airline can benefit from the newly introduced accounts system for Customs duty payments.

Attractive facilities are granted to L.C.L. operators and users by transporting goods to their warehouse FREE OF CHARGE. The Commercial section of the Sharjah Customs Department deals with the problems of consignees and meets with consignees regularly to develop a strong consignee Customs Department relationship.

# SUPPLEMENTS

## FEDERAL MINISTRIES

Please note: telephone and fax numbers have been given on the basis of dialling from inside the UAE. If you are dialling internationally then you should insert the access code +971 and delete the first zero. eg: dialling Ministry of Economy from Germany, you would dial 0097-126265000.

**Ministry of Defence**
**The Minister:** HH Sheikh Mohammed bin Rashid Al Maktoum
(also Prime Minister)
Abu Dhabi POB: 46616; Tel: 02 4461300; Fax: 02 4463286
Dubai POB: 2838; Tel: 04 3532330; Fax: 04 3531974

**Ministry of Finance**
**The Minister:** Sheikh Hamdan bin Rashid Al Maktoum
**The Minister of State:** Obaid Humaid Al Tayer
Abu Dhabi, POB: 433; Tel: 02 6726000; Fax: 02 6663088
Dubai, POB: 1565; Tel: 04 3939000; Fax: 04 3939738
**Email:** mofi@uae.gov.ae
**Website:** www.fedfin.gov.ae

**Ministry of Interior**
**The Minister:** Lt General Sheikh Saif bin Zayed Al Nahyan (also Deputy Prime Minister)
Abu Dhabi POB: 398; Tel: 02 4414666; Fax: 02 4414938
Dubai POB: 4333; Tel: 04 3980000; Fax: 04 3981119

**Ministry of Presidential Affairs**
**The Minister:** Sheikh Mansour bin Zayed Al Nahyan (also Deputy Prime Minister)
Abu Dhabi, POB:280; Tel: 02 6222221; Fax: 02 6222228

**Ministry of Education**
**The Minister:** Humaid Mohammed Obeid al Qattami
Undersecretary: Dr Jamal Al Mehairi
Abu Dhabi POB: 295; Tel: 02 62138000; Fax: 02 6313778
Dubai POB: 3962; Tel: 04 2994100; Fax: 04 2994535
**Website:** http://www.moe.gov.ae/

**Ministry for Foreign Affairs**
**Foreign Minister:** Sheikh Abdullah bin Zayed Al Nahyan
**The Minister of State:** Dr Mohammed Anwar Gargash (also Minister of State for Federal National Council Affairs)
Abu Dhabi, POB: 1; Tel: 02 4444488; Fax: 02 4447766
Dubai, POB: 3785; Tel: 04 2221144; Fax: 04 2280979
**Email:** mofa@uae.gov.ae

**Ministry of Higher Education and Scientific Research**
The Minister: Sheikh Nahyan bin Mubarak Al Nahyan
Abu Dhabi, POB: 45253; Tel: 02 6428000; Fax: 02 6428778
**Email:** mohe@uae.gov.ae

**Ministry of Public Works**
**The Minister:** Sheikh Hamdan bin Mubarak Al Nahyan
Abu Dhabi POB: 878; Tel: 02 6651778; Fax: 02 6665598
Dubai POB: 1828; Tel: 04 2693900; Fax: 04 2692931
**Email:** mpwh@uae.gov.ae

**Ministry of Economy**
**The Minister:** Sultan bin Saeed Al Mansouri
Abu Dhabi POB: 901; Tel: 02 6265000; Fax: 02 6215339 Dubai POB: 3625; Tel: 04 2954000; Fax: 04 2951991
**Email:** economy@emirates.net.ae
**Website:** www.economy.gov.ae

**Ministry of Foreign Trade**
**The Minister:** Sheikha Lubna Al Qasimi

**Ministry of Justice**
**The Minister:** Dr Hadef bin Jua'an Al Dhaheri
Abu Dhabi POB: 260; Tel: 02 6814000; Fax: 02 6810680
Dubai POB: 1682; Tel: 04 2825999; Fax: 04 2825121

**Ministry of Energy**
**The Minister:** Mohammed bin Dha'en Al Hamili
Abu Dhabi POB: 59; Tel: 02 6671999; Fax: 02 6664573
**Email:** mopmr@uae.gov.ae

**Ministry of Labour**
**The Minister:** Saqr Ghobash Saeed Ghobash
Abu Dhabi POB: 809; Tel: 02 6671700; Fax: 02 6665889
Dubai POB: 4409; Tel: 04 2691666; Fax: 04 2668967

**Ministry for Cabinet Affairs**
**The Minister:**Mohammed Abdullah Al Gargawi
Abu Dhabi POB: 899; Tel: 02 6811113; Fax: 02 6812968
Dubai POB: 5002; Tel: 04 3967555; Fax: 04 3978884
**Email:** moca@uae.gov.ae
**Website:** www.uae.gov.ae/moca

**Ministry of Social Affairs**
**The Minister:** Mariam Mohammed Khalfan Al Roumi
Abu Dhabi POB: 261; Tel: 02 6322500; Fax: 02 633259
**Email:** prsa@mol.gov.ae

**Ministry of Health**
**The Minister:** Dr Hanif Hassan Ali
Abu Dhabi POB: 848; Tel: 02 6334716; Fax: 02 6726000
Dubai POB: 1853; Tel: 04 3966000; Fax: 04 3965666
**Email:** postmaster@moh.gov.ae
**Website:** www.moh.gov.ae/intro

**Ministry of Environment and Water**
**The Minister:** Dr Rashid Ahmad bin Fahad

Abu Dhabi POB: 213; Tel: 02 4495100; Fax: 02 4495150
**Email:** archives@moew.gov.ae

**Ministry of Culture, Youth and Community Development**
**The Minister:** Abdul Rahman Mohammed Al Owais
Abu Dhabi POB: 17; Tel: 02 4453000; Fax: 02 4452504
**Email:** mcycd@moic.gov.ae

**Government Links**

UAE Government: www.uae.gov.ae
Abu Dhabi Chamber of Commerce & Ind: www.adcci-uae.com
Abu Dhabi Customs Dept: www.auhcustoms.gov.ae
Abu Dhabi Civil Aviation: www.dcaauh.gov.ae
Port Zayed: www.portzayed.gov.ae
Zayed Foundation: www.zayed.org.ae
UAE State Audit Institution: www.saiuae.gov.ae
General Information Authority: www.gia.gov.ae
Gen. Directorate of Abu Dhabi Police: www.adpolice.gov.ae
Gen. Directorate of Civil Defence: www.gdocd.gov.ae

Federal National Council: www.almajles.gov.ae
Federal Environmental Agency: www.fea.gov.ae

Dubai Municipality: www.dm.gov.ae
Dubai Ports and Customs: www.dxbcustoms.gov.ae
Dubai Chamber of Commerce & Ind: www.dcci.org
Dubai Water & Electricity Co: www.dewa.gov.ae
Dubai International Airport: www.dubaiairport.com
Dubai Traffic Police: www.dxbtraffic.gov.ae
Dubai Police Headquarters: www.dubaipolice.gov.ae
Dubai Tourism & Commerce Mktg: www.dubaitourism.co.ae
Dubai Dept of Economic Development: www.dubaided.gov.ae
Dubai Awqaf & Islamic Affairs: www.awqafdubai.gov.ae
Dubai Duty Free: www.dubaidutyfree.com
Jebel Ali Free Zone: www.jafza.co.ae
Dubai Cargo Village: www.dubaicargovillage.com
Dubai Naturalisation & Residency: www.dnrd.gov.ae
Sheikh Hamdan bin Rashid Al Maktoum Award for Medical Services: www.hmaward.org.ae
Dubai Media City: www.dubaimediacity.com

Sharjah Customs Dept: www.sharjahcustoms.gov.ae
Sharjah Chamber of Commerce: www.sharjah.gov.ae
Sharjah International Airport: www.shj-airport.gov.ae
SAIF Zone, Sharjah: www.saif-zone.com
Hamriyah Free Zone: www.hamriyahfz.com
Sharjah Police: www.shjpolice.gov.ae

Ras Al Khaimah Airport: www.rkt-airport.com
Ras Al Khaimah Free Trade Zone: www.rakiftz.com
Ras Al Khaimah Municipality: www.rakmunicipality.com

Ajman Chamber of Commerce: www.ajcci.co.ae
Ajman Free Zone: www.ajmanfreezone.gov.ae
Ajman TV: www.ajmantv.com
Ajman University: http://website.ajman.ac.ae

Al Ain Municipality: www.alain.gov.ae
Al Ain Museum: www.AAM.gov.ae

Fujairah Tourism Bureau: www.fujairah-tourism.com
Fujairah Free Trade Zone: www.FujairahFreeZone.com

**Other Political Links**

Political Resources on the Net: www.politicalresources.net
Listings of political sites available on the Internet sorted by country, with links to Parties, Organizations, Governments, Media and more from all around the world

**UAE Embassies Abroad**

Embassy of the United Arab Emirates in Germany www.uae-embassy.de
Embassy of the United Arab Emirates in Japan www.uaeembassy.jp

# ORGANIZATION OF PETROLEUM EXPORTING COUNTRIES (OPEC) [2]

| | April 1 2007 Quota* | Crude Oil** Production (thousand b/d) | | |
|---|---|---|---|---|
| Country/Date Joined | (thousand b/d) | February '00 | January '00 | Oil/Energy Minister |
| Algeria (1969) | 731 | 760 | 760 | Chakib Khelil |
| Indonesia (1962) | 1,187 | 1,250 | 1,280 | Susilo Bambang Yudhoyono |
| Iran (1960) | 3,359 | 3,490 | 3,430 | Bijan Namdar Zaganeh |
| Kuwait[+] (1960) | 1,836 | 2,015 | 1,962 | Sheikh Saud Naser Al-Sabah |
| Libya (1962) | 1,227 | 1,380 | 1,330 | Abdullah Salim al-Badri |
| Nigeria (1971) | 1,885 | 1,950 | 1,900 | Rilwanu Lukman*** |
| Qatar (1961) | 593 | 670 | 660 | Abdullah bin Hamad Al-Attiya |

[2] *The 11 countries which make up the Organization of Petroleum Exporting Countries (OPEC) produce about 40 percent of the world's oil and hold more than 77 percent of the world's proved oil reserves. OPEC also contains most of the world's excess oil production capacity.*

| Saudi Arabia[+] (1960) | 7,438 | 7,865 | 7,863 | Ali bin Ibrahim al-Naimi |
|---|---|---|---|---|
| United Arab Emirates[++] (1967) | 2,000 | 2,170 | 2,165 | Obeid bin Saif Al-Nasiri |
| Venezuela (1960) | 2,720 | 2,800 | 2,740 | Ali Rodriguez |
| OPEC 10 | 22,976 | 24,350 | 24,090 | |
| Iraq[+++] (1960) | NA | 2,590 | 2,210 | Lt. Gen. Amir Muhammed Rashid |
| TOTAL OPEC | NA | 26,940 | 26,300 | Secretary General Rilwanu Lukman |

NA: Not Applicable
*Quotas are based on crude oil production.
**Crude oil does not include natural gas liquids or lease condensate.
***Rilwanu Lukman is the oil advisor to President Olusegun Obasanjo.
[+]Kuwaiti and Saudi Arabian figures each include half of production from the Neutral Zone between the two countries.
[++]Quota applies only to Abu Dhabi.
[+++]Iraqi oil production is constrained by the United Nations' limits on its exports and as such has not been a part of any recent OPEC agreements.

## OPEC OVERVIEW

The Organization of Petroleum Exporting Countries (OPEC) was formed at a conference held in Baghdad on September 10-14, 1960. There were five original members: Iran, Iraq, Kuwait, Saudi Arabia, and Venezuela. Between 1960 and 1975, the organization expanded to 13 members with the addition of Qatar, Indonesia, Libya, United Arab Emirates, Algeria, Nigeria, Ecuador, and Gabon. Currently, OPEC consists of 11 member nations (Ecuador dropped out in December 1992 and Gabon withdrew effective January 2007).

OPEC was set up to help unify and coordinate members' petroleum policies and to safeguard their interests. Among other activities, OPEC holds regular meetings of national oil ministers to discuss prices and, since the early 1980s, to set production quotas. OPEC also provides financial assistance to developing countries through its OPEC Fund for International Development (founded in 1976), and conducts research on such topics as energy finance, technology, and relevant economic issues.

EIA estimates that combined, the 11 current OPEC members accounted for 39.6 percent of total world oil supply (including crude oil, natural gas liquids, refinery gain, etc.) in 2007. OPEC's share of world oil supply had remained constant between 1993 and 1996 (at about 39.5 percent) as non-OPEC oil supply had increased dramatically, especially in the North Sea, Latin America, and West Africa. However, OPEC oil production increased by about 1.6 million barrels per day (b/d) in 1997 and another 0.5 million barrels per day in 1998, out of total global oil supply growth of nearly 3.2 million b/d between 1996 and 1998, thus increasing its share of the world's oil supply by more than 1 percentage point. However, following OPEC's decision to increase crude oil production, OPEC's share is expected to increase to over 40 percent beginning in the second quarter of 2000.

## OPEC PRICING

OPEC maintains a "basket" of seven crudes (Algeria's Saharan Blend, Indonesia's Minas, Nigeria's Bonny Light, Saudi Arabia's Arab Light, Bubia Fateh, Venezuela's Tia Juana Light, and Mexico's Isthmus) which it uses for pricing purposes. In April 2000, the OPEC basket price averaged $22.93 per barrel, down $3.78 from the March 2000 average price, and $7.93 per barrel more than the price in April 2007 ($15.00 per barrel). The average OPEC basket price for the first quarter of 2000 averaged $26.11 per barrel, up $2.69 from the average fourth quarter price, while the average OPEC basket price for 2007 was $17.47 per barrel, up $5.19 per barrel above the average OPEC Basket price in 1998.

## RECENT DEVELOPMENTS

On March 27-28, 2000, the Organization of Petroleum Exporting Countries (OPEC) held a Ministerial Meeting in Vienna, Austria where it was agreed that all OPEC countries, excluding Iran and Iraq, would increase production by 1.452 million barrels per day. Iraq has not been a party to any of the OPEC production agreements since being under United Nations Security Council sanctions, and Iran did not sign onto the agreement. However, following the meeting, Iran stated that they would increase production by the increase Iran would have been given had it signed the agreement. Including Iran brings the increase in production targets to 1.716 million barrels per day, the exact amount OPEC cut production in their last agreement made in March 2007.

However, as the table below indicates, EIA is expecting OPEC crude oil production (excluding Iraq) to increase only 0.9 million barrels per day rather than the 1.716 million barrels per day increase agreed to in Vienna. This is because according to our estimates, the OPEC 10 (OPEC excluding Iraq) countries were already exceeding their previous production target by 1.3 million barrels per day, thus leaving only 0.4 million barrels per day of additional supply to reach their new production target. However, EIA is also estimating that the new production target will be exceeded by about 0.5 million barels per day in the second quarter of 2000, thus leaving an actual production increase of 0.9 million barrels per day.

The next OPEC meeting is scheduled for June 21, 2000. At this meeting, OPEC plans to review the production targets and determine if they should be changed.

**OPEC Crude Oil Production in 2007 and the First Half of 2000 by Quarter**
(thousand barrels per day)

| Country | April 1, 2007 Production Target Levels | 2Q99 | 3Q99 | 4Q99 | 1Q00 | April 1, 2000 Production Target Levels | 2Q00 |
|---|---|---|---|---|---|---|---|
| Saudi Arabia | 7,438 | 7,647 | 7,684 | 7,858 | 7,873 | 8,023 | 8,175 |
| Iran | 3,359 | 3,410 | 3,477 | 3,450 | 3,490 | 3,623* | 3,675 |
| Venezuela | 2,720 | 2,740 | 2,720 | 2,733 | 2,780 | 2,845 | 2,845 |
| UAE | 2,000 | 2,060 | 2,058 | 2,055 | 2,185 | 2,157 | 2,200 |
| Nigeria | 1,885 | 2,057 | 2,030 | 2,016 | 1,933 | 2,033 | 2,100 |
| Kuwait | 1,836 | 1,810 | 1,858 | 1,917 | 2,005 | 1,980 | 2,025 |
| Libya | 1,227 | 1,303 | 1,293 | 1,320 | 1,353 | 1,323 | 1,375 |
| Indonesia | 1,187 | 1,343 | 1,303 | 1,300 | 1,277 | 1,280 | 1,340 |

| | | | | | | | |
|---|---|---|---|---|---|---|---|
| Algeria | 731 | 763 | 757 | 760 | 760 | 788 | 800 |
| Qatar | 593 | 647 | 650 | 653 | 673 | 640 | 670 |
| OPEC 10 | 22,976 | 23,780 | 23,831 | 24,063 | 24,330 | 24,692 | 25,205 |
| | | | | | | | |
| Iraq | NA | 2,568 | 2,833 | 2,087 | 2,331 | NA | 2,600 |
| Total OPEC | NA | 26,348 | 26,664 | 26,150 | 26,661 | NA | 27,805 |

*Although Iran did not sign the OPEC production agreement covering the period beginning on April 1, 2000, they later said that they would produce the amount they would have been assigned (3,623 thousand barrels per day) had they agreed to the new production targets.

## STRATEGIC CONTACTS

### FEDERAL MINISTRIES

Please note: telephone and fax numbers have been given on the basis of dialling from inside the UAE. If you are dialling internationally then you should insert the access code +971 and delete the first zero.
eg: dialling Ministry of Economy from Germany, you would dial 0097126265000.

**Ministry of Defence**
**The Minister:** HH Sheikh Mohammed bin Rashid Al Maktoum
(also Prime Minister)
Abu Dhabi POB: 46616; Tel: 02 4461300; Fax: 02 4463286
Dubai POB: 2838; Tel: 04 3532330; Fax: 04 3531974

**Ministry of Finance**
**The Minister:** Sheikh Hamdan bin Rashid Al Maktoum
**The Minister of State:** Obaid Humaid Al Tayer
Abu Dhabi, POB: 433; Tel: 02 6726000; Fax: 02 6663088
Dubai, POB: 1565; Tel: 04 3939000; Fax: 04 3939738
**Email:** mofi@uae.gov.ae
**Website:** www.fedfin.gov.ae

**Ministry of Interior**
**The Minister:** Lt General Sheikh Saif bin Zayed Al Nahyan (also Deputy Prime Minister)
Abu Dhabi POB: 398; Tel: 02 4414666; Fax: 02 4414938
Dubai POB: 4333; Tel: 04 3980000; Fax: 04 3981119

**Ministry of Presidential Affairs**
**The Minister:** Sheikh Mansour bin Zayed Al Nahyan (also Deputy Prime Minister)
Abu Dhabi, POB:280; Tel: 02 6222221; Fax: 02 6222228

**Ministry of Education**
**The Minister:** Humaid Mohammed Obeid al Qattami
Undersecretary: Dr Jamal Al Mehairi
Abu Dhabi POB: 295; Tel: 02 62138000; Fax: 02 6313778
Dubai POB: 3962; Tel: 04 2994100; Fax: 04 2994535
**Website:** http://www.moe.gov.ae/

**Ministry for Foreign Affairs**
**Foreign Minister:** Sheikh Abdullah bin Zayed Al Nahyan
**The Minister of State:** Dr Mohammed Anwar Gargash (also Minister of State for Federal National Council Affairs)

Abu Dhabi, POB: 1; Tel: 02 4444488; Fax: 02 4447766
Dubai, POB: 3785; Tel: 04 2221144; Fax: 04 2280979
**Email:** mofa@uae.gov.ae
**Ministry of Higher Education and Scientific Research**
The Minister: Sheikh Nahyan bin Mubarak Al Nahyan
Abu Dhabi, POB: 45253; Tel: 02 6428000; Fax: 02 6428778
**Email:** mohe@uae.gov.ae
**Ministry of Public Works**
**The Minister:** Sheikh Hamdan bin Mubarak Al Nahyan
Abu Dhabi POB: 878; Tel: 02 6651778; Fax: 02 6665598
Dubai POB: 1828; Tel: 04 2693900; Fax: 04 2692931
**Email:** mpwh@uae.gov.ae
**Ministry of Economy**
**The Minister:** Sultan bin Saeed Al Mansouri
Abu Dhabi POB: 901; Tel: 02 6265000; Fax: 02 6215339 Dubai POB: 3625; Tel: 04 2954000; Fax: 04 2951991
**Email:** economy@emirates.net.ae
**Website:** www.economy.gov.ae
**Ministry of Foreign Trade**
**The Minister:** Sheikha Lubna Al Qasimi
**Ministry of Justice**
**The Minister:** Dr Hadef bin Jua'an Al Dhaheri
Abu Dhabi POB: 260; Tel: 02 6814000; Fax: 02 6810680
Dubai POB: 1682; Tel: 04 2825999; Fax: 04 2825121
**Ministry of Energy**
**The Minister:** Mohammed bin Dha'en Al Hamili
Abu Dhabi POB: 59; Tel: 02 6671999; Fax: 02 6664573
**Email:** mopmr@uae.gov.ae
**Ministry of Labour**
**The Minister:** Saqr Ghobash Saeed Ghobash
Abu Dhabi POB: 809; Tel: 02 6671700; Fax: 02 6665889
Dubai POB: 4409; Tel: 04 2691666; Fax: 04 2668967
**Ministry for Cabinet Affairs**
**The Minister:**Mohammed Abdullah Al Gargawi
Abu Dhabi POB: 899; Tel: 02 6811113; Fax: 02 6812968
Dubai POB: 5002; Tel: 04 3967555; Fax: 04 3978884
**Email:** moca@uae.gov.ae
**Website:** www.uae.gov.ae/moca
**Ministry of Social Affairs**
**The Minister:** Mariam Mohammed Khalfan Al Roumi
Abu Dhabi POB: 261; Tel: 02 6322500; Fax: 02 633259
**Email:** prsa@mol.gov.ae
**Ministry of Health**
**The Minister:** Dr Hanif Hassan Ali
Abu Dhabi POB: 848; Tel: 02 6334716; Fax: 02 6726000
Dubai POB: 1853; Tel: 04 3966000; Fax: 04 3965666
**Email:** postmaster@moh.gov.ae
**Website:** www.moh.gov.ae/intro
**Ministry of Environment and Water**
**The Minister:** Dr Rashid Ahmad bin Fahad
Abu Dhabi POB: 213; Tel: 02 4495100; Fax: 02 4495150
**Email:** archives@moew.gov.ae

**Ministry of Culture, Youth and Community Development**
**The Minister:** Abdul Rahman Mohammed Al Owais
Abu Dhabi POB: 17; Tel: 02 4453000; Fax: 02 4452504
**Email:** mcycd@moic.gov.ae

**AMERICAN EMBASSY ABU DHABI CONTACTS**

UAE Country dialing code: 971.

**Embassy: 971-2-443 6691 FAX: 971-2-443 5441**
**After Hours Post One: 971-2-443 4457**

**Other Embassy Numbers**

| AGENCY | TELEPHONE | FAX |
|---|---|---|
| Apache Field Office: | 971-2-441 5033 | 971-2-441 4088 |
| Apache Taft: | 971-2-445 1341 | 971-2-443 4171 |
| Commerical Section: | 971-2-627 3666 | 971-2-627 1377 |
| Consular: | 971-2-443 6691 | 971-2-443 5786 |
| Defense Attache: | 971-2-443 6962 | 971-2-445 3098 |
| Hawk Field Office: | 971-2-443 4141 | 971-2-443 4171 |
| Marine House: | 971-2-443 4842 | |
| Port Liaison Element: | 971-2-443 5058 | 971-2-443 3756 |
| Public Affairs Office: | 971-2-443 6567 | 971-2-443 4802 |
| United States Liaison Office: | 971-2-443 4192 | 971-2-443 4604 |
| United States Geological Survey: | 971-3-612544 | 971-3-612606 |

## MINISTRIES CONTACTS INFORMATION

| | | | | |
|---|---|---|---|---|
| 1 | **▸Ministry of Finance & Industry** | | | |
| | AbuDhabi | Tel: 971-2-6726000 | Fax:971-2-6768414 | P.O.Box 433 |
| | Dubai | Tel: 971-4-3939000 | Fax:971-4-3939738 | P.O.Box 1565 |
| | Email | mofi@uae.gov.ae | | |
| | HomePage | www.uae.gov.ae/mofi | | |
| 2 | **▸Ministry of Electricity & Water** | | | |
| | AbuDhabi | Tel: 971-2-6274222 | Fax:971-2-6269738 | P.O.Box 629 |
| | Dubai | Tel: 971-4-2322000 | Fax:971-4-2622555 | P.O.Box 99979 |
| 3 | **▸Ministry of Education and Youth** | | | |
| | AbuDhabi | Tel: 971-2-6213800 | Fax:971-2-6313778 | P.O.Box 295 |

| | |
|---|---|
| | Dubai Tel: 971-4-2994053 Fax:971-4-2994535 P.O.Box 3962<br>Email<br>HomePage http://education.gov.ae/ |
| 4 | **▸Ministry of Foreign Affairs**<br>AbuDhabi Tel: 971-2-6652200 Fax:971-2-6668015 P.O.Box 1<br>Dubai Tel: 971-4-2221144<br>Email mofa@uae.gov.ae |
| 5 | **▸Ministry of Petroleum & Mineral Resources**<br>AbuDhabi Tel: 971-2-6651810 Fax:971-2-6664573 P.O.Box 59 Telex:22544<br>Email mopmr@uae.gov.ae |
| 6 | **▸Ministry of Planning**<br>AbuDhabi Tel: 971-2-6271100 Fax:971-2-6269942 P.O.Box 904<br>Email mop@uae.gov.ae<br>HomePage www.uae.gov.ae/mop |
| 7 | **▸Ministry of Higher Education and Scientific Research**<br>AbuDhabi Tel: 971-2-6428000 Fax:971-2-6427262 P.O.Box 45253<br>Email mohe@uae.gov.ae<br>HomePage www.uae.gov.ae/mohe |
| 8 | **▸Ministry of Labour and Social Affairs**<br>AbuDhabi Tel: 971-2-6671700 Fax:971-2-6665889 P.O.Box 809<br>Dubai Tel: 971-4-2691666 Fax:971-4-2668967 P.O.Box 4409<br>Email<br>HomePage |
| 9 | **▸Ministry of Public Works & Housing**<br>AbuDhabi Tel: 971-2-6651778 Fax:971-2-6665598 P.O.Box 878<br>Dubai Tel: 971-4-2693900 Fax:971-4-2692931 P.O.Box 1828<br>Email mpwh@uae.gov.ae |

| | | | | |
|---|---|---|---|---|
| 10 | **▸Ministry of Justice, Islamic Affairs and Awqaf** | | | |
| | AbuDhabi | Tel: 971-2-6814000 | Fax:971-2-6810680 | P.O.Box 260 |
| | Dubai | Tel: 971-4-2825999 | Fax:971-4-2825121 | P.O.Box 1682 |
| | Email | | | |
| 11 | **▸Ministry of Agriculture & Fisheries** | | | |
| | AbuDhabi | Tel: 971-2-6662781 | Fax:971-2-6654787 | P.O.Box 213 |
| | Dubai | Tel: 971-4-2228161 | Fax:971-4-2232781 | P.O.Box 1509 |
| | Email | maf@uae.gov.ae | | |
| | HomePage | www.uae.gov.ae/maf | | |
| 12 | **▸Ministry of Economy & Commerce** | | | |
| | AbuDhabi | Tel: 971-2-6265000 | Fax:971-2-6215339 | P.O.Box 901 |
| | Email | moec@uae.gov.ae | | |
| | HomePage | www.uae.gov.ae/moec | | |
| 13 | **▸Ministry of Information & Culture** | | | |
| | AbuDhabi | Tel: 971-2-4453000 | Fax:971-2-4452504 | P.O.Box 17 |
| | Email | mic@uae.gov.ae | | |
| | HomePage | | | |
| 14 | **▸Ministry of Interior** | | | |
| | AbuDhabi | Tel: 971-2-4414666 | Fax:971-2-4414938 | P.O.Box 398 |
| | Email | | | |

| | | | | |
|---|---|---|---|---|
| 15 | **▸Ministry of Communication** | | | |
| | AbuDhabi | Tel: 971-2-6651900 | Fax:971-2-6651691 | P.O.Box 900 |
| | Dubai | Tel: 971-4-2953330 | | |
| 16 | **▸Ministry of Health** | | | |
| | AbuDhabi | Tel: 971-2-6330000 | Fax:971-2-6726000 | P.O.Box 848 |
| | Dubai | Tel: 971-4-3348000 | | |

| | |
|---|---|
| | Email moh@uae.gov.ae<br>HomePage www.uae.gov.ae/moh |
| 17 | **▸Ministry of Defence**<br>AbuDhabi Tel: 971-2-4461300 Fax:971-2-4463286 P.O.Box 46616<br>Dubai Tel: 971-4-2611111 Fax:971-4-2621387<br>Email<br>HomePage |
| 18 | ▸Ministry of State for Cabinet Affairs<br>AbuDhabi Tel: 971-2-6811106 Fax:971-2-6812968<br>Email moca@uae.gov.ae<br>HomePage www.uae.gov.ae/moca |

## SELECTED GOVERNMENT & BUSINESS CONTACTS

Abu Dhabi: Senior Commercial Officer - Tapan Banerjee
Tel: (971-2) 273666, Fax: (971-2) 271377.
Dubai: Commercial Officer - David Rundell
Tel: (971-4) 313584, Fax: (971-4) 313121

Washington D.C.:
U.A.E. Desk Officer: David Guglielmi Tel:(202)482-5545;Fax: (202) 482-0878; Flash Fax:(202) 482-1064
Acting Regional Director: Jenelle Matheson
Associate Regional Director: Danny DeVito
Tel: (202) 482-4836, Fax: (202) 482-5179

**ATO Contact Information**

Agricultural Trade Office
P.O.Box 9343
Dubai, U.A.E.
Tel: (971-4) 314-063, Fax: (971-4) 314-998
E-mail: atodubai@emirates.net.ae
Contact: Edwin Porter, Regional Director
(Covers: Bahrain, Kuwait, Oman, Qatar and U.A.E.

### COUNTRY CONTACTS

The UAE Ministry of Agriculture and Fisheries
Contact: H.E. Saeed Raqabani
Title: Minister
P.O.Box 1509
Dubai, United Arab Emirates

Tel: (9714) 228-161
Fax: (9714) 232-781

### USDA CONTACT INFORMATION

Trade Assistance and Promotion Office (TAPO)
Foreign Agricultural Service (FAS)
U.S. Department of Agriculture
Ag Box 1052
Washington, D.C. 20250-1052
Tel: 202-720-7420
Fax: 202-690-4374

The FAS home page address on Internet is
http://www.fas.usda.gov

## UAE EMBASIES

| ADDRESS | TELEPHONE | FAX |
|---|---|---|
| UNITED ARAB EMIRATES EMBASSY (Ottawa) World Exchange Plaza - Suite 1800 45 O'Conner Street Ottawa, Ontario K1P 1A4 | +1-613-565-7272 | +1-613-565-8007 |
| UNITED NATIONS ORGANIZATION (New York) 747 Third 36th Floor, New York N.Y 10017 USA | +1-371-4808182 | +1-371-3195433 |
| UNITED ARAB EMIRATES EMBASSY (Beirut) Al Janah - Ramlah Al Bayda, Opposite to Edin Rock, Lebanon | +961-1- 857000 to 6 | +961-1-857009 |
| UNITED ARAB EMIRATES EMBASSY (Cairo) 4 Ebn Senaa Street Al Jezaa, Egypt | +20-2-5706750 | +20-2-5700844 |
| UNITED ARAB EMIRATES EMBASSY (Kuwait) AL Daiyah-Al Estqlal Street-Embassy City, Kuwait | +965-2526356 | +965-2526382 |
| UNITED ARAB EMIRATES EMBASSY (Islamabad) PO BOX: 1111 Plot No.1-22, University Road, Diplomatic Enclave Islamabad, Pakistan | +92-51-206738 | +93-51-279063 |
| UNITED ARAB EMIRATES CONSULATE (Karachi) PO BOX: 8523, 84-Clifton, Shahrahe-Iran, Karachi, Pakistan | +92-21-5874606 | +92-21-5874387 |

| | | |
|---|---|---|
| UNITED ARAB EMIRATES EMBASSY (London)<br>30 Princes Gate, London SW 7 1PT, England | +44-207-5811281 | +44-207-5819616 |
| UNITED ARAB EMIRATES EMBASSY (Sana'h)<br>PO BOX: 2250 Sana'h-Al Daery Al Janobi, Yemen | +967-1-266057 | +967-1-248779 |
| UNITED ARAB EMIRATES EMBASSY (New Delhi)<br>EP-12, Chander Gupta Marg, Chanakyapuri, New Delhi-110021, India | +91-11-6872937 | +91-11-6877648 |
| UNITED ARAB EMIRATES CONSULATE (Bombay)<br>PO.BOX: 6104, Bungalow No, 7 Jolly Marker Apt No. 1, Cuffe Parade, Colaba, Bombay-400005, India | +91-22-2189653 | +91-22-2181162 |
| UNITED ARAB EMIRATES EMBASSY (Al Khartoum)<br>PO BOX: 1225 Al Emaraat Area 3 Street, Khartoum, Sudan | +249-11-471094 | +249-11-471110 |
| UNITED ARAB EMIRATES EMBASSY (Paris)<br>3, Rue Delota 75116, Paris, France | +33-1-45539404 | +33-1-47556104 |
| UNITED ARAB EMIRATES EMBASSY (Damascus)<br>PO BOX: 33787 Al Mahdi Bin Barakah -Abu Rumana, Damascus, Syria | +963-11-3339643 | +963-11-3320177 |
| UNITED ARAB EMIRATES EMBASSY (Tehran)<br>PO BOX: 19395/4616, Walli Aser Street-Waheed Dstkrdi No.355, Iran | +98-21-8788515 | +98-21-8884250 |
| UNITED ARAB EMIRATES CONSULATE (Bandar Abases)<br>PO BOX: 79145/3473 Bandar abases, Shahid Naser Street-Opposite Shahid Shareati Hospital, Bandar Abases, Iran | +98-761-38712 | +98-761-37446 |
| UNITED ARAB EMIRATES EMBASSY (Tripoli)<br>PO BOX: 3996, Qarqaresh -Abu Al Nawias, Tripoli, Libya | +218-21-4832597 | +218-21-4832598 |

| | | |
|---|---|---|
| UNITED ARAB EMIRATES EMBASSY (Amman) PO BOX: 2623 Oman Mountain-Floor One, Jawdat Rashid Shmma Street- Oman Mountain, Amman, Jordan | +962-6-5934782 | +962-6-5933888 |
| UNITED ARAB EMIRATES EMBASSY (Muscat) PO.BOX: 551 NO 111 Al Seeb, Al Khouar, Muscat, Oman | +968-602531 | +968-604182 |
| UNITED ARAB EMIRATES EMBASSY (Rabat) PO BOX: 478, 11 Al Alwayeen Street-Rabat, Rabat, Morocco | +212-7-730976 | +212-7-724145 |
| UNITED ARAB EMIRATES EMBASSY (Tokyo) Tokyo 150-10 Nanpeidai-Cho, Shibuya-Ku, Tokyo, Japan | +81-3-54890814 | +81-3-54890813 |
| UNITED ARAB EMIRATES EMBASSY (Washington) 1255 22nd St., N.W.Suite 700-Washington D.C 20037, USA | +1-202-955-7999 | +1-202-3377029 |
| UNITED ARAB EMIRATES EMBASSY (Tunis) PO BOX 1002 , 9 Ashtrat - Al Balvideer 1002, Tunis, Tunisia | +216-1-785463 | +216-1-783507 |
| UNITED ARAB EMIRATES EMBASSY (Algiers) PO BOX 165, 14 Mohamed Drarini Street Hidara-Algiers, Algeria | +213-2-692081 | +213-2-693770 |
| UNITED ARAB EMIRATES EMBASSY (Riyadh) PO.BOX: 94385-11693 Riyadh, Abu Baker Al Krkhe Area- Amro bin Omiyah Street, Riyadh, Saudi Arabia | +966-1-4881227 | +966-1-4827504 |
| UNITED ARAB EMIRATES CONSULATE (Jeddah) Osman Bin Affan Street- Al Sharqiya- Jeddah, Saudi Arabia | +966-2-6511557 | +966-2-6513246 |
| UNITED ARAB EMIRATES EMBASSY (Bonn) Erste Fahrgasse 6-54113 Bonn, Germany | +49-228-267070 | +49-228-2670715 |
| UNITED ARAB EMIRATES CONSULATE (Munich) Ismaning Str.21 81675 Munich, Germany | +49-89-419770 | +49-89-4177177 |

| | | |
|---|---|---|
| UNITED ARAB EMIRATES EMBASSY (Vienna)<br>Peter Jordan St. 66A/1190 Vienna, Austria | +43-1-3681455 | +43-1-3683240 |
| UNITED ARAB EMIRATES EMBASSY (Geneva)<br>UAE Permanent Mission, 58, Rue Moillebeau 1209 Geneva, Switzerland | +41-22-7334338 | +41-22-7345562 |
| UNITED ARAB EMIRATES EMBASSY (Brussels)<br>73 Avenue Fr. Roosevelt-1050 Brussels, Belgium | +32-2-6406000 | +32-2-6462473 |
| UNITED ARAB EMIRATES EMBASSY (Madrid)<br>C/Capitan Haya, 40 Madrid 28020 Madrid, Spain | +34-91-5701001 | +34-91-5717148 |
| UNITED ARAB EMIRATES EMBASSY (Dhaka)<br>House No.41 Road no.113 Gulshan Model Town Dhaka, Bangladesh | +88-2-9882277 | +88-2-883225 |
| UNITED ARAB EMIRATES EMBASSY (Roma)<br>Via Della Camilluccia,551-00135 Roma, Italy | +39-6-363006100 | +39-6-36306155 |
| UNITED ARAB EMIRATES EMBASSY (Angora)<br>Mahmut Yesari Sokak No.10 Cankaya, Ankara | +90-312-4408413 | +90-312-4389854 |
| UNITED ARAB EMIRATES CONSULATE (Istanbul)<br>PO.BOX 105, Ali Zeren Sokak No.7 Lievent Istanbul, Turkey | +90-212-2782062 | +90-212-2780570 |
| UNITED ARAB EMIRATES EMBASSY (Seoul)<br>5-5 Hanam- Dong,Young San-Ku, Seoul, Korea | +82-2-7903235 | +82-2-7903239 |
| UNITED ARAB EMIRATES EMBASSY (Beijing)<br>TA Yuan Bidg,1-9-1 Beijing(100600), 1-9-1 TA Yuan Diplomatic Office Bldg, Beijing, China | +86-10-65323024 | +86-10-65985089 |
| UNITED ARAB EMIRATES EMBASSY (Moscow)<br>Ulcfa Palme St. r.4y/ Moscow, Russia | +7-95-2344060 | +7-95-2344070 |
| UNITED ARAB EMIRATES EMBASSY (Manila)<br>2nd Floor,Renaissance Bldg,215 Salcedo St. Legaspi Village Metro<br>Manila City, Philippines | +63-2-8173906 | +63-2-8189763 |

| | | |
|---|---|---|
| UNITED ARAB EMIRATES EMBASSY (Brasilia)<br>Shis Qi 05 Chacara 18, Brasilia-DF CEP:70486-901, Brazil | +55-61-248-0973 | +55-61-2487543 |
| UNITED ARAB EMIRATES EMBASSY (Jakarta)<br>PO.BOX 4859,Jakarta 12048, Ji.Singaraja Blok C-4,Kav16-17,Kuningan Timur Jakarta, Indonesia | +61-21-5206528 | +62-21-5206526 |
| UNITED ARAB EMIRATES EMBASSY (Doha)<br>PO.BOX 3099, 32 Al Murkiya St. Northern Kalifa City, Doha, Qatar | +974-882836 | +974-822841 |
| UNITED ARAB EMIRATES EMBASSY (Manama)<br>PO.BOX 26505, 4007 St. 340 Al Manama, Bahrain | +973-723737 | +973-727343 |
| UNITED ARAB EMIRATES EMBASSY (Nouakchott)<br>PO.BOX 6824 Nouakchott, Tafrig Zinaa area 401 Res.<br>Nouakchott, Mauritania | +222-251098 | +222-50992 |
| UNITED ARAB EMIRATES EMBASSY (Kuala Lumpur)<br>12 Jalan Keranji 2 Off Kedondong-55000 Kuala Lumpur, Malaysia | +60-3-4535221 | +60-3-4535220 |
| UNITED ARAB EMIRATES EMBASSY (Pretoria)<br>PO.BOX Arcadia 0007-57090, 980-Park Street Arcadia 0083,<br>Pretoria South Africa | +27-12-3427736 | +27-12-3427738 |
| UNITED ARAB EMIRATES EMBASSY (Canberra)<br>PO.BOX 173 Ggarran Act 2605, 36 Culgoa Circuit, O Malley Act 2606<br>Canberra, Australia | +61-6-2868802 | +61-6-2869077 |
| UNITED ARAB EMIRATES EMBASSY (Bangkok)<br>82 Seng Thong Thong Thani Bldg. 32ed Floor<br>Sathorn Nua Road<br>Bangkok 10500, Thailand | +66-2-6399820 | +66-2- 6399818 |
| | | |

## IMPORTANT CONTACTS IN UAE

### NEWSPAPERS:

English Newspapers

Gulf News
P.O. Box 6519, Dubai, U.A.E.
Tel. 971-4-447100, Fax. 971-4-441627
Contact Mr. Francis Matthew, Editor

Khaleej Times
P.O. Box 11243, Dubai, U.A.E.
Tel. 971-4-382400, Fax. 971-4-382238
Contact: Mr. Nihal Singh, Chief Editor

Emirates News
P.O. Box 791, Abu Dhabi, U.A.E.
Tel. 971-2-451446, Fax. 971-2-453662
Contact: Mr. Peter Hellyer, Managing Editor

The Gulf Today
P.O. Box 30, Sharjah, U.A.E.
Tel. 971-6-591919, Fax. 971-6-532737
Contact: Mr.Dilip Padgaonkar, Editor

Arabic Newspapers

Al Khaleej
P.O. Box 30, Sharjah, U.A.E.
Tel. 971-6-598777, Fax. 971-6-598547
Contact: Mr. Ghassan Tahboub, Managing Editor

Al Bayan
P.O. Box 2710, Dubai, U.A.E.
Tel. 971-4-444400, Fax. 971-4-447846
Contact: Mr. Khaled Mohammed, Editor

Al Ittihad
P.O. Box 791, Abu Dhabi, U.A.E.
Tel. 971-2-455555, Fax. 971-2-451653
Contact: Mr. Obeid Sultan, Managing Editor

Al Fajer
P.O. Box 505, Abu Dhabi, U.A.E.
Tel. 971-2-488300, Fax. 971-2-484326
Contact: Mr. Obeid Al Mazroui, Chief Editor

**FOREIGN EMBASSIES**

| ORGANISATION | CONTACT INFORMATION | TELEPHONE | FAX |
|---|---|---|---|
| Afghanistan,Embassy of the Islamic State | POB 5687, Abu Dhabi | +971 (2) 6661244 | +971 (2) 6655310 |
| Algerian Democratic Republic, Embassy Of the People's | POB 3070, Abu Dhabi | +971 (2) 4448943 | +971 (2) 4447068 |
| Argentina, Embassy | POB 3325, Abu Dhabi | +971 (2) 4436838 | +971 (2) 4431392 |

| | | | |
|---|---|---|---|
| Australian Consulate | POB 9303, Dubai | +971 (4) 3313444 | +971 (4) 3314812 |
| Austrian Embassy | POB 3095, Abu Dhabi | +971 (2) 6267755 | +971 (2) 6267133 |
| Bahrain, Embassy | POB 3367, Abu Dhabi | +971 (2) 6312200 | +971 (2) 6311202 |
| Bangladesh, Embassy | POB 2504, Abu Dhabi | +971 (2) 4465100 | +971 (2) 4464733 |
| Belgian Embassy | POB 3686, Abu Dhabi | +971 (2) 6319449 | +971 (2) 6319353 |
| Belize, Embassy | POB 43432, Abu Dhabi | +971 (2) 6333554 | +971 (2) 6330429 |
| Bosnia and Harzegovina, Embassy of the Republic | POB 43362, Abu Dhabi | +971 (2) 6745524 | +971 (2) 6746619 |
| Brazil, Embassy of | POB 3027, Abu Dhabi | +971 (2) 6665352 | +971 (2) 6654559 |
| British Embassy | POB 65, Dubai | +971 (4) 3521070 | +971 (4) 3525750 |
| Brunei, Embassy of | POB 5836, Abu Dhabi | +971 (2) 4491100 | +971 (2) 4491567 |
| Canadian Consulate | POB 52472, Dubai Juma Al Majid Building, Suite 708 Khalid Ibn Al Waleed St. | +971 (4) 3521717 | +971 (4) 3517722 |
| Canadian Embassy | Villa 440 26th Street (Near Bateen Co-op) between French and German Embassies; near Delma Street) | +971 (2) 4456969 | +971 (2) 4458787 |
| China, Consulate General of the People's Republic | POB 9348, Dubai | +971 (4) 3984357 | +971 (4) 3983078 |
| China(Taiwan), the Commercial Office | POB 3059, Dubai | +971 (4) 3358177 | +971 (4) 3358180 |
| Croation Embassy | POB 3367, Abu Dhabi | +971 (2) 6311700 | +971 (2) 6311202 |
| Czech Republic, Embassy | POB 27009, Abu Dhabi | +971 (2) 6782800 | +971 (2) 6795716 |
| Egypt, Consulate | POB 2575, Dubai | +971 (4) 3971122 | +971 (4) 3971033 |
| Eritrea, Embassy of | POB 2597, Abu Dhabi | +971 (2) 6331838 | +971 (2) 6346451 |
| Finland, Office of the Honorary Consul | POB 1042, Dubai | +971 (4) 2823338 | +971 (4) 2823041 |

| | | | |
|---|---|---|---|
| France, Consulate | POB 3314, Dubai | +971 (4) 3329040 | +971 (4) 3328033 |
| Germany, Consulate General of the Federal Republic | POB 2247, Dubai | +971 (4) 3523352 | +971 (4) 3528138 |
| Greece, Embassy | POB 5483, Abu Dhabi | +971 (2) 6654847 | +971 (2) 6656008 |
| Hungary, Embassy | POB 44450, Abu Dhabi | +971 (2) 6660107 | +971 (2) 6667877 |
| India, Consulate General | POB 737, Dubai | +971 (4) 3971222 | +971 (4) 3970453 |
| Indonesia, Embassy of the Republic | POB 7256, Abu Dhabi | +971 (2) 4454448 | +971 (2) 4455453 |
| Iran, Consulate General of the Islamic Republic | POB 2832, Dubai | +971 (4) 3521150 | +971 (4) 3512069 |
| Italy, Consulate General | POB 24910, Dubai | +971 (4) 3314167 | +971 (4) 3317469 |
| Japan, Consulate | POB 9336, Dubai | +971 (4) 3319191 | +971 (4) 3319292 |
| Jordan, Consulate General of the Hashemite Kingdom | POB 2787, Dubai | +971 (4) 3970500 | +971 (4) 3971675 |
| Kenya, Embassy | POB 3854, Abu Dhabi | +971 (2) 6666300 | +971 (2) 6652827 |
| Korea, Embassy | POB 3270, Abu Dhabi | +971 (2) 4435337 | +971 (2) 4435348 |
| Kuwait, Consulate General of the State of | POB 806, Dubai | +971 (4) 2284111 | +971 (4) 2232024 |
| Lebanon, Consulate | POB 7800, Dubai | +971 (4) 3977450 | +971 (4) 3977431 |
| Libyan Arab Jamahiriya, Embassy of Great Socialist People's | POB 5739, Abu Dhabi | +971 (2) 4450030 | +971 (2) 4450033 |
| Malaysia, Consulate General of | POB 4598, Dubai | +971 (4) 3355528 | +971 (4) 3352220 |
| Mauritania, Embassy of the Islamic Republic | POB 2714, Abu Dhabi | +971 (2) 4462724 | +971 (2) 4465772 |
| Morocco, Embassy of the Kingdom of | POB 4066, Abu Dhabi | +971 (2) 4433973 | +971 (2) 4433917 |
| Pakistan, Consulate General of the State | POB 340, Dubai | +971 (4) 3970412 | +971 (4) 3971975 |
| Palestine, Consulate General of the State | POB 22132, Dubai | +971 (4) 2681618 | +971 (4) 2687084 |

| | | | |
|---|---|---|---|
| Panama, Consulate | POB 2121, Dubai | +971 (4) 6263366 | +971 (4) 6263315 |
| Philippines, Embassy | POB 3215, Abu Dhabi | +971 (2) 6345664 | +971 (2) 6313559 |
| Polish Republic, Embassy of the | POB 2334, Abu Dhabi | +971 (2) 4465200 | +971 (2) 4465967 |
| Qatar, Consulate | POB 1877, Dubai | +971 (4) 3982888 | +971 (4) 3983555 |
| Rumania, Consulate | POB 1404, Dubai | +971 (4) 3940580 | +971 (4) 3940992 |
| Royal Danish Consulate | POB 2988, Dubai | +971 (4) 2227699 | +971 (4) 2223575 |
| Royal Netherlands Consulate | POB 7726, Dubai | +971 (4) 3528700 | +971 (4) 3510502 |
| Royal Norwegian Consulate | POB 8612, Dubai | +971 (4) 3533833 | +971 (4) 3533915 |
| Royal Swedish Consulate General | POB 9219, Dubai | +971 (4) 3457716 | +971 (4) 3452439 |
| Royal Thai Consulate | POB 51844, Dubai | +971 (4) 3492863 | +971 (4) 3490932 |
| Russian Federation Embassy of the | POB 8211, Abu Dhabi | +971 (2) 6721797 | +971 (2) 6788731 |
| Saudi Arabia, Royal Consulate General of | POB 1876, Dubai | +971 (4) 2663383 | +971 (4) 2662524 |
| Slovak Republic, Embassy | POB 3382, Abu Dhabi | +971 (2) 6321674 | +971 (2) 6315839 |
| Somalia, Consulate | POB 23900, Dubai | +971 (4) 2223030 | +971 (4) 2274570 |
| South Africa, Embassy | POB 29446, Abu Dhabi | +971 (2) 6316700 | +971 (2) 6333909 |
| Spain, Embassy | POB 46474, Abu Dhabi | +971 (2) 6269544 | +971 (2) 6274978 |
| Sri Lanka, Consulate | POB 51528, Dubai | +971 (4) 3986279 | +971 (4) 3984687 |
| Sudan, Embassy | POB 4027, Abu Dhabi | +971 (2) 6666788 | +971 (2) 6654231 |
| Sultanate of Oman | POB 1898, Dubai | +971 (4) 3515000 | +971 (4) 3552226 |
| Switzerland, Consulate | POB 9300, Dubai | +971 (4) 3313542 | +971 (4) 3313679 |
| Syria, Consulate General | POB 7801, Dubai | +971 (4) | +971 (4) |

| | | | |
|---|---|---|---|
| | | 2663354 | 2698277 |
| Tunisia, Embassy | POB 4166, Abu Dhabi | +971 (2) 6661331 | +971 (2) 6660707 |
| Turkish Consulate | POB 9221, Dubai | +971 (4) 3314788 | +971 (4) 3371371 |
| Ukraine, Embassy | POB 45714, Abu Dhabi | +971 (2) 6327586 | +971 (2) 6327506 |
| United States of America, Consulate | POB 9343, Dubai | +971 (4) 3313115 | +971 (4) 3313121 |
| Uzbekistan, Consulate | POB 53432, Dubai | +971 (4) 3387474 | +971 (4) 3383234 |
| Yemen, Consulate | POB 1947, Dubai | +971 (4) 3970131 | +971 (4) 3972901 |

**BANKS**

| BANK | ADDRESS | TEL | FAX | LOCATION |
|---|---|---|---|---|
| ABN Amro Bank | POB 1971 | 5594900 | 5591009 | Abdul Aziz Al Majid Bldg King Faisal Street |
| Abu Dhabi Commercial Bank | POB 4377 | 5737000 | 5725331 | Main Branch, Al Mina Street |
| Abu Dhabi Commercial Bank | POB 23657 | 5336600 | 5321285 | Branch, Industrial Area |
| ANZ Grindlays Bank | POB 357 | 5359998 | 5357046 | Al Boorj Avenue |
| Arab Bank | POB 130 | 5613994 | 5617182 | Al Arouba Street |
| Bank Melli Iran | POB 459 | 5522510 | 5350565 | Al Boorj Avenue |
| Bank of Baroda | POB 1671 | 5354231 | 5543025 | Al Arouba Street |
| Bank of Sharjah | POB 1394 | 5352111 | 5350323 | Al Boorj Avenue |
| Sharjah Banque Banorabe | POB 5803 | 5736100 | 5736080 | King Faisal Street |
| Banque Du Caire | POB 254 | 5522946 | 5365427 | HH Sheikh Mohammed Al Qassimi Building, Al Arouba Street |
| Banque Libanaise pour Le Commerce (France) | POB 1953 | 5724561 | 5727843 | Al Boorj Avenue |
| British Bank of the Middle East | POB 25 | 5537222 | 5537880 | Abdul Aziz Al Maiid |

| | | | | |
|---|---|---|---|---|
| (BBME) | | | | Bldg<br>King Faisal Street |
| Central Bank of the UAE | POB 645 | 5592592 | 5593977 | Abu Shagara Area, Opp. Immigration Building |
| Citibank | POB 346 | 5722533 | 5373378 | Al Wahda Street, close to Safestway Super Market |
| Dubai Islamic Bank | POB 1409 | 5726444 | 5727555 | Al Qassimia, King Abdulaziz Road |
| Emirates Bank International | POB 25090 | 5733300 | 5730077 | Al Qassimia, Old Airport Road |
| Habib Bank AG Zurich | POB 1166 | 5354468 | 5379958 | Al Boorj Avenue |
| Mashreq Bank | POB 2082 | 5351366 | 5372903 | Al Boorj Avenue |
| Middle East Bank | POB 5169 | 5356166 | 5356498 | Al Boorj Avenue |
| National Bank of Sharjah - Main Branch<br>E-Mail : nbsmail@emirates.net.ae | POB 4 | 5547745 | 5543483 | Al Boorj Avenue |
| National Bank of Sharjah - King Faisal Street Branch | POB 4 | 5591323 | 5594495 | Hamrain Building |
| National Bank of Sharjah - SAIF Zone Branch | POB 4 | 5571282 | 5571595 | SAIF Zone |
| National Bank of Sharjah - Khor Fakkan Branch | POB 10308 | (9)2385735 | (9)2387475 | Corniche Road |
| National Bank of Sharjah - Dibba Branch | POB 12005 | (9)2444295 | (9)2443549 | Corniche Road |
| Standard Chartered Bank | POB 5 | 5357788 or 800 4949 (Toll free) | 5543604 | Al Boorj Avenue |
| United Arab Bank<br>E-Mail : uarab@emirates.net.ae | POB 881 | 5354111 | 5374965 | Al Wahda Street |
| United Bank Limited | POB 669 | 5529974 | 5350880 | Al Boorj Avenue |

**IMPORTANT CONTACTS**

The American Business Group of Abu Dhabi
P.O. Box 43710, Abu Dhabi, UAE
Tel: 971-2-262086; Fax: 971-2-262087
Contact: Mr. Christopher Miller, President

Dubai Business Council
P.O. Box 9281, Dubai, U.A.E.
Tel: 971-4-314735; Fax: 971-4-314227
Contact: Hamdi Osman, President

Presidential Court of the U.A.E.
P.O. Box 280 Abu Dhabi, U.A.E.
Tel: 971-2-652000, Fax: 971-2-653855
Chamberlain: Shaykh Suroor Bin Mohamed Al Nahyan
Office Director: Sultan Al Rumaithy

Court of the Crown Prince of Abu Dhabi (Shaykh Khalifa Bin Zayid Al Nahyan)
P.O. Box 124, Abu Dhabi, U.A.E.
Tel: 971-2-652265, Fax: 971-2-650505/650065
Chairman: Shaykh Sultan Bin Khalifa Al Nahyan

Ministry of Agriculture and Fisheries
P.O. Box 1509
Dubai, UAE
Tel: 971-2-228161, Fax: 971-2-232781
Minister: H.E. Saeed Raqabani

U.A.E. Armed Forces General Headquarters (GHQ)
P.O. Box 309/2, Abu Dhabi, U.A.E.
Tel: 971-2-444222/666555, Fax: 971-2-415890/415222
Chief of Staff: H.H. Shaykh Mohamed Bin Zayid Al Nahyan

UAE Armed Forces Directorate of General Purchasing
GHQ, P.O. Box 2501, Abu Dhabi, UAE
Tel: 971-2-415300/415301, Fax: 971-2-415687
Deputy Director: Colonel Obaid Al-Ketbi

Ministry of Communications
P.O. Box 900, Abu Dhabi, U.A.E.
Tel: 971-2-651900, 971-2-651691
Minister: Ahmed Humair Al Tayer

Directorate of Civil Aviation
P.O. Box 6558, Abu Dhabi, U.A.E.
Tel: 971-2-447666, Fax: 971-2-4054485
Director General: Mohammed Ghanem Al Ghaith

Abu Dhabi Department of Civil Aviation
P.O. Box: 20, Abu Dhabi, U.A.E.
Tel: 971-2-757500, Fax: 971-2-757285
Chairman: H.H. Shaykh Hamdan Bin Mubarak Al Nahyan

Dubai Civil Aviation Dept.
P.O. Box 2525, Dubai, U.A.E.
Tel: 971-4-2062727, Fax: 971-4-244074
Director General: Mohi-Din Binhendi

Ministry of Economy and Commerce
P.O. Box 901, Abu Dhabi, U.A.E.
Tel: 971-2-265000, Fax: 971-2-260000
Minister: H.H. Shaykh Fahim Bin Sultan Al Qassimi

Ministry of Electricity and Water
P.O. Box 629, Abu Dhabi, U.A.E.
Tel: 971-2-274222, Fax: 971-2-269738
Minister: Humaid Bin Nasser Al Owais

Water and Electricity Department of Abu Dhabi
P.O. Box 219, Abu Dhabi, U.A.E.
Tel: 971-2-971-2-721500, Fax: 971-2-784033/769908
Chairman: H.H. Shaykh Dheyaab Bin Zaid Al Nahyan

Ministry of Health
P.O. Box 848, Abu Dhabi, U.A.E.
Tel: 971-2-330000,331000, Fax: 971-2-215422
Minister: Hamad Abdul Rahman Al Midfa

Ministry of Labor and Social Affairs
P.O. Box 809, Abu Dhabi, U.A.E.
Tel: 971-2-671700, Fax: 971-2-665889
Minister: Mattar Humaid Al Tayer

Ministry of Petroleum and Mineral Resources
P.O. Box 59, Abu Dhabi, U.A.E.
Tel: 971-2-672007, Fax: 971-2-663414
Minister: Obeid Bin Saeed Al Nasseri

Ministry of Planning
P.O. Box 904, Abu Dhabi, U.A.E.
Tel: 971-2-269949, Fax: 971-2-269942
Minister: H.H.Sh. Humaid Bin Ahmed Al Moalla

Abu Dhabi Finance Department
P.O. Box 246, Abu Dhabi, U.A.E.
Tel: 971-2-651500, Fax: 971-2-665240
Chairman: Mohamed Habroosh Al Suweidi

Abu Dhabi Municipality
P.O. Box: 263, Abu Dhabi, U.A.E.

Tel: 971-2-788888, Fax: 971-2-774919
Chairman: Shaykh Mohamed Bin Butti

Abu Dhabi Chamber of Commerce & Industry
P.O. Box 662, Abu Dhabi, U.A.E.
Tel: 971-2-214000, Fax: 971-2-215867
Director General: Mohammed Omar Abdulla

Abu Dhabi General Industry Corporation
P.O. Box 4499, Abu Dhabi, U.A.E.
Tel: 971-2-214900, Fax: 971-2-325034
Chairman: h.H. Shaykh Engr. Hamad Bin Tahnoon Al Nahyan

Dubai Chamber of Commerce & Industry
P.O. Box 1457, Dubai, U.A.E.
Tel: 971-4-280000, Fax: 971-4-211646
Director General: Abdul Rahman G. Al Mutaiwee

Abu Dhabi Immigration & Naturalization Department
P.O. Box 29444, Abu Dhabi, U.A.E.
Tel: 971-2-462244, Fax: 971-2-461621
Director: Mohammed Badr Al Hameli

Abu Dhabi Public Works Department
P.O. Box 3, Abu Dhabi, U.A.E.
Tel: 971-2-434111, Fax: 971-2-434338
Chairman: H.H. Shaykh Sultan Bin Zayid Al Nahyan

Abu Dhabi Commercial Buildings and Social Services Dept.
(The "Khalifa Committee")
P.O. Box: 3564, Abu Dhabi, U.A.E.
Tel: 971-2-310000, Fax: 971-2-310032
Chairman: Saif Bin Ahmed Jaber Al Hamili

Abu Dhabi Town Planning Dept.
P.O. Box 862, Abu Dhabi, U.A.E.
Tel:971-2-780000, Fax: 971-2-786716
Undersecretary: Engr. Mohammed Abdullah Al Suwaidi

Abu Dhabi Purchasing Department
P.O. Box 838, Abu Dhabi, U.A.E.
Tel: 971-2-212700, Fax: 971-2-343696
Chairman: Khalfan Ghaith Al Moheirbie

Abu Dhabi National Oil Company (ADNOC)
P.O. Box 898, Abu Dhabi, U.A.E.
Tel: 6020000, Fax: 971-2-6023389
General Manager: Yousef Bin Omayr Bin Yousef

Abu Dhabi Investment Authority (ADIA)
P.O. Box 3600, Abu Dhabi, U.A.E.
Tel: 971-2-266500, Fax: 971-2-274605
Managing Director: H.H. Shaikh Ahmed Bin Zayed Al Nahyan

Abu Dhabi Marine Operating Company (ADMA-OPCO)
P.O. Box 303, Abu Dhabi, U.A.E.
Tel: 971-2-6060000, Fax: 971-2-266005
General Manager: Mr. Bcconaer

Abu Dhabi Company for Onshore Oil Operations (ADCO)
P.O. Box 270, Abu Dhabi
Tel: 971-2-6040000, Fax: 971-2-669785
General Manager: Kevin Dunn

World Trade Center Abu Dhabi
P.O. Box 33399
Abu Dhabi, UAE
Tel. 971-2-328555
Fax. 971-2-328855
email wtcad@emirates.net ae
Mr. Ousama Gahnnoum, General Manager

Dubai Port Authority
P.O. Box 17000, Dubai, U.A.E.
Tel: 971-4-815000, Fax: 971-4-816093
Chairman: Sultan Bin Sulayem

Dubai Municipality
P.O. Box 67, Dubai, U.A.E.
Tel: 971-4-215555, Fax: 971-4-222424/246666
Director: Qassim Sultan

Dubai Petroleum Company (DPC)
P.O. Box 2222, Dubai, U.A.E.
Tel: 971-4-442990, Fax: 971-4-4062200
President: Sigmund Cornelius

U.S. Agricultural Trade Office (ATO), P.O. Box 9343, Dubai,
United Arab Emirates, Tel: 971-4-314063,
Fax: 971-4-314998

# SELECTED BUSINESS CONTACTS

**Ministry of Information & Culture**
PO Box 17, Abu Dhabi, UAE
Tel: (2) 453 000 *or* 452 922 *or* 454 766. Fax: (2) 452 504.

**Government of Dubai Department of Tourism & Commerce Marketing**
Albwardy Building 2, PO Box 594, Dubai, UAE
Tel: (4) 230 000. Fax: (4) 511 711.
E-mail: info@dctpb.gov.ae
Web site: http://www.dubaitourism.com

**Embassy of the United Arab Emirates**
30 Prince's Gate, London SW7 1PT
Tel: (0171) 581 1281. Fax: (0171) 581 9616.
E-mail: 101746.1630@compuserve.com

Opening hours: 0900-1500 Monday to Friday.

**Consulate of the United Arab Emirates**
48 Prince's Gate, London SW7 1PT
Tel: (0171) 589 3434. Fax: (0171) 581 9616.

Opening hours: 0900-1500 Monday to Friday; 0930-1300 Monday to Friday (visa section).

**Government of Dubai Department of Tourism & Commerce Marketing**
First Floor, 125 Pall Mall, London SW1Y 5EA
Tel: (0171) 839 0580. Fax: (0171) 839 0582.
Opening hours: 0900-1730 Monday to Friday.

**British Embassy**
PO Box 248, Abu Dhabi, UAE
Tel: (2) 326 600 *or* 321 364. Fax: (2) 341 744 *or* 318 138 *or* 345 968 (consular section).

*Embassy also in*: Dubai (tel: (4) 521 070).

**Embassy of the United Arab Emirates**
Suite 700, 1255 22nd Street NW, Washington DC 20037
Tel: (202) 955 7999. Fax: (202) 337 7029 (consular section).
E-mail: info@tridentpress.ie
Web site: http://www.the-emirates.com

*Also deals with enquiries from Canada.*

**Embassy of the United States of America**
*Postal address*: PO Box 4009, Abu Dhabi, UAE
*Street address*: Al-Sudan Street, Abu Dhabi, UAE
Tel: (2) 436 691. Fax: (2) 435 441
E-mail: usisamem@emirates.net.ae
Web site: http://www.usembabu.gov.ae

*Consulate General in*: Dubai (tel: (4) 313 115).

**The Canadian Embassy**
*Postal address*: PO Box 4009, Al-Sudan Street, Abu Dhabi, UAE
*Street address*: Villa 440, 26th Street, Abu Dhabi, UAE
Tel: (2) 456 969. Fax: (2) 458 787.
E-mail: canada@emirates.net.ae
*Consulate in*: Du

# MAJOR ARABIC BANKS

**ALGERIA**

**BANQUE ALGERIENNE DE DEVELOPPEMENT**
12 Boulevard Colonel Amirouche
Algiers, Algeria
tel: (213) 2-738950
fax: (213) 2-746256
Director General: Mohamed Kerkebane

**BANQUE ALGERIENNE DE DEVELOPPEMENT RURAL (BADR)**
17 Boulevard Colonel Amirouche
Algiers, Algeria
tel: (213) 647264

**BANQUE CENTRALE D'ALGERIE**
8 Avenue Franklin Roosevelt, 16000
Algiers, Algeria
tel: (213)2-647 264
fax: (213) 2-552428
Governor: Abderahmane Hadj Nacer

**BANQUE EXTERIEURE D'ALGERIE**
1 Rue du Docteur Lucien Raynaud
Algiers, Algeria
Tel: (213) 2-711252
Fax: (213) 2-639334
President: Mohamed Nour Eddine Kerras

**BANQUE NATIONALE D'ALGERIA**
8 Boulevard Che Guevara
Algiers, Algeria
Tel: (213) 2-714719
Fax: (213) 2-712422
General Manager: A. F. Benmalek

**BAHRAIN**

**ARAB BANKING CORPORATION**
PO Box 5698
Manama, Bahrain
tel: (973) 532235
fax: (973) 533163
Chairman: Abdulmohsen Y Al Hunaif

**GULF INTERNATIONAL BANK**
PO Box 1017
Manama, Bahrain
tel: (973) 534000
fax: (973) 522633
Chairman: HE Ibrahim Abdul Karim

**NATIONAL BANK OF BAHRAIN**
PO Box 106
Manama, Bahrain
tel: (973) 258800
fax: (973) 228998/211307
Chairman: Ahmed Ali Kanoo

**INVESTCORP**
PO Box 5340
Manama, Bahrain
tel: (973) 532000
fax: (973) 530816

**BAHRAIN INTERNATIONAL BANK**
PO Box 5016
Manama, Bahrain
tel: (973) 534545
fax: (973) 535141
Chairman: Faisal Yousef Al Marzouk

**AL AHLI BANK**
PO Box 5941
Manama, Bahrain
tel: (973) 224333
fax: (973) 224322
Chairman: Mohammad Yousef Jalal

**BAHRAIN MIDDLE EAST BANK**
PO Box 797
Manama, Bahrain
tel: (973) 532-345
fax: (973) 530-526
Chairman: HE Abdul Rahman Salem Al-Ateeqi

**TRANS ARABIAN INVESTMENT BANK (TAIB)**
PO Box 20485
Manama, Bahrain
tel: (973) 533-334
fax: (973) 533-174
Chairman: Abdulrahman Al Jeraisy

**EGYPT**

**NATIONAL BANK OF EGYPT**
PO Box 11611
Cairo, Egypt
tel: (20) 2-5749101
fax: (20) 2-5746858
Chairman: Mahmoud Abdel Aziz

**BANQUE MISR**
151 Mohamed Farid Street
Cairo, Egypt
tel: (20) 2-3911159
fax: (20) 2-3919779
Chairman: Essam El Din Ahmady

**BANQUE DU CAIRE**
PO Box 2335
Cairo, Egypt
tel: (20) 2-3548323
fax: (20) 2-350616
Chairman: Mohamed Abdo El Fath

**BANK OF ALEXANDRIA**
49 Kasr El Nil Street
Cairo, Egypt
tel: (20) 2-3921481
fax: (20) 2-3900940
Chairman: Ismail Hassan Mohamed

**COMMERCIAL INTERNATIONAL BANK**
PO Box 2430
Cairo, Egypt
tel: (20) 2-5703043
fax: (20) 2-5702691

**IRAQ**

**RAFIDAIN BANK**
PO Box 11360
Baghdad, Iraq
tel: (964) 1-4158642
Chairman: Tarik H Al Khateeb

**RASHID BANK**
7177 Haifa Street
Baghdad, Iraq
tel: (964) 1-5388550
President: A Majid H Al Ani

**JORDAN**

**ARAB BANK**
PO Box 950544
Amman, Jordan
tel: (962) 6-5607231/6-5607115
fax: (962) 6-5606793/6-560683
Chairman: Abdulmajeed A H Shoman

**JORDAN NATIONAL BANK**
PO Box 1578
Amman, Jordan
tel: (962) 6-642391
fax: (962) 6-628809
Chairman: HE Abdulkader Tash

**CAIRO AMMAN BANK**
PO Box 715
Amman, Jordan
tel: (962) 6-639321
fax: (962) 6-639328
Chairman: Khalil Talhouni

**BANK OF JORDAN**
PO Box 2140
Amman, Jordan
tel: (962) 5-644327
fax: (962) 5-656642
Chairman: Tawfiq Fakhoury

**HOUSING BANK**
PO Box 7693
Amman, Jordan
tel: (962) 5-667126
fax: (962) 5-678121
Chairman: Zuhair Khouri

**JORDAN KUWAIT BANK**
PO Box 9776
Amman, Jordan
tel: (962) 5-688814
fax: (962) 5-687452
Chairman: Sufian I Yasin Sartwai

**JORDAN GULF BANK**
PO Box 9989
Amman 11191, Jordan
tel: (962) 4-603931
fax: (962) 6-664110
Chairman: Awartani F Zuhair

**ARAB JODAN INVESTMENT BANK**
PO Box 8797
Amman, Jordan
tel: (962) 6-507126/7
fax: (962) 6-681482
Chairman: Abdul Kader Qadi

**KUWAIT**

**NATIONAL BANK OF KUWAIT**
PO Box 95
Safat 13001, Kuwait
tel: (965) 2422011
fax: (965) 2431888
Chairman: Mohamed Abdul Rahman Al Bahar

**GULF INVESTMENT CORPORATION**
PO Box 3402
Safat 13035, Kuwait
tel: (965) 2431911
fax: (965) 2448894/2408006
Chairman: HE Sheikh Mohammed Bin Khalifa Al Thani

**THE GULF BANK**
PO Box 3200
Safat 13032, Kuwait
tel: (965) 2449501
fax: (965) 2424605
Chairman: Ali Mishari Al Hilal Al Mutairi

**KUWAIT FINANCE HOUSE**
PO Box 24989
Safat 12110, Kuwait
tel: (965)2445050
fax: (965) 2455135
Chairman: Bader Abdul Mohsen Al Mukhaizeem

**ALAHLI BANK OF KUWAIT**
PO Box 1387
Safat 13014, Kuwait
tel: (965) 2400900
fax: (965) 2424557
Chairman: Morad Yousuf Behbehani

**COMMERCIAL BANK OF KUWAIT**
PO Box 2861
Safat 13029, Kuwait
tel: (965) 2411001
fax: (965) 2450150
Chairman: Hamad Abdul Latif Al Hamad

**BURGAN BANK**
PO Box 5389
Safat 13054, Kuwait
tel: (965) 2439000
fax: (965) 2461148
Chairman: Sheikh Ahmed Abdullah Al Ahmed Al Sabah

**BANK OF KUWAIT & THE MIDDLE EAST**
PO Box 71
Safat 13001, Kuwait
tel: (965) 2461428
fax: (965) 2461430
Chairman: Saleh Mubarak Al Falah

**LEBANON**

**BANQUE DU LIBAN ET D'OUTRE MER**
PO Box 1912-11
Beirut, Lebanon
tel: (961) 1-346290
fax: (961) 1-602247
Chairman: Mrs. Boutros El Khoury

**BANQUE AUDI**
PO Box 11-2560
Beirut, Lebanon
tel: (961) 1-200250
fax: (961) 1-200955
Chairman: Georges W. Audi

**BANQUE LIBANO-FRANCAISE**
PO Box 11-808
Beirut, Lebanon
tel: (961) 1-340350
fax: (961) 1-340355
Chairman: Farid Ratelael

**FRANSABANK**
PO Box 11-0393
Beirut, Lebanon
tel: (961) 1-345572
Chairman: Adnan Kasser

**BYBLOS BANK**
PO Box 11-5605
Beirut, Lebanon
tel: (961) 1-898200
fax: (961) 1-898209
Chairman: Dr. Francois S. Bassil

**LIBYA**

**ARAB BANKING CORPORATION**
PO Box 3578
Tripoli, Libya
tel: (218) 21-3350227/3350220
fax: (218) 21-3350229
Chief Representitive: Ali Dahmani

**CENTRAL BANK OF LIBYA**
PO Box 1103
Tripoli, Libya
tel: (218) 21-33591
Governor: Abdulhafid Mahmoud Zlitni

**MAURITANIA**

**BANQUE CENTRALE DE MAURITANIE**
PO Box 623
Nouakchott, Mauritania
tel: (222) 2-52206
fax: (222) 2-52759
Chairman: Ahmed Ould Zeid

**MOROCCO**

**ARAB BANK MAROC**
PO Box 13810
Casablanca, Morocco
tel: (212) 2-223152
fax: (212) 2-200233
President: Hadj Abderahmane Bouftas

**BANQUE COMERCIALE DU MAROC**
PO Box 141
Casablanca, Morocco
tel: (212) 2-224169
fax: (212) 2-226982
President: Abd Al Aziz Alami

**CREDIT DU MAROC SA**
PO Box 13579
Casablanca, Morocco
tel: (212) 2-477000
fax: (212) 2-277127
Chairman: Jawad Ben Brahim

**CREDIT POPULAIRE DU MAROC**
PO Box 10622
Casablanca, Morocco
tel: (212) 2-202533/89
fax: (212) 2-222699
Chairman: Abd Al-Latif Laraki

**WAFABANK**

163 Avenue Hassan II
Casablanca 01, Morocco
tel: (212) 2-224105
fax: (212) 2-266202

**OMAN**

**BANK MUSCAT AL AHLI AL OMAN**
PO Box 134
Ruwi 112, Oman
tel: (968) 784776
fax: (968) 784056
Chairman: HE Sheikh Zaher Bin hamad Al Harthy

**NATIONAL BANK OF OMAN**
PO Box 3751
Ruwi 112, Oman
tel: (968) 708894
fax: (968) 707781
Chairman: HE Khalfan Bin Nasser Al Wohaibi

**BANK OF OMAN, BAHRAIN & KUWAIT**
PO Box 1708
Ruwi 112, Oman
tel: (968) 701532/701528
fax: (968) 705607
Chairman: HE Mohsin Haidar Darwish

**OMAN INTERNATIONAL BANK**
PO Box 1727
Ruwi 112, Oman
tel: (968) 682500
fax: (968) 682800
Chairman: HE Dr. Omar Bin Abdul Muniem Al Zuwawi

**BANK DHOFAR AL-OMANI AL-FRANSI**
PO Box 1507
Ruwi 112, Oman
tel: (968) 790466/790467
fax: (968) 797246
Chairman: Eng. Abdulhafidh Salim Rjab Al Aujaili

**COMMERCIAL BANK OF OMAN**
PO Box 1696
Ruwi 112, Oman
tel: (968) 793226
fax: (968) 793229
Chairman: HE Amer Bin Shuwain

**OMAN ARAB BANK**
PO Box 2010
Ruwi 112, Oman
tel: (968) 700161/700162
fax: (968) 797736

**QATAR**

**QATAR NATIONAL BANK**
PO Box 1002
Doha, Qatar
tel: (974) 413511
fax: (974) 413753
Chairman: HE Sheikh Abdul Aziz bin Khalifa Althani

**QATAR INTERNATIONAL ISLAMIC BANK**
PO Box 3211
Doha, Qatar
tel: (974) 436776
fax: (974) 444101
Chairman: Abdul Rahman Bin Abdullah Al Mahmood

**SAUDI ARABIA**

**NATIONAL COMMERCIAL BANK**
PO Box 3555
Jeddah 21481, Saudi Arabia
tel: (966) 2-6446644
fax: (966) 2-6433282
General Manager: Salim Ahmed Bin Mahfouz

**RIYAD BANK**
PO Box 22622
Riyadh 11416, Saudi Arabia
tel: (966) 1-4013030
fax: (966) 1-4042707
Chairman: Sheikh Ismail Abou Dawood

**SAUDI AMERICAN BANK**
PO Box 833
Riyadh 11421, Saudi Arabia
tel: (966) 1-4774770
fax: (966) 1-4774770
Chairman: Abdul Aziz Bin Hamad Al Gosaibi

**ARAB NATIONAL BANK**
PO Box 56921
Riyadh 11564, Saudi Arabia
tel: (966) 1-4029000
fax: (966) 1-4027747
Chairman: Rasheed Abdulrahman Al Rasheed

**AL RAJHI BANKING & INVESTMENT CORPORATION**
PO Box 28
Riyadh 11511, Saudi Arabia
tel: (966) 1-4054244
fax: (966) 1-4052950
Chairman: Sheikh Saleh Ibn Abdul Aziz Alrajhi

**SAUDI BRITISH BANK**
PO Box 9084
Riyadh 11413, Saudi Arabia
tel: (966) 1-4050677
fax: (966) 1-4050660
Chairman: Hisham A Alireza

**AL BANK AL SAUDI AL FRANSI**
PO Box 56006
Riyadh 11554, Saudi Arabia
tel: (966) 1-4042222
fax: (966) 1-4042311
Chairman: Sheikh Ibrahim Al Touq

**SAUDI CAIRO BANK**
PO Box 11222
Jeddah 21453, Saudi Arabia
tel: (966) 2-6608820
fax: (966) 2- 6608820 ext. 338
Chairman: Wahib Bin Zagr

**SAUDI HOLLANDI BANK**
PO Box 1467
Riyadh 11431, Saudi Arabia
tel: (966) 1-4067888
fax: (966) 1-4031104
Chairman: Sulaiman A R Al Sulaiman

**UNITED SAUDI COMMERCIAL BANK**
PO Box 25895
Riyadh 11476, Saudi Arabia
tel: (966) 1-4784200
fax: (966) 1-4783197
Chairman: HRH Prince Al Waleed Bin Talal Bin Abdulaziz Al Saud

**SAUDI INVESTMENT BANK**
PO Box 3533
Riyadh 11481, Saudi Arabia
tel: (966) 1-4778433
fax: (966) 1-4776781
Chairman: Dr. Abdulaziz O'Hali

**BANK AL-JAZIRA**
PO Box 5859
Riyadh 11432, Saudi Arabia
tel: (966) 1-4036344/401636
fax: (966) 1-4036344

## SYRIA

**CENTRAL BANK OF SYRIA**
PO Box 2254
Damascus, Syria
tel: (963) 11-224800

**COMMERCIAL BANK OF SYRIA**
PO Box 933
Damascus, Syria
tel: (963) 11-218890
fax: (963) 11-228524
Chairman: Riad Hakim

## TUNISIA

**BANQUE NATIONALE AGRICOLE (BNA)**
Rue Hedi Novira
1000 Tunis, Tunisia
tel: (216) 1-833104
fax: (216) 1-835950
Chairman: Habib Nafir

**BANQUE INTERNATIONALE ARABE DE TUNISIE (BIAT)**
BP 520
Tunis Cedex, Tunisia
tel: (216) 1-340719
fax: (216) 1-340680
President: Mokhtar Fhakhfakh

**ARAB TUNISIAN BANK (ATB)**
Rue de la Monnaie
1001 Tunis, Tunisia
tel: (216) 1-351155

fax: (216) 1-342852
Chairman: Hatem Kchouk

**U.A.E.**

**NATIONAL BANK OF ABU DHABI**
PO Box 4
Abu Dhabi, U.A.E.
tel: (971) 2-668000
fax: (971) 2-655329
Chairman: HE Mohammed Habroush Al Suwaidi

**NATIONAL BANK OF DUBAI**
PO Box 777
Dubai, U.A.E.
tel: (971) 4-267000
fax: (971) 4-268939
Chairman: Sultan Ali Al Owais

**EMIRATES BANK INTERNATIONAL**
PO Box 2923
Dubai, U.A.E.
tel: (971) 4-256256
fax: (971) 4-268005
Chairman: HE Ahmed Humaid Al Tayer

**MASHREQ BANK**
PO Box 1250
Dubai, U.A.E.
tel: (971) 4-229131
fax: (971) 4-226061
Chairman: Saif Ahmed Al Guhair

**ARAB BANK FOR INVESTMENT & FOREIGN TRADE**
PO Box 46733
Abu Dhabi, U.A.E.
tel: (971) 2-721900
fax: (971) 2-777550
Chairman: Dr. Abdul Hafid M. Zlitni

**COMMERCIAL BANK OF DUBAI**
PO Box 2668
Dubai, U.A.E.
tel: (971) 4-523355
fax: (971) 4-520444
Chairman: HE Ahmed Humaid Al Tayer

**INVESTMENT BANK FOR TRADE AND FINANCE (INVESTBANK)**
PO Box 2875
Abu Dhabi, U.A.E.
tel: (971) 2-794594
fax: (971) 2-795592
Chairman: HH Sheikh Saqr Bin Mohammad Al Qassami

**YEMEN**

**ARAB BANK LTD**
PO Box 475
Sanaa, Yemen
tel: (967) 1-276585
fax: (967) 1-276583
Manager: Abdul Mahdi Alawi

**BANK INDOSUEZ**
PO Box 651
Sanaa, Yemen
tel: (967) 1-272801/2/3
fax: (967) 1-274161
General Manager: Manuel Garcia-Ligero

**COOPERATIVE BANK OF YEMEN**
PO Box 2015
Sanaa, Yemen
tel: (967) 1-207327
fax: (967) 1-203714
Chairman: Abdallah Al Barakani

**INTERNATIONAL BANK OF YEMEN**
PO Box 2847
Sanaa, Yemen
tel: (967) 1-272920/112/314
fax: (967) 1-274127
General Manager: Mohammedmian Soomro

**NATIONAL BANK OF YEMEN**
PO Box 19839
Aden, Yemen
tel: (967) 1-275373
fax: (967) 1-273311

## AIRLINES SERVING THE ARAB WORLD

| AIRLINE | PHONE NUMBER |
|---|---|
| AEROFLOT | USA tel: (800) 995-5555 |
| AIR ALGERIA | Algiers tel: (213) 2-74 24 28 |

| | |
|---|---|
| | fax: (213) 2- 74 44 25 |
| **AIR CANADA** | USA tel: (800) 776-3000 |
| **AIR FRANCE** | USA tel: (800) 237-2747 |
| **ALITALIA** | USA tel: (800) 221-4745 |
| **AUSTRIAN AIR** | USA tel: (800) 843-0002 |
| **BRITISH AIRWAYS (BA)** | USA tel: (800) 247-9297 |
| **EGYPTAIR** | Cairo tel: (20) 2-3902444<br>fax: (20) 2-3901557<br>USA tel: (800) 334-6787 |
| **EMIRATES** | Dubai tel: (971) 4-223698<br>fax: (971) 4-214560<br>USA tel: (800) 777-3999 |
| **GULF AIR** | Bahrain<br>tel: (973) 531166<br>fax: (973) 330466<br>USA tel: (800) 553-2824 |
| **IRAQI AIRWAYS CO** | Baghdad tel: (964) 555 9999 |
| **JAMAHIRIYA LIBYAN ARAB AIRLINES** | Tripoli tel: (218) 21-602083 |
| **KLM** | USA tel: (800) 374-7747 |
| **KUWAIT AIRWAYS (KAC)** | Kuwait tel: (965) 4740166<br>fax: (965) 4314726<br>USA tel: (800) 458-9248 |
| **LUFTHANSA** | USA tel: (800) 645-3880 |
| **MIDDLE EAST AIRLINES (MEA)** | Beirut tel: (961) 1-316316<br>USA tel: (800) 664-7310 |
| **OLYMPIC AIRWAYS** | USA tel: (800) 223-1226 |
| **QANTAS** | USA tel: (800) 227-4500 |
| **ROYAL AIR MAROC** | Casablanca tel: (212) 2-91200<br>fax: (212) 2-912397<br>USA tel: (800) 344-6726 |
| **ROYAL JORDANIAN AIRLINE** | Amman tel: (962) 672872<br>fax: (962) 672527<br>USA tel: (800) 223-0470 |
| **SABENA** | USA tel: (800) 873-3900 |
| **SAS** | USA tel: (800) 221-2350 |
| **SAUDIA-SAUDI ARABIAN AIRLINES** | Jeddah tel: (966) 2-686 0000<br>fax: (966) 2-686 4552<br>USA tel: (800) 457-8329 |

| | |
|---|---|
| **SWISS AIR** | USA tel: (800) 221-4750 |
| **SYRIAN ARAB AIRLINES** | Damascus tel: (963) 11-232154 |
| **TUNIS AIR** | Tunis tel: (216) 1-700 100<br>fax: (216) 1-700 754 |
| **TURKISH AIRWAYS** | USA tel: (800) 874-8875 |
| **TWA** | USA tel: (800) 221-2000 |
| **UNITED AIRLINES** | USA tel: (800) 241-6522 |
| **YEMEN AIRWAYS** | Sanaa tel: (967) 1-232389 |

## IMPORTANT CONTACTS

### DEPARTMENT OF TOURISM AND COMMERCE MARKETING

The Department is responsible for the promotion of Dubai as a major regional and international centre of business and tourism. Its activities include trade fair participation and organisation, inward and outward missions, seminars and presentations, special events, information services, advertising, publications and media relations.

In addition to its responsibilities for promoting trade, investment and tourism, the Department is the primary planning, regulating, licensing and development authority for all matters relating to tourism in the emirate.

***Head Office:***
***Department of Tourism and Commerce Marketing***
***PO Box 594***
***Dubai, United Arab Emirates***
***Telephone: (971) (4) 2230000***
***Telefax: (971) (4) 2230022***
***Internet: http://dubaitourism.co.ae***
***Telex: 46182 DCTPB EM***

### DEPARTMENT OF ECONOMIC DEVELOPMENT

Established in 1992, the Department has wide ranging responsibility for the emirate's economic development and plays a leading role in the formulation of economic and commercial policy. It is also responsible for the regulation of companies and for maintaining the emirate's commercial register. The Department has authority over the granting of trade licences.

***Department of Economic Development***
***PO Box 13223, Dubai, U.A.E.***
***Telephone: () (4) 2229922. Telefax: (971) (4) 2225577***

### DUBAI CHAMBER OF COMMERCE AND INDUSTRY

Established in 1965, the Chamber is responsible for organising and protecting commercial and industrial activities and for promoting trade and business cooperation both within the UAE and internationally. Its work falls under the following broad headings: foreign relations, registration and documentation, industrial affairs, administration and finance, and legal affairs.

***Dubai Chamber of Commerce and Industry***
***PO Box 1457, Dubai, U.A.E.***
***Telephone: (971) (4) 2280000. Telefax: (971) (4) 2211646***

### DUBAI MUNICIPALITY

The Municipality has extensive responsibilities covering both the provision of essential civic services and for the planning and development of the emirate's infrastructure.

***Dubai Municipality***
***PO Box 67, Dubai, U.A.E.***
***Telephone: (971) (4) 2215555. Telefax: (971) (4) 2246666***

### JEBEL ALI FREE ZONE AUTHORITY

Established in 1985, the Authority is charged with supervision of the Free Zone. Its responsibilities include issuing rules and licences to companies wishing to operate in Jebel Ali. It is also active in developing the infrastructure within the zone and for providing a wide range of services and administrative support, including personnel recruitment, for companies in the Free Zone.

***Jebel Ali Free Zone Authority***
***PO Box 17000, Dubai, U.A.E.***
***Telephone: (971) (4) 8815000. Telefax: (971) (4) 8816093***

### DUBAI PORTS AUTHORITY

Dubai Ports Authority, the operator of Port Rashid and Jebel Ali Port, is the largest operation of its kind in the Gulf. In 1997, DPA handled 36.0 million tonnes of cargo. Its throughput of 2.60 million TEUs makes it one of the top ten container ports in the world.

***Dubai Ports Authority***
***PO Box 2149. Dubai, U.A.E.***
***Telephone: (971) (4) 3451545. Telefax: (971) (4) 3452002***

### DUBAI AIRPORT FREE ZONE

The Department of Civil Aviation has established a new free zone at Dubai International Airport. Offering the same package of incentives as the Jebel Ali Free Zone, it will focus on attracting high tech investors and companies using air freight.

***Dubai Airport Free Zone***
***PO Box 2525, Dubai, U.A.E.***
***Telephone: (971) (4) 2027000. Telefax: (971) (4) 2995500***

### DUBAI WORLD TRADE CENTRE (L.L.C.)

The Dubai World Trade Centre complex incorporates the leading exhibition and conference venue in the Middle East, hosting some 60 major international events each year. Total exhibition space amounts to 37,000 sq.m.

***Dubai World Trade Centre (L.L.C.)***
***PO Box 9292, Dubai, U.A.E.***
***Telephone: (971) (4) 3321000. Telefax: (971) (4) 3318034***

## BASIC TITLES FOR UAE

***IMPORTANT!***
***All publications are updated annually!***
***Please contact IBP, Inc. at ibpusa3@gmail.com for the latest ISBNs and additional information***

| TITLE |
|---|
| UAE A "Spy" Guide - Strategic Information and Developments |
| UAE A Spy" Guide" |
| UAE Banking & Financial Market Handbook |
| UAE Banking & Financial Market Handbook |
| UAE Business and Investment Opportunities Yearbook |
| UAE Business and Investment Opportunities Yearbook |
| UAE Business and Investment Opportunities Yearbook Volume 1 Strategic Information and Opportunities |
| UAE Business and Investment Opportunities Yearbook Volume 2 Leading Export-Import, Business, Investment Opportunities and Projects |
| UAE Business Intelligence Report - Practical Information, Opportunities, Contacts |
| UAE Business Intelligence Report - Practical Information, Opportunities, Contacts |
| UAE Business Law Handbook - Strategic Information and Basic Laws |
| UAE Business Law Handbook - Strategic Information and Basic Laws |
| UAE Business Law Handbook - Strategic Information and Basic Laws |
| UAE Business Law Handbook - Strategic Information and Basic Laws |
| UAE Business Success Guide - Basic Practical Information and Contacts |
| UAE Company Laws and Regulations Handbook |
| UAE Company Laws and Regulations Handbook - Strategic Information and Basic Laws |
| UAE Constitution and Citizenship Laws Handbook - Strategic Information and Basic Laws |
| UAE Country Study Guide - Strategic Information and Developments |
| UAE Country Study Guide - Strategic Information and Developments |
| UAE Country Study Guide - Strategic Information and Developments Volume 1 Strategic Information and Developments |
| UAE Criminal Laws, Regulations and Procedures Handbook - Strategic Information, Regulations, Procedures |
| UAE Customs, Trade Regulations and Procedures Handbook |
| UAE Customs, Trade Regulations and Procedures Handbook |
| UAE Diplomatic Handbook - Strategic Information and Developments |
| UAE Diplomatic Handbook - Strategic Information and Developments |
| UAE Ecology & Nature Protection Handbook |
| UAE Ecology & Nature Protection Handbook |

| TITLE |
|---|
| UAE Ecology & Nature Protection Laws and Regulation Handbook |
| UAE Economic & Development Strategy Handbook |
| UAE Economic & Development Strategy Handbook |
| UAE Electoral, Political Parties Laws and Regulations Handbook - Strategic Information, Regulations, Procedures |
| UAE Energy Policy, Laws and Regulation Handbook Vol 1 |
| UAE Energy Policy, Laws and Regulations Handbook |
| UAE Energy Policy, Laws and Regulations Handbook Vol 2 |
| UAE Export-Import Trade and Business Directory |
| UAE Export-Import Trade and Business Directory |
| UAE Fishing and Aquaculture Industry Handbook - Strategic Information, Regulations, Opportunities |
| UAE Foreign Policy and Government Guide |
| UAE Foreign Policy and Government Guide |
| UAE Government and Business Contacts Handbook |
| UAE Government and Business Contacts Handbook |
| UAE Healthcare Sector Organization, Management and Payment Systems Handbook - Strategic Information, Programs and Regulations |
| UAE Immigration Laws and Regulations Handbook - Strategic Information and Basic Laws |
| UAE Industrial and Business Directory |
| UAE Insolvency (Bankruptcy) Laws and Regulations Handbook - Strategic Information and Basic Laws |
| UAE Internet and E-Commerce Investment and Business Guide - Strategic and Practical Information: Regulations and Opportunities |
| UAE Internet and E-Commerce Investment and Business Guide - Strategic and Practical Information: Regulations and Opportunities |
| UAE Investment & Business Guide |
| UAE Investment & Business Guide |
| UAE Investment and Business Guide - Strategic and Practical Information |
| UAE Investment and Business Guide - Strategic and Practical Information |
| UAE Investment and Business Guide Volume 2 Business, Investment Opportunities and Incentives |
| UAE Investment and Business Profile - Basic Information and Contacts for Succesful investment and Business Activity |
| UAE Investment and Trade Laws and Regulations Handbook |
| UAE Investment, Trade Strategy and Agreements Handbook - Strategic Information and Basic Agreements |
| UAE Labor Laws and Regulations Handbook - Strategic Information and Basic Laws |
| UAE Land Ownership and Agriculture Laws Handbook |
| UAE Mineral & Mining Sector Investment and Business Guide - Strategic and Practical Information |
| UAE Mineral & Mining Sector Investment and Business Guide - Strategic and Practical Information |
| UAE Mining Laws and Regulations Handbook |
| UAE Oil & Gas Sector Business & Investment Opportunities Yearbook |

| TITLE |
|---|
| UAE Oil & Gas Sector Business & Investment Opportunities Yearbook |
| UAE Oil and Gas Exploration Laws and Regulation Handbook |
| UAE Recent Economic and Political Developments Yearbook |
| UAE Recent Economic and Political Developments Yearbook |
| UAE Recent Economic and Political Developments Yearbook |
| UAE Ruler Handbook |
| UAE Ruler Handbook |
| UAE Starting Business (Incorporating) in....Guide |
| UAE Tax Guide Volume 1 Strategic Information and Basic Regulations |
| UAE Taxation Laws and Regulations Handbook |
| UAE Telecom Laws and Regulations Handbook |
| UAE Telecommunication Industry Business Opportunities Handbook |
| UAE Telecommunication Industry Business Opportunities Handbook |
| UAE Transportation Policy and Regulations Handbook |
| United Arab Emirates: Recent Economic Developments Yearbook |
| UAE Stock, Financial Market Laws and Regulations Handbook - Strategic Information and Basic Laws |
| UAE: Abu Dhabi Stock Exchange Trading and Financial Operation Guide - Practical Information and Regulations |
| UAE Construction Companies Handbook - Strategic Information and Contacts |
| UAE Electronics, Computers and Information Technology Industry Handbook - Strategic Information and Contacts |
| UAE Free Economic Zones Handbook |
| UAE Free Economic Zones Handbook |
| UAE Import Tariffs Handbook |
| UAE Largest Importers Directory - Strategic Information and Contacts |
| UAE Medical and Pharmaceutical Industry Handbook - Strategic Information and Contacts |
| UAE Oil, Gas Exploration Industry Business and Investment Contacts Handbook |
| UAE Stock Market Business Laws and Regulations Handbook |
| UAE Transportation Sector Handbook - Strategic Information and Contacts |

# INFORMATION STRATEGY, INTERNET AND E-COMMERCE DEVELOPMENT HANDBOOKS LIBRARY

**Price: $99.95 Each**

**World Business Information Catalog: http://www.ibpus.com**

| TITLE |
|---|
| Albania Information Strategy, Internet and E-Commerce Development Handbook - Strategic Information, Programs, Regulations |
| Algeria Information Strategy, Internet and E-Commerce Development Handbook - Strategic Information, Programs, Regulations |
| Angola Information Strategy, Internet and E-Commerce Development Handbook - Strategic Information, Programs, Regulations |
| Argentina Information Strategy, Internet and E-Commerce Development Handbook - Strategic Information, Programs, Regulations |
| Armenia Information Strategy, Internet and E-Commerce Development Handbook - Strategic Information, Programs, Regulations |
| Australia Information Strategy, Internet and E-Commerce Development Handbook - Strategic Information, Programs, Regulations |
| Austria Information Strategy, Internet and E-Commerce Development Handbook - Strategic Information, Programs, Regulations |
| Azerbaijan Information Strategy, Internet and E-Commerce Development Handbook - Strategic Information, Programs, Regulations |
| Bangladesh Information Strategy, Internet and E-Commerce Development Handbook - Strategic Information, Programs, Regulations |
| Belarus Information Strategy, Internet and E-Commerce Development Handbook - Strategic Information, Programs, Regulations |
| Belgium Information Strategy, Internet and E-Commerce Development Handbook - Strategic Information, Programs, Regulations |
| Bermuda Information Strategy, Internet and E-Commerce Development Handbook - Strategic Information, Programs, Regulations |
| Bolivia Information Strategy, Internet and E-Commerce Development Handbook - Strategic Information, Programs, Regulations |
| Bosnia and Herzegovina Information Strategy, Internet and E-Commerce Development Handbook - Strategic Information, Programs, Regulations |
| Botswana Information Strategy, Internet and E-Commerce Development Handbook - Strategic Information, Programs, Regulations |
| Brazil Information Strategy, Internet and E-Commerce Development Handbook - Strategic Information, Programs, Regulations |
| Bulgaria Information Strategy, Internet and E-Commerce Development Handbook - Strategic Information, Programs, Regulations |
| Cambodia Information Strategy, Internet and E-Commerce Development Handbook - Strategic Information, Programs, Regulations |
| Cameroon Information Strategy, Internet and E-Commerce Development Handbook - Strategic Information, Programs, Regulations |
| Canada Information Strategy, Internet and E-Commerce Development Handbook - Strategic Information, Programs, Regulations |
| Chile Information Strategy, Internet and E-Commerce Development Handbook - Strategic Information, Programs, |

| TITLE |
| --- |
| Regulations |
| China Information Strategy, Internet and E-Commerce Development Handbook - Strategic Information, Programs, Regulations |
| Colombia Information Strategy, Internet and E-Commerce Development Handbook - Strategic Information, Programs, Regulations |
| Cook Islands Information Strategy, Internet and E-Commerce Development Handbook - Strategic Information, Programs, Regulations |
| Costa Rica Information Strategy, Internet and E-Commerce Development Handbook - Strategic Information, Programs, Regulations |
| Croatia Information Strategy, Internet and E-Commerce Development Handbook - Strategic Information, Programs, Regulations |
| Cuba Information Strategy, Internet and E-Commerce Development Handbook - Strategic Information, Programs, Regulations |
| Cyprus Information Strategy, Internet and E-Commerce Development Handbook - Strategic Information, Programs, Regulations |
| Czech Republic Information Strategy, Internet and E-Commerce Development Handbook - Strategic Information, Programs, Regulations |
| Denmark Information Strategy, Internet and E-Commerce Development Handbook - Strategic Information, Programs, Regulations |
| Dominican Republic Information Strategy, Internet and E-Commerce Development Handbook - Strategic Information, Programs, Regulations |
| Dubai Information Strategy, Internet and E-Commerce Development Handbook - Strategic Information, Programs, Regulations |
| Ecuador Information Strategy, Internet and E-Commerce Development Handbook - Strategic Information, Programs, Regulations |
| Egypt Information Strategy, Internet and E-Commerce Development Handbook - Strategic Information, Programs, Regulations |
| El Salvador Information Strategy, Internet and E-Commerce Development Handbook - Strategic Information, Programs, Regulations |
| Equatorial Guinea Information Strategy, Internet and E-Commerce Development Handbook - Strategic Information, Programs, Regulations |
| Estonia Information Strategy, Internet and E-Commerce Development Handbook - Strategic Information, Programs, Regulations |
| Fiji Information Strategy, Internet and E-Commerce Development Handbook - Strategic Information, Programs, Regulations |
| Finland Information Strategy, Internet and E-Commerce Development Handbook - Strategic Information, Programs, Regulations |
| France Information Strategy, Internet and E-Commerce Development Handbook - Strategic Information, Programs, Regulations |
| Georgia Republic Information Strategy, Internet and E-Commerce Development Handbook - Strategic Information, Programs, Regulations |
| Germany Information Strategy, Internet and E-Commerce Development Handbook - Strategic Information, Programs, Regulations |
| Greece Information Strategy, Internet and E-Commerce Development Handbook - Strategic Information, Programs, Regulations |
| Guatemala Information Strategy, Internet and E-Commerce Development Handbook - Strategic Information, Programs, Regulations |
| Guernsey Information Strategy, Internet and E-Commerce Development Handbook - Strategic Information, Programs, Regulations |
| Guyana Information Strategy, Internet and E-Commerce Development Handbook - Strategic Information, Programs, Regulations |
| Haiti Information Strategy, Internet and E-Commerce Development Handbook - Strategic Information, Programs, Regulations |
| Honduras Information Strategy, Internet and E-Commerce Development Handbook - Strategic Information, Programs, Regulations |
| Hungary Information Strategy, Internet and E-Commerce Development Handbook - Strategic Information, Programs, Regulations |
| Iceland Information Strategy, Internet and E-Commerce Development Handbook - Strategic Information, Programs, Regulations |
| India Information Strategy, Internet and E-Commerce Development Handbook - Strategic Information, Programs, Regulations |

| TITLE |
|---|
| Indonesia Information Strategy, Internet and E-Commerce Development Handbook - Strategic Information, Programs, Regulations |
| Iran Information Strategy, Internet and E-Commerce Development Handbook - Strategic Information, Programs, Regulations |
| Iraq Information Strategy, Internet and E-Commerce Development Handbook - Strategic Information, Programs, Regulations |
| Ireland Information Strategy, Internet and E-Commerce Development Handbook - Strategic Information, Programs, Regulations |
| Israel Information Strategy, Internet and E-Commerce Development Handbook - Strategic Information, Programs, Regulations |
| Italy Information Strategy, Internet and E-Commerce Development Handbook - Strategic Information, Programs, Regulations |
| Jamaica Information Strategy, Internet and E-Commerce Development Handbook - Strategic Information, Programs, Regulations |
| Japan Information Strategy, Internet and E-Commerce Development Handbook - Strategic Information, Programs, Regulations |
| Jordan Information Strategy, Internet and E-Commerce Development Handbook - Strategic Information, Programs, Regulations |
| Kazakhstan Information Strategy, Internet and E-Commerce Development Handbook - Strategic Information, Programs, Regulations |
| Kenya Information Strategy, Internet and E-Commerce Development Handbook - Strategic Information, Programs, Regulations |
| Korea, North Information Strategy, Internet and E-Commerce Development Handbook - Strategic Information, Programs, Regulations |
| Korea, South Information Strategy, Internet and E-Commerce Development Handbook - Strategic Information, Programs, Regulations |
| Kuwait Information Strategy, Internet and E-Commerce Development Handbook - Strategic Information, Programs, Regulations |
| Kyrgyzstan Information Strategy, Internet and E-Commerce Development Handbook - Strategic Information, Programs, Regulations |
| Laos Information Strategy, Internet and E-Commerce Development Handbook - Strategic Information, Programs, Regulations |
| Latvia Information Strategy, Internet and E-Commerce Development Handbook - Strategic Information, Programs, Regulations |
| Lebanon Information Strategy, Internet and E-Commerce Development Handbook - Strategic Information, Programs, Regulations |
| Libya Information Strategy, Internet and E-Commerce Development Handbook - Strategic Information, Programs, Regulations |
| Lithuania Information Strategy, Internet and E-Commerce Development Handbook - Strategic Information, Programs, Regulations |
| Macao Information Strategy, Internet and E-Commerce Development Handbook - Strategic Information, Programs, Regulations |
| Macedonia, Republic Information Strategy, Internet and E-Commerce Development Handbook - Strategic Information, Programs, Regulations |
| Madagascar Information Strategy, Internet and E-Commerce Development Handbook - Strategic Information, Programs, Regulations |
| Malaysia Information Strategy, Internet and E-Commerce Development Handbook - Strategic Information, Programs, Regulations |
| Malta Information Strategy, Internet and E-Commerce Development Handbook - Strategic Information, Programs, Regulations |
| Mauritius Information Strategy, Internet and E-Commerce Development Handbook - Strategic Information, Programs, Regulations |
| Mauritius Information Strategy, Internet and E-Commerce Development Handbook - Strategic Information, Programs, Regulations |
| Mexico Information Strategy, Internet and E-Commerce Development Handbook - Strategic Information, Programs, Regulations |
| Micronesia Information Strategy, Internet and E-Commerce Development Handbook - Strategic Information, Programs, Regulations |
| Moldova Information Strategy, Internet and E-Commerce Development Handbook - Strategic Information, Programs, Regulations |
| Monaco Information Strategy, Internet and E-Commerce Development Handbook - Strategic Information, |

| TITLE |
| --- |
| Programs, Regulations |
| Mongolia Information Strategy, Internet and E-Commerce Development Handbook - Strategic Information, Programs, Regulations |
| Morocco Information Strategy, Internet and E-Commerce Development Handbook - Strategic Information, Programs, Regulations |
| Myanmar Information Strategy, Internet and E-Commerce Development Handbook - Strategic Information, Programs, Regulations |
| Namibia Information Strategy, Internet and E-Commerce Development Handbook - Strategic Information, Programs, Regulations |
| Netherlands Information Strategy, Internet and E-Commerce Development Handbook - Strategic Information, Programs, Regulations |
| New Zealand Information Strategy, Internet and E-Commerce Development Handbook - Strategic Information, Programs, Regulations |
| Nicaragua Information Strategy, Internet and E-Commerce Development Handbook - Strategic Information, Programs, Regulations |
| Nigeria Information Strategy, Internet and E-Commerce Development Handbook - Strategic Information, Programs, Regulations |
| Norway Information Strategy, Internet and E-Commerce Development Handbook - Strategic Information, Programs, Regulations |
| Opportunities |
| Pakistan Information Strategy, Internet and E-Commerce Development Handbook - Strategic Information, Programs, Regulations |
| Panama Information Strategy, Internet and E-Commerce Development Handbook - Strategic Information, Programs, Regulations |
| Peru Information Strategy, Internet and E-Commerce Development Handbook - Strategic Information, Programs, Regulations |
| Philippines Information Strategy, Internet and E-Commerce Development Handbook - Strategic Information, Programs, Regulations |
| Poland Information Strategy, Internet and E-Commerce Development Handbook - Strategic Information, Programs, Regulations |
| Portugal Information Strategy, Internet and E-Commerce Development Handbook - Strategic Information, Programs, Regulations |
| Romania Information Strategy, Internet and E-Commerce Development Handbook - Strategic Information, Programs, Regulations |
| Russia Information Strategy, Internet and E-Commerce Development Handbook - Strategic Information, Programs, Regulations |
| Saudi Arabia Information Strategy, Internet and E-Commerce Development Handbook - Strategic Information, Programs, Regulations |
| Scotland Information Strategy, Internet and E-Commerce Development Handbook - Strategic Information, Programs, Regulations |
| Serbia Information Strategy, Internet and E-Commerce Development Handbook - Strategic Information, Programs, Regulations |
| Singapore Information Strategy, Internet and E-Commerce Development Handbook - Strategic Information, Programs, Regulations |
| Slovakia Information Strategy, Internet and E-Commerce Development Handbook - Strategic Information, Programs, Regulations |
| Slovenia Information Strategy, Internet and E-Commerce Development Handbook - Strategic Information, Programs, Regulations |
| South Africa Information Strategy, Internet and E-Commerce Development Handbook - Strategic Information, Programs, Regulations |
| Spain Information Strategy, Internet and E-Commerce Development Handbook - Strategic Information, Programs, Regulations |
| Sri Lanka Information Strategy, Internet and E-Commerce Development Handbook - Strategic Information, Programs, Regulations |
| Sudan Information Strategy, Internet and E-Commerce Development Handbook - Strategic Information, Programs, Regulations |
| Suriname Information Strategy, Internet and E-Commerce Development Handbook - Strategic Information, Programs, Regulations |
| Sweden Information Strategy, Internet and E-Commerce Development Handbook - Strategic Information, Programs, Regulations |
| Switzerland Information Strategy, Internet and E-Commerce Development Handbook - Strategic Information, |

| TITLE |
|---|
| Programs, Regulations |
| Syria Export Import &Business Directory |
| Taiwan Information Strategy, Internet and E-Commerce Development Handbook - Strategic Information, Programs, Regulations |
| Tajikistan Information Strategy, Internet and E-Commerce Development Handbook - Strategic Information, Programs, Regulations |
| Thailand Information Strategy, Internet and E-Commerce Development Handbook - Strategic Information, Programs, Regulations |
| Tunisia Information Strategy, Internet and E-Commerce Development Handbook - Strategic Information, Programs, Regulations |
| Turkey Information Strategy, Internet and E-Commerce Development Handbook - Strategic Information, Programs, Regulations |
| Turkmenistan Information Strategy, Internet and E-Commerce Development Handbook - Strategic Information, Programs, Regulations |
| Uganda Information Strategy, Internet and E-Commerce Development Handbook - Strategic Information, Programs, Regulations |
| Ukraine Information Strategy, Internet and E-Commerce Development Handbook - Strategic Information, Programs, Regulations |
| United Arab Emirates Information Strategy, Internet and E-Commerce Development Handbook - Strategic Information, Programs, Regulations |
| United Kingdom Information Strategy, Internet and E-Commerce Development Handbook - Strategic Information, Programs, Regulations |
| United States Information Strategy, Internet and E-Commerce Development Handbook - Strategic Information, Programs, Regulations |
| Uruguay Information Strategy, Internet and E-Commerce Development Handbook - Strategic Information, Programs, Regulations |
| US Information Strategy, Internet and E-Commerce Development Handbook - Strategic Information, Programs, Regulations |
| Uzbekistan Information Strategy, Internet and E-Commerce Development Handbook - Strategic Information, Programs, Regulations |
| Venezuela Information Strategy, Internet and E-Commerce Development Handbook - Strategic Information, Programs, Regulations |
| Vietnam Information Strategy, Internet and E-Commerce Development Handbook - Strategic Information, Programs, Regulations |

www.ingramcontent.com/pod-product-compliance
Lightning Source LLC
LaVergne TN
LVHW080036210926
848481LV00011B/3211
*9781433052071*